CliffsNotes®

GRE®
General Test

CRAM PLAN™

2nd Edition

CliffsNotes®

GRE®
General Test
CRAM PLAN™

2nd Edition

Carolyn Wheater, Jane R. Burstein, and Catherine McMenamin

WILEY

Wiley Publishing, Inc.

About the Authors

Carolyn Wheater teaches middle-school and upper-school mathematics at the Nightingale-Bamford School in New York City. Educated at Marymount Manhattan College and the University of Massachusetts, Amherst, she has taught math and computer technology for 30 years to students from preschool through college. **Jane Burstein** is currently an instructor at Hofstra University. Educated at S.U.N.Y. Stony Brook and Hofstra University, she taught English at Herricks High School for 36 years. She is an author of *CliffsNotes SAT Cram Plan, CliffsNotes ACT Cram Plan, CliffsNotes GMAT Cram Plan,* and *CliffsNotes AFQT Cram Plan.* **Catherine McMenamin** has an M.A. in art history from Columbia University. She lives and teaches in New York City.

Acknowledgements

Carolyn would like to thank Elizabeth Kuball, who is everything an author could hope for in an editor. She is also grateful to her daughter, Laura Wheater, who proofreads the math and catches the mistakes, and to her husband, Jim Wheater, for his infinite patience. Jane thanks her husband for his patience; her children for their often humorous suggestions; her friend and colleague Barbara Hoffman for her assistance; and her editor, Elizabeth Kuball, for her expertise.

Editorial

Acquisition Editor: Greg Tubach

Project Editor: Elizabeth Kuball

Copy Editor: Elizabeth Kuball

Technical Editors: Mike McAsey, Mary Jane Sterling, Barb Swovelin

Composition

Proofreader: Sossity R. Smith

Wiley Publishing, Inc., Composition Services

CliffsNotes® GRE® General Test Cram Plan™, 2nd Edition

Published by:
Wiley Publishing, Inc.
111 River Street
Hoboken, NJ 07030-5774
www.wiley.com

Copyright © 2011 Wiley, Hoboken, NJ

Published simultaneously in Canada

Library of Congress Control Number: 2011930283
ISBN: 978-0-470-87873-6 (pbk)
ISBN: 978-1-118-04859-7 (ebk)

Printed in the United States of America
10 9 8 7 6 5 4 3 2

Table of Contents

Introduction

If you're preparing to take the GRE, this is not your first encounter with standardized testing. You've likely taken the SAT or ACT for your undergraduate admission, so you have some expectations for the GRE. From your previous test-taking experience, you probably realize that the goal is to test your reasoning and critical-thinking skills, and the content, whether verbal or mathematical, is only the vehicle for that assessment. Without firm control of that vehicle, however, you won't be able to demonstrate your reasoning skills effectively. To approach the GRE with confidence, you need to review the content and practice the style of questions you'll find on the test. *CliffsNotes GRE General Test Cram Plan* is designed to help you achieve your best possible score on the GRE, whether you have two months, one month, or one week to prepare.

About the Test

The GRE is comprised of three sections:

- **Analytical Writing:** Within the Analytical Writing section, you'll be asked to complete two writing tasks: an "Analyze an Issue" task and an "Analyze an Argument" task.
- **Verbal Reasoning:** The Verbal Reasoning section includes critical-reading questions, text completions, and sentence equivalences.
- **Quantitative Reasoning:** The Quantitative Reasoning questions may appear as multiple-choice, quantitative-comparison, or numeric-entry questions.

  In the answer keys for the Diagnostic Test and Full-Length Practice Test, you'll find spaces to enter your responses to some of the Quantitative Reasoning questions. On the computer-based test, you'll simply type your answer into a box on-screen. On the paper-based test, you'll be asked to enter your answer in a grid, filling in an oval or square for each digit or character in your answer. Read the directions for filling in those grids carefully, and remember that although there are boxes above the grid in which to write your answer, you must also fill in the ovals or squares to receive credit for the answer.

The format of the GRE

Most people will take the GRE on a computer. For those geographical areas where the computer-based test is not available, the paper-based test is offered.

The computer-based test

The current computer-based test is an adaptive test—one that allows the computer to tailor the test to the ability of the individual test-taker. The test allots a set time for each section and bases your score on the number of questions you answer in that time period and on their level of difficulty. You're presented first with medium-difficulty questions, which are scored as you answer them. Based on your responses, the computer assigns you questions of higher, lower, or equal difficulty. Your score is based on the number of questions you answer correctly, as well as on the difficulty of the question, with the more difficult questions earning more points. As a result, the number of questions you answer may be different from the number answered by another test-taker.

Beginning August 1, 2011, you'll be able to change and edit questions within a section. You'll also be able to "mark and review"—that is, bookmark a question that you'd like to return to later. The new technology allows you to move forward and backward within a section so you can change or edit answers or skip questions and then return to them. After you complete a section, however, you can't return to it. For the Analytical Writing section, you'll type your essays on the computer, using a simplified word processor that includes basic functions common to all word-processing software (such as inserting, deleting, cutting, and pasting).

The Computer-Based GRE				
Section	Subject	Number of Questions	Type of Question	Time Allotted
1	Analytical Writing	1	"Analyze an Issue" task	30 minutes
2	Analytical Writing	1	"Analyze an Argument" task	30 minutes
3	Verbal Reasoning	Approximately 20, in 2 sections	Multiple choice, including text completions, sentence equivalences, and critical-reading questions	30 minutes per section
4	Quantitative Reasoning	Approximately 20, in 2 sections	Multiple choice and quantitative comparisons	35 minutes per section
5	Experimental	Varies	Varies	Varies

Note: You will have 3 hours and 45 minutes in which to work on the computer-based test. The sections are in any order. During the time allowed for one section, you may work only on that section. As soon as you begin a section, an on-screen clock will begin to count down the time you have left in that particular section. You'll also receive an alert signal when you have five minutes remaining in the section.

The paper-based test

The paper-based test was once the standard, but today it's used only in areas where computer-based testing is not available. The paper-based test has a predetermined number of questions of each type for the Verbal Reasoning and Quantitative Reasoning sections. The following table shows the breakdown of the paper-based test on which the Full-Length Practice Test is patterned.

The Paper-Based GRE				
Section	Subject	Number of Questions	Type of Question	Time Allotted
1	Analytical Writing	2	1 "Analyze an Issue" task and 1 "Analyze an Argument" task	30 minutes per essay
2	Quantitative Reasoning	30	15 quantitative comparisons and 15 multiple-choice questions	35 minutes
3	Verbal Reasoning	20	Text completions, sentence equivalences, and critical-reading questions	30 minutes
4	Verbal Reasoning	20	Text completions, sentence equivalences, and critical-reading questions	30 minutes
5	Quantitative Reasoning	30	15 quantitative comparisons and 15 multiple-choice questions	35 minutes
6	Experimental	Varies	Varies	Varies

How the test has changed

In August 2011, the GRE General Test will be replaced by the Revised GRE General Test. The changes in the test are designed to make the test questions mirror the kinds of thinking skills required by rigorous graduate school programs. The new version of the computer-based test also incorporates such user-friendly features as an on-screen calculator and a "mark and review" option that allows you to skip a question, change your answer, or return to earlier questions.

The revised test also provides a new score scale: Verbal Reasoning and Quantitative Reasoning scores are now calculated on a 130-to-170-point scale in one point increments (as compared to the old 200-to-800-point scales reported in ten-point increments). The six-point scale of the Analytical Writing section remains a six-point scale.

Question types

There are three main types of Verbal Reasoning questions:

- **Text-completion questions:** In the text-completion category, all the questions ask you to choose an answer that correctly completes the sentence. Some text-completion questions have one only blank; others have two or three blanks. For questions with more than one blank, the answer choices appear in columns, and you select answers from the columns corresponding to the numbered blanks.

- **Sentence-equivalence questions:** In sentence-equivalence questions, you're given one sentence with one blank and a list of answer choices. You're asked to choose two answer choices that correctly complete the sentence and result in two sentences similar in meaning.

- **Reading-comprehension questions:** In the reading-comprehension category, you'll find three types of questions:

  - Traditional multiple-choice questions, in which you're given five choices, and you select one answer

  - Multiple-choice questions, in which you're given three choices, and you select all the correct answers

  - Select-in-passage questions, in which you have to click on the sentence in the reading passage that answers the question

There are four main types of Quantitative Reasoning questions:

- **Multiple-choice questions in which you select one answer:** These are the traditional multiple-choice questions, in which you're given five choices, and you select one answer.

- **Multiple-choice questions in which you select more than one answer:** In these questions, you're given a variety of choices, and you select all the correct answers. You may or may not be told how many answers to choose.

- **Numeric-entry questions:** These questions don't provide you with answer choices. Instead, you arrive at the answer and enter it in a single box (for integers and decimals) or in two boxes (one for the numerator of a fraction and the other for the denominator of a fraction).

- **Quantitative-comparison questions:** In these questions, you're given two quantities—one in Column A and the other in Column B—and you determine which quantity is greater. If Column A is greater, you choose A; if Column B is greater, you choose B; if the quantities are equal, you choose C; and if it's impossible to determine which is greater, you choose D.

Scoring

Your scores for the multiple-choice sections are determined by the number of questions for which you select the best answer or answers from the choices given. Questions for which you mark no answer are not counted in scoring. Nothing is subtracted from a score if you answer a question incorrectly. Therefore, to maximize your scores, it's better for you to guess than not to respond at all.

The 2011 revision of the GRE introduces a new scoring system. You'll receive a score for each section of the test, and the scale for those scores has changed:

- **Verbal Reasoning:** Scores will be reported on a scale of 130 to 170 in one-point increments.
- **Quantitative Reasoning:** Scores will be reported on a scale of 130 to 170 in one-point increments.
- **Analytical Writing:** Scores will be reported on a scale of 0 to 6 in half-point increments.

Where to take the GRE

The GRE is administered at test centers year-round, by appointment. For the computer-based test, you'll be able to choose a day and time to take the test, subject to availability. For the paper-based test, you're limited to certain testing dates. For more information on testing sites and dates for both computer-based and paper-based tests, go to www.ets.org/gre/general/register/centers_dates.

You'll need to arrive at the test center 30 minutes before your appointment. Bring your admission ticket and a photo ID. Except for pens and pencils, no personal items may be brought into the testing room. You'll be provided with a place to store other items, including cellphones, calculators, and electronic devices, but you won't be able to access them again until the test is over. You'll be given scratch paper, and you may not remove that paper from the testing room.

You'll be given a calculator to use for the paper-based test. For the computer-based test, the computer will have an on-screen calculator for your use during the test.

About This Book

CliffsNotes GRE General Test Cram Plan is designed to guide you through a thorough and well-organized preparation for the GRE General Test. Whether your test date is two months away, one month away, or just a week away, *CliffsNotes GRE General Test Cram Plan* helps you address your weaknesses and approach the test with confidence.

Begin with the Diagnostic Test, a compact simulation of the questions you can expect to find on the Verbal Reasoning and Quantitative Reasoning sections of the GRE. Check your work against the answers and solutions provided. The Verbal Reasoning questions are organized by type, allowing you to determine which style of question you need to practice. The Quantitative Reasoning questions are mixed by subject, and the answers include cross-references to the sections that review the content of the question. After you've scored your Diagnostic Test, look for patterns of strengths and weakness. As you begin your review, pay special attention to any areas of weakness you've identified; these are your target areas.

After you've identified your target areas, the two-month, one-month, and one-week cram plans will show you how to do a systematic study of the subject reviews, while practicing the question formats used on the GRE. The two-month cram plan gives you seven weekly tasks and a day-by-day plan for the week before the test. Like the two-month cram plan, the one-month cram plan includes weekly assignments and a daily breakdown for the last week, but it organizes the material and highlights key areas to make best use of the available time. If you have only one week to prepare for the test, the one-week cram plan will guide you day by day through the essential topics and practice.

After you've had time to read and practice the material in the subject reviews, the Full-Length Practice Test will give you a clear assessment of your readiness. Patterned after the paper-based GRE, this simulated GRE includes directions and timings that mimic the real test, as well as solutions and explanations to help you correct your errors.

With diagnosis, planning, practice, and assessment, *CliffsNotes GRE General Test Cram Plan* provides the information, skills, and tactics you need to approach the GRE with confidence and to achieve your best possible score.

I. Diagnostic Test

Section 1: Verbal Reasoning

Time: 30 minutes

20 questions

Directions (1–6): For each blank, select the word or phrase that best completes the text. (Your answer will consist of one, two, or three letters, depending on the number of blanks in each question.)

1. With a _____ common among those to whom short-term fixes are expedient, Senator Noah Julian refused to consider a complete overhaul of the election funding issue.

   A. aestheticism
   B. myopia
   C. skepticism
   D. inventiveness
   E. paranoia

2. Settling into what he thought would be cosmopolitan suburban community, Seth was confounded by the _____ of his neighbors.

   A. erudition
   B. urbanity
   C. insularity
   D. gentility
   E. affluence

3. In his interesting preface, Mr. Shorthouse alludes to William Smith's philosophical novel, *Thorndale.* As a picture of thought developments in the early Victorian period, the work has special historical interest for the (1) _____ and theological student; in this respect, it may be (2) _____ to Pater's *Marius the Epicurean,* which also vividly reproduces the intellectual ferment of an earlier age.

Blank 1	Blank 2
philosophical	abstracted
secular	adapted
antithetical	likened

4. Indeed, it is a source of common (1) _____ among engineers, who smirk that the average layman cannot differentiate between the man who runs a locomotive and the man who designs a locomotive. In ordinary (2) _____, both are called engineers.

Blank 1	Blank 2
irritation	parlance
wrath	colloquialism
amusement	hyperbole

1

5. The *Sheaf Gleaned in French Fields* is certainly the most imperfect of Toru Dutt's writings, but it is not the least interesting. It is a wonderful mixture of strength and weakness, of genius (1) _____ great obstacles and of talent succumbing to ignorance and inexperience. That it should have been performed at all is so extraordinary that we forget to be surprised at its (2) _____. The English verse is sometimes (3) _____; at other times the rules of our prosody are absolutely ignored, and it is obvious that the Hindu poetess was chanting to herself a music that is discord in an English ear.

Blank 1	Blank 2	Blank 3
performing	constancy	exquisite
overriding	propinquity	gauche
recapitulating	unevenness	unintelligible

6. One step in social order leads to another, and thus is furnished a means of utilizing without waste all of the individual and social forces. Yet how irregular and (1) _____ are the first steps of human progress. A step forward, followed by a long period of readjustment of the conditions of life; a movement forward here and a (2) _____ force there. Within this irregular movement we discover the true course of human progress. One tribe, on account of peculiar advantages, makes a special discovery, which places it in the (3) _____ and gives it power over others.

Blank 1	Blank 2	Blank 3
catastrophic	retarding	echelon
dramatic	dominating	nadir
faltering	impulsive	ascendancy

Directions (7–12): Questions follow each of the passages. Using only the stated or implied information in each passage, answer the questions.

Questions 7–9 are based on the following passage.

The Vietnam War began in 1956 and ended in 1975. It had dire consequences for millions of Americans. The American military pushed forward to South Vietnam to assist its government against the communist regime, who were supported by North Vietnam. By the late 1960s, the United States entered this war in which almost 60,000 Americans would die. Two million Vietnamese lives may have been lost, including those of many thousands of civilians, due to intensive bombing by the opponents. Also, a highly toxic chemical caused defoliation, the elimination of vegetation. The Vietnam War is estimated to have cost approximately $200 billion.

Returning Vietnam veterans, approximately 2.7 million in all, did not receive a positive welcome from American civilians. Instead, they returned to widespread public opposition. Their moral opposition to the war made it difficult for many Americans to show support for these veterans.

A few years after the Vietnam War, veterans started a fund for construction of a memorial to those who had died; they raised nearly $9 million. A competition was held for the proper design, with the proviso that the memorial should not express any political view of the war.

In a funerary design course at Yale University, 21-year-old architecture student Maya Lin submitted a proposal for the design competition for the memorial. The popular conception of a war memorial recalled the heroic equestrian statues of Civil War generals, but in Lin's opinion, such representations were too simplified. Her design consisted of two walls of polished black granite built into the earth, set in the shape of a shallow V. Carved into the stone are the names of all the men and women killed in the war or still missing, in chronological order by the date of their death or disappearance. Rising up 10 feet high, the names begin and continue to that wall's end, resuming at the point of the opposite wall and ending at the place where the names began. Visitors can easily access the wall and touch the names, an integral part of Lin's design.

After the judges evaluated thousands of entries for this competition in the spring of 1981, Maya Lin won. The public's reaction to this particular design was sharply divided, reflecting their opposing feelings about this war. Yet more than one million visitors view the memorial each year.

7. What is the author's primary purpose of the passage?

   A. To propose ideas about Maya Lin's submission from Yale University
   B. To dissect the Vietnam Memorial's proposition
   C. To discuss the history of the design of the Vietnam Memorial and the response to it
   D. To critique the judges reviewing Lin's sculptural proposal
   E. To discuss the history of the Vietnam War and its aftermath

8. Select the sentence that presents Lin's reasons for not creating a conventional war memorial.

9. What details in the narrative suggest that it was possible to fulfill the requirement that the monument express no political view of the war?

   A. Those opposing it said it degraded the memory of those who had given their lives to this cause.
   B. The United States government wanted a memorial that would honor the dead.
   C. Carved into the stone are the names of all the men and women killed in the war or still missing, in chronological order by the date of their death or disappearance.
   D. One wall points toward the Washington Monument and the other wall points toward the Lincoln Memorial, bringing the Vietnam Memorial into proper historical reference.
   E. Many Americans were unwilling to confront the war's many painful issues.

Questions 10–11 are based on the following passage.

Alfred Tennyson was born August 6, 1809, at Somersby, a little village in Lincolnshire, England. His father was the rector of the parish; his mother, whose maiden name was Elizabeth Fytche, and whose character he touched in his poem "Isabel," was the daughter of a clergyman; and one of his brothers, who later took the name of Charles Turner, also was a clergyman. The religious nature in the poet was a constant element in his poetry, secrets to an observation that was singularly keen, and a philosophic reflection that made Tennyson reveal in his poetry an apprehension of the laws of life, akin to what Darwin was disclosing in his contemporaneous career.

In his early "Ode to Memory," Tennyson has translated into verse the consciousness that woke in him in the secluded fields of his Lincolnshire birthplace. For companionship, he had the large circle of his home, for he was one of eight brothers and four sisters; and in that little society there was not only the miniature world of sport and study, but a very close companionship with the large world of imagination.

Frederick Tennyson was already at Cambridge when Charles and Alfred went to that university in 1828 and were matriculated at Trinity College. Alfred Tennyson acquired there, as so many other notable Englishmen, not only intellectual discipline, but that close companionship with picked men that is engendered by the half-monastic seclusion of the English university.

Tennyson regarded his post as Poet Laureate in the light of a high poetic and patriotic ardor. Starting with his first laureate poem "To the Queen," the record of Tennyson's career from this time forward is marked by the successive publication of his works.

10. According to the passage, what role does religion play in Tennyson's poetry?

   A. It plays a direct role as his poetry is mostly piously devotional in substance.

   B. Rejection of orthodoxy is a constant refrain in Tennyson's poetry based on nature.

   C. It plays a significant role based on the poet's religious nature and pastoral observation.

   D. It does not play a crucial role, even though Tennyson grew up with clergymen as relatives.

   E. Religion was studied at Trinity College and weaved into verse at that time.

11. It can be inferred from the passage that the author regards Tennyson as which of the following? Consider each of the three choices and select all that apply.

   A. Being influenced by his family's role in society and religion as well as the patriotic fervor of peers

   B. Receiving national recognition for his talents and his beliefs

   C. Acquiring more than a purely intellectual education at university

Question 12 is based on the following passage.

The mores, or customs, of man began at a very early time and have been a persistent ruling power in human conduct. Through tradition they are handed down from generation to generation, to be observed with more or less fidelity as a guide to the art of living. Every community, whether primitive or developed, is controlled to a great extent by the prevailing custom. It is common for individuals and families to do as their ancestors did. This habit is frequently carried to such an extent that the deeds of the fathers are held sacred from which no one dare to depart. Isolated communities continue year after year to do things because they had always done so, holding strictly to the ruling custom founded on tradition, even when some better way was at hand.

12. The author of the passage would probably consider which of the following to be similar to the paradigm he describes?

   A. Young Japanese do not perceive family as something that provides "meaning" in their lives, unlike young Americans, Chinese, and Swedes.

   B. When asked to rank their values by order of importance, many German youths placed obedience last.

   C. Young men of the Inuit tribe often leave their families to seek employment in large cities.

   D. A ritual face-painting ceremony of prepubescent females continues in an isolated Amazonian community, long after the reason for its institution is lost.

   E. A French artist paints a scene intended to evoke pathos; however, most American viewers find levity in its content.

Directions (13–16): Select *two* of the choices from the list of six that best complete the meaning of the sentence as a whole. The two words you select should produce completed sentences that are most alike in meaning. To receive credit for the question, both answers must be correct. No partial credit will be given; your answer must consist of two letters.

13. The art world rejects the much-touted youthful artist, finding that her _____ work lacks the maturity for serious consideration.

    A. puerile
    B. abstract
    C. jejune
    D. aesthetic
    E. impressionable
    F. clumsy

14. Rejoinders at the open debate quickly became rancorous; each candidate resorted to _____ to malign the opposition.

    A. aspersion
    B. pedantry
    C. elucidation
    D. exaltation
    E. solicitude
    F. calumny

15. Long touted as the epitome of *beaux-arts* architecture, the garishly elaborate decorations in the restored mansion of the former dictator struck Ella and her colleagues from the design studio as more _____ than palatial.

    A. meretricious
    B. magnificent
    C. ostentatious
    D. beneficent
    E. illusory
    F. antediluvian

16. As the _____ strains of the dirge filled the concert hall, many in the audience were reminded of the recent passing of the preeminent conductor who so often had graced the podium.

    A. sanguine
    B. plaintive
    C. clandestine
    D. lugubrious
    E. subjective
    F. explosive

Directions (17–20): Questions follow each of the passages. Using only the stated or implied information in each passage, answer the questions. For questions with five choices, select one answer choice. For questions with three choices, select all the choices that apply.

Questions 17–18 are based on the following passage.

Her image accompanied me even in places the most hostile to romance. On Saturday evenings when my aunt went marketing I had to go to carry some of the parcels. We walked through the flaring streets, jostled by drunken men and bargaining women, amid the curses of laborers, the shrill litanies of shop-boys who stood on guard by the barrels of pigs' cheeks, the nasal chanting of street-singers, who sang a ballad about the troubles in our native land. These noises converged in a single sensation of life for me: I imagined that I bore my chalice safely through a throng of foes. Her name sprang to my lips at moments in strange prayers and praises which I myself did not understand. My eyes were often full of tears (I could not tell why) and at times a flood from my heart seemed to pour itself out into my bosom. I thought little of the future. I did not know whether I would ever speak to her or not or, if I spoke to her, how I could tell her of my confused adoration. But my body was like a harp and her words and gestures were like fingers running upon the wires.

17. In this passage, what does the narrator undergo? Consider each of the three choices and select all that apply.

    A.   A quasi-religious experience while grocery shopping
    B.   An imagined revelation of himself as heroic figure
    C.   A prolonged confession of his ardor to his loved one

18. The passage provides information about all of the following *except:*

    A.   When the market is open
    B.   What is sold in the market
    C.   What kinds of songs are sung on the streets
    D.   How the boy assists a family member
    E.   The musical instrument that the boy plays

Questions 19–20 are based on the following passage.

Among the men and women prominent in the public life of America, there are but few whose names are mentioned as often as that of Emma Goldman. Yet the real Emma Goldman is almost quite unknown. The sensational press has surrounded her name with so much misrepresentation and slander, it would seem almost a miracle that, in spite of this web of calumny, the truth breaks through and a better appreciation of this much maligned idealist begins to manifest itself. There is but little consolation in the fact that almost every representative of a new idea has had to struggle and suffer under similar difficulties. Is it of any avail that a former president of a republic pays homage at Osawatomie to the memory of John Brown? Or that the president of another republic participates in the unveiling of a statue in honor of Pierre Proudhon, and holds up his life to the French nation as a model worthy of enthusiastic emulation? Of what avail is all this when, at the same time, the *living* John Browns and Proudhons are being crucified? The honor and glory of a Mary Wollstonecraft or of a Louise Michel are not enhanced by the City Fathers of London or Paris naming a street after them—the living generation should be concerned with doing justice to the *living* Mary Wollstonecrafts and Louise Michels. Posterity assigns to men like Wendel Phillips and Lloyd Garrison the proper niche of honor in the temple of human emancipation; but it is the duty of their contemporaries to bring them due recognition and appreciation while they live.

19. Which of the following, if true, most seriously undermines the author's main point?

    A. In 1978, Reverend Martin Luther King, Jr., was posthumously awarded the United Nations Prize in the field of human rights.

    B. Shirin Ebadi, the 56-year-old first Iranian female judge, won the 2003 Nobel Peace Prize for her efforts to improve human rights.

    C. Pierre Proudhon, a self-proclaimed anarchist who urged "a society without authority," became a member of the French Parliament.

    D. Until the 20th century, Mary Wollstonecraft received more recognition for her unorthodox lifestyle than for her treatise on the rights of women.

    E. John Brown, an American abolitionist, was labeled a "misguided fanatic" by President Abraham Lincoln.

20. In the second sentence of the passage, *real* most nearly means:

    A. Concrete
    B. Actual
    C. Factual
    D. Tangible
    E. Original

IF YOU FINISH BEFORE TIME IS CALLED, CHECK YOUR WORK ON THIS SECTION ONLY. DO NOT WORK ON ANY OTHER SECTION IN THE TEST.

Section 2: Quantitative Reasoning

Time: 60 minutes

50 questions

Numbers: All numbers used are real numbers.

Figures: Figures are intended to provide useful positional information, but they are not necessarily drawn to scale. Unless a note states that a figure is drawn to scale, you should not solve these problems by estimating sizes or by measurements. Use your knowledge of math to solve the problems. Angle measures can be assumed to be positive. Lines that appear straight can be assumed to be straight. Unless otherwise indicated, figures lie in a plane.

Directions (1–18): You are given two quantities, one in Column A and one in Column B. You are to compare the two quantities and choose one of the following:

    A.   The quantity in Column A is greater.
    B.   The quantity in Column B is greater.
    C.   The two quantities are equal.
    D.   The relationship cannot be determined from the information given.

---

x and y are integers greater than 0

$$\left(\frac{x}{y}\right)^2 > \frac{x}{y} \text{ and } \left(\frac{y}{x}\right)^2 < \frac{y}{x}$$

	Column A	**Column B**
1.	x	y

$$a \otimes b = a^2 - b$$
$$a \odot b = a + b^2$$

	Column A	**Column B**
2.	$(3 \otimes 4) \odot 5$	$3 \otimes (4 \odot 5)$

The number 4.2953 is to be rounded to the nearest thousandth

	Column A	**Column B**
3.	The digit in the thousandths place of the rounded number	The digit in the hundredths place of the rounded number

$$3 < a < b < 4$$

Column A	Column B
4. $33\frac{1}{3}\%$ of a	25% of b

$$\frac{n}{5} = \frac{p}{3}$$

Column A	Column B
5. $\dfrac{n+1}{5}$	$\dfrac{p+1}{3}$

Five times the difference between a and b is 25

Column A	Column B
6. Six times the difference between a and b	36

$$n \geq 0$$

Column A	Column B
7. $\sqrt{n^2}$	$\left(\sqrt{n}\right)^2$

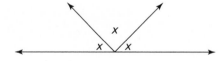

Column A	Column B
8. x	90

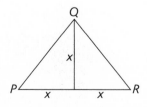

Column A	Column B
9. The area $\triangle PQR$	Half the area of a circle of radius x

	Column A	Column B
10.	The length of a side of a square whose perimeter is 24	The length of the longer side of a rectangle whose perimeter is 24

A and B are points in the coordinate plane

$$A = (-x, y)$$
$$B = (x, -y)$$

	Column A	Column B
11.	The distance from the origin to point A	The distance from the origin to point B

	Column A	Column B
12.	$\left(x^3\right)^5 \left(x^4\right)^5$	$\left(x^7\right)^5$

a and b are integers

$$1 < a < b < 10$$

	Column A	Column B
13.	The number of multiples of a that are greater than 20 but less than 80	The number of multiples of b that are greater than 20 but less than 80

The mean of p, q, and r is 20

	Column A	Column B
14.	The mean of p, q, r, and 40	30

	Column A	Column B
15.	The number of integers between 0 and 50 that are multiples of both 3 and 5	4

$$X = \{3, 4, 5\}$$
$$Y = \{4, 5, 6\}$$

	Column A	Column B
16.	The number of distinct products that can be formed by multiplying one element of X by one element of Y	The number of distinct sums that can be formed by adding one element of X and one element of Y

	Column A		Column B
17.	The number of weeks in 427 days		The number of months in 5 years

	Column A		Column B
18.	$\frac{1}{2} \div \frac{3}{4} + \frac{1}{3}$		$\frac{1}{2} + \frac{3}{4} \div \frac{1}{3}$

Directions (19–50): Unless otherwise directed, select a single answer choice. For numeric-entry questions, enter a number in the box(es) below the question. Equivalent forms of the correct answer, such as 2.5 and 2.50, are all correct. Fractions do not need to be reduced to lowest terms. Enter the exact answer unless the question asks you to round your answer.

Questions 19–22 are based on the following table.

Speed (mph)	Braking Distance (feet)
20	21
30	47
40	82
50	128
60	185

19. The stopping distance for a car is the distance the car travels between the time the driver realizes a stop is required and the time the car comes to a complete stop. The stopping distance is the total of reaction distance and braking distance. The reaction distance, the distance the car travels in the time it takes the driver to realize that a stop is necessary and to apply the brakes, is 1.1 feet for each mile per hour of the speed of the car. The braking distance is the additional distance the car will travel between the time the brake is applied and the time the car reaches a complete stop. The table shows the braking distance for a car traveling at different speeds. What is the stopping distance, in feet, for a car traveling at 30 mph?

20. How much longer, in feet, is the stopping distance for a car traveling at 60 mph than for one traveling at 40 mph?

A. 22
B. 55
C. 103
D. 125
E. 141

21. If total stopping distance for a car traveling at 50 mph is expressed as a rate in feet per mile per hour, the rate will be how many feet per mile per hour?

A. 2.56
B. 2.67
C. 3.15
D. 3.66
E. 4.18

11

22. Based on the information given, choose all the true statements below.

    A. An increase in speed from 20 mph to 40 mph more than doubles the stopping distance.
    B. An increase in speed from 30 mph to 50 mph more than doubles the stopping distance.
    C. An increase in speed from 40 mph to 60 mph more than doubles the stopping distance.

23. If a particle travels 2.4×10^7 cm/second, how long will it take to travel 7.2×10^9 cm, in seconds?

    A. 3.0×10^{-2}
    B. 3.0×10^2
    C. 3.0×10^7
    D. 3.0×10^9
    E. 4.8×10^{63}

24. $\triangle XYZ$ is isosceles with $\overline{XY} \cong \overline{YZ}$. If $m\angle Y = 36°$, what is the measure of $\angle X$?

    A. 36°
    B. 54°
    C. 60°
    D. 72°
    E. 144°

25. If the sum of two numbers is 12 and their difference is 2, what is their product?

    ☐

26. The length of a rectangle is 4 inches more than its width. If the perimeter is 20 inches, what is the area of the rectangle, in square inches?

    A. 20
    B. 96
    C. 64
    D. 21
    E. 32

27. If $x|y-3| < 0$, choose all the true statements.

    A. $x < 0$
    B. $y < 0$
    C. $y < 3$
    D. $y < -3$
    E. $y \neq 3$

28. A game booth at the carnival gave stuffed bears as prizes. The bears were identical except for color. Eight bears were brown, six were white, and four were black. A bear is selected at random for each winner. What is the probability that the first winner will receive a black bear?

    A. $\frac{1}{4}$
    B. $\frac{2}{9}$
    C. $\frac{2}{7}$
    D. $\frac{1}{2}$
    E. $\frac{2}{3}$

29. $5.4 \times 10^{-3} =$

    A. 0.0054
    B. 0.054
    C. 0.54
    D. 540
    E. 5,400

30. A rectangular solid has two faces that are squares with sides of 5. The other four faces of the solid are rectangles that are 5 by 8. Find the volume of the solid.

    ☐

31. For all values of t for which it is defined, the expression $\dfrac{t^2 + 7t + 10}{t^2 - 4}$ can be simplified to:

   A. $\dfrac{7t + 10}{-4}$

   B. $\dfrac{t + 5}{t - 2}$

   C. $\dfrac{t + 5}{t + 2}$

   D. $\dfrac{-5}{2}$

   E. $\dfrac{t + 3}{t}$

32. If $290 \le 45 - 7w < 990$, choose all the statements that could be true.

   A. $w > -135$
   B. $w < -35$
   C. $w = -35$
   D. $7w > -945$
   E. $-245 \le 7w$

33. A right triangle has legs 15 cm and 20 cm long. Find the length of the hypotenuse.

   A. 25 cm
   B. 11.25 cm
   C. 33 cm
   D. 35 cm
   E. 18 cm

34. What is the area of the circle defined by the equation $(x - 4)^2 + (y + 9)^2 = 1$?

   A. π
   B. 2π
   C. 3π
   D. 4π
   E. 9π

35. How many solutions are there to the equation $4x^2 - 36 = 0$?

   A. 0
   B. 1
   C. 2
   D. 3
   E. 4

36. The average grade of a class of N students is 80 and the average grade of a class of P students is 70. When the two classes are combined, the average is 76. What is $\dfrac{P}{N}$?

37. A shoe store routinely sells shoes for 50% more than its cost. At the end of each season, it clears out the remaining stock by selling it at 10% below cost. If a pair of shoes regularly sold for $75, what would you pay for them at the end-of-season sale?

   A. $67.50
   B. $37.50
   C. $45.00
   D. $101.25
   E. $30.00

38. If the average (mean) of x and 10 is equal to the average (mean) of x, 3, 14, and 16, find the value of x.

   A. 10
   B. 11
   C. 12
   D. 13
   E. 14

39. The hollow cylinder shown has a radius of 3 and a height of 8.

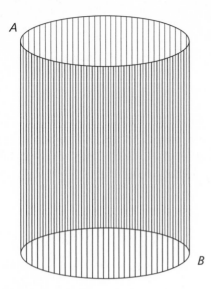

What is the straight-line distance from point A on the upper rim to point B on the lower rim?

A. $\sqrt{73}$
B. 11
C. 48π
D. 10
E. 20.5

40. In rectangle $QRST$, point P is the midpoint of side RS. If the area of quadrilateral $QRPT$ is 30, what is the area of rectangle $QRST$?

A. 40
B. 60
C. 80
D. 100
E. 120

41. Let $x \otimes y$ be defined as the product of the integers from x to y. For example, $3 \otimes 7 = 3 \times 4 \times 5 \times 6 \times 7$. What is the value of $\frac{2 \otimes 5}{6 \otimes 8}$?

42. If $6t = 3v - 9$, choose all the expressions that correctly represent v as a function of t.

A. $v = 6t + 12$
B. $v = 2t + 9$
C. $v = 6t + 3$
D. $v = 2t + 3$
E. $v = \frac{6t + 9}{3}$
F. $v = 6t + 6$

43. If 70% of the senior class had part-time jobs and there are 480 seniors, how many seniors did *not* have part-time jobs?

A. 144
B. 160
C. 240
D. 288
E. 336

44. Find the area of the shaded region, in square centimeters, if the rectangle is 24 cm long and 8 cm high.

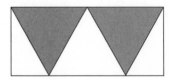

A. 192
B. 96
C. 64
D. 48
E. 24

45. What is the length of the diagonal of a square whose area is 169 square inches?

    A. $169\sqrt{2}$ inches

    B. $169\sqrt{3}$ inches

    C. $13\sqrt{2}$ inches

    D. $13\sqrt{3}$ inches

    E. $\dfrac{43\sqrt{2}}{2}$ inches

46. If n is divided by 5, the remainder is 1. Choose all the true statements from the choices below.

    A. If $3n$ is divided by 5, the remainder is 3.

    B. If $4n$ is divided by 2, the remainder is 2.

    C. If $6n$ is divided by 5, the remainder is 1.

    D. If $6n$ is divided by 3, the remainder is 0.

    E. If $7n$ is divided by 5, the remainder is 1.

47. Four children received a gift of candy, which they shared equally. The oldest child then gave half of his share to his youngest sister. Another brother kept three-fourths of his share and gave the rest to the youngest sister. What fraction of the candy did the youngest sister receive?

    A. $\dfrac{1}{16}$

    B. $\dfrac{3}{16}$

    C. $\dfrac{1}{2}$

    D. $\dfrac{5}{16}$

    E. $\dfrac{7}{16}$

48. On Monday, Jennifer placed 1 cent in her piggy bank. On Tuesday, she put 2 cents in. On Wednesday, she added 4 cents, and on Thursday, she added 8 cents. If Jennifer continues this saving pattern, how much will be in her piggy bank after ten days?

    ☐

49. The difference between the measure of an interior angle of a regular hexagon and the measure of an external angle of a regular pentagon is

    A. 12°

    B. 36°

    C. 48°

    D. 60°

    E. 90°

Question 50 refers to the following table.

Building	Steps	Total Seconds
CN Tower (Toronto)	1,776	687
Taipei 101 (Taiwan)	2,046	653
Willis Tower (Chicago)	2,109	822
Empire State Building (New York)	1,576	625
Hancock Tower (Chicago)	1,632	637
Boston Place (Boston)	697	272

50. Many tall buildings sponsor annual races in which participants run up the stairs to the building's top floor or observation deck. The table lists the number of steps climbed and the first-place finisher's time in seconds for some of these races. Based on the information in the table, which race's winner ran fastest?

    A. Willis Tower

    B. Taipei 101

    C. Empire State Building

    D. Hancock Tower

    E. Boston Place

IF YOU FINISH BEFORE TIME IS CALLED, CHECK YOUR WORK ON THIS SECTION ONLY. DO NOT WORK ON ANY OTHER SECTION IN THE TEST.

Answer Key

Section 1: Verbal Reasoning

1. B
2. C
3. philosophical, likened
4. amusement, parlance
5. overriding, unevenness, exquisite
6. faltering, retarding, ascendancy
7. C
8. The popular conception of a war memorial recalled the heroic equestrian statues of Civil War generals, but in Lin's opinion, such representations were too simplified.
9. C
10. C
11. A, B, C
12. D
13. A, C
14. A, F
15. A, C
16. B, D
17. A, B
18. E
19. B
20. B

Section 2: Quantitative Reasoning

1. A
2. A
3. B
4. A
5. B
6. B
7. C
8. B
9. B
10. B
11. C
12. C
13. A
14. B
15. B
16. A
17. A
18. B
19. 80
20. D
21. D
22. A, B
23. B
24. D
25. 35
26. D
27. A, E
28. B
29. A
30. 200
31. B
32. A, B, C, D
33. A
34. A
35. C
36. $\frac{2}{3}$
37. C
38. D
39. D
40. A
41. $\frac{5}{14}$
42. D, E
43. A
44. B
45. C
46. A, C, D
47. E
48. $10.23
49. C
50. B

Answer Explanations

Section 1: Verbal Reasoning

1. **B** The context clue that the senator finds short-term fixes expedient suggests *myopia,* which means near-sightedness or short-sightedness. The other choices don't make sense in the sentence. *(See Chapter V, Section B.)*

2. **C** The phrase *what he thought would be cosmopolitan* suggests that the community wasn't what Seth expected. Insular (narrow-minded or concerned only with local matters) is the opposite of cosmopolitan (sophisticated, broad in outlook, international in scope). The other choices don't follow the logic of the sentence. *(See Chapter V, Section B.)*

3. **philosophical, likened** *Philosophical* is the best choice for Blank 1 because the first sentence describes *Thorndale* as a philosophical novel. In addition, the second sentence refers to it as a "picture of thought developments." It is *likened* (Blank 2) to *Marius the Epicurean* because that "also reproduces the intellectual ferment. . . ." The other choices don't follow the logic of the sentence. *(See Chapter V, Section C.)*

4. **amusement, parlance** That engineers "smirk" suggests that they feel *amusement* (Blank 1). *Parlance* is the best choice for Blank 2 because it means the language of people in a particular profession. The other choices don't follow the logic of the sentence. *(See Chapter V, Section C.)*

5. **overriding, unevenness, exquisite** The passage asserts that Dutt's writings are a "mixture of strength and weakness." This sets up a series of contrasts and creates the logic of "genius *overriding* (Blank 1) great obstacles." The contrasts continue with the work being "so extraordinary that we forget to be surprised at its *unevenness*" (Blank 2) and with the verse being sometimes *exquisite* (Blank 3) while "at other times the rules of our prosody are absolutely ignored." The other choices don't follow the logic of the sentence. *(See Chapter V, Section C.)*

6. **faltering, retarding, ascendancy** The second sentence begins with "Yet," which sets up a contrast to the first sentence. Thus, while "one step leads to another," the steps are "irregular and *faltering*" (Blank 1). Blank 2 must be a negative word, *retarding,* to contrast with "a movement forward." To have "power over others" suggests that Blank 3 is *ascendancy.* The other choices don't follow the logic of the sentence. *(See Chapter V, Section C.)*

7. **C** The author's primary purpose is to discuss the design of the memorial and to explain the response of the American public. Choice A isn't discussed in the passage. Choice B is inaccurate; no proposition is mentioned. Choice D is wrong because the judges aren't critiqued in the passage. Choice E is too general and inaccurate. *(See Chapter VIII, Section B1.)*

8. **The popular conception of a war memorial recalled the heroic equestrian statues of Civil War generals, but in Lin's opinion, such representations were too simplified.** In this sentence, Lin rejects the traditional figural representations that have been popular in the past. In her view, they oversimplify the human cost of the war.

9. **C** Having all the names of those who died carved into the wall conveys a nonpolitical recognition of service. Choices A, B, D, and E all express political positions. *(See Chapter VIII, Section B1.)*

10. **C** According to the passage, Tennyson infused his poetry with his religious beliefs and his love of nature. Choice A is incorrect; it's too extreme because the passage doesn't state that Tennyson was piously devotional. Choices B and D are contradicted by the information in the passage. Choice E is irrelevant. *(See Chapter VIII, Section B1.)*

11. **A, B, C** All the statements can be inferred from the information in the passage. *(See Chapter VIII, Section B2.)*

12. **D** The paradigm or model set up in the passage is one of traditions being handed down from generation to generation, year after year. The tradition of ritual face-painting best fits this paradigm. Choice A deviates from the paradigm. Choice B is somewhat irrelevant and somewhat contradictory. Choice C is antithetical to the paradigm. Choice E is completely irrelevant. *(See Chapter VIII, Section B1.)*

13. **A, C** "Lacks maturity" is the clue that the youthful artist is *puerile* or *jejune* (childish or immature). None of the other choices fits the context. *(See Chapter VI, Section A; Chapter VII.)*

14. **A, F** "Rancorous" and "malign" are the clues that the candidates resorted to *aspersion* or *calumny* (slander). *(See Chapter VI, Section B; Chapter VII.)*

15. **A, C** "Garishly elaborate decorations" is the clue to *meretricious* (superficially attractive in a vulgar manner) or *ostentatious* (marked by a vulgar display of wealth). *(See Chapter VI, Section A; Chapter VII.)*

16. **B, D** A dirge is a funeral song or hymn, which suggests *lugubrious* or *plaintive* (gloomy or mournful) strains. *(See Chapter VI, Section B; Chapter VII.)*

17. **A, B** The quasi-religious nature of the experience is suggested by all the allusions to religion: "litanies," "chalice," "prayers," "adoration." The boy imagines himself a hero as he "bore his chalice safely through a throng of foes." Choice C is incorrect because it is directly contradicted by the penultimate sentence: "I did not know whether I would ever speak to her or not or, if I spoke to her, how I could tell her of my confused adoration." *(See Chapter VIII, Section B2.)*

18. **E** The passage alludes to the boy's body as a "harp," but he never says he plays an instrument. All the other choices are contained in the passage. The market is open on Saturdays; pigs' cheeks are sold in the market; the street-singers sing ballads; and the boy carries parcels for his aunt. *(See Chapter VIII, Section B1.)*

19. **B** The author's main point is that most outstanding reformers have suffered during their lifetimes, only to be honored after their deaths. Choice B, an example of a woman honored during her lifetime, undermines the author's premise. None of the other choices counters the author's main point. *(See Chapter VIII, Section B1.)*

20. **B** In the context of the passage, *real* means *actual*. The passage suggests that her life story has been misrepresented so much that the "real/actual" woman remains unknown. None of the other choices fits the context as well as *actual*. *(See Chapter VIII, Section B1.)*

Section 2: Quantitative Reasoning

1. **A** Because $\left(\dfrac{x}{y}\right)^2 > \dfrac{x}{y}$ and $\left(\dfrac{y}{x}\right)^2 < \dfrac{y}{x}$, $\dfrac{x}{y}$ must be greater than 1 and $\dfrac{y}{x}$ must be less than 1, so $x > y$. *(See Chapter X, Sections D and H.)*

2. **A** $(3 \otimes 4) \odot 5 = (3^2 - 4) \odot 5 = (9 - 4) \odot 5 = 5 \odot 5 = 5 + 5^2 = 5 + 25 = 30$, but
$3 \otimes (4 \odot 5) = 3 \otimes (4 + 5^2) = 3 \otimes (4 + 25) = 3 \otimes 29 = 3^2 - 29 = 9 - 29 = -20$. *(See Chapter XIII, Section B.)*

3. **B** The number 4.2953 rounded to the nearest thousandth is 4.295. The digit in the thousandths place is 5 and the digit in the hundreds place is 9. *(See Chapter X, Section F.)*

4. **A** If $3 < a < b < 4$, $1 < 33\frac{1}{3}\%$ of $a < \frac{4}{3}$ and $\frac{3}{4} < 25\%$ of $b < 1$. 25% of $b < 1 < 33\frac{1}{3}\%$ of a. *(See Chapter X, Section G.)*

5. **B** $\frac{n}{5} = \frac{p}{3}$ $3n = 5p$ $n = \frac{5p}{3}$ $n + 1 = \frac{5p}{3} + 1 = \frac{5p+3}{3}$ $\frac{n+1}{5} = \frac{5p+3}{3 \cdot 5} = \frac{p+\frac{3}{5}}{3}$. *(See Chapter X, Section E.)*

6. **B** If 5 times the difference between a and b is 25, then the difference between a and b is 5, so 6 times the difference between a and b is 30. *(See Chapter XI, Section A.)*

7. **C** $\sqrt{n^2} = |n|$, which is just n, because $n \geq 0$ and $\left(\sqrt{n}\right)^2 = n$. *(See Chapter X, Section I.)*

8. **B** The three angles must total 180°, and because all three are equal, x must equal 60°. *(See Chapter XII, Section B.)*

9. **B** The area of $\triangle PQR = \frac{1}{2}(2x)(x) = x^2$ and half the area of a circle of radius $x = \frac{1}{2}\pi \cdot x^2$. Because half of π is greater than one, $\frac{1}{2}\pi \cdot x^2 > x^2$. *(See Chapter XII, Sections E and F.)*

10. **B** The length of a side of the square can be determined to be $24 \div 4 = 6$, but the longer side of the rectangle will be greater than 6. In order to have a rectangle that is not a square and, thus, has a longer side, there must be a shorter side that is less than 6 and a longer side that is greater than 6. *(See Chapter XII, Section C.)*

11. **C** The distance from the origin to point $A = \sqrt{(-x-0)^2 + (y-0)^2} = \sqrt{x^2 + y^2}$. The distance from the origin to point $B = \sqrt{(x-0)^2 + (-y-0)^2} = \sqrt{x^2 + y^2}$. *(See Chapter XII, Section H.)*

12. **C** $\left(x^3\right)^5 \left(x^4\right)^5 = x^{15} x^{20} = x^{35}$ and $\left(x^7\right)^5 = x^{35}$. *(See Chapter X, Section H.)*

13. **A** Because you're given little information about a and b, trying various possibilities won't be efficient. Instead, consider that the larger the number, the farther apart its multiples will fall, and so the fewer multiples will fall in a fixed range. For example, multiples of 9 between 20 and 80 include 27, 36, 45, 54, 63, and 72—a total of six. But multiples of 8 number seven: 24, 32, 40, 48, 56, 64, and 72. *(See Chapter X, Section C.)*

14. **B** If the mean of p, q, and r is 20, the sum of p, q, and r is 60; therefore, the sum of p, q, r, and 40 is 100 and the mean of p, q, r, and 40 is $100 \div 4 = 25$. *(See Chapter XIII, Section A.)*

15. **B** Integers that are multiples of both 3 and 5 are multiples of 15, so they include 15, 30, and 45—a total of three. *(See Chapter X, Section C.)*

16. **A** Three elements in X and three elements in Y mean that there are nine products and nine sums, but they may not all be distinct. Products include 3×4, 3×5, 3×6, 4×4, 4×5, 4×6, 5×4, 5×5, and 5×6. Only 4×5 and 5×4 are duplicated, so there are eight distinct products. The possible sums are $3 + 4$, $3 + 5$, $3 + 6$, $4 + 4$, $4 + 5$, $4 + 6$, $5 + 4$, $5 + 5$, and $5 + 6$, giving only five distinct sums. *(See Chapter XIII, Section C.)*

17. **A** The number of weeks in 427 days is $427 \div 7 = 61$, and the number of months in 5 years is $5 \times 12 = 60$. *(See Chapter X, Section B.)*

18. B Order of operations is a concern here, as are the fractions. $\frac{1}{2} \div \frac{3}{4} + \frac{1}{3} = \frac{2}{3} + \frac{1}{3} = 1$ while $\frac{1}{2} + \frac{3}{4} \div \frac{1}{3} = \frac{2}{4} + \frac{9}{4} = \frac{11}{4}$. *(See Chapter X, Sections A and D.)*

19. 80 The stopping distance is the reaction distance plus the braking distance. The reaction distance is 1.1 feet for each mile per hour of speed, so $1.1 \times 30 = 33$ feet. Add to that the braking distance of 54 feet, for a total of $33 + 47 = 80$ feet. *(See Chapter XIII, Section A.)*

20. D The stopping distance for a car traveling at 60 mph is $66 + 185 = 251$ feet. The stopping distance for a car traveling at 40 mph is $44 + 82 = 126$ feet. The difference is $251 - 126 = 125$ feet. *(See Chapter XIII, Sections A and D.)*

21. D The stopping distance for a car traveling at 50 mph is $1.1 \times 50 + 128 = 55 + 128 = 183$ feet. Divide that by 50 to get a rate of 3.66. *(See Chapter XIII, Sections A and D.)*

22. A, B The stopping distances are 43 feet at 20 mph, 80 feet at 30 mph, 126 feet at 40 mph, 183 feet at 50 mph, and 251 feet at 60 mph. 126 is more than 2×43, 183 is more than 2×80, but 251 is less than 2×126. *(See Chapter XIII, Sections A and D.)*

23. B Distance divided by rate equals time, so $\frac{7.2 \times 10^9}{2.4 \times 10^7} = \frac{7.2}{2.4} \times \frac{10^9}{10^7} = 3 \times 10^2 = 300$ seconds. *(See Chapter X, Section F; Chapter XIII, Section D.)*

24. D If $\triangle XYZ$ is isosceles with $\overline{XY} \cong \overline{YZ}$, $\angle Y$ is the vertex angle. If $m\angle Y = 36°$, then each of the congruent base angles measures $\frac{180 - 36}{2} = \frac{144}{2} = 72°$. *(See Chapter XII, Section B.)*

25. 35 If x and y represent the two numbers, $x + y = 12$ and $x - y = 2$. Adding the equations, $2x = 14$ and $x = 7$. So, $y = 12 - 7 = 5$, and the product $xy = 35$. *(See Chapter XI, Section B.)*

26. D $L = 4 + W$ and $P = 2L + 2W = 2(4 + W) + 2W = 20$. Solving the equation $8 + 4W = 20$ gives $W = 3$ so $L = 7$ and the area is $L \cdot W = 21$ square inches. *(See Chapter XII, Section C.)*

27. A, E The absolute value of any expression behaves as a positive, so the fact that $x|y - 3| < 0$ tells you that $x < 0$. You can't make a determination about y, except to say that it isn't equal to 3. If y were equal to 3, the product would be 0. *(See Chapter XI, Section A.)*

28. B The probability that a winner will receive a black bear = the number of black bears divided by the total number of bears. $P(\text{black bear}) = \frac{4}{18} = \frac{2}{9}$. *(See Chapter XIII, Section C.)*

29. A Move the decimal point three places to the left. *(See Chapter X, Section F.)*

30. 200 The volume of a rectangular solid is length $\times$ width $\times$ height. Taking the square face as the base and 8 as the height, $V = 5 \times 5 \times 8 = 200$ cubic units. *(See Chapter XII, Section G.)*

31. B $\frac{t^2 + 7t + 10}{t^2 - 4} = \frac{(t+5)(t+2)}{(t+2)(t-2)} = \frac{t+5}{t-2}$. *(See Chapter XI, Section D.)*

32. A, B, C, D If $290 \le 45 - 7w < 990$ then $245 \le -7w < 945$ and $-35 \ge w > -135$. *(See Chapter XI, Section A.)*

33. A Use the Pythagorean theorem: $c = \sqrt{a^2 + b^2} = \sqrt{15^2 + 20^2} = \sqrt{225 + 400} = \sqrt{625} = 25$. A quicker method is to recognize that these values are multiples of a Pythagorean triple. *(See Chapter XII, Section B.)*

34. A The equation describes a circle with center at $(4, -9)$ and a radius of 1. Only the radius is important to the question. Area is $\pi r^2 = \pi$. *(See Chapter XII, Sections F and H.)*

35. C $4x^2 - 36 = 0 \rightarrow 4x^2 = 36 \rightarrow x^2 = 9 \rightarrow x = \pm 3$. *(See Chapter XI, Section D.)*

36. $\frac{2}{3}$ If the average of N grades is 80, then the total of all the grades in that group is $80N$. The total of the grades in the class of P students is $70P$. When the classes are combined, $\frac{80N + 70P}{N + P} = 76$. While one equation is not sufficient to solve for N or P, it is enough to express the relationship between N and P. Cross-multiply and simplify, and work toward an equation with $\frac{P}{N}$ on one side. Cross-multiplying gives you $80N + 70P = 76(N + P)$ or $80N + 70P = 76N + 76P$, which becomes $4N = 6P$. Then $\frac{P}{N} = \frac{4}{6}$, which reduces to $\frac{2}{3}$. *(See Chapter XIII, Section A.)*

37. C The regular price of $75 is 150% of cost, so cost is $75 \div 1.50 = 50. At the end of the season, it will sell for 90% of cost, or $0.90 \times 50 = 45. *(See Chapter X, Section G.)*

38. D The mean of x and 10 is equal to $\frac{x+10}{2}$ and the mean of x, 3, 14, and 16 is $\frac{x+3+14+16}{4} = \frac{x+33}{4}$. If $\frac{x+10}{2} = \frac{x+33}{4}$, then $\frac{2(x+10)}{4} = \frac{x+33}{4}$ and $2(x + 10) = x + 33$. Solving, $2x + 20 = x + 33 \rightarrow x = 13$. *(See Chapter XIII, Section A.)*

39. D A radius of 3 means a diameter of 6, and the diameter and height form the legs of a right triangle, whose hypotenuse, the straight-line distance from A to B, can be found by the Pythagorean theorem: $c = \sqrt{a^2 + b^2} = \sqrt{6^2 + 8^2} = \sqrt{100} = 10$. *(See Chapter XII, Sections B and F.)*

40. A Drawing the diagram will be helpful.

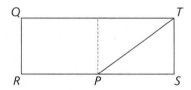

If a perpendicular were drawn to P, it would divide the rectangle in half, so the area of quadrilateral $QRPT$ is three-fourths of the area of the rectangle. *(See Chapter XII, Section C; Chapter X, Section D.)*

41. $\frac{5}{14}$ Applying the definition, $\frac{2 \otimes 5}{6 \otimes 8} = \frac{\cancel{2} \cdot \cancel{3} \cdot \cancel{4} \cdot 5}{\cancel{6} \cdot 7 \cdot \cancel{8}_2} = \frac{5}{14}$. *(See Chapter XIII, Section B.)*

42. D, E If $6t = 3v - 9$, add 9 to both sides to get $6t + 9 = 3v$. Divide by 3 to get $\frac{6t+9}{3} = v$ and simplify to get $2t + 3 = v$. *(See Chapter XI, Section A.)*

43. A 70% of $480 = \frac{7}{10} \times 480 = 7 \times 48 = 336$ and $480 - 336 = 144$. Alternately, if 70% had jobs, 30% did not, so $\frac{3}{10} \times 480 = 3 \times 48 = 144$. *(See Chapter X, Section G.)*

44. B The area of the rectangle is $24 \times 8 = 192$ square centimeters, but each of the shaded triangles has a height of 8 and a base of half of 24. The combined area of the two triangles is, which is 96 cm², or half the area of the rectangle. *(See Chapter XII, Section E.)*

45. C If the area of the square is 169 square inches, each side is 13 inches, so the diagonal is $13\sqrt{2}$. *(See Chapter XII, Sections C and D.)*

46. **A, C, D** N is one more than a multiple of five, a number of the form $5p + 1$, so multiplying N by 73 will produce a number of the form $15p + 3$. Dividing $15p + 3$ by 5 produces $\frac{15p+3}{5} = 3p + \frac{3}{5}$, so the remainder is 3. Then $4N = 20p + 4$, and dividing by 2 gives you $10p + 2$ with a remainder of zero. $6N = 30p + 6$, divided by 5, gives you $6p + 1$ and a remainder of 1, but if you divide it by 3, you get $10p + 2$ with a remainder of 0. $7N = 35p + 5$ divided by 5 is $7p + 1$ with a remainder of 0. *(See Chapter X, Section C.)*

47. **E** If the four children shared the candy equally, each began with $\frac{1}{4}$ of the candy. The oldest brother gave $\frac{1}{2} \cdot \frac{1}{4} = \frac{1}{8}$ of the candy to the youngest sister. The other brother gave $\frac{1}{4} \cdot \frac{1}{4} = \frac{1}{16}$ of the candy to her. So the youngest sister had $\frac{1}{4} + \frac{1}{8} + \frac{1}{16} = \frac{4}{16} + \frac{2}{16} + \frac{1}{16} = \frac{7}{16}$ of the candy. *(See Chapter X, Section D.)*

48. **$10.23** It's possible to calculate each day's addition to savings and then add, but it may be faster to look for a pattern in the cumulative sum. On day 1, she deposits 1¢, for a total of 1¢. On day 2, she deposits 2¢ for a total of 3¢. On day 3, she deposits 4¢ for a total of 7¢. Each day's total is 1¢ less than the next day's deposit. Calculate the deposit for the 11th day and subtract one to find the ten-day total. On the 11th day, she would deposit 2^{10} cents, or $10.24, so the ten-day total is $10.23. *(See Chapter XIII, Section F.)*

49. **C** The measure of an interior angle of a regular hexagon is $\frac{180(6-2)}{6} = 120°$. The measure of an exterior angle of a regular pentagon is $\frac{360}{5} = 72°$. The difference is $120° - 72° = 48°$. *(See Chapter XII, Section D.)*

50. **B** Actually calculating speeds would be time-consuming. Using a rough estimation, most of the runners covered fewer than three steps per second, but the winner of the Taipei 101 climbed more than three steps per second. *(See Chapter XIII, Sections A and D.)*

	Quantitative	Verbal	Writing
8 weeks before the test	**Study time:** 2½ hours ❏ Take the **Diagnostic Test** and review the answer explanations. ❏ Based on your test results, identify difficult topics and their corresponding chapters. These chapters are your targeted chapters.		

	Study time: 2 hours
	❏ **Arithmetic:** Chapter X
	   ❏ Read Sections A–C and H–I.
	   ❏ As you review, build a list of formulas and rules to memorize.
	   ❏ Do practice questions 1–5.
		Study time: 1 hour
		❏ **Text Completion:** Chapter V
		   ❏ Read Introduction.
		   ❏ Read Sections A–C.
		❏ **Vocabulary Review:** Chapter VII
		   ❏ Read through the list. Put any unfamiliar words on index cards.
		   ❏ Study vocabulary words abash–conjoin.
			Study time: 1 hour
			❏ **Analytical Writing:** Chapter IX
			   ❏ Read the chapter.
			   ❏ Pay attention to the difference between the "Analyze an Issue" task and the "Analyze an Argument" task.

7 weeks before the test	**Study time:** 2 hours
	❏ **Arithmetic:** Chapter X
	   ❏ Read Sections D–G.
	   ❏ Add any new formulas and rules to your list.
	   ❏ Do practice questions 1–5.
	❏ Review one of your target chapters.
	   ❏ Do questions 6–10 in this chapter.
		Study time: 1 hour
		❏ **Text Completion:** Chapter V
		   ❏ Do practice questions 1–20.
		❏ **Vocabulary Review:** Chapter VII
		   ❏ Study vocabulary words connoisseur–flaunt.
			Study time: 30 minutes
			❏ **Analytical Writing:** Chapter IX
			   ❏ Review the chapter.
			   ❏ Focus on the "Analyze an Argument" task.

6 weeks before the test	**Study time:** 2 hours
	❏ **Algebra:** Chapter XI
	   ❏ Read Sections A–D.
	   ❏ Add any new formulas and rules to your list.
	   ❏ Do practice questions 1–5.
	❏ Review one of your target chapters.
	   ❏ Do questions 6–10 in this chapter.
		Study time: 1 hour
		❏ **Sentence Equivalence:** Chapter VI
		   ❏ Read Introduction.
		   ❏ Read Sections A–C.
		   ❏ Do practice questions 1–10.
		❏ **Vocabulary Review:** Chapter VII
		   ❏ Study vocabulary words flippant–loquacious.
			Study time: 30 minutes
			❏ **Analytical Writing:** Chapter IX
			   ❏ Review the chapter.
			   ❏ Focus on the "Analyze an Issue" task.

continued

	Quantitative	Verbal	Writing

5 weeks before the test	**Study time:** 2 hours
	❑ **Geometry:** Chapter XII
	  ❑ Read Sections A–E.
	  ❑ Add any new formulas and rules to your list.
	  ❑ Do practice questions 1–5.
		Study time: 1 hour
		❑ **Sentence Equivalence:** Chapter VI
		  ❑ Do practice questions 11–30.
		❑ **Vocabulary Review:** Chapter VII
		  ❑ Study vocabulary words lugubrious–prodigal.
			Study time: 1½ hours
			❑ **Analytical Writing:** Chapter IX
			  ❑ Practice an "Analyze an Issue" task.

4 weeks before the test	**Study time:** 2 hours
	❑ **Geometry:** Chapter XII
	  ❑ Read Sections F–H.
	  ❑ Add any new formulas and rules to your list.
	  ❑ Do practice questions 1–5.
	❑ Review one of your target chapters.
	  ❑ Do practice questions 6–10 in this chapter.
		Study time: 1½ hours
		❑ **Reading Comprehension:** Chapter VIII
		  ❑ Read Introduction.
		  ❑ Read Sections A–C.
		  ❑ Do practice questions 1–7.
		❑ **Vocabulary Review:** Chapter VII
		  ❑ Study vocabulary words prodigious–self-effacing.
			Study time: 1½ hours
			❑ **Analytical Writing:** Chapter IX
			  ❑ Practice an "Analyze an Argument" task.

3 weeks before the test	**Study time:** 2 hours
	❑ **Applications:** Chapter XIII
	  ❑ Read Sections A–C.
	  ❑ Add any new formulas and rules to your list.
	  ❑ Do practice questions 1–5.
	❑ Review one of your target chapters.
	  ❑ Do practice questions 6–10 in this chapter.
		Study time: 1 hour
		❑ **Reading Comprehension:** Chapter VIII
		  ❑ Do practice questions 8–15.
		❑ **Vocabulary Review:** Chapter VII
		  ❑ Study vocabulary words shrewd–zealous.
			Study time: 1 hour
			❑ **Analytical Writing:** Chapter IX
			  ❑ Analyze the "Analyze an Argument" task to see how you could substantiate or back up your reasoning better with examples.
			  ❑ Redo the task based on your analysis.

2 weeks before the test	**Study time:** 2½ hours ❑ Take the **Practice Test** and review answer explanations. ❑ Based on your test results, identify difficult topics and their corresponding chapters. These chapters are your targeted areas.		

	Study time: 2 hours
	❑ **Applications:** Chapter XIII
	  ❑ Read Sections D–F.
	  ❑ Add any new formulas and rules to your list.
	  ❑ Do practice questions 1–5.
	❑ Review one of your target chapters.
	  ❑ Do practice questions 6–10 in this chapter.
		Study time: 1 hour
		❑ **Text Completion:** Chapter V
		  ❑ Reread the chapter.
		  ❑ Review Section A.
		  ❑ Redo any practice questions you got wrong the first time.
		❑ **Vocabulary Review:** Chapter VII
		  ❑ Study vocabulary words abash–curtail.
			Study time: 1 hour
			❑ **Analytical Writing:** Chapter IX
			  ❑ Analyze the "Analyze an Issue" task to see how you could substantiate or back up your reasoning better with examples.
			  ❑ Redo the task based on your analysis.

	Quantitative	Verbal	Writing

7 days before the test	**Study time:** 30 minutes
	❏ **Arithmetic:** Chapter X
	  ❏ Read Sections C and G.
	  ❏ Redo any questions you got wrong the first time.
	❏ Review your list of formulas and rules.
		Study time: 1 hour
		❏ **Sentence Equivalence:** Chapter VI
		  ❏ Reread the chapter.
		  ❏ Redo any practice questions you got wrong the first time.
		❏ **Vocabulary Review:** Chapter VII
		  ❏ Study vocabulary words dearth–fundamental.
			Study time: 1 hour
			❏ **Analytical Writing:** Chapter IX
			  ❏ Review Sections A–B.

6 days before the test	**Study time:** 30 minutes
	❏ **Algebra:** Chapter XI
	  ❏ Read Section B.
	  ❏ Redo any questions you got wrong the first time.
	❏ Review your list of formulas and rules.
		Study time: 1 hour
		❏ **Reading Comprehension:** Chapter VIII
		  ❏ Reread the chapter.
		  ❏ Redo any practice questions you got wrong the first time.
		❏ **Vocabulary Review:** Chapter VII
		  ❏ Study vocabulary words garner–itinerant.
			Study time: 30 minutes
			❏ **Analytical Writing:** Chapter IX
			  ❏ Practice an "Analyze an Argument" task and score yourself.

5 days before the test	**Study time:** 30 minutes
	❏ **Geometry:** Chapter XII
	  ❏ Read Sections B–C.
	  ❏ Redo any questions you got wrong the first time.
	❏ Review your list of formulas and rules.
		Study time: 1½ hours
		❏ **Vocabulary Review:** Chapter VII
		  ❏ Study vocabulary words jargon–mystical.
			Study time: 45 minutes
			❏ **Analytical Writing:** Chapter IX
			  ❏ Practice an "Analyze an Issue" task and score yourself.

4 days before the test	**Study time:** 30 minutes.
	❏ **Geometry:** Chapter XII
	  ❏ Read Section G.
	  ❏ Redo any questions you got wrong the first time.
	❏ Review your list of formulas and rules.
		Study time: 1 hour
		❏ **Vocabulary Review:** Chapter VII
		  ❏ Study vocabulary words nadir–pusillanimous.
			Study time: 1 hour
			❏ **Analytical Writing:** Chapter IX
			  ❏ Read Section D1.

3 days before the test	**Study time:** 30 minutes
	❏ **Applications:** Chapter XIII
	  ❏ Read the chapter.
	  ❏ Redo any questions you got wrong the first time.
	❏ Review your list of formulas and rules.
		Study time: 1 hour
		❏ **Vocabulary Review:** Chapter VII
		  ❏ Study vocabulary words quandary–turpitude.
			Study time: 1 hour
			❏ **Analytical Writing:** Chapter IX
			  ❏ Read Section D2.

continued

	Quantitative	Verbal	Writing

2 days before the test	**Study time: 30 minutes**
	❏ **Applications:** Chapter XIII
	   ❏ Read Section D.
	   ❏ Redo any questions you got wrong the first time.
		Study time: 45 minutes
		❏ **Vocabulary Review:** Chapter VII
		   ❏ Study vocabulary words ubiquitous– zealous.
			Study time: 30–45 minutes
			❏ **Analytical Writing:** Chapter IX
			   ❏ Pick the type of task you need to work on most ("Analyze an Argument" or "Analyze an Issue"), and write it with a timer.

1 day before the test	**Study time:** 1 hour
	❏ Review your target chapters.
	   ❏ Review questions in these chapters that you got wrong before, and make sure you understand your errors.
	❏ Review your list of formulas and rules one last time before bed.
		Study time: 30 minutes
		❏ **Vocabulary Review:** Chapter VII
		   ❏ Review any vocabulary words that you still don't know.
			Study time: 1 hour
			❏ **Analytical Writing:** Chapter IX
			   ❏ Read the chapter.
			   ❏ Rewrite your essay to a score-6 level.

Morning of the test	**Reminders:**
	❏ Allow yourself enough time to reach the testing center with some time to spare, so that you have a chance to relax before you're scheduled to begin testing.
	❏ Dress in layers so you can adjust if you find the testing room too hot or too cold.
	❏ Have a good meal before the test, but don't overeat.
	❏ Take the following items with you on test day:
	   ❏ Your admission ticket and photo ID
	   ❏ Several pens and no. 2 pencils
	   Scrap paper will be provided to you. You may not bring anything else into the testing room.
	❏ Try to go outside for a few minutes and walk around before the test.
	❏ Most important: Stay calm and confident during the test. Take deep, slow breaths if you feel nervous. You can do it!		

III. One-Month Cram Plan

	Quantitative	Verbal	Writing
4 weeks before the test	**Study time:** 2½ hours ❏ Take the **Diagnostic Test** and review the answer explanations. ❏ Based on your test results, identify difficult topics and their corresponding chapters. These chapters are your targeted chapters.		

	Study time: 2 hours
	❏ **Arithmetic:** Chapter X
	  ❏ Read the chapter.
	  ❏ As you review, build a list of formulas and rules to memorize.
	  ❏ Do practice questions 1–5.
		Study time: 2 hours
		❏ **Text Completion:** Chapter V
		  ❏ Read Introduction.
		  ❏ Read Sections A–C.
		  ❏ Do practice questions 1–20.
		❏ **Vocabulary Review:** Chapter VII
		  ❏ Read through the list. Put any unfamiliar words on index cards.
		  ❏ Study vocabulary words abash–flaunt.
			Study time: 1 hour
			❏ **Analytical Writing:** Chapter IX
			  ❏ Read the chapter.
			  ❏ Pay attention to the difference between the "Analyze an Issue" task and the "Analyze an Argument" task.
			  ❏ Read Section A.

3 weeks before the test	**Study time:** 2 hours
	❏ **Algebra:** Chapter XI
	  ❏ Read the chapter.
	  ❏ Add any new formulas and rules to your list.
	  ❏ Do practice questions 1–5.
		Study time: 2 hours
		❏ **Sentence Equivalence:** Chapter VI
		  ❏ Read Introduction.
		  ❏ Read Sections A–C.
		  ❏ Do practice questions 1–10.
		❏ **Vocabulary Review:** Chapter VII
		  ❏ Study vocabulary words flippant–prodigal.
			Study time: 1 hour
			❏ **Analytical Writing:** Chapter IX
			  ❏ Practice an "Analyze an Issue" task, with a timer.

2 weeks before the test	**Study time:** 2 hours
	❏ **Geometry:** Chapter XII
	  ❏ Read the chapter.
	  ❏ Add any new formulas and rules to your list.
	  ❏ Do practice questions 1–5.
		Study time: 2 hours
		❏ **Sentence Equivalence:** Chapter VI
		  ❏ Review the chapter.
		  ❏ Do practice questions 11–30.
		❏ **Vocabulary Review:** Chapter VII
		  ❏ Study vocabulary words prodigious–zealous.
			Study time: 1 hour
			❏ **Analytical Writing:** Chapter IX
			  ❏ Practice an "Anayze an Argument" task, with a timer.

continued

	Quantitative	Verbal	Writing

7 days before the test	**Study time:** 30 minutes
	❏ **Applications:** Chapter XIII
	  ❏ Read Sections A–B.
	  ❏ Add any new formulas and rules to your list.
	  ❏ Do practice questions 1–5.
		Study time: 1 hour
		❏ **Reading Comprehension:** Chapter VIII
		  ❏ Read Introduction.
		  ❏ Read Sections A–C.
		  ❏ Do practice questions 1–7.
			Study time: 30 minutes
			❏ **Analytical Writing:** Chapter IX
			  ❏ Practice an "Analyze an Argument" task, and score yourself.
			  ❏ Read Section A.

6 days before the test	**Study time:** 1 hour
	❏ **Applications:** Chapter XIII
	  ❏ Read Sections C–D.
	  ❏ Add any new formulas and rules to your list.
	  ❏ Do practice questions 1–5.
		Study time: 1 hour
		❏ **Reading Comprehension:** Chapter VIII
		  ❏ Do practice questions 8–15.
		❏ **Vocabulary Review:** Chapter VII
		  ❏ Study vocabulary words abash–flaunt.
			Study time: 45 minutes
			❏ **Analytical Writing:** Chapter IX
			  ❏ Practice an "Analyze an Issue" task, and score yourself.

5 days before the test	**Study time:** 30 minutes
	❏ **Applications:** Chapter XIII
	  ❏ Read Sections E–F.
	  ❏ Add any new formulas and rules to your list.
	  ❏ Do practice questions 1–5.
		Study time: 1 hour
		❏ **Text Completion:** Chapter V
		  ❏ Review the chapter.
		❏ **Vocabulary Review:** Chapter VII
		  ❏ Study vocabulary words flippant–prodigal.
			Study time: 30 minutes
			❏ **Analytical Writing:** Chapter IX
			  ❏ Correct your essays, and add examples or rewrite awkward sentences.

4 days before the test	**Study time:** 1 hour
	❏ Review your target chapters.
	  ❏ Redo any questions you got wrong the first time.
	❏ Study your list of rules and formulas.
		Study time: 1 hour
		❏ **Sentence Equivalence:** Chapter VI
		  ❏ Review the chapter.
		❏ **Vocabulary Review:** Chapter VII
		  ❏ Study vocabulary words prodigious–self-effacing.
			Study time: 1 hour
			❏ **Analytical Writing:** Chapter IX
			  ❏ Read Section D.

3 days before the test	**Study time:** 30 minutes
	❏ Review your target chapters.
	  ❏ Do practice questions 6–10 in these chapters.
	❏ Study your list of rules and formulas.
		Study time: 1 hour
		❏ **Reading Comprehension: Chapter VIII**
		  ❏ Review the chapter.
		❏ **Vocabulary Review:** Chapter VII
		  ❏ Study vocabulary words shrewd–zealous.
			Study time: 45 minutes
			❏ **Analytical Writing:** Chapter IX
			  ❏ Pick the type of task you need to work on most ("Analyze an Argument" or "Analyze an Issue"), and write it with a timer.

2 days before the test	**Study time:** 2½ hours ❏ Take the **Practice Test** and review answer explanations. ❏ Based on your test results, identify difficult topics and their corresponding chapters. These chapters are your targeted areas.		

	Quantitative	Verbal	Writing
1 day before the test	**Study time:** 30 minutes ❑ Review your target chapters. ❑ Review your list of formulas and rules one last time before bed.	**Study time:** 45 minutes ❑ **Text Completion:** Chapter V 　❑ Review the chapter. ❑ **Sentence Equivalence:** Chapter VI 　❑ Review the chapter. ❑ **Reading Comprehension:** Chapter VIII 　❑ Review the chapter. ❑ **Vocabulary Review:** Chapter VII 　❑ Review all vocabulary words.	**Study time:** 30 minutes ❑ **Analytical Writing:** Chapter IX 　❑ Reread Section D. 　❑ Revise your essays to improve score.
Morning of the test	**Reminders:** ❑ Allow yourself enough time to reach the testing center with some time to spare, so that you have a chance to relax before you're scheduled to begin testing. ❑ Dress in layers so you can adjust if you find the testing room too hot or too cold. ❑ Have a good meal before the test, but don't overeat. ❑ Take the following items with you on test day: 　❑ Your admission ticket and photo ID 　❑ Several pens and no. 2 pencils 　Scrap paper will be provided to you. You may not bring anything else into the testing room. ❑ Try to go outside for a few minutes and walk around before the test. ❑ Most important: Stay calm and confident during the test. Take deep, slow breaths if you feel nervous. You can do it!		

IV. One-Week Cram Plan

	Quantitative	Critical Reading	Writing
7 days before the test	**Study time:** 2½ hours ❏ Take the **Diagnostic Test** and review the answer explanations. ❏ Based on your test results, identify difficult topics and their corresponding chapters. These chapters are your targeted chapters. *Note:* In one week, you can't study every detail of every chapter. Expect to give most material a quick reading and focus your efforts on your targeted chapters.		

6 days before the test	**Study time:** 1 hour
	❏ **Arithmetic:** Chapter X
	  ❏ Read the chapter.
	  ❏ As you review, build a list of formulas and rules to memorize.
	  ❏ Focus on your targets or on Sections C and E.
	  ❏ Do practice questions 1–10.
		Study time: 1 hour
		❏ **Text Completion:** Chapter V
		  ❏ Read the chapter.
		  ❏ Do practice questions 1–20
		❏ **Vocabulary Review:** Chapter VII
		  ❏ Study vocabulary words abash–diffidence.
			Study time: 45 minutes
			❏ **Analytical Writing:** Chapter IX
			  ❏ Read the chapter.
			  ❏ Practice an "Analyze an Issue" task, with a timer.

5 days before the test	**Study time:** 1 hour
	❏ **Algebra:** Chapter XI
	  ❏ Read the chapter.
	  ❏ Add any new formulas and rules to your list.
	  ❏ Focus on your targets or on Section A.
	  ❏ Do practice questions 1–10.
		Study time: 1 hour
		❏ **Sentence Equivalence:** Chapter VI
		  ❏ Read the chapter.
		  ❏ Do practice questions 1–10.
		❏ **Vocabulary Review:** Chapter VII
		  ❏ Study vocabulary words dilatory–inimitable.
			Study time: 30 minutes
			❏ **Analytical Writing:** Chapter IX
			  ❏ Practice an "Analyze an Argument" task, with a timer.

4 days before the test	**Study time:** 1 hour
	❏ **Geometry:** Chapter XII
	  ❏ Read the chapter.
	  ❏ Add any new formulas and rules to your list.
	  ❏ Focus on your targets or on Sections C and G.
	  ❏ Do practice questions 1–10.
		Study time: 1 hour
		❏ **Sentence Equivalence:** Chapter VI
		  ❏ Review the chapter.
		  ❏ Do practice questions 11–30.
		❏ **Vocabulary Review:** Chapter VII
		  ❏ Study vocabulary words innocuous–prodigal.
			Study time: 1 hour
			❏ **Analytical Writing:** Chapter IX
			  ❏ Analyze the "Analyze an Issue" task to see how you could substantiate or back up your reasoning better with examples.
			  ❏ Rewrite the essay based on your analysis.

	Quantitative	Critical Reading	Writing

3 days before the test	**Study time:** 1 hour
	❑ **Applications:** Chapter XIII
	❑ Read the chapter.
	   ❑ Add any new formulas and rules to your list.
	   ❑ Focus on your targets or on Section A.
	   ❑ Do practice questions 1–10.
		Study time: 1 hour
		❑ **Reading Comprehension:** Chapter VIII
		   ❑ Read the chapter.
		   ❑ Do practice questions 1–15.
		❑ **Vocabulary Review:** Chapter VII
		   ❑ Study vocabulary words prodigious–zealous.
			Study time: 1 hour
			❑ **Analytical Writing:** Chapter IX
			   ❑ Analyze the "Analyze an Argument" task to see how you could substantiate or back up your reasoning better with examples.
			   ❑ Rewrite the essay based on your analysis.

2 days before the test	**Study time:** 2½ hours ❑ Take the **Practice Test** and review answer explanations. ❑ Based on your test results, identify difficult topics and their corresponding chapters. These chapters are your targeted areas.		

1 day before the test	**Study time:** 1 hour
	❑ Review your target chapters.
	❑ Redo any questions you got wrong the first time.
	❑ Review your list of formulas and rules one last time before bed.
		Study time: 1 hour
		❑ **Text Completion:** Chapter V
		   ❑ Review the chapter.
		   ❑ Redo any questions you got wrong the first time.
		❑ **Sentence Equivalence:** Chapter VI
		   ❑ Review the chapter.
		   ❑ Redo any questions you got wrong the first time.
		❑ **Reading Comprehension:** Chapter VIII.
		   ❑ Review the chapter.
		   ❑ Redo any questions you got wrong the first time.
		❑ **Vocabulary Review:** Chapter VII
		   ❑ Review all vocabulary words.
			Study time: 1½ hours
			❑ **Analytical Writing:** Chapter IX
			   ❑ Write an "Analyze an Issue" task and an "Analyze an Argument" task, with a timer.
			   ❑ Score yourself.

Morning of the test	**Reminders:**
	❑ Allow yourself enough time to reach the testing center with some time to spare, so that you have a chance to relax before you're scheduled to begin testing.
	❑ Dress in layers so you can adjust if you find the testing room too hot or too cold.
	❑ Have a good meal before the test, but don't overeat.
	❑ Take the following items with you on test day:
	   ❑ Your admission ticket and photo ID
	   ❑ Several pens and no. 2 pencils
	   Scrap paper will be provided to you. You may not bring anything else into the testing room.
	❑ Try to go outside for a few minutes and walk around before the test.
	❑ Most important: Stay calm and confident during the test. Take deep, slow breaths if you feel nervous. You can do it!		

V. Text Completion

Text completion questions measure your ability to complete the meaning of a sentence or several sentences by choosing a word or words that most logically fit with the context clues in the sentence. In this section, you're tested on your vocabulary, your critical thinking skills, and your language usage skills.

Each question presents you with a short passage of one to five sentences with one to three blanks. Your task is to read the passage and fill in the blanks by selecting the best word or phrase for each blank from among the choices. For questions with one blank, you'll have five choices; for questions with two or three blanks, you'll choose from among three choices for each blank. For these multiple-blank questions, you must be correct in *all* your choices; you get *no credit* for partially correct answers. For example, if you get two out of the three blanks correct, but one blank incorrect, you'll receive no credit for the question.

A. Text Completion Strategies

When working on text completion questions, follow these steps:

1. **Read the sentence carefully and analyze the sentence structure.**

   Focus on words or phrases that set up the logic of the sentence. Ask yourself questions: Does the sense of the sentence indicate a series of parallel ideas? Is there a word that signals a switch that suggests you're looking for opposites?

2. **Focus on finding the context clues embedded in the sentence.**

   Look for words or phrases in the sentence that set up relationships (for example, similarity, opposition, or cause and effect) or give hints about the missing words. You don't have to find the missing words in order; sometimes you have a clearer idea about the meaning of a word in the second or third blank. Find that word and then work backward to the first blank.

   In multiple-blank questions, use the logic of the sentence and the relationships among the words to guide you.

3. **As you read the sentence, pay particular attention to *signal words* (introductory or transitional words that establish relationships within the sentence).**

4. **Use process of elimination to eliminate the incorrect choices.**

5. **Zero in on the best answer.**

6. **Reread the sentence after you've chosen an answer or answers and check the logic again.**

Here are some words that signal a **contrast or contradiction:**

despite	even though	rather than
however	nevertheless	instead
in spite of	but	
although	yet	

Here are some words that signal **ideas that are similar:**

in addition	moreover	for example
and	furthermore	likewise

Here are some words that signal a **cause-and-effect relationship:**

because	therefore	since
thus	consequently	
as a result	hence	

B. One-Blank Text Completions

When you're answering one-blank text completion questions, follow these strategies:

- **As you read the sentence, think about the word or words you might logically use to fill in the blanks before you look at the words in the choices.** This will help you narrow down the choices. You may find the exact word you were thinking of or a similar word among the choices.

- **Consider the structure of the sentence.** For example, if there is a clause followed by a colon, the words after the colon are an explanation.

- **Ask yourself: Is the missing word a positive word or a negative word? Is it a praising word or a criticizing word?** Use this thinking to help you narrow down your choices.

- **Don't eliminate a word because you think it's the wrong part of speech.** The answer choices are *always* the correct part of speech. One of the choices may be a word you're accustomed to using as a verb, but in this particular sentence, it's used as a noun. For example, the word *dispatch* is most commonly used as a verb meaning to send off or to transmit, but it also can be used as a noun to mean quickness: "He sent out the package with dispatch."

Here is a sample one-blank text completion question.

EXAMPLE:

Presenting a lecture on matters far too abstruse and _____ for his audience of laypersons, the physicist used quotidian analogies to create an accessible presentation.

- A. inane
- B. egalitarian
- C. momentous
- D. arcane
- E. sophomoric

The correct answer is **D.** *Arcane* means esoteric or capable of being understood only by a select few. The sentence contains several context clues. First, the lecture is *abstruse,* which means difficult to understand. In addition, the physicist used *quotidian* (commonplace, ordinary) analogies to make his presentation accessible to an audience of *laypersons* (nonprofessionals). The logic of the clues should lead you to understand that the missing word must describe something that most nonscientists would find hard to comprehend. Using process of elimination, you can eliminate choice A (inane means stupid or silly). Choice B, egalitarian (believing in equality), is also incorrect. Choice C, momentous (important), is possible but not the best choice given the clues in the sentence. Choice E, sophomoric, means childish or immature and is opposite in meaning to the missing word.

C. Multiple-Blank Text Completions

When you're answering the multiple-blank text completion questions, follow the same general strategies as you would for one-blank questions. In addition, consider the following:

- The passages are usually longer (up to five sentences) and may require more critical thinking on your part to follow the writer's logic. Focus and concentrate on the writer's presentation of ideas.
- When you choose what appears to be the best answer for each blank in the sentence, also consider the relationships among the two or three words or phrases. Think about the impact your choice in one blank has on your subsequent choices.
- After you've selected your two or three answers, be sure to reread the sentence very carefully to determine that all your choices are appropriate for the logic and coherence of the passage.

Here are two sample multiple-blank text completions.

EXAMPLES:

1. Beginning in 2005, several strains of the influenza virus have been (1) _____ viruses that most likely originated in China and Vietnam. Their (2) _____ was generated by the increase in both business and leisure travel to Asia.

Blank 1	Blank 2
decimated by	dissemination
decomposed in	derivation
seeded by	diminution

The correct answers are **seeded by** and **dissemination.** The context suggests that the recent strains of the influenza virus have come from Asia and have been spread by an increase in travel to that area. The passage doesn't indicate that the virus has been destroyed, so *decimated by* is not correct for Blank 1. The logic of the passage doesn't support a virus having *decomposed in* another virus. *Derivation* is not generated by an increase in travel, so that doesn't fit in Blank 2. A *diminution* is not generated by an increase in travel, so that doesn't fit in Blank 2.

2. The conductor of the symphony orchestra was famous for being (1) _____ in his public appearances. His private persona, however, was in sharp contrast to these wildly frenetic performances. His personal correspondence, for example, was characterized by (2) _____, and his family life, notable for its (3) _____.

Blank 1	Blank 2	Blank 3
agile	measured thoughtfulness	serenity
diffident	stylistic exuberance	turmoil
boisterous	rhetorical gaucherie	pedantry

The correct answers are *boisterous, measured thoughtfulness,* and *serenity.* The sentence sets up a contrast between the conductor's public and private lives. The context clue *wildly frenetic* sets up the logic of the contrast. If the conductor's performances are frenetic, then *boisterous* is the best word for Blank 1. To contrast with this behavior, his private life (including his family and his correspondence) must be more *serene* and thoughtful. *Stylistic exuberance* doesn't fit in Blank 2 because it doesn't provide the contrast to *frenetic.* The sentence doesn't suggest that he is a clumsy letter writer so *rhetorical gaucherie* isn't correct. Neither *turmoil* nor *pedantry* fits in Blank 3 because neither is the opposite of *frenetic.*

Practice

Directions (1–20): For each blank, select the word or phrase that best completes the text. (Your answer will consist of one, two, or three letters, depending on the number of blanks in each question.)

1. Dr. Stein diligently studied quantum physics with the intention of joining the _____ of elite scientists who would confer on important issues in this field of study.

   A. posse
   B. coterie
   C. chasm
   D. conspiracy
   E. contumely

2. The remote (1) _____ moors in Bronte's gothic novel *Wuthering Heights* are the ideal backdrop to the (2) _____ love story of a group of highly emotional individuals.

Blank 1	Blank 2
lugubrious	insouciant
mellifluous	tumultuous
acquiescent	parsimonious

3. As investors became more (1) _____ about the economic outlook, their plans for expansion became more (2) _____.

Blank 1	Blank 2
salutary	diaphanous
sanguine	aggrandized
dejected	seditious

4. In every society, even the most primitive, some form of musical expression exists. From the percussive sounds of prehistoric man beating on a hollow log to the magnificent symphonies of Beethoven, music (1) _____ a need for artistic expression in human society. The universal appeal of musical expression suggests that it is (2) _____ to our psychological makeup. We use music to express feelings of love, despair, fear, hope, and splendor; yet, at the same time, music can (3) _____ these same feelings in us.

Blank 1	Blank 2	Blank 3
repudiates	yoked	engender
satisfies	antithetical	undermine
inures	insensitive	verbalize

5. We would have thought that the commentator's remarks regarding the _____ in the recent campaign were hyperbolic had we not seen evidence of political trickery.

   A. chicanery
   B. effrontery
   C. subtlety
   D. solidarity
   E. meticulousness

6. The poetry of George Herbert is surprising in that it is both (1) _____ and (2) _____; his verse humbly expresses his devotional beliefs in images that are often imbued with playful wit.

Blank 1	Blank 2
pious	pedestrian
secular	trite
dogmatic	jocular

7. When it was discovered in 1938, the coelacanth, a fish previously thought to have been extinct for thousands of years, (1) _____ marine biologists and (2) _____.

Blank 1	Blank 2
electrified	reinforced preconceived notions
exacerbated	overturned long-held beliefs
impugned	mitigated current expectations

8. Feeling he lacked the _____ needed to become a financial analyst, Manuel sought more advanced training in high-level economic theory.

   A. vacuity
   B. jocosity
   C. frugality
   D. equanimity
   E. perspicacity

9. The Tunguska explosion was a powerful explosion that occurred in central Siberia in 1908 near the Tunguska River. At the time, the bizarre and catastrophic nature of the blast engendered (1) _____ visions among the (2) _____ inhabitants of that remote region. Herds of reindeer within a few miles of the blast (3) _____; nomads were thrown from their tents miles away; all vegetation within a 2,000-square-mile radius was destroyed.

Blank 1	Blank 2	Blank 3
myopic	superstitious	survived unscathed
prosaic	affluent	were instantaneously incinerated
apocalyptic	sedulous	caused many fatalities

10. Ice sculptures, though often quite beautiful and extravagant displays, are necessarily an _____ art form.

    A. evocative
    B. ephemeral
    C. abstemious
    D. idiosyncratic
    E. effusive

11. One of the features that make the study of the Renaissance so fascinating is that, in that age, the stream of personal record, which had been driven underground, its course choked and hidden beneath the fallen masonry of the Roman Empire, emerges again (1) _____ and flows in ever-increasing volume. For reconstruction of the past, we are no longer limited to charters and institutions, or the mighty works of men's hands. In place of a mental output, rigidly confined within (2) _____ modes of thought and expression, we have a literature that reflects the varied phases of human life, that can discard romance and look upon the commonplace; and instead of dry and meager chronicles, rarely producing evidence at first hand, we have rich store of memoirs and private letters, by means of which we can form real pictures of individuals—approaching almost to (3) _____ and intimacy—and regard the same events from many points of view.

Blank 1	Blank 2	Blank 3
stymied	lithe	objective asceticism
unimpeded	protean	subjective acquaintance
debilitated	unbending	callous insensitivity

12. To preserve credibility as a biographer, the author forbore to (1) _____ the hard fortunes of his hero and maintained (2) _____ to the main drift of the original chronicle.

Blank 1	Blank 2
ascertain	fidelity
scrutinize	sophistry
mitigate	empiricism

13. Instead of believing in the infallible wisdom of the common people, George Washington regarded them as inflammatory _____ and tried to save the republic from them.

   A. progenitors
   B. archetypes
   C. dolts
   D. pugilists
   E. elitists

14. The whole point of the story of Cinderella, the most widely and constantly charming of all stories, is that the Fairy Prince lifts Cinderella above her cruel sisters and stepmother, and so enables her to lord it over them. The same idea (1) _____ practically all other folk stories; the essence of each of them is to be found in the ultimate triumph and (2) _____ of its protagonist.

Blank 1	Blank 2
underlies	extirpation
undermines	exaltation
underplays	exhortation

15. Gustave Le Bon has put forward the doctrine that the individual man, cheek by jowl with the multitude, drops down an intellectual peg or two, and so tends to show the mental and emotional reactions of his (1) _____. It is thus that he explains the well-known violence and imbecility of crowds. The crowd, as a crowd, performs acts that many of its members, as individuals, would never be guilty of. Its average intelligence is very low; it is inflammatory, vicious, idiotic, almost (2) _____. Crowds, properly worked up by skillful (3) _____, are ready to believe anything, and to do anything.

Blank 1	Blank 2	Blank 3
pundits	erudite	demagogues
rivals	ascetic	recluses
inferiors	simian	recidivists

16. The orator tried to sway his audience with _____ arguments, but most of the listeners discerned the subterfuge behind his rhetoric.

   A. abysmal
   B. scrupulous
   C. lambent
   D. inane
   E. specious

17. Joseph Conrad, according to critic H. L. Mencken, grounds his work firmly upon this sense of cosmic implacability, this confession of _____ and conviction that human life is a seeking without a finding, that its purpose is impenetrable, that joy and sorrow are alike meaningless.

    A. sanctity
    B. unintelligibility
    C. aspiration
    D. determinism
    E. verisimilitude

18. The author still plods along in the laborious, oblivious way he first marked out for himself; he is quite as undaunted by (1) _____ praise as by bludgeoning, malignant (2) _____.

Blank 1	Blank 2
indigent	abuse
effusive	encomium
improvident	accolades

19. After years of frugality, the heirs of the late tycoon, reveling in their newfound affluence, eschewed (1) _____ in favor of (2) _____.

Blank 1	Blank 2
husbandry	alacrity
effrontery	profligacy
perfidy	mendacity

20. Because computer-generated digital painting is still neither totally accepted nor completely rejected as an art form by curators, its placement in museums remains _____.

    A. aggrandized
    B. arbitrary
    C. ubiquitous
    D. aesthetic
    E. importunate

Answers

1. **B** A *coterie* is an exclusive group of people who share common interests. It fits with the context clue in the sentence, *elite scientists who would confer on important issues.* Choice A, *posse,* also can mean a group of people; however, it is more casual and doesn't convey the proper tone for a group of scientists. All the other choices are inappropriate for the sentence: choice C, *chasm,* means a deep hole in the earth or a gap; choice D, *conspiracy,* means a group plan to commit an illegal act; and choice E, *contumely,* means insulting language or treatment.

2. **lugubrious, tumultuous** *Remote moors* suggests a gloomy setting and *lugubrious* means gloomy or mournful. A group of highly emotional individuals should lead you to *tumultuous love story.* All the other choices aren't logical with these context clues: *mellifluous* means pleasant sounding, *acquiescent* means passively agreeing, *insouciant* means nonchalant or carefree, and *parsimonious* means stingy.

3. **sanguine, aggrandized** The relationship between these two words must present a logical progression in the sentence: As investors become more cheerfully optimistic (or *sanguine*), they'll enlarge (or *aggrandize*) their plans for expansion. None of the other choices makes logical sense in the sentence: *salutary* means healthful, *dejected* means very unhappy or disappointed, *diaphanous* means transparent or vague, and *seditious* means treasonous.

4. **satisfies, yoked, engender** The first sentence should lead you to understand that music is important to human beings because it satisfies a need for artistic expression and is connected (or *yoked*) to our psychological makeup. The parallel points in the last paragraph are that music both expresses and engenders feelings. The passage presents the positive relationship between music and human beings, so none of the negative choices fits the context. *Repudiates* means rejects, and *inures* means to harden to or become immune to the effects of. *Antithetical* means opposite, and *insensitive* means thoughtless. *Undermine* means to weaken, and *verbalize* means to speak. None of these choices makes sense in the passage.

5. **A** The context clue in the sentence is *trickery:* Having seen evidence of trickery, we accept the commentator's remarks about trickery (or *chicanery*). None of the other choices fits the clue in the sentence: choice B, *effrontery,* means boldness or nerve; choice C, *subtlety,* means indirectness or something suggested; choice D, *solidarity,* means unity; choice E, *meticulousness,* means extreme carefulness or precision.

6. **pious, jocular** The sentence contains two context clues: *devotional beliefs* and *playful wit. Pious* (religiously devoted) fits in Blank 1, and *jocular* (having a joking manner) fits in Blank 2. *Secular* means not concerned with religion, so it's the opposite of what you're looking for. *Dogmatic* means expressing rigid opinions; it doesn't fit as well as *pious.* Neither *pedestrian* (dull or uninspired) nor *trite* (overused) is logical to describe playful wit.

7. **electrified, overturned long-held beliefs** The main clue in the sentence is that the coelacanth was *previously thought to be extinct.* One would expect scientists to be very excited (or *electrified*) about the unexpected discovery, which overturned long-held beliefs. *Exacerbated* (made worse) and *impugned* (criticized as false) don't fit the logic of the sentence. *Reinforced preconceived notions* is the opposite of what is indicated in the sentence, as is *mitigated current expectations.*

8. **E** If Manuel sought more training, then it's logical that he believed that he lacked *perspicacity* (acuteness of perception). None of the other choices fits the context clue of seeking high-level training in economic theory: choice A, *vacuity,* means emptiness or meaninglessness; choice B, *jocosity,* means humorousness; choice C, *frugality,* means economy or thriftiness; and choice D, *equanimity,* means poise or composure.

9. **apocalyptic, superstitious, were instantly incinerated** A powerful, unexplained explosion would give rise to *apocalyptic* (predictive of disaster and destruction of biblical proportions) visions. For Blank 2, *superstitious* is the only possible choice. *Affluent* means wealthy, and *sedulous* means hard-working and attentive. The emphasis in the passage is on destruction, so it's logical that the reindeer *were instantaneously incinerated* (burned). They wouldn't have *survived unscathed.* Finally, the reindeer wouldn't have *caused many fatalities;* the blast did.

10. **B** It's logical to assume that an ice sculpture on display can't last very long; it would, thus, be *ephemeral* (lasting only a brief time). Choice A might have been a tempting choice, but although it's possible for an ice sculpture to be *evocative,* it is not necessarily so. The other choices don't fit in the logic of the sentence: choice C, *abstemious,* means moderate or nonindulgent; choice D, *idiosyncratic,* means having odd personal habits or quirks; and choice E, *effusive,* means overflowing with emotion.

11. **unimpeded, unbending, subjective acquaintance** The first sentence of the passage uses the image of a stream that had been choked but now is able to flow; that makes *unimpeded,* rather than *stymied* (blocked) or *debilitated* (weakened), a logical choice for Blank 1. For Blank 2 the clue is *rigidly confined,* which should lead you to *unbending. Lithe* (effortless graceful) and *protean* (able to change form) don't work in Blank 2. For Blank 3 the clue is *a rich store of memoirs and private letters,* which should lead you to *subjective acquaintance* rather than *objective asceticism* or *callous insensitivity,* neither of which expresses personal intimacy.

12. **mitigate, fidelity** If a biographer wants to preserve credibility, he must be truthful. The author *forbore* (held back) and refused to *mitigate* (excuse or lessen) the hard fortunes of the subject and maintained *fidelity* (faithfulness) to history. *Ascertain* (determine with certainty) and *scrutinize* (examine carefully) are opposite in meaning to the sense of the sentence. *Sophistry* (false reasoning) and *empiricism* (reliance on observation and experimentation) don't work in Blank 2.

13. **C** The sentence begins with *Rather than,* which means that Washington believed the common people were the opposite of those who have infallible wisdom. A *dolt* is a stupid person. A *progenitor,* choice A, is a ancestor; an *archetype,* choice B, is an original model; a *pugilist,* choice D, is a fighter; and an *elitist,* choice E, is one who believes in the superiority of a group of people.

14. **underlies, exaltation** The sentence suggests that the theme of the Cinderella story is the foundation of most folk stories; thus, this basic plot and the "ultimate triumph" or *exaltation* (happiness or raising up) of the main character *underlie* them. Neither *undermines* (weakens) or *underplays* (minimizes) fits the context. You also can eliminate *extirpation* (the complete removal or destruction) and *exhortation* (a strong urging) from Blank 2 because neither fits the concept of the "ultimate triumph."

15. **inferiors, simian, demagogues** The clue *drops down* should lead you to inferiors rather than to *pundits* (experts) or *rivals.* The word in Blank 2 must follow the sense of the fourth sentence: "Its average intelligence is very low; it is inflammatory, vicious, idiotic. . . ." *Erudite* (scholarly) and *ascetic* (practicing austerity and self-denial) don't fit, but *simian* (behavior characteristic of monkeys or apes) does. For Blank 3, you must look for one who is most likely to work up a crowd; that should lead you to *demagogues* (leaders who gain power by appealing to a crowd's emotions) rather than *recluses* (hermits) or *recidivists* (chronic criminals).

16. **E** The clue *subterfuge behind his rhetoric* should lead you to *specious* (appearing true but actually false). Choice A, *abysmal* (horrible); choice B, *scrupulous* (honest); choice C, *lambent* (gleaming); and choice D, *inane* (stupid or silly) don't fit the context.

17. **B** To fill in this blank, you must consider the whole context of the sentence. Conrad can't find the purpose in human life or in the universe; thus, he confesses to a universal sense of *unintelligibility* (the impossibility of understanding it all). Choice A, *sanctity* (holiness) is not appropriate, nor is choice C, *aspiration.* Choice D, *determinism* (a belief that everything has a cause), is the opposite of what Conrad believes. Choice E, *verisimilitude* (having the appearance of truth), doesn't make sense in the sentence.

18. **effusive, abuse** The sentence sets up a contrast between praise and its opposite in Blank 2, *abuse*. For Blank 1, only *effusive* (overflowing with emotion) will make sense. *Indigent* (poor) and *improvident* (unconcerned about the future) don't fit the context. Because Blank 2 must be the opposite of *praise,* both *encomium* (an expression of high praise) and *accolades* (signs of praise) are incorrect.

19. **husbandry, profligacy** The clue "reveling in their newfound affluence" suggests that the heirs have *eschewed* (avoided) *husbandry* (economy) and pursued *profligacy* (wastefulness). Neither *effrontery* (audacity) nor *perfidy* (treachery) works in Blank 1. Neither *alacrity* (cheerful readiness) nor *mendacity* (untruthfulness) works in Blank 2.

20. **B** The clue in the sentence is that *computer-generated digital painting is still neither totally accepted nor completely rejected,* so its placement in museums would be at the whim of the curator, an *arbitrary* decision. Choice A, *aggrandized* (enlarged), and choice C, *ubiquitous* (present everywhere), contradict the clue. Although you may associate the word *aesthetic* (choice D) with art, it doesn't fit the logic of the sentence. Choice E, *importunate* (demanding and persistent), also doesn't fit the logic of the sentence.

VI. Sentence Equivalence

Sentence equivalence questions measure your ability to find two words that complete the meaning of a sentence. You'll be presented with a sentence with one blank followed by six choices. You must find the two words that most logically fit with the context clues in the sentence as a whole and create completed sentences that are alike in meaning. In this section, you're tested on your vocabulary, your critical thinking skills, and your language usage skills.

The key to the sentence equivalence questions is to find the two words in the choices that are closest to each other in meaning. In other words, you're looking for synonyms or words that are most nearly synonymous. To receive credit for these questions, both of your choices must be correct. You'll receive *no credit* if you select only one of the correct answers.

Use the vocabulary list in Chapter VII to help you prepare for the sentence equivalence questions. The more words you know, the easier these questions will be.

A. Sentence Equivalence Strategies

When working on sentence equivalence questions, follow these steps:

1. **Read the sentence carefully and analyze the sentence structure and the context clue(s).**

   As you read the sentence, think about the word you might logically use to fill in the blank before you look at the words in the choices. This will help you narrow the choices. You may find the exact word you were thinking of or a similar word among the choices.

   As you read the sentence, pay particular attention to *signal words* (introductory or transitional words that establish relationships within the sentence). Refer to Chapter V for lists of signal words.

2. **Use process of elimination to eliminate the incorrect choices.**

   Ask yourself: Should the missing word be a positive word or a negative word? Is it a praising word or a criticizing word? Use this thinking to help you narrow your choices to the best two.

   Remember that you're looking for two choices that are very similar in meaning, perhaps even synonyms. This may also help you eliminate incorrect choices.

   Don't eliminate a word because you think it's the wrong part of speech. The choices are always the correct part of speech. One of the choices may be a word you're accustomed to using as an adjective, but in this particular sentence, it's used as a verb. For example, the word *legitimate* is most commonly used as an adjective meaning legal or conforming to acknowledged standards, but it also can be used as a verb to mean to argue or prove that a claim is lawful or reasonable.

3. **Reread the sentence after you've chosen your answers, and check the logic again.**

   Make sure that both words you've chosen maintain the same meaning of the sentence.

B. Vocabulary

The sentence equivalence questions on the GRE test your understanding of vocabulary words and how they're used in context. The test-makers know that the ability to understand and use appropriate language is important in all aspects of life—in the business world, in graduate school, and in daily life. The best way to accomplish this successfully is to read, read, read! The more you read, the better you get at it. And, the more widely and deeply you read, the more varied the vocabulary you'll encounter. So, for the next few days, weeks, or months, plan to read as much as you can in a variety of subject areas.

Reading is the best long-term tool to increase your command of the difficult vocabulary that appears on the GRE. So, what should you read and how should you read? Follow these tips:

- **Vary your reading materials.** A wealth of print and online material is available on every topic you can possibly conceive of. You just have to motivate yourself to find out what someone else has written about the topic, and you'll open up new worlds. And, if you're reading about a topic that fascinates you, you won't find reading painful or time-consuming.

- **Read with an open mind.** If you begin to read an article or a book with a set of preconceived ideas about the topic, you may miss something. Try to open your mind to the writer and follow his or her ideas. This process may require you to consider the subject matter in a new light, but that's the right idea. Learning is a lifelong process—don't miss an opportunity to educate yourself.

- **Question as you read.** Intellectual curiosity is the sign of a good mind at work. Sometimes a comment by a writer will cause you to wonder or question his or her point. Don't doubt yourself. Seek out ways to satisfy your need to know. Do some research; go online or to the library.

- **Study the vocabulary.** Once you've embarked on this pathway to a better vocabulary and reading skills, apply yourself to the task. Write down on the front of index cards any unfamiliar words you encounter in your reading, and write the definitions on the back. Now you have a personal set of flash cards to use in conjunction with the vocabulary list in Chapter VII.

C. Synonym Clusters

You also can build your vocabulary for the sentence equivalence section of the GRE by studying *synonym clusters* (words that are similar in meaning). Try using index cards to help you study. Begin by writing a heading on the top of the card with the meaning of the words in the synonym cluster. Then list all the words that are similar in meaning to the word in the heading.

Here are some synonym clusters you should familiarize yourself with:

Afraid	Arrogant
Adjectives: aghast, alarmed, apprehensive, cowardly, cowed, craven, distressed, frightened, horrified, petrified, shocked, terrified, timid	Adjectives: bombastic, conceited, egotistical, haughty, imperious, overbearing, peremptory, presumptuous, pretentious, pompous, proud, snobbish, supercilious, vainglorious
Bold or Courageous	**Noisy**
Adjectives: adventurous, audacious, courageous, daring, dauntless, fearless, forceful, intrepid, resolute, valiant, valorous	Adjectives: blatant, boisterous, clamorous, deafening, obstreperous, raucous, rowdy, strident, vociferous

Words of Praise	Words of Criticism
Nouns: accolade, acclaim, adulation, approbation, commendation, encomium, eulogy, kudos, laudation, panegyric, reverence Verbs: celebrate, commemorate, exalt, extol, laud, revere, worship	Nouns: censure, disapprobation, disapproval, disparagement, obloquy, opprobrium, shame Verbs: abuse, assail, bash, belittle, berate, blame, carp, castigate, censure, chastise, chide, condemn, denounce, disparage, excoriate, fulminate, impugn, malign, reprehend, reprimand, reprobate, revile, scathe, vilify
Stubborn	**Changeable**
Adjectives: adamant, inflexible, intractable, intransigent, obdurate, obstinate, recalcitrant	Adjectives: arbitrary, capricious, erratic, fickle, fluctuating, inconsistent, irresolute, mercurial, mutable, vacillating, variable, volatile, whimsical
Wordy or Talkative	**Quiet or Reserved**
Adjectives: effusive, garrulous, loquacious, prolix, redundant, verbose, voluble	Adjectives: brief, brusque, concise, curt, laconic, pithy, reticent, succinct, taciturn, terse, uncommunicative
Harmful	**Short-Lived**
Adjectives: baleful, baneful, deleterious, detrimental, inimical, injurious, lethal, malicious, nocuous, noxious, pernicious, sinister, virulent	Adjectives: ephemeral, evanescent, fleeting, fugitive, impermanent, transient, transitory
Hatred	**Hard-Working or Skillful**
Nouns: anathema, animosity, animus, antipathy, aversion, malevolence, odium, repugnance, repulsion Verbs: abhor, abominate, deprecate, despise, detest, execrate, loathe	Adjectives: adept, adroit, agile, assiduous, apt, competent, dextrous, diligent, facile, indefatigable, industrious, persistent, proficient, sedulous, unflagging, unrelenting
Slow-Moving or Lazy	**Showy or Flashy**
Adjectives: exanimate, indolent, inert, lackadaisical, languid, languorous, lethargic, otiose, sluggish, slothful, somnolent, torpid	Adjectives: affected, conspicuous, flamboyant, garish, gaudy, meretricious, ostentatious, pretentious, tawdry
To Soothe or Relieve	**Calmness or Poise**
Verbs: abate, allay, alleviate, ameliorate, appease, assuage, extenuate, mitigate, palliate, placate, propitiate, temper	Nouns: aplomb, composure, equanimity, nonchalance, poise, quietude, sang-froid Adjectives: equable, halcyon, imperturbable, pacific, placid, quiescent, sedate, serene, tranquil, unflappable
Happy or Joyful	**Sad**
Adjectives: blithesome, ecstatic, effervescent, elated, enraptured, expansive, festive, gladsome, heartening, jocund, jocose, jovial, jubilant, mirthful, rapturous, sanguine, transported, upbeat	Adjectives: distressing, doleful, dolorous, lamentable, grievous, grim, heartbreaking, hurting, lugubrious, melancholy, mournful, pitiful, plaintive, regretful, rueful, sorrowful, tragic, woeful, wretched
	Angry
	Adjectives: affronted, antagonized, bitter, chafed, choleric, convulsed, cross, displeased, enraged, exacerbated, ferocious, fierce, fiery, fuming, furious, galled, hateful, heated, huffy, ill-tempered, impassioned, incensed, indignant, inflamed, infuriated, irascible, irate, ireful, irritable, maddened, nettled, offended, outraged, piqued, provoked, raging, resentful, riled, splenetic, storming, sulky, sullen, vexed, wrathful

Practice

Directions (1–10): Choose the two words that are most similar in meaning to the keyword.

1. Loquacious

   A. Concise
   B. Diligent
   C. Garrulous
   D. Prolix
   E. Inert
   F. Jovial

2. Snobby

   A. Arrogant
   B. Ephemeral
   C. Haughty
   D. Terse
   E. Noxious
   F. Malignant

3. Inimical

   A. Indignant
   B. Voluble
   C. Sedulous
   D. Pernicious
   E. Torpid
   F. Deleterious

4. Fleeting

   A. Unflagging
   B. Ephemeral
   C. Pithy
   D. Arrogant
   E. Transitory
   F. Aloof

5. Audacious

    A. Reticent
    B. Fearless
    C. Valuable
    D. Craven
    E. Dauntless
    F. Benevolent

6. Berate

    A. Delay
    B. Laud
    C. Extol
    D. Despise
    E. Castigate
    F. Reprimand

7. Praise

    A. Censure
    B. Encomium
    C. Duplicity
    D. Repulsion
    E. Adulation
    F. Calumny

8. Antipathy

    A. Eulogy
    B. Acclaim
    C. Malevolence
    D. Odium
    E. Commiseration
    F. Conciliation

9. Clamorous

    A. Supercilious
    B. Aghast
    C. Obstreperous
    D. Pedantic
    E. Vociferous
    F. Incipient

10. Obstinate

    A. Capricious
    B. Whimsical
    C. Obdurate
    D. Fulsome
    E. Fallacious
    F. Intractable

Directions (11–30): Select *two* of the choices from the list of six that best complete the meaning of the sentence as a whole. The two words you select should produce completed sentences that are most alike in meaning.

11. No longer as _____ as he had been when he was younger, the aging gymnast merely described rather than demonstrated demanding stunts.

    A. disputative
    B. somnolent
    C. adept
    D. modest
    E. tenuous
    F. agile

12. Although many decry the current state of the American education system, few parents treat their child's teacher with _____.

    A. eloquence
    B. acumen
    C. contempt
    D. mettle
    E. derision
    F. jocosity

13. Although she was by nature reticent and reluctant to speak in public, the biologist answered questions about her breakthrough with an _____ that surprised and pleased her colleagues.

    A. apprehension
    B. equanimity
    C. effacement
    D. obduracy
    E. anxiety
    F. aplomb

14. Leaving no doubt as to her intentions, the senator's _____ remarks revealed her firm commitment to long-term environmental precautions.

   A. tenuous
   B. unequivocal
   C. vacillating
   D. whimsical
   E. indisputable
   F. blithe

15. The film, denounced by many critics as so sentimental as to be _____, left most audience members in tears.

   A. maudlin
   B. jocose
   C. abstemious
   D. perverse
   E. transitory
   F. treacly

16. The chair of the department issued a warning that those instructors who were _____ in handing in their students' grades in a timely manner would be censured.

   A. felicitous
   B. remiss
   C. indulgent
   D. stringent
   E. derelict
   F. scrupulous

17. Although many executives in the cash-strapped company were leery of the ramifications of the upcoming employee evaluations, the two grandsons of the company founder remained _____ in their attitudes.

   A. tremulous
   B. smug
   C. supine
   D. complacent
   E. abashed
   F. craven

18. When Professor North attended the lecture given by the word-renowned physicist, she found that far from the _____ presentation she expected, the lecture was quite accessible.

    A.   arcane
    B.   fundamental
    C.   auspicious
    D.   dolorous
    E.   succinct
    F.   recondite

19. A silent landing and camouflaged gear allowed the advance guard a _____ entry into enemy territory.

    A.   furtive
    B.   egalitarian
    C.   obstreperous
    D.   surreptitious
    E.   halcyon
    F.   ebullient

20. The editors found that the latest version of the historical survey was marred by _____ inclusions that digressed from the central issue.

    A.   germane
    B.   utilitarian
    C.   intrinsic
    D.   peripheral
    E.   inherent
    F.   tangential

21. The plant manager was shocked by the _____ of the workers who questioned his judgment regarding the implementation of new safety procedures.

    A.   conventionality
    B.   reticence
    C.   audacity
    D.   effrontery
    E.   timorousness
    F.   caginess

22. The company accountant was intimidated by the _____ attitude of the internal revenue auditors who refused to return his attempts at cordiality.

   A. stable
   B. hostile
   C. affable
   D. fraudulent
   E. empathetic
   F. glacial

23. The emperor had a strong dislike of flattery, regarding those who sought to influence him through praise as _____.

   A. connoisseurs
   B. pundits
   C. sycophants
   D. dilettantes
   E. toadies
   F. demagogues

24. Had Professor Burns included even a(n) _____ of evidence, his theory would have been received with serious consideration rather than derision.

   A. plethora
   B. modicum
   C. proclivity
   D. occlusion
   E. iota
   F. panegyric

25. Always the charlatan, Charlie tried to confuse his listeners with _____ evidence.

   A. specious
   B. pithy
   C. cogent
   D. substantiated
   E. irreproachable
   F. spurious

26. Sophie attended a series of lectures on the evolution of fashion as a way of satisfying her _____ fine clothing.

    A. disdain for
    B. predilection for
    C. ambivalence toward
    D. penchant for
    E. abhorrence of
    F. embellishment of

27. Never known for careful deliberation of the case before rendering a decision, the judge often trusted his visceral response and _____ issued his rulings.

    A. intentionally
    B. ponderously
    C. precipitately
    D. sententiously
    E. impetuously
    F. genially

28. Alex's bulky and solidly defined musculature, more suggestive of a weight lifter than a ballroom dancer, belied his _____ movements on the dance floor.

    A. supple
    B. lithe
    C. bulky
    D. gauche
    E. rigid
    F. phlegmatic

29. Passing through the narrow gap in the remote area of the mountains, the explorers found not the _____ wilderness they expected, but a bustling community surrounding a hive of industrial activity.

    A. measured
    B. populous
    C. civilized
    D. hazardous
    E. unsullied
    F. pristine

30. Most employers are loath to promote workers who are _____; they prefer to sponsor those who are steadfast and resolute.

    A.   implacable
    B.   immutable
    C.   staid
    D.   capricious
    E.   mercurial
    F.   conscientious

Answers

For the meanings of all the words in these questions, see Chapter VII.

1. **C, D** *Loquacious* means talkative and is most similar in meaning to *garrulous* and *prolix.*

2. **A, C** *Snobby* means overly proud and is most similar in meaning to *arrogant* and *haughty.*

3. **D, F** *Inimical* means harmful and is most similar in meaning to *deleterious* and *pernicious.*

4. **B, E** *Fleeting* means passing by quickly and is most similar in meaning to *ephemeral* and *transitory.*

5. **B, E** *Audacious* means bold and is most similar in meaning to *fearless* and *dauntless.*

6. **E, F** *Berate* means to scold or criticize and is most similar in meaning to *castigate* and *reprimand.*

7. **B, E** *Praise* means words that speak highly of and is most similar in meaning to *encomium* and *adulation.*

8. **C, D** *Antipathy* means hatred and is most similar in meaning to *malevolence* and *odium.*

9. **C, E** *Clamorous* means noisy and is most similar in meaning to *obstreperous* and *vociferous.*

10. **C, F** *Obstinate* means stubborn and is most similar in meaning to *obdurate* and *intractable.*

11. **C, F** The logic of the sentence contrasts the gymnast's earlier state (*adept* and *agile*) with his present state (aging) and capable of only describing rather than demonstrating. One who can no longer demonstrate is not as physically able as he once was.

12. **C, E** The context clues in this sentence are all in the logic and the vocabulary. The introductory word *Although* sets up a contrast between the generally negative attitude of "many" (suggested by the verb *decry,* meaning to criticize openly) and the parents. Thus, few parents treat their child's teachers with contempt or derision (scorn). None of the other choices is negative; they don't provide the required contrast in the sentences.

13. **B, F** The sentence begins with *Although,* which sets up a contrast between *reticent and reluctant to speak in public* and the missing word. The missing word must then be *equanimity* (poise) or *aplomb* (self-confidence).

14. **B, E** The clues in the sentence are that the senator left *no doubt as to her intentions* and *revealed her firm commitment.* Her remarks were, therefore, *unequivocal* (without doubt) and *indisputable* (impossible to doubt).

15. **A, F** The clues in the sentence lead to you select a word that means very sentimental; both *maudlin* and *treacly* mean overly sentimental.

16. **B, E** The logic of the sentence suggests that those instructors who don't hand in their grades on time are careless or neglectful. Both *remiss* and *derelict* fit the logic of the sentence.

17. **B, D** The sentence sets up a contrast between the *leery* (wary or suspicious) employees and the grandsons of the founder who are far more secure in their positions. They are *smug* and *complacent* (satisfied and secure in their positions).

18. **A, F** The lecture was *accessible,* far from *arcane* and *recondite* (understood only by experts).

19. **A, D** *A silent landing and camouflaged gear* suggests the need for stealth, especially when entering enemy territory. Both *furtive* and *surreptitious* mean secretive or stealthy.

20. **D, F** The clue *digressed from the central issue* should lead you to *peripheral* and *tangential,* words that mean not relevant or central to the issue at hand.

21. **C, D** The plant manager would be shocked by questions characterized by *audacity* or *effrontery,* words that mean boldness or nerve.

22. **B, F** The clues in the sentence are that the accountant was intimidated and that the auditors did not return the accountant's cordiality. The words that best fit this context are *hostile* and *glacial* (coldly hostile).

23. **C, E** An emperor who has *a strong dislike of flattery* would consider those who praise him to be *sycophants* or *toadies* (fawning flatterers).

24. **B, E** The fact that Professor Burns's theory was met with derision suggests that it didn't contain a *modicum* or *iota* (single small bit) of evidence.

25. **A, F** The clue is that Charlie is a *charlatan* (a fraud or false expert); hence, he would use *specious* (having the appearance of truth but actually false) or *spurious* (not genuine) evidence to confuse his listeners.

26. **B, D** If Sophie is attending lectures on the evolution of fashion, she must have a *predilection* or *penchant* (strong liking) for fine clothing.

27. **C, E** A judge who is not known for careful deliberation but rather for *visceral* (intuitive or gut) response would most likely make decisions *precipitately* (rashly) or *impetuously* (impulsively).

28. **A, B** The description of Alex as having the body of a weight lifter *belied* (contradicted) his *supple* and *lithe* (flexible and graceful) movements on the dance floor.

29. **E, F** The context clues lead you to understand that the explorers expected to find an *unsullied* (unblemished) and *pristine* (untouched) wilderness; they instead found a *bustling community surrounding a hive of industrial activity.*

30. **E, F** Because the sentence contains the clue that employers are *loath* (reluctant) to promote these workers, you're looking for the opposite of *steadfast and resolute: capricious* (fickle, impulsive) and *mercurial* (unpredictable).

VII. Vocabulary

Try to familiarize yourself with as many of these vocabulary words as possible. First, highlight all the unfamiliar words. Then, try to memorize as many of the unfamiliar words as you can. The best study technique is to put each unfamiliar word on an index card and write the definition on the back. Then divide them into small groups and learn one group of words at a time. As you study, say the words out loud. That way, you're using your ears and your eyes to help you retain the definition in your memory.

abash: To embarrass; to make ashamed

aberration: An abnormality

abet: To aid in the commission (usually of a crime)

abhor: To hate

abjure: To formally renounce

abnegate: To renounce

abrasive: Rough; coarse

abrogate: To put an end to

abscond: To depart suddenly and secretly

abstemious: Characterized by self-denial or abstinence

abstruse: Difficult to understand

acclaim: Praise

acquiesce: To comply; to agree; to submit

acumen: Quickness of intellectual insight

admonition: Gentle scolding or warning

affable: Good-natured; easy to approach

affectation: Pretension; unnatural behavior designed to impress others

aggrandize: To enlarge; to improve

aghast: Horrified; astonished

agile: Able to move quickly, physically or mentally

alacrity: Cheerful willingness or promptness

alleviate: To relieve; to make less hard to bear

aloof: Reserved; distant

altruism: Unselfishness; charitableness

amalgamate: To mix or blend together

ambiguous: Having a double meaning

ameliorate: To relieve; to make better

amiable: Friendly

anarchy: Lack of control; absence of government

animosity: Hatred

antipathy: Hatred

aplomb: Self-confidence

apocryphal: Of doubtful authority or authenticity

apparition: Ghostly sight

appease: To soothe

approbation: Approval

arboreal: Pertaining to trees

arcane: Difficult to understand; known to only a few

ardor: Passion

argot: Language used by a particular group

articulate: Eloquent; able to express oneself well

ascetic: One who practices self-denial and excessive abstinence

ascribe: To assign as a quality or attribute

asperity: Harshness; roughness

assail: To attack violently

assiduous: Unceasing; persistent

assuage: To relieve

astute: Keen in discernment

attenuate: To make or become weaker

audacious: Bold; fearless

auspicious: Favorable

austere: Severely simple; strict; harsh

authoritarian: Demanding; despotic

avarice: Greed

avid: Eager

baleful: Malignant

banal: Commonplace; trite

baneful: Causing harm

bellicose: Warlike

belligerent: Displaying a warlike spirit

benefactor: One who does kindly and charitable acts

benevolence: An act of kindness or generosity

benign: Good; kind

berate: To scold severely

bewilder: To confuse

blandishment: Flattery

blithe: Carefree; joyous

boisterous: Lively; rowdy; overexcited

bolster: To support

bombast: Pompous or inflated language

boorish: Rude

brazen: Bold; blatant

brevity: Briefness

burgeon: To grow; to flourish

burnish: To make brilliant or shining

cabal: A plot; a group of plotters

cacophony: A disagreeable or discordant sound

cagey: Cautious; secretive

cajole: To convince by flattering speech

callow: Immature; young and inexperienced

calumny: Slander

candid: Straightforward; honest

cantankerous: Grouchy; irritable

capacious: Roomy

capitulate: To surrender

castigate: To punish

caustic: Sarcastic; severe

censure: To criticize severely

chagrin: Embarrassment; dismay

charlatan: A fraud; a quack

chauvinist: One who is sure of the superiority of his position

chicanery: The use of trickery to deceive

circumspect: Prudent; cautious

circumstantial: Based on inference rather than conclusive proof

cloying: Excessively sweet

coerce: To force

cogent: Strongly persuasive

collusion: A secret agreement for a wrongful purpose

comedic: Amusing

compendious: Concise

complaisant: Willing to please

compound: To combine; to intensify

comprehensive: All-inclusive; broad in scope

compromise: Meet halfway; expose to danger or disgrace

compunction: Uneasiness caused by guilt or remorse

conciliatory: Tending to reconcile

concord: Harmony

conflagration: A great fire

congeal: To coagulate

congenial: Agreeable; friendly

conjoin: To join together

connoisseur: An expert judge of art, especially one with thorough knowledge and sound judgment

console: To comfort

conspicuous: Clearly visible

constrict: To bind

consummate: (v.) To complete; (adj.) supreme, total

contemplative: Calm and thoughtful

contentious: Argumentative

contrite: Remorseful

contumacious: Rebellious

contumely: Contempt

conundrum: A riddle

conviction: A strongly held belief

copious: Plentiful

corroboration: Confirmation

covetous: Desirous

cow: To frighten into submission

craven: Cowardly

credulous: Easily deceived

cupidity: Greed

curmudgeon: An ill-tempered person

curtail: To cut off; to cut short

dearth: Scarcity

debacle: Disaster

deferential: Respectful

deleterious: Hurtful

delineate: To outline; to sketch

demagogue: A leader who gains power by appealing to emotions

demur: To hesitate

denounce: To condemn; to criticize harshly

deplete: To reduce; to lessen

depraved: Wicked; morally corrupt

dereliction: Careless neglect

deride: To ridicule

derivative: Coming from some origin; not original

descry: To catch sight of

desiccant: A drying agent

desultory: Haphazard

detrimental: Harmful

deter: To frighten away

diaphanous: Transparent; vague

diatribe: A bitter or malicious criticism

didactic: Pertaining to teaching

diffidence: Shyness; lack of self-confidence

dilatory: Tending to cause delay

dilettante: A dabbler in art or knowledge

discern: To distinguish; to see clearly

disconsolate: Hopelessly sad

discreet: Cautious; prudent

discrete: Separate; distinct

dissemble: To hide by putting on a false appearance

disseminate: To scatter; to distribute

dissent: Disagreement

dissipate: To disappear; to be wasteful

divulge: To tell something previously private or secret

dogmatic: Stubbornly opinionated; making statements without argument or evidence

dolorous: Sad; painful

dolt: A stupid person

draconian: Very harsh; severe

droll: Humorous

dubious: Doubtful; skeptical; questionable

duplicity: Deceitfulness; dishonesty

ebullient: Showing enthusiasm

eclectic: Coming from a variety of sources

edify: To educate; to enlighten

effervescent: Bubbly; enthusiastic

effrontery: Boldness; audacity

effulgence: Bright light

egalitarian: Believing in equality

elucidate: To clarify

elusive: Tending to escape

embellish: To add decoration

embezzle: To misappropriate secretly

empirical: Based on observation

encomium: High praise

encumbrance: A burdensome and troublesome load

enervate: To weaken

engender: To produce

enigma: A riddle; a puzzle

enmity: Hatred

epistle: A letter

equable: Equal; serene

equanimity: Calmness; composure

equivocate: To be deliberately vague or misleading

eradicate: To destroy thoroughly

erratic: Irregular

erroneous: Incorrect

erudite: Scholarly; very learned

eschew: To avoid

espouse: To endorse

eulogy: Words of praise

euphonious: Pleasant sounding

evanescent: Existing briefly; ephemeral; fleeting

evince: To show clearly

evoke: To call or summon forth

exacerbate: To make worse

exalt: To praise; to worship

excoriation: Severe criticism

execrate: To detest

exculpate: To free from blame

expedient: Useful; advantageous

explicate: To explain; to clarify

explicit: Clear; unambiguous

expostulate: To express disagreement

expropriate: To deprive of possession

expunge: To erase; to remove from a record

expurgate: To cleanse; to purify

extant: Still existing and known

extenuate: To make less severe

extinct: No longer in existence

extirpate: To rip out; to destroy

extol: To praise in the highest terms

extraneous: Irrelevant

facetious: Amusing

facile: Easy

fallacious: Illogical

fatuous: Idiotic; stupid

fawn: To seek favor by flattery

feckless: Lacking purpose

fecund: Fertile

felicitous: Favorable

fervid: Intense; passionate

fetter: To shackle

fidelity: Faithfulness

flag: To decline in energy

flamboyant: Flashy; showy

flaunt: To show off

flippant: Frivolous; inappropriately lacking in seriousness

flout: To treat with contempt

forbearance: Patience

forswear: To renounce

foster: To encourage

frenetic: Frantic

frivolity: Silly and trivial behavior or activities

frugal: Economical

fulmination: Bitter protest

fulsome: Excessive to the point of disgusting

fundamental: Basic; central

garner: To earn; to gather

garrulous: Talkative; chatty

gaucherie: Socially awkward remark or action

gentility: Refinement; courtesy

germane: Relevant

glean: To pick out carefully

grandiloquence: Pompous language

gregarious: Sociable, outgoing

guile: Duplicity

gullible: Credulous

halcyon: Calm and peaceful

harangue: A tirade

harbinger: First sign; messenger

hedonism: Pursuit of pleasure

heed: To pay attention to

heinous: Odiously sinful

heresy: An opinion or doctrine that opposes accepted beliefs or principles

hybrid: Cross breed; mixture

hypocrisy: Extreme insincerity

hubris: Excessive pride

iconoclasm: A challenge to or overturning of traditional beliefs, customs, or values

idiosyncrasy: A habit peculiar to an individual; a quirk

idyll: An experience of serene happiness

ignoble: Low in character or purpose

ignominious: Shameful

illicit: Unlawful

illusory: Deceptive; misleading

immaculate: Clean; without spot or blemish

imminent: Close at hand

immutable: Unchangeable

impassive: Unmoved by or not exhibiting feeling

impecunious: Having no money

impede: To block; to obstruct

imperious: Insisting on obedience; arrogant

imperturbable: Calm

impervious: Impenetrable

impetuous: Impulsive

implacable: Incapable of being pacified

implicate: To hint at or suggest involvement

implicit: Implied

importune: To beg

imprecation: A curse

impromptu: Anything done or said on the spur of the moment

improvident: Lacking foresight or thrift

impudent: Rash; impulsive

impugn: To oppose; to attack

impute: To attribute

inadvertent: Accidental

inane: Silly

incessant: Unceasing

inchoate: In the early stages; unformed

incipient: Initial; beginning of development

incite: To rouse to a particular action

incisive: Sharp; perceptive

incongruous: Unsuitable for the time, place, or occasion

incorrigible: Incapable of being corrected or reformed

inculcate: To teach by frequent repetitions

indelible: Permanent; not removable

indigence: Poverty

indigenous: Native

indignant: Angry at unfairness

indolence: Laziness

indomitable: Unconquerable

indulgent: Yielding to the desires of oneself or those under one's care

ineffable: Unable to be expressed in words

ineluctable: Impossible to avoid

inept: Not fit; not capable

inevitable: Unavoidable

inexorable: Unrelenting

ingenuous: Candid; frank; open in character

inimical: Adverse

inimitable: Impossible to imitate

innocuous: Harmless

inscrutable: Impenetrably mysterious or profound

insinuate: To imply

insipid: Tasteless

insouciant: Carefree

instigate: To start; to cause trouble

insurrection: Active resistance to authority

intractable: Stubbornly resistant to control

intransigent: Unyielding

intrepid: Fearless; bold

introspection: The act of observing and analyzing one's own thoughts and feelings

inundate: To flood

inure: To harden or toughen by use or exposure

invective: Abusive language

inveterate: Habitual

invidious: Showing or feeling envy

inviolable: Secure from attack

invincible: Unable to be conquered, subdued, or overcome

iota: A small or insignificant amount

irascible: Prone to anger

irate: Moved to anger

ire: Anger

irksome: Annoying

irrefutable: Certain; undeniable

irreproachable: Above criticism; flawless

irresolution: Indecisiveness

itinerant: Wandering

jargon: Language of a specialist; pretentious language

jocular: Inclined to joke

jovial: Merry

judicious: Prudent

lackadaisical: Listless

languid: Relaxed

lascivious: Lustful

lassitude: Lack of vitality or energy

laudable: Praiseworthy

legacy: A bequest

levity: Lack of seriousness; lightness

licentious: Immoral

lionize: To treat as a celebrity

listless: Inattentive

lithe: Supple

loquacious: Talkative

lugubrious: Indicating sorrow; mournful

lustrous: Shining

malevolence: Ill will

malign: To speak evil of; to slander

malleable: Pliant

maudlin: Foolishly and tearfully sentimental

melancholy: Sad

mendacious: Untrue

mendicant: A beggar

meretricious: Superficially attractive

mesmerize: To hypnotize

meticulous: Careful; painstaking; fussy

mettle: Courage

microcosm: The world or universe on a small scale

mien: The external appearance or manner of a person

mirth: Laughter; happiness

miser: A stingy person

misnomer: A name wrongly or mistakenly applied

modicum: A small amount

mollify: To soothe

momentous: Highly significant

mordant: Sarcastically biting

moribund: On the point of dying

morose: Gloomy

multifarious: Having great diversity or variety

mundane: Worldly; ordinary

munificent: Extraordinarily generous

myriad: A large indefinite number

mystical: Spiritual; magical

nadir: The lowest point

nefarious: Wicked; evil

negligent: Careless

neophyte: A beginner

noisome: Very offensive, particularly to the sense of smell

nonchalant: Carefree; coolly indifferent

nondescript: Having no distinguishing characteristics

nonplussed: Confused; surprised

noxious: Hurtful

nugatory: Worthless

obdurate: Stubborn

obloquy: Denunciation; disgrace

obfuscate: To confuse; to make unnecessarily complicated

obscure: Hard to understand; indistinct; not known

obsequious: Showing a servile readiness; slavish obedience

obstreperous: Boisterous

obtrude: To push oneself on others

obtuse: Thick-headed; stubborn

obviate: To clear away; to prevent

odious: Hateful

officious: Meddling in what is not one's concern

ominous: Threatening

onerous: Burdensome; oppressive

onus: A burden; a responsibility

opalescent: Shimmering milky colors

opportunist: One who takes advantage of something, especially in a devious way

opprobrium: Shame; disgrace

opulent: Lavish

ostentation: A showy display

ostracism: Exclusion from society

palatial: Magnificent; palace-like

palliate: To relieve; to ease

panacea: A cure-all

panegyric: Extravagant praise

paradigm: Pattern; model

paragon: A model of excellence

pariah: A social outcast

parsimonious: Cheap; stingy

partisan: Showing devotion to a party or one side of an issue

pathos: The quality that arouses emotion or sympathy

paucity: Scarcity; lack

pedantic: Too concerned with correct rules and accuracy; plodding

pedestrian: Dull; ordinary; humdrum

penchant: A strong liking

penurious: Excessively cheap or stingy

peremptory: Authoritative; dictatorial

perfidy: Treachery; traitorousness

perfunctory: Just going through the motions; mechanical

peripheral: Tangential; unimportant; minor

perjury: Lying under oath

perspicacity: Perceptiveness

perturb: To bother; to disturb

perverse: Stubbornly unreasonable; contrary

permeate: To pervade

pernicious: Harmful; poisonous

perspicacity: Sharp insightfulness or discernment

perturbation: Mental excitement; confusion

petulant: Childish irritability

pervasive: Widespread

phlegmatic: Sluggish; lacking energy

pious: Religious

pithy: Brief and to the point

placate: To calm; to appease

plaintive: Mournful

platitude: A written or spoken statement that is dull or commonplace

plethora: Excess; abundance

poignant: Emotionally painful

pluralism: Different groups with different beliefs existing within one society

ponderous: Unusually weighty or forcible

portent: Anything that indicates what is to happen; an omen or sign

posit: To put forward

pragmatic: Practical

precarious: Perilous; risky; unstable

preclude: To prevent

precocious: Advanced for one's age

predilection: Tendency; special liking

predominate: To be chief in importance

premature: Coming too soon

presage: To foretell

prescience: Knowledge of events before they take place

presumptuous: Overly confident; arrogant

prevalent: Widespread

prevaricate: To avoid giving an honest answer; to be deliberately misleading

primordial: Existing at the beginning of time

pristine: Pure; unspoiled

probity: Virtue; integrity

proclivity: A natural inclination

procrastination: Delay

prodigal: Wasteful; extravagant

prodigious: Immense

profligacy: Extremely wasteful; having low moral standards

profound: Showing great perception; having deep meaning

profuse: Produced or displayed in overabundance

prolix: Wordy

propinquity: Nearness in space or time

propitiatory: Appeasing

prosaic: Unimaginative

protracted: Lengthened

provident: Providing for the future

prudence: Caution

puerile: Childish

pugnacious: Quarrelsome

punctilious: Strictly observant of the rules prescribed by law or custom

pundit: Expert

pusillanimous: Cowardly

quandary: A puzzling predicament

quibble: A trivial objection

quiescence: Being quiet, still, or at rest; inactive

quixotic: Chivalrous or romantic to a ridiculous or extravagant degree

quotidian: Of an everyday character; ordinary

raconteur: Storyteller

ramify: To divide or subdivide into branches or subdivisions

rancor: Bitterness

rapacious: Greedy

recalcitrant: Stubbornly resistant

recant: To withdraw formally one's belief (in something previously believed or maintained)

recidivism: The tendency to relapse into crime

recluse: One who lives in retirement or seclusion

recondite: Understood by only a select few; arcane; esoteric

recuperate: To recover

regale: To delight

relegate: To demote

remiss: Careless; negligent

remonstrate: To argue strongly

renovate: To restore

repast: A meal

repose: Rest; relaxation

reproach: To scold

repudiate: To refuse to have anything to do with; to reject

repulsive: Grossly offensive

resilience: The ability to bounce back, cope, or adapt

respite: Interval of rest

reticent: Reserved; unwilling to communicate

retrograde: Moving backward in space or time

revelatory: Revealing an emotion or quality

revere: To respect highly; to worship

ritual: An established pattern of behavior, often ceremonial

sagacious: Wise; perceptive

salutary: Beneficial

sanction: To approve authoritatively

sanguine: Cheerfully confident; optimistic

sardonic: Scornfully or bitterly sarcastic

satiate: To satisfy fully the appetite or desire of

scintillating: Dazzling; sparkling

scrupulous: Precise; having moral integrity

secular: Nonreligious

sedulous: Diligent; persistent

self-effacing: Modest; humble

shrewd: Characterized by skill at understanding and profiting from circumstances

sluggard: A person habitually lazy or idle

smug: Self-satisfied

solace: Comfort

solvent: Having sufficient funds

somnolent: Sleepy

sophistry: False reasoning

sophomoric: Immature

soporific: Causing sleep

sordid: Filthy; morally degraded

sparse: Thinly spread

specious: Something that has the appearance of truth but is actually false

spurious: Not genuine

spurn: To reject

squalid: Dirty; poverty-stricken

squander: To waste

stanch: To stop the flowing of; to check

stingy: Cheap; unwilling to spend money

stringent: Strict; severe

stymie: To hinder

sublime: Supreme

subsume: To include in something larger

subterranean: Underground

subterfuge: A deceitful maneuver

subtle: Slight; understated

succinct: Concise

sumptuous: Rich; costly

supercilious: Haughty; arrogant

superfluous: More than is needed

suppress: To prevent from being disclosed or published

surfeit: Excess

sybarite: One who loves luxuries

sycophant: A servile flatterer

taciturn: Quiet; not talkative

tangential: Peripheral; not central

tedious: Boring; monotonous

temerity: Boldness; nerve

terse: Brief; concise

timorous: Lacking courage

toady: Obsequious flatterer

torpid: Dull; sluggish

tout: To praise; to try to attract customers

tractable: Easily led or controlled

tranquil: Calm; peaceful

transitory: Existing for a short time only

tremulous: Fearful; trembling

trepidation: Fear

trite: Made commonplace by frequent repetition

truculence: Ferocity

tumult: Noisy commotion

turbid: In a state of turmoil; muddled

turbulent: Moving violently

turgid: Swollen

turpitude: Wickedness

ubiquitous: Being present everywhere

unctuous: Insincerely earnest

undermine: To subvert in an underhand way; to weaken

undulate: To move like a wave or in waves

unerring: Without flaw

upbraid: To scold

urbane: Suave; elegant

vapid: Dull; uninteresting

vehement: Characterized by strong anger or passion; violent

venal: Mercenary; corrupt

venerate: To worship

venial: Forgivable; pardonable

veracity: Truthfulness

verbose: Wordy

vestige: A remaining trace of something gone

vigilant: Alert; watchful

vilify: To condemn; to slander

vindictive: Vengeful

vindicate: To free from blame

vitiate: To corrupt

vociferous: Forcefully loud

volatile: Unstable; explosive

voluble: Talkative

voluminous: Large; long; prolific

whimsical: Fanciful; lighthearted; quirky

zealous: Unreservedly enthusiastic

VIII. Reading Comprehension

The reading comprehension portion of the GRE is designed to test your ability to recall and sometimes infer (or read between the lines) to find facts and analyze concepts from a dense and often uninteresting reading passage. Even though it can be tedious, here's the good news: Everything you need to know to answer the questions is contained in the passage! You don't need any outside knowledge of the subject in order to do well on these questions.

Being able to read and understand information is obviously a big part of graduate school regardless of your course of study. The reading comprehension portions of the GRE test your ability to comprehend and make sense of information on topics that may or may not be familiar to you or of interest to you.

Reading comprehension topics tend to come from the social sciences, physical sciences, and arts and humanities. The questions test your ability to draw inferences and evaluate the meaning of the passage and to be able to refer to the passage and search for specific information. You'll encounter a total of about ten passages on the two verbal sections. Each passage will be followed by one to six questions, with one question on the screen at a time. The passage stays in view on the screen until you've answered all related questions for that passage so that you can refer to it as you work through the questions.

Most of the questions fall into the following categories:

- Main purpose
- Supporting ideas
- Inferences
- Application
- Structure
- Style and tone

A. Reading Comprehension Strategies

Here are strategies for successfully completing the GRE critical reading passages:

- **Always read actively.** Focus on what the author is trying to tell you. Think as you read—don't allow your mind to drift. Have a mental dialogue with the text.
- **If you're confused by a sentence or a paragraph, don't reread.** The sentence or paragraph may become clearer as you read, or there may not be any questions about that part of the passage. If you have to reread, do so as you answer the questions.
- **Stay interested in the passage.** Link the passage in your mind to a familiar topic. This strategy will help you stay focused
- **Take notes on scrap paper as you read.** These do not have to be extensive: just jot down the main idea of each paragraph or plot a cause-and-effect relationship.

- **Watch for key words and phrases that indicate a shift or transition in the passage**. A passage may appear to present a position that the author supports; then the author will begin a sentence with *but* or *however* and negate the previous position.

- **Don't allow your personal feelings or your own knowledge about the topic to influence your answers.** Always go back to what is stated in or implied by the text for support for your answer.

- **Read *all* the choices before you select an answer.** Use the process of elimination as you read the choices. If you're sure an answer is wrong, eliminate it. When you've read all the choices, look again only at the choices that you haven't eliminated, and evaluate their accuracy. Don't be fooled by an answer that makes a correct statement but does not answer the specific question. A statement may be true based on the information in the passage, but it may still be the wrong answer because it doesn't answer the question you're being asked.

- **Don't second-guess questions that appear to be too easy.** The test is constructed with a range of questions, and, especially at the beginning, an answer may simply be accessible.

- **Be on the lookout for *except* questions.** For *except* questions, four of the answers will be right. In these questions, you're looking for the *wrong* answer.

- **Take your time on the first few questions.** Because the GRE is adaptive, it adjusts to your level of ability. You want to be sure to get the first few questions right so the computer will keep increasing the difficulty. Difficult questions are worth more points than easy questions, so be careful and accurate on those first few questions.

B. Multiple-Choice Questions

There are two types of multiple choice questions: those in which you must select one answer and those in which you must select one or more answers.

1. Select one answer choice

The questions in which you must select one answer are the traditional multiple-choice reading comprehension questions you've encountered on the SAT, the ACT, or other standardized tests throughout your academic career. You're presented with a question and five possible answer choices. Based on what is stated in or implied by the passage, you select the best answer from among the five choices.

Here is a sample question. Read the passage and select the best answer to the question.

EXAMPLE:

> The nerves of the human body translate, or enable the mind to translate, the impressions of the world into facts of consciousness and thought. Different nerves are suited to the perception of different impressions. We do not see with the ear, nor do we hear with the eye. Each nerve, or group of nerves, selects and responds to those for the perception of which it is specially organized. The optic nerve passes from the brain to the back of the eyeball; there it spreads out to form the retina, a web of nerve filaments on which the images of external objects are projected by the optical portion of the eye. This nerve is limited to visual perception and is oblivious to other stimuli.

According to the passage, the retina is best defined as:

A. An impression of the world
B. A part of the brain
C. A web of perception
D. A meshwork of nerve filaments
E. The anterior portion of the eyeball

The correct answer is **D.** The question is a supporting idea or detail question. You're looking for a detail or definition within the passage. Skim through the paragraph looking for key words. You should see the word *retina* in the fifth sentence of the paragraph. Following the word *retina,* you'll find an explanation of it: *a web of nerve filaments.* Now evaluate the five answer choices. Choice A is not correct because *an impression of the world* is not *a web of filaments.* A retina is also not *a part of the brain,* so eliminate choice B. Choice C is a little tricky because it contains the word *web,* but the definition in the paragraph is not *a web of perception.* Choice D is correct—a *meshwork* is the same as a *web.* Choice E might tempt you because the retina is a part of the eyeball, but it is in the back of the eyeball, not in the *anterior* (front) part.

2. Select one or more answer choices

The questions in which you must select one or more answers present a question and give you three answer choices. You're asked to select all the answers that are correct. You may select one, two, or all three choices. In order to receive credit for these questions, you must select *all* the correct responses. You'll receive no credit if your answer is partially correct.

Here is a sample question. Read the passage and consider each of the three choices. Select all the answers that apply.

EXAMPLE:

In matters intellectual and artistic, Newland Archer felt himself distinctly the superior of these chosen specimens of old New York society; he had probably read more, thought more, and even seen a good deal more of the world than any other man of the number. Singly, they betrayed their inferiority; but grouped together, they represented "New York," and the habit of masculine solidarity made him accept their doctrine on all the issues called moral. He instinctively felt that in this respect it would be troublesome—and also rather bad form—to strike out for himself.

Which of the following statements about Newland Archer can be inferred from this passage? Consider each of the three choices and select all that apply.

A. As a newcomer to New York, he is awed by both the urbanity and the artistic education of the people around him.
B. He understands that he must underplay his intellectual eminence to fit into the social strata with which he has affiliated himself.
C. He intuits that despite his inherent superiority, his safest strategy is to follow the lead of others in moral matters.

The correct answer is **B** and **C**. To answer this question correctly, you have to understand the character of Newland Archer. He feels superior to the other men in New York society, but he feels that the safest course for him in moral matters is to follow the group. Choice A is incorrect because there is no evidence that Archer is a newcomer or is awed by the other men in his social circle. Choice B is correct because Archer has "read more, thought more, and even seen a good deal more of the world than any other man of the number," but he knows he can't flaunt his superiority if he wants to blend into the group of men. Choice C is supported by the last sentence in the paragraph—". . . it would be troublesome—and also rather bad form—to strike out for himself"—so he'll follow the other men in moral issues.

C. Select-in-passage

These questions ask you to use the mouse to click a sentence in the passage that meets the requirements of each question. You must read through the passage, find the sentence that will answer the question, and click anywhere on that sentence. Clicking on the sentence will highlight it; that click will complete your answer to the question.

Here is a sample question. Read the passage and answer the question.

EXAMPLE:

> Like Dreiser, Conrad is forever fascinated by the "immense indifference of things," the tragic vanity of the blind groping that we call aspiration, the profound meaninglessness of life—fascinated, and left wondering. One looks in vain for an attempt at a solution of the riddle in the whole canon of his work. Dreiser, more than once, seems ready to take refuge behind an indeterminate sort of mysticism, even a facile supernaturalism, but Conrad, from first to last, faces squarely the massive and intolerable fact. His stories are not chronicles of men who conquer fate, nor of men who are unbent and undaunted by fate, but of men who are conquered and undone. Each protagonist is a new Prometheus, with a sardonic ignominy piled upon his helplessness. Each goes down a Greek route to defeat and disaster, leaving nothing behind him save an unanswered question. I can scarcely recall an exception. Kurtz, Lord Jim, Razumov, Nostromo, Captain Whalley, Yanko Goorall, Verloc, Heyst, Gaspar Ruiz, Almayer: one and all they are destroyed and made a mock of by the blind, incomprehensible forces that beset them.

> Select the sentence that indicates the futility of searching throughout Conrad works for an answer to the enigma of the meaning of life.

You should select the second sentence: **One looks in vain for an attempt at a solution of the riddle in the whole canon of his work.** This sentence indicates the futility (looks in vain) for the answer to the question of the meaning (or meaninglessness) of life.

Practice

Directions (1–15): Questions follow each of the passages. Using only the stated or implied information in each passage, answer the questions.

Questions 1–3 refer to the following passage.

The planet's largest terrestrial ecosystem is an environment that completely encircles the Earth's northern pole. Called the Taiga Forest in the northern region (closest to the Arctic) and the Boreal Forest in the southern region, this immense area covers 4.6 million square miles and includes much of Russia and Canada, and parts of Norway, Sweden, Finland, and the United States. Conifer forests dominate this region. The paucity of nutrients in the soil keeps the types of trees rather limited; there are only about 30 types of trees in the Boreal and Taiga forests, in contrast with the highly diversified tropical rain forests, which can have hundreds of different species of trees in small areas. The unique, challenging environment leads to a somewhat homogenous forest.

The soil content of this region is ideal for conifer trees that are well suited for this harsh environment. These efficient gymnosperms are highly adapted to conserving nutrients, an important characteristic in a land where the soil is highly acidic, thin, often frozen for much of the year, and lacking in nutrients. Conifers need fewer nutrients than other trees do, because they shed their needles every three or four years or more and, thus, are less dependent on nutrients for annual needle growth.

Water conservation is another adaptive technique employed by coniferous trees. Because they can't access water from the soil for much of the year, retaining the water they do have is crucial for survival. Conifer needles are encased in a protective, waxy coat that retards evaporation, and the *stomata* (the pores on the needles' surface) are depressed rather than flush with the surface, so less moisture is lost due to wind and evaporation, a process called *transpiration.*

1. An appropriate title for this passage could be:

   A. Conifers Thrive and Dominate in the Boreal and Taiga Forests
   B. Life in the Boreal Forest
   C. Harsh Conditions in the Northern Regions of the Planet Result in Limited Flora and Fauna
   D. Conifers Require Limited Amounts of Water and Nutrients for Growth
   E. Lack of Nutrients in Forests

2. What adaptive techniques are particular to conifer trees in the region discussed in the passage? Consider each of the three choices and select all that apply.

   A. A waxy coating on the needles protect against moisture loss requiring less water.
   B. Conifers shed their needles annually.
   C. These trees have stomata that don't store nutrients.

3. Select the sentence that explains the reason for the limited diversity of trees in the ecosystem described in the passage.

Questions 4–7 refer to the following passage.

The fungal kingdom is enormous and has a unique and vital ecological niche. Mushrooms are the fruiting bodies of fungi, and some form beneficial relationships with living plants. Others degrade, colonize, and sometimes kill their hosts. Fungi, along with bacteria, fulfill the role in nature of breaking down and recycling material by reducing complex organic compounds into simple building blocks, thus enabling plants to reuse them. Fungi are divided into three categories based on their relationship to their substrate.

Parasitic fungi are mushrooms that feed on living organisms. A comparatively small amount of fungi fall into this category, including the *Cordyceps, Asterophora,* and *Sparassis crispa* species. Although these mushrooms are pernicious and can do great damage to their hosts, they are now recognized for their ability to create new habitats for other organisms. Some mushrooms are parasitic only under certain conditions and saprophytic under others; honey mushrooms are one example.

Saprophytic fungi subsist on dead or decaying matter such as wood, soil, grass, dung, and debris. By utilizing their mycelial network to weave between the cell walls of plants and secrete enzymes and acids, they are able to transform the large molecular complexes into simpler ones. After the matter has been decomposed, the result is a return of carbon, hydrogen, nitrogen, and minerals back into the ecosystem. Most saprophytes are woodland species such as shiitakes and oysters. Primary decomposers are the first to begin the decomposition process; secondary decomposers arrive after previous fungi have partially broken down the substrate to a condition in which they can thrive. The common cultivated button mushroom is an example of a secondary saprophytic mushroom.

Mycorrhiza is the term to describe the symbiotic associations between fungi and the rootlets of trees and plants. Ecologists recognize that the health of a forest is directly related to the presence, abundance, and variety of mycorrhizal associations. These rootlets provide the fungus with organic compounds and moisture while the fungus assists the roots in the absorption of inorganic nitrogen and other minerals, and essential elements including phosphorus, copper, and zinc. This process is believed to aid in the resistance of certain diseases. Improved plant growth and reproductive fitness are other ways that plants and trees benefit from this relationship.

4. What is the primary point of the article?

   A. A variety of mushrooms play different ecological roles.
   B. Fungi are a critical part of the ecosystem.
   C. Mushrooms are healthy to eat because they contain enzymes and they can contribute carbon, hydrogen, and nitrogen minerals.
   D. *Mycorrhiza* is the term to describe the symbiotic relationship between fungi and the rootlets of trees and plants.
   E. Organic compounds and moisture assist the roots of all fungi.

5. What is the result after saprophytic matter has been decomposed?

   A. Hydrogen, carbon, nitrogen, and minerals return to the ecosystem.
   B. Mushrooms secrete enzymes and acids.
   C. Nutrient-dense soil is created.
   D. Matter such as wood, grass, and soil is regenerated.
   E. Simple molecular complexes are transformed into more complex ones.

6. The passage suggests that fungi perform which of the following beneficial purposes? Consider each of the three choices and select all that apply.

   A. They reduce complex organic compounds into simpler units that can be reused.
   B. They are deleterious to their hosts by feeding on living organisms.
   C. They create new home environments for other organisms.

7. Select the sentence that presents paradoxical characteristics of fungi.

Questions 8–10 refer to the following passage.

A seminal piece of music widely regarded as a masterpiece of the 20th century had an inauspicious debut. Igor Stravinsky's ballet score *Le Sacre du Printemps,* or *Rite of Spring,* premiered in 1913 at Paris's Theatre des Champs-Élysées to a woefully unprepared audience. Both the music and the performance of the dancers, choreographed by Vaslav Nijinksy, were a radical departure from what the audience had come to expect and they responded by laughing, hissing, cat-calling, and causing a near riot. Stravinsky's story of a pagan sacrificial ritual was accompanied by ferociously dissonant, avant-garde music, unusual dance costumes, and strange choreography. It was an abrupt, decisive break from the harmonious, melodious past and a brazen introduction to the modern era. The audience had a visceral reaction from the moment of the bassoon's opening notes, the instrument pushed jarringly to its highest register. The string section playing a single dissonant chord 23 times in succession in a loud, pulsating manner, and the large percussion section pounded out primitive rhythms.

8. Which of the following is *not* true?

    A. Igor Stravinsky intended to shock his audience.
    B. The audience responded negatively to the piece.
    C. The audience quickly appreciated the dissonant music.
    D. The score was a cacophony of sound.
    E. The score was a cacophony of rhythm.

9. The main point of this paragraph can be summed up as:

    A. *Rite of Spring* was a good representation of a typical ballet score of that era.
    B. Stravinsky was a rebel.
    C. The audience of 1913 France was not prepared for this avant-garde style of music.
    D. Classical ballet music is normally accompanied by melodious music.
    E. Classical ballet music is normally accompanied by rhythmic music within a mathematical framework.

10. Select the sentence that illustrates the pejorative reaction of the first audience to view *Le Scare du Printemps.*

Questions 11–15 refer to the following passage.

What is the origin of the prejudice against humor? Why is it so dangerous, if you would keep the public confidence, to make the public laugh? Is it because humor and sound sense are essentially antagonistic? Has humanity found by experience that the man who sees the fun of life is unfitted to deal sanely with its problems? I think not. No man had more of the comic spirit in him than William Shakespeare, and yet his serious reflections, by the sheer force of their sublime obviousness, have pushed their way into the race's arsenal of immortal platitudes. So, too, with Aesop, and with Balzac, and with Dickens, to come down the scale. All of these men were fundamentally humorists, and yet all of them achieved what the race has come to accept as a penetrating sagacity. Contrariwise, many a haloed pundit has had his occasional guffaw. Lincoln, had there been no Civil War, might have survived in history chiefly as the father of the American smutty story—the only original art form that America has yet contributed to literature. Huxley, had he not been the greatest intellectual duelist of his age, might have been its greatest satirist. Bismarck, pursuing the gruesome trade of politics, concealed the devastating wit of a Molière; his surviving epigrams are truly stupendous. And Beethoven, after soaring to the heights of tragedy in the first movement of the Fifth Symphony, turned to the sardonic bull-fiddling of the *scherzo.*

11. It can be inferred from the passage that the writer would agree with which of the following statements?

   A. Humor is dangerous because it ridicules many of the tenets held sacred by the public.
   B. The qualities of being funny and having penetrating sagacity are mutually exclusive.
   C. Any individual who sees the humor of everyday life is unable to deal with its myriad problems in a rational way.
   D. Even saintly experts have been known to yield to the temptation of humor.
   E. Lincoln's great speeches are the only original American art form.

12. The phrase *To come down the scale* in the seventh sentence suggests the author's belief that

   A. In the great works of literature, humor is a less important quality than more serious considerations.
   B. Shakespeare's comic reflections are both sublime and immortal.
   C. The antagonism between humor and sobriety is an essential conflict that hasn't been resolved, even by the greatest writers in the English language.
   D. The combination of humor and music has lifted the human spirit throughout the ages.
   E. Shakespeare is a writer of greater eminence than Aesop, Balzac, or Dickens.

13. The tone of this passage is best described as:

   A. Whimsical and amusing
   B. Trenchant and cogent
   C. Hostile and mordant
   D. Indignant and unforgiving
   E. Tentative and objective

14. Which of the following best describes the structure of the passage? Consider each of the three choices and select all that apply.

   A. Assertion followed by specific illustration
   B. Generalization followed by a survey of contrasting viewpoints
   C. Personal anecdote followed by historical evidence

15. Select the sentence in which the writer gives an answer to one of the questions he posed in the first four sentences.

Answers

1. **A** Given the options, choice A would be the most appropriate title for this reading passage. Although some of the other options may be true statements based on the information presented, choice A is the best because the passage is primarily about how conifers adapt and thrive in this environment.

2. **A** The only answer that is accurate is choice A. Conifer needles have a waxy coating that protects against moisture loss, so these trees can live in an environment without a lot of rain water. The other answers are not true—conifers shed their needles every three or four years, not annually, and the stomata does store nutrients.

3. **The paucity of nutrients in the soil keeps the types of trees rather limited; there are only about 30 types of trees in the Boreal and Taiga forests, in contrast with the highly diversified tropical rain forests, which can have hundreds of different species of trees in small areas.** The fourth sentence explains the reason for the limited diversity in the ecosystem.

4. **B** Although all the answer choices are true, choice B is the correct answer because the *main* point of this passage is that fungi play a critical role in the ecosystem.

5. **A** After the matter has been decomposed by the saprophytic mushrooms, hydrogen, carbon, nitrogen, and minerals are returned to the ecosystem. This is clearly stated in the passage.

6. **A, C** The passage indicates that the beneficial functions of fungi include reducing complex organic compounds into simpler units that can be reused and creating new home environments for other organisms. Choice B is not a beneficial function; it is deleterious.

7. **Although these mushrooms are pernicious and can do great damage to their hosts, they are now recognized for their ability to create new habitats for other organisms.** This sentence presents apparently contradictory characteristics of fungi: by damaging some organisms, the fungi make way for new habitats for other organisms.

8. **C** The audience did not quickly learn to appreciate the dissonant music.

9. **C** It is clear from the passage that the audience at the premiere of the *Rite of Spring* was not accustomed to this type of music and choreography.

10. **Both the music and the performance of the dancers, choreographed by Vaslav Nijinksy, were a radical departure from what the audience had come to expect and they responded by laughing, hissing, cat-calling, and causing a near riot.** This sentence best illustrates the pejorative reaction of the initial audience.

11. **D** The only choice that is supported by the passage is choice D. The writer mentions many great writers who have employed humor in their writing. In fact, he states, "many a haloed pundit has had his occasional guffaw." All the other choices are contradicted by the information in the passage.

12. **E** After discussing Shakespeare, the writer mentions three other authors with the quip "to come down the scale." This suggests his belief that these authors are somewhat lower on the scale of great writing than Shakespeare. Thus, Shakespeare is a writer of greater eminence than Aesop, Balzac, or Dickens.

13. **B** The tone of the passage is best described as forceful and direct with a sharp wit. Choice B is the best answer. Each of the other choices has at least one word that is inaccurate: The tone of the passage is not whimsical (although it might be considered amusing). It isn't hostile, indignant, or tentative. *Remember:* Both words in the answer must be accurate in order for it to be the correct answer.

14. **A** Only choice A, assertion followed by specific illustration, is an accurate description of the organization of the passage. The passage doesn't contain a survey of opposing viewpoints or a personal anecdote.

15. **I think not.** This is the writer's answer to the question that he poses in the fourth sentence.

IX. Analytical Writing

The Analytical Writing section of the GRE tests your critical thinking skills and analytical writing abilities. It assesses your ability to express and substantiate complicated ideas, analyze an argument, and write a clear and cogent essay. It does not assess specific content knowledge; instead, it tests your ability to think on the spot, form a thesis, and substantiate that thesis with evidence.

The Analytical Writing section consists of two separately timed analytical writing tasks:

- **A 30-minute "Analyze an Issue" task:** You must write an essay on a topic that presents an issue of broad interest. You can discuss the issue from any perspective(s) you choose, as long as you provide relevant reasons and specific examples to clarify and substantiate your views. Your task is to make a well-reasoned, well-written argument in support of your position on the issue. The graders don't have a particular "right" answer in mind; they'll focus on your ability to recognize the complexity of the issue and to formulate and articulate a reasonable position.

- **A 30-minute "Analyze an Argument" task:** For this essay you must critique a given argument by discussing how well reasoned you find it. You have to analyze and evaluate the logic of the argument and the quality and relevance of the evidence used for support rather than agree or disagree with the position it presents.

The two tasks are complementary in that one requires you to construct your own argument by taking a stance and giving evidence to support your views on the issue, whereas the other requires you to critique someone else's argument by assessing its claims and evaluating the evidence given. This requires critical thinking and persuasive writing skills that university faculty value as important for success in graduate school.

Before you take the GRE, you need to spend some time preparing for the Analytical Writing section. The GRE Web site provides a pool of topics from which your questions will be taken (www.ets.org/gre/revised_general/prepare/analytical_writing). Review the list of possible essay topics, the scoring rubric, the test-taking strategies, and the scored sample essay responses and reader commentary. In the Analytical Writing section, the topics relate to a broad range of subjects from humanities to fine arts to the social and/or physical sciences. *Remember:* No topic requires specific content knowledge. Topics only test analytical writing and critical thinking rather than a particular subject matter. Practice writing and organizing an essay with specific examples, as well as analyzing a position's reasoning and evidence.

A. Analytical Writing Topics

There are too many topics for us to list them all here, but in the following sections, we provide a sampling of some of the topics you may see on the GRE. *Remember:* Be sure to go online (www.ets.org/gre/revised_general/prepare/analytical_writing) and click on each writing task to view the complete list of topics and study them in advance of taking the GRE. You can even print all the topics to make the studying easier.

1. "Analyze an Issue" topics

For the "Analyze an Issue" task, you'll be given one of the following instructions:

- Consider the extent to which you agree or disagree with the claim in the statement and write a response in which you explain your reasoning for the position. As you develop your position, evaluate the ramifications of the issue and the way these possibilities have shaped your position.

- Consider the extent to which you agree or disagree with the recommendation and write a response that explains your reasoning for the position you have taken. As you develop your perspective, explain the advantages and disadvantages of adopting the recommendation in the claim.

- Consider the extent to which you agree or disagree with the claim, and write an essay in which you address the opposing viewpoint. In developing and supporting your position, evaluate the logic of the counterarguments to your position.

- Consider the two views presented in the issue. Write an essay in which you discuss which position on the issue you find you are better able to support. Be sure to evaluate both sides of the issue in your essay.

- Consider the policy presented in the issue. Write a response in which you discuss your position on the policy and explain your reasoning. In developing and supporting your position, you should consider the possible consequences of implementing the policy and explain how these consequences have shaped your position.

Here are some of the general topics or ideas you might find:

- Politics should not be about pursuing ideals, but instead its aims should be to find a common thread among people and reach a reasonable argument.

- Technology enables one to access information immediately; however, it steals humans of the ability to contemplate deeply since we feel unable to compete with computers.

- Artistic innovations are more valuable than scientific inventions in modern-day civilization.

- Contemporary technology in today's society gives us fractious information at rapid speed, and society can lose perspective in this fast-moving, fragmented world.

- The intellect—such as analytical reasoning and cognitive ability—deserves more attention today.

- Productivity is effective and teamwork thrives when people work together toward a common goal.

- The past does not help when one is looking for guidance in our new and complex world.

- Society values artists more than critics because artists create something worthy of praise. (*Note:* A *critic* is one who evaluates works of art, such as novels, films, music, paintings, and so on.)

- Only experts, not generalists, can provide a valuable critique.

2. "Analyze an Argument" topics

For the "Analyze an Argument" task, you'll be given one of the following instructions:

- In a well-reasoned essay, discuss what specific evidence is needed to evaluate the argument and explain how the evidence would weaken or strengthen the argument.

- In a well-reasoned essay, examine the stated and/or unstated assumptions of the argument. Consider how the argument depends on these assumptions, and what the implications are for the argument if the assumptions prove unwarranted.

- In a well-reasoned essay, discuss what questions would need to be answered in order to decide whether the recommendation and the argument on which it is based are logical and practical. Consider how the answers to these questions would help to evaluate the recommendation.

- In a well-reasoned essay, discuss what questions would need to be answered in order to decide whether the advice and the argument Hot on which it is based are logical and practical. Consider how the answers to these questions would help to evaluate the advice.

- In a well-reasoned essay, discuss what questions would need to be answered in order to decide whether the recommendation is likely to have the predicted result. Be sure to explain how the answers to these questions would help to evaluate the recommendation.

- In a well-reasoned essay, discuss what questions would need to be answered in order to decide whether the prediction and the argument on which it is based are logical and practical. Be sure to explain how the answers to these questions would help to evaluate the prediction.

- In a well-reasoned essay, discuss one or more alternative explanations that could be the equal of the proposed explanation and explain how your explanation(s) can justifiably account for the evidence presented in the argument.

- In a well-reasoned essay, discuss what questions would need to be addressed in order to decide whether the conclusion and the argument on which it is based are logical and practical. Consider how the answers to the questions would help to evaluate the conclusion.

Here are some of the topics you might find:

- The following appeared in a letter from the owner of the Shadeland Station apartment complex to its manager:

  "One month ago, all the sinks on the first ten floors of Shadeland Station were changed to restrict the water flow to half of its original force. Although actual readings of water usage before and after the adjustment are not yet available, this modification will obviously result in a considerable savings for Shadeland Corporation, because the corporation pays for the water. Except for a few complaints about low water pressure in the bathrooms and kitchens, no problems with sinks have been reported since the change. Clearly, restricting water flow throughout all the 30 floors of Shadeland Station will increase our profits further."

  In a well-reasoned essay, discuss one or more alternative explanations that could be the equal of the proposed explanation and explain how your explanation(s) can justifiably account for the evidence presented in the argument.

- The following recommendation was presented by the human resources department to the trustees of the Best Jeans Company:

  "In the last two quarters of this fiscal year, under the leadership of our president, J. Y. Kearney, our profits have fallen considerably. Thus, we should ask for his resignation in return for a munificent severance package. In Jeff's place, we should appoint Catherine Mack. Catherine is currently president of Starlight Hot Jewelry, a company whose profits have increased considerably over the past several years. Although we will have to pay twice the salary for this replacement, it will be well worth it because we can expect our profits to increase significantly."

  In a well-reasoned essay, discuss what questions would need to be answered in order to decide whether the recommendation is likely to have the predicted result. Be sure to explain how the answers to these questions would help to evaluate the recommendation.

B. The Scoring of the Analytical Writing Section

Each essay response is scored on a 6-point scale with holistic scoring, which means that each response is judged as a whole. Readers don't separate the response into sections and award a certain number of points for a particular component (such as organization, grammar, and so on), but they do assign scores based on the quality of the response taking into account its characteristics overall. Organization (or the lack thereof) will be part of the readers' general impression of the response and will, therefore, contribute to the score.

GRE readers are college and university faculty experienced in teaching courses with an emphasis on writing and critical-thinking skills. All GRE readers have undergone careful training, passed qualifying tests, and demonstrated that they are able to maintain scoring accurately.

The essay score given by the reader is reviewed by a computerized program developed by ETS, which monitors the human reader. When the computer evaluation and the reader's score agree, the reader's score is used as the final score. If they disagree by a certain amount, a second reader scores the essay, and the final score is the average of the two readers' scores. The primary emphasis in scoring the Analytical Writing section is on critical thinking and analytical writing skills.

Following is a breakdown of the various score ranges.

- **5.5 to 6: Superb Essay**
  - Supports an opinion on the issue with insightful examples and organization or a fine critique of the argument
  - Generally well written and organized with strong vocabulary, logical reasoning, and clarity of style
  - Mechanics of writing are solid with proper grammar and spelling
- **4.5 to 5: Solid Essay**
  - Supports an opinion on the issue with solid examples or a strong critique of the argument
  - Generally well written and organized with varied vocabulary, logical reasoning, and clarity of style
  - Mechanics of writing are good with only minor flaws in grammar and spelling
- **3.5 to 4: Good Essay**
  - Supports an opinion on the issue with good examples
  - Generally well written and organized with logical reasoning and a clear style
  - Mechanics are okay
- **2.5 to 3: Fair Essay**
  - Partially supports an opinion on the issue with insightful examples and organization or a fine critique of the argument
  - Generally disorganized with an unclear style and lacking organization
  - Poor mechanics of writing or awkward grammatical structure and weak spelling
- **1.5 to 2: Poor Essay**
  - Barely supports an opinion on the issue with few or no examples and weak organization or a poor argument
  - Generally poorly written and lacking in organization and clarity
  - Many grammar and spelling mistakes

- **0.5 to 1: Deficient Essay**
  - Fails to support an opinion on the issue with examples and lacks any organization or logic of the argument
- **0: No Score Essay**
  - Irrelevant or missing topic or argument
  - Copies or plagiarizes writing
  - Undecipherable language or written in another language

C. Analytical Writing Strategies

It is very important to budget your time wisely. Within the 30-minute time limit for the "Analyze an Issue" task, you need to give yourself enough time to think about the issue, outline or plan a response, and then compose an essay. Within the 30-minute time limit for the "Analyze an Argument" task, you need to allow enough time to analyze the argument, organize a critique, and compose your response.

Here are specific steps to help you write a cohesive essay within the time allotted:

1. **Brainstorm.**

   Take five minutes to think about as many ideas as you can to support your position. On a separate piece of paper, list your ideas, definitions, theories, reasons, and examples that support and refute your point. Then read over your notes and choose the best three to five ideas as a foundation for your essay.

2. **Outline.**

   Now that you have your ideas, organize them in a logical sequence. ***Remember:*** Good organization is key. Think about how a GRE reader will grade it, and make sure to include essential examples that support your thesis.

3. **Draft or write.**

   Use the standard format: introduction, supporting paragraphs, and conclusion. It is important that your composition is focused and well substantiated. Write the introduction and conclusion first, and then draft the body paragraphs.

4. **Proofread and edit.**

   Leave five minutes to reread for errors of spelling, grammar, and organization and make sure you have clear transitions.

Edit and proofread at the end of each timed task to check for obvious errors. Although an occasional spelling or grammatical error will not significantly affect your score (GRE readers who grade your writing understand the time constraints of this section and will consider your response a "first draft"), obvious and persistent errors will weaken the overall effectiveness of your writing and lower your score.

Following the third section, you'll have the opportunity to take a ten-minute break. There is a one-minute break between the other test sections. You might want to get up, stretch, and replenish any materials such as scratch paper during each scheduled break.

The following sections provide more specific strategies for each task.

1. The "Analyze an Issue" task

Because the "Analyze an Issue" task is meant to assess writing and critical thinking skills and not specific knowledge of one subject area, it is best to prepare for it by practicing writing responses and critiquing your response based on these tips:

- Use solid reasons, evidence, and examples to support your position on an issue.
- Use critical thinking skills. ***Remember:*** It is not your position on the issue that matters but rather how effectively you substantiate it.

A smart way to prepare for the "Analyze an Issue" task is to practice writing on some of the published topics and read the commentary about sample responses along with scoring.

Think about these questions:

- What is the primary or main issue?
- Why is the argument sound (or why is it not sound)? Do you agree with the argument?
- Does the issue make reasonable or unreasonable assumptions?
- Are the conditions of the claim reasonable?
- Is further explanation needed to explain terms for the reader?
- Are the reasons that support it sound?
- What are some strong examples—both hypothetical and real—to substantiate the argument? Which are the best examples?

2. The "Analyze an Argument" task

The "Analyze an Argument" task differs from the "Analyze an Issue" task in that your task is to critique and analyze the writer's argument, not present your own opinion or ideas on the subject. You'll be given one short passage, and you'll have 30 minutes to write an essay on how well the argument is supported. These passages intentionally contain assumptions and holes in their arguments; you need to identify these assumptions and holes. Then you need to present your case on why you think the author has erroneously reached his conclusion and offer your suggestions on how to write a better response.

This section tests two skills that are crucial for success in graduate school: your analytical writing skills and your critical thinking skills. Regardless of your course of study in school, critical thinking and analytical writing are tools you'll rely upon often.

Your score will be based on the following:

- How well you identify and analyze the argument
- The structure of your response (how well organized it is, how well your ideas are developed, and supported, and how well you present your case)
- Your use of standard written English

Prepare ahead of time for this portion of the GRE by giving yourself 30 minutes to write critiques to "Analyze an Argument" tasks. With each practice critique you write, you'll learn how to wisely divide your half-hour into reading the essay, making notes, writing your response, and proofreading your work.

The main components of an "Analyze an Argument" task are the following:

- **Premise:** The premise, or proposition, is what the author concludes from the information given.
- **Assumptions:** Assumptions are what the author assumes, drawing inferences and insinuations based on the material.
- **Conclusion:** This is the conclusion that the author arrives at based on the facts and assumptions.

Use your scratch paper to organize yourself before you begin writing. Ask yourself:

- Are there any holes in the author's logic? Is he jumping to conclusions based on the evidence presented, or are valid assumptions being made based on the material?
- What is the author's premise or point? Is the premise logically convincing?
- Why does the author reach the conclusion that he does? What evidence or proof supports the author's claims?
- Can you think of an alternate explanation that may also be true given the material presented? Does this explanation confirm or contradict the author's?
- Are there any gaps—assumptions or faulty logic in the argument? Is the author over-generalizing? How specifically is the author's premise weakened?
- Is the author jumping to conclusions? Is he assuming causal relationships between two pieces of evidence that aren't necessarily true? What can one logically conclude based on the information provided in the passage?
- What are your ideas for strengthening the author's argument?

Make an outline using the standard format.

- **First paragraph (introduction):** What is the author's premise? Explain that the argument isn't well-reasoned.
- **Supporting paragraphs:** Highlight the most obvious flaws in the author's argument. Why is the author wrong? What crucial piece of information is missing for the author to be able to confidently make that claim? Support your critique well.

  Continue on with another paragraph or two identifying other mistakes. Would additional information strengthen the author's premise, or weaken it?
- **Summary:** Summarize your assessment of the argument. Use good examples on how you would suggest that the author improve his point.

Be direct and concise. This is not the place for flowery language or to showcase your large vocabulary. You will be graded on how well you argue your case, present facts that support your case, and express yourself. Your response should be well articulated and insightful and highlight your command and facility of the English language.

Remember: Give yourself a few minutes at the end to go back and reread your essay. Edit and proofread and, most important, ensure that your ideas are well supported and that your writing is well organized and clear.

D. Sample Essay Responses

1. The "Analyze an Issue" task

In this section, we provide examples of varying levels of essays, all written in response to the following:

> In any area of accomplishment, it is highly unlikely that one can make a significant contribution without first being strongly influenced by preceding achievements.

> Write an essay in which you consider the extent to which you agree or disagree with the statement and explain your reasoning for the position you take. In developing and supporting your position, you should consider ways in which the statement might or might not hold true. Be sure to explain how these factors shape your position.

Sample level-6 essay

A significant contribution to any cause requires time, effort, and determination, all of which are not only inspired by precedents but also supported by previous knowledge. Sometimes minor additions, even snippets of information, have provided the spark that has paved the way for momentous break-throughs. Whether it is a single piece of a larger puzzle or an entire concept, every innovator needs to draw from previous investigations in order to advance in his or her field. It is impossible to make a significant contribution without being strongly influenced by past achievements. That being said, some important discoveries are so ground-breaking that they appear to have sprung "full-grown from the brow of Zeus" or from the brain of some brilliant investigator.

Newton and Leibnitz are generally credited with the discovery of calculus, but they were not solitary pioneers: Their calculations are based on advanced mathematics, which is, in turn, derived from the continuity-based mathematics of medieval thinkers like Galileo. The medievals based their formulas on the Greek precursors, men like Democritus and others. Building upon the principles of those great mathematicians who preceded him, Newton proposed the three laws of motion and contrived his own explanation of complex, integral calculus to explain these laws. While Newton gets much of the credit, and justly so, he constructed his computations on a foundation that extends backwards for thousands of years.

Just as Newton followed a path carved for him by his predecessors, so Thomas Edison was able to build on previous knowledge for his invention of the light bulb. Had Benjamin Franklin not discovered how to harness electricity and Joseph Swan not done experiments in England with carbon filaments, Edison might never have succeeded in illuminating America. Edison was not alone in his quest for electrical applications. Other scientists in this country and in England were experimenting with filaments, attempting to find the best electrical conductor that could maintain a sustained glow. Perhaps it was just chance or luck that allowed Edison to be the first find the right material, but he lives in history as the discoverer of the light bulb.

Innovations build off other innovations. We depend upon the past to spark our inspiration and to instill us with the confidence to break new ground. Indeed, it is rare to find a great leader in any field who does not acknowledge a debt to those who have gone before. The possibilities of tomorrow are always built on the realities of yesterday.

Reader commentary: The above essay was graded a 6. It is well organized and effectively supported with relevant examples. The writer demonstrates a clear understanding of the task and has written a thoughtful essay. The writing is cogent and the language is clear and concise. The essay follows the standard essay format (opening paragraph, supporting paragraphs, conclusion), and the sentences flow smoothly from one idea to the next.

Sample level-4 essay

Ever since elementary school, we have learned that in order to excel in a subject, we have to first comprehend the subject. Although I agree with this, I do not agree that one must be "strongly influenced by past achievements" in that subject in order to contribute to that field. While in some professions, such as government positions, one must understand the past to leave one's mark in the present, but one is mostly influenced by one's own experiences, one's encounters with others, and in health care, the people in the top positions extract the benefits of other professions, such as an airline check list, to use as groundwork for a surgical checklist for sanitation. Overall, one desires to scar the field of their interest, not by learning about past achievements in that field, but by one's own experiences and experiences.

Ever since I can remember, my mother has asked my father questions about his profession, Senior Project Manager for Turner Construction Company in airport projects, for advice on how to revise her department of Quality Management in North Shore Long Island Jewish Hospital Sectors. This is just one of the many examples of how in many areas of study, people look to the successes in other fields, hoping to mold those successes in their own field. My mother recently told me that one of the major reasons why the hospital has decreased unsanitary conditions in the operating room is because her department looked at the airline department's checklist for safety and decided to create their own surgical checklist for doctors in the operating room. Even in the field of psychology, psychologists have used the scientific method utilized in the science field for experiments, to conduct their own experiments on human behavior, such as Stanley Milgrim in the 1960s when he conducted the electric shock experiment in which he would observe how far a human could be pushed to potentially kill another human being in the presence of an authority figure. Overall, many fields take the past accomplishments of other fields and mend them to their own liking; they are obviously not influenced by their own field's past accomplishments, but rather the accomplishments of other fields that could potentially aid to further better their field.

Although one is influenced heavily by one's own experiences, expectations, and other accomplishments in various areas of life, there are times when one must understand the past accomplishments of other fields in order to leave a significant mark on that field forever. The government of the United States is one that is "by the people and for the people" and "derives its power from the people," but the top leaders in government must extensively study the history of the government in order to realize what they can contribute that would be beneficial to the country as a whole. In David Gergen's novel, "Eyewitness to Power: The Essence of Leadership from Nixon to Clinton," it stresses the importance of how a President must first understand the past in order to contribute to the future. As an example, Gergen says how Nixon used to study the past successes of government and past failures to see how he could benefit the country and move the country on a path to success, like Woodrow Wilson. Nixon, like all other presidents, have studied comprehensively the past presidencies to see what contributed to either to rise or the downfall of the nation, so they could significantly put the country on the path to success. In the field of government, a politician in general must comprehend the past in order to move the country forward in the future. Even though this one field of government must be influenced by the past contributions in that specific field, the rest of the fields are highly influenced by other sectors and other factors that are out of the control of their own field.

Even though, as James Madison stated in the Federalist 10, "for every faction there will be an opposing faction," it is essential to realize that most of the accomplishments in the world have been due to the accomplishments in other areas of life. The essential question is: What is stronger, the heart or the brain? In many cases, the heart is the stronger of the two and the heart will dictate where to go in the future and what a person should do; in essence, the brain does not have as much influence on personal decisions like the heart does. All in all, it is the heart and the heart's desire that has the most influence on a person, not the words in a textbook and a lecture that a professor gives.

Reader commentary: The above essay was graded a 4. It is an example of an energetic attempt to address the task that becomes lost in its own wordiness, the major error in this essay. In attempting to answer the question, the writer struggles to express himself clearly. He tries to disagree with the position in the prompt and ends up qualifying it ("there are times when one must understand the past accomplishments of other fields in order to leave a significant mark on that field forever"). The final reference to James Madison is rather cryptic, and it leads the writer into a maudlin "heart versus brain" conclusion that mars the effectiveness of the essay.

Sample level-2 essay

The more knowledge a person has, the better the contribution that person can make to the world. If you have a strong background, you could use that knowledge to your advantage. There have been many leaders who have gained acquired knowledge and then from there they have managed to lead people who agree with their ideas. Martin Luther King an example of a leader who studies the art of passive protesting. The United State's as a whole is its own leader and this is due to the fact that many Americans understand the history of our past allowing us to see what mistakes can be avoided in the long run.

Martin Luther King was part of the Civil rights movement. He contributed a lot to this movement because he believed in change. He was no ordinary leader because he stood out. People recognized him when they saw him. The fact is he had strong beliefs and principles that held his ground. He weas never fickle and his ideas where supported on knowledge and experience. Today Martin Luther King is known for his work and many can agree that his strong ideas that where supported by his knowledge and experience allowed him to accomplish even further goals.

By having background on a topic and being influences will allow anyone to form a strong opinion that is favored by background information. The more knowledge you have on a topic the better it is to have a strong theory because there is more knowledge to support your ideas allowing for others to understand you ideas.

Reader commentary: This essay is graded a 2. It attempts to address the prompt but is marred by so much repetition and disorganized thinking that it is an unsuccessful response. It contains many awkward and unparallel sentences ("By having background on a topic and being influences will allow anyone to form a strong opinion that is favored by background information"). It is filled with generalizations ("Today Martin Luther King is known for his work . . .") and contains too many spelling, punctuation, and grammatical errors. The errors are enough to create a major distraction, and the writer does not demonstrate any critical thinking or analytical writing skills.

2. The "Analyze an Argument" task

In this section, we provide examples of varying levels of essays, all written in response to the following:

> A recent five-year study of the sleeping habits of a selection of people challenges the belief that receiving at least eight hours of sleep a night is healthy. People in this study who reported sleeping eight or more hours a night had a higher rate of specific health problems than the subjects who slept seven hours a night on average. People who reported sleeping five hours a night had only a minimal increase in health issues compared to those who slept eight hours a night. It is apparent that people should try to sleep seven hours each night; therefore, getting too much sleep is worse for one's health than getting too little sleep.

Write a response in which you discuss the soundness of the conclusion. Discuss what questions would need to be addressed in order to decide whether the conclusion and the argument on which it is based are reasonable. Be sure to consider how the answers to the questions would help to evaluate the conclusion.

Sample level-6 essay

The passage above claims that people should aim to get seven hours of sleep each night because, in the cited study, those who reported sleeping more than eight hours or less than seven had higher rates of health issues. There is not sufficient data presented here for the author to draw the conclusion that all people should sleep for seven hours to get maximum health benefits. Numerous important variables are absent from the information presented that would substantiate the author's conclusion.

The author does not give crucial facts regarding the study; without this information, it is impossible to safely state that people should sleep seven hours per night. When was the study conducted? How many people were involved? What were the ages and genders of the subjects? These are all critical pieces of information. We are also unaware of other health risk factors such as diet, stress levels, alcohol consumption, whether the person smoked; all of these variables have a major impact on a person's overall health, and sleep is but one variable. Only comparing the number of hours of sleep people received and ignoring these other factors is specious logic.

Another glaring omission is the health of the subjects prior to the study beginning. People who are healthier tend to need less sleep than people whose health is compromised in some way, so it is not clear which came first: Did the participants who slept longer do so because they had health problems, or did the fact that they slept longer than eight hours make them unhealthy? It can't be determined based on the limited information given.

In addition, we are not privy to what kind of health problems the study's subjects suffer from. It is not clear if the health issues are mental or physiological. Sleep clearly impacts both mental and physical health, but the causal relationship between health and sleep is not evident based on this particular study. There is also no mention of the degrees of health problems between those who slept for eight hours or more versus those who slept less than seven hours, other than saying that the difference was "slight." It is too simplistic to suggest that people are better off sleeping too little rather than too much as it ignores other important factors.

The author is not necessarily incorrect in his conclusion, but as mentioned above, there isn't enough information present to adequately prove his thesis. The writer needs to present more facts about the study and its participants in order to substantiate the idea that seven hours of sleep is ideal for most people. It is a mistake to make such a sweeping generalization based on the limited information presented.

Reader commentary: The above essay was graded a 6 based on the fact that it is well organized, the writer has a mastery of English, and the ideas are well supported. The language is clear and concise; it follows the standard essay format (opening paragraph, supporting paragraphs, conclusion) and is well executed in its critique of the author's argument.

Sample level-4 essay

The author claims that people need seven hours of sleep each night in order to be healthy based on a study of people who reported higher rates of health problems if they slept more than eight hours, or less than seven. The author draws the conclusion based on scant evidence and makes assumptions on insufficient facts.

In order to give more credence to the statement that people would be healthiest if they slept for seven hours each night but it is too black and white. The study leaves out crucial information that would make his argument more valid. A sound study would include more information about the subject's lifestyle including their age, sex, stress levels, and eating and drinking habits.

The author is also assuming a cause-and-effect relationship between health and sleep that is not well supported. One can't conclude that those who slept the most were unhealthy because they slept longer, perhaps they slept longer because they were depressed, didn't feel well, didn't have to be up early in the morning—and it could be merely coincidental that this group reported higher rates of health problems.

For the author's premise to be valid more information is necessary. The logic is somewhat faulty and conclusions are being drawn based on a lot of assumptions and guesses versus being supported by solid data.

Reader commentary: The above essay was graded a 4 because it showed competent use of English, had some mistakes but not enough to confuse the reader, and had valid critiques of the argument that were satisfactorily supported. To be a stronger critique there should be fewer grammatical errors and a stronger critique of the errors in the argument.

Sample level-2 essay

I think that in order for this authors argument to be stronger it should give more background information on the subjects so we'd know if he was comparing apples with apples. There's a lot of stuff missing. From the information presented it is not clear why some people, who were unhealthy slept more, maybe they were not health to begin with or maybe sleeping more did make them unhealthier. Its hard to say.

This argument isn't very convincing. It should have more information so we can have a clue as to why the author is making the claims he makes. It would also be helpful to now some facts about the people in the study, such as what was their health like, what they suffered from and why sleeping less than seven hours made them unhealthy. Maybe sleeping more really is better for us if we are healthy to begin with but it's hard to say.

We'd need better facts for this to be a stronger argument. Right now its weak.

Reader commentary: This essay is graded a 2 because it is disorganized and contains too many spelling, punctuation, and grammatical errors (subjects don't agree with the verbs, the possessive is not used when it should be, and so on). The errors are enough to create a major distraction, and the writer does not demonstrate any critical thinking or analytical writing skills.

X. Arithmetic

Changes to the GRE in 2011 will include the addition of an on-screen calculator for use in the Quantitative Reasoning sections. As a result, you can expect fewer questions that test your ability to perform calculations and more questions that test your understanding of concepts.

> **Tip: Relying too much on the calculator can waste time, so try to handle simple calculations with mental math whenever possible, and save the calculator for longer calculations and larger numbers.**

Producing correct answers—whether by mental math or by calculator—requires an understanding of arithmetic, which is the subject of this chapter.

A. Order of Operations

Arithmetic problems can involve many operations, and if those operations are performed in different orders, the resulting answers could be different. Because only one answer can be correct, there are rules about the order in which arithmetic operations should be performed. The order of operations is a set of rules that tells us how to evaluate expressions. Some people remember this order by the acronym **PEMDAS**; others use a sentence to help them remember. *Please Excuse My Dear Aunt Sally* is one favorite.

The letters in **PEMDAS** are meant to help you remember to:

- Simplify expressions inside **P**arentheses.
- Evaluate powers, or numbers with **E**xponents.
- **M**ultiply and **D**ivide, moving from left to right.
- **A**dd and **S**ubtract, moving from left to right.

Multiplication and division have the same priority. Do multiplication or division as you meet them as you work across the line, instead of doing all the multiplication and then all the division. The same is true for addition and subtraction. Do them as you come to them. Do not give addition a higher rank than subtraction.

EXAMPLE:

> Find the simplest value for $8 \times [2 \times (4 + 3)^2 - 20 + 12] \div 4$.

The correct answer is **180.** Grouping symbols take precedence. So, work from the inside out:

$8 \times [2 \times (4 + 3)^2 - 20 + 12] \div 4$	Add 4 + 3.
$8 \times [2 \times (7)^2 - 20 + 12] \div 4$	Square 7.
$8 \times [2 \times 49 - 20 + 12] \div 4$	Multiply 2×49.
$8 \times [98 - 20 + 12] \div 4$	Subtract 98 − 20.
$8 \times [78 + 12] \div 4$	Add 78 + 12.
$8 \times [90] \div 4$	Multiply 8×90.
$720 \div 4$	Divide 720 ÷ 4.
180	You get the answer: 180.

Most calculators follow the order of operations automatically, evaluating $3 + 2 \times 5$ as 13, for example, not as 25. You need to use parentheses when you want to override the normal order of operations—for example, to get the calculator to do $(3 + 2) \times 5$.

Practice

Directions (1–2): You are given two quantities, one in Column A and one in Column B. You are to compare the two quantities and choose one of the following:

A.   The quantity in Column A is greater.
B.   The quantity in Column B is greater.
C.   The two quantities are equal.
D.   The relationship cannot be determined from the information given.

	Column A	Column B
1.	$4 - 3 \times 4 + 3$	$(4 - 3) \times (4 + 3)$

	Column A	Column B
2.	$4 - 3(4 + 3)$	$(4 - 3) \times 4 + 3$

Directions (3–10): Unless otherwise directed, select a single answer choice. For numeric-entry questions, enter a number in the box(es) below the question. Equivalent forms of the correct answer, such as 2.5 and 2.50, are all correct. Fractions do not need to be reduced to lowest terms. Enter the exact answer unless the question asks you to round your answer.

3. Select the two expressions that produce a result equal to $5 \times 3 - 7 \times 3$.

   A. $5 \times (3 - 7) \times 3$
   B. $(5 \times 3) - (7 \times 3)$
   C. $5 \times (3 - 7 \times 3)$
   D. $5 - 7 \times 3$
   E. $(5 - 7) \times 3$

4. Choose all the expressions that are less than 100.

   A. $5^2 - 2 \times 7 - 3$
   B. $5^2 - (2 \times 7) - 3$
   C. $5^2 - 2 \times (7 - 3)$
   D. $5^2 - (2 \times 7 - 3)$
   E. $(5^2 - 2) \times 7 - 3$
   F. $(5^2 - 2) \times (7 - 3)$
   G. $5^2 - [2 \times (7 - 3)]$

5. The expression $[(66 - 54) \div 3 + 10 \div 5 - (6 - 2^2)]$ is equal to

   A. 14
   B. 4
   C. 3
   D. 0.8
   E. −10

6. The product of 15 and 4, minus the quotient of 30 and 5, is equal to

   A. 25
   B. 35
   C. 54
   D. 17
   E. 66

7. Eight times 9, plus 10 times 11, minus the product of 2 squared and 5 squared is

   A. 81
   B. 82
   C. 153
   D. 873
   E. 802

8. $a - b + b \times (b^3 - a) \div b$ must be equal to

    A. $a - (b + b) \times (b^3 - a) \div b$
    B. $-b + b^3$
    C. $-b^3$
    D. $a \times (b^3 - a) \div b$
    E. $a \times (b^4 - a) \div b$

9. $17 - (8 - 3)(2 + 1) \div 5 =$

                                                    [   ]

10. $7 + 3^2 \div 2 - 6 =$

                                                    [   ]

Answers

1. **B** The correct answer is B, because $(4 - 3) \times (4 + 3) = 1 \times 7 = 7$, which is greater than $4 - 3 \times 4 + 3 = 4 - 12 + 3 = -8 + 3 = -5$.

2. **B** The correct answer is B, because $(4 - 3) \times 4 + 3 = 1 \times 4 + 3 = 4 + 3 = 7$, which is greater than $4 - 3(4 + 3) = 4 - 3(7) = 4 - 21 = -17$.

3. **B, E** In $5 \times 3 - 7 \times 3$, the multiplications should be done first, so any choice that places parentheses around the multiplication will have the same value. Therefore, choice B is equivalent. Choice A, $5 \times (3 - 7) \times 3$, performs the subtraction before the multiplication, giving a result of -60, and $5 \times (3 - 7 \times 3)$ becomes $5 \times (3 - 21)$ or -90. Choices D and E seem to be missing a number, but the placement of the parentheses in choice E brings the distributive property into play. Choice D, which does the multiplication first, is not equivalent, but choice E is $(5 - 7) \times 3 = -2 \times 3 = -6$.

4. **A, B, C, D, F, G** Don't spend time doing the entire calculation for each answer choice. Simplify enough that you can make an estimate of the size. Choice A becomes $5^2 - 2 \times 7 - 3 = 25 - 14 - 3$, which is less than 25, so clearly less than 100. The placement of the parentheses in choice B does not change the order of operations, so choice B is identical to choice A. Choices C and D do alter the order, but $5^2 - 2 \times (7 - 3) = 25 - 2 \times 4$ still leaves a number less than 25, as does $5^2 - (2 \times 7 - 3) = 25 - (14 - 3)$. Choice E, $(52 - 2) \times 7 - 3 = (25 - 2) \times 7 - 3$, requires you to multiply the 23 that results from the parentheses by 7, giving you a result well over 100, so the final subtraction will not change that. Choice F comes close to 100, but $(52 - 2) \times (7 - 3) = (25 - 2) \times 4$, but 23×4 is just a bit less than 100. Choice G, $52 - [2 \times (7 - 3)] = 25 - [2 \times 4]$, is also less than 25 and, therefore, less than 100.

5. **B** The correct answer is choice B, because $[(66 - 54) \div 3 + 10 \div 5 - (6 - 2^2)] = [(66 - 54) \div 3 + 10 \div 5 - (6 - 4)] = [12 \div 3 + 10 \div 5 - 2] = [4 + 10 \div 5 - 2] = [4 + 2 - 2] = 4$.

6. **C** The correct answer is choice C, because the product of 15 and 4 is 60 and the quotient of 30 and 5 is 6, so $60 - 6 = 54$. (***Remember:*** The product is the result of multiplication, and the quotient is the result of division.)

7. **B** The correct answer is choice B, because 8 times 9, plus 10 times 11, minus the product of 2 squared and 5 squared is $8 \times 9 + 10 \times 11 - (2^2 \times 5^2) = 72 + 110 - (4 \times 25) = 182 - 100 = 82$.

8. **B** $a - b + b \times (b^3 - a) \div b$ eliminates the option of using a calculator and forces you to analyze whether the expressions are equivalent. The expression in parentheses is evaluated first; then it's multiplied by b and the result is divided by b. Those operations cancel each other, so $a - b + b \times (b^3 - a) \div b = a - b + b^3 - a = -b + b^3$.

9. **14** $17 - (8 - 3)(2 + 1) \div 5 = 17 - (5)(3) \div 5 = 17 - 15 \div 5 = 17 - 3 = 14$.

10. **5.5** $7 + 3^2 \div 2 - 6 = 7 + 9 \div 2 - 6 = 7 + 4.5 - 6 = 11.5 - 6 = 5.5$.

B. Integers

Integers are positive and negative whole numbers and zero. The rules for arithmetic with integers apply to other positive and negative numbers as well, like $+4\frac{3}{5}$ or -7.5. Remember that larger numbers are farther to the right on the number line. For negative numbers, larger means closer to zero (-4 is larger than -5).

1. Absolute value

The *absolute value* of the number is the distance of the number from zero, without regard to direction. Absolute value is often thought of as "the number without its sign." The symbol for the absolute value of x is $|x|$. Both 5 and -5 have an absolute value of 5, because both are five units from zero, so $|5| = 5$ and $|-5| = 5$. One number is positive and one is negative because one is above zero and one is below zero, but absolute value is not concerned with direction.

2. Addition

To add integers, look at the signs and at the absolute values. If the signs are the same, add the absolute values and keep the sign.

$+3 + +5 = +8$	Both numbers are positive, so add $3 + 5$ and make the answer positive.
$-9 + -2 = -11$	Both numbers are negative, so add $9 + 2$ and make the answer negative.

If the signs are *different,* subtract the absolute values, and take the sign of the number with the larger absolute value.

$+3 + -5 = -2$	Signs are different, so subtract $5 - 3 = 2$. Because $|-5| > |+3|$, take the sign of -5.
$-14 + +25 = +11$	Signs are different, so subtract $25 - 14 = 11$. Because $|+25| > |-14|$, take the sign of $+25$.

3. Subtraction

Don't subtract. When a problem calls for subtraction, change the sign of the second number and follow the rules for adding.

$-5 - +3 = -5 + -3 = -8$	Subtracting a positive is adding a negative.
$-4 - -5 = -4 + +5 = +1$	Subtracting a negative is adding a positive.

4. Multiplication and division

The rules for signs are identical whether you're multiplying or dividing. If the signs are the same, the answer is positive. If the signs are different, the answer is negative.

$+2 \times +5 = +10$	Positive × positive = positive
$+4 \times -7 = -28$	Positive × negative = negative
$-3 \times +9 = -27$	Negative × positive = negative
$-6 \times -8 = +48$	Negative × negative = positive

Practice

Directions (1–2): You are given two quantities, one in Column A and one in Column B. You are to compare the two quantities and choose one of the following:

A. The quantity in Column A is greater.
B. The quantity in Column B is greater.
C. The two quantities are equal.
D. The relationship cannot be determined from the information given.

	Column A	Column B
1.	-12×4	12×-4

	Column A	Column B
2.	$\dfrac{-16}{8}$	$\dfrac{16}{-2 \times 4}$

Directions (3–10): Unless otherwise directed, select a single answer choice. For numeric-entry questions, enter a number in the box(es) below the question. Equivalent forms of the correct answer, such as 2.5 and 2.50, are all correct. Fractions do not need to be reduced to lowest terms. Enter the exact answer unless the question asks you to round your answer.

3. Choose all the expressions that are equal to –18.

   A. $-8 - 10$
   B. -3×6
   C. $-4 + 14$
   D. 2×-9
   E. $36 \div -2$
   F. $(-9)^2$
   G. $-90 \div 5$
   H. $-20 + 38$

4. Choose the three expressions that are equal to $4 + -3 - (-5 - 8)$.

   A. -2×-7
   B. 2×-7
   C. -4×-3
   D. -4×3
   E. $6 \times 4 - 10$
   F. $6 \times (4 - 10)$
   G. $-8 \times 3 - 5 \times 2$
   H. $-8 \times 3 + 5 \times 2$
   I. $8 \times 3 + 5 \times -2$
   J. $-8 \times 3 + 6 \times -8$

5. Find the simplest answer for $-4 - 5 - -5 - 8 + 12 - -4$.

   A. -4
   B. -2
   C. 0
   D. 2
   E. 4

6. Each day, Jon records the temperature at 2 p.m. On Monday, the temperature was 62°. On Tuesday, it was 4° higher, but on Wednesday, it dropped 7°. On Thursday, there was no change, but on Friday, the temperature rose 10°. What was the temperature on Friday?

   A. 59°
   B. 62°
   C. 65°
   D. 69°
   E. 73°

7. When Carl went out for the wrestling team, he started a program of diet and exercise. In the first month of the season, he gained 9 pounds. In the second month, he lost 3 pounds. In the third month, he gained 6 pounds. What was the average monthly change in Carl's weight?

   A. +12 pounds
   B. −6 pounds
   C. +6 pounds
   D. −4 pounds
   E. +4 pounds

8. The sum of –7 and –4 times the quotient of –8 and +2 is equal to which of the following?

   A. 0
   B. –23
   C. 9
   D. 44
   E. –44

9. Simplify: $\dfrac{(5\times{}^-7)-(2\times{}^-10)+1}{({}^-3\times5)+({}^-2\times{}^-4)}$.

10. The expression $x \, \Delta \, y$ is defined as follows:

   If the sum of x and y is positive, add –7 to the sum.

   If the sum of x and y is negative, divide the sum by –2.

   If the sum of x and y is 0, subtract 3 from the sum.

   Find $-4 \, \Delta \, 3$.

Answers

1. **C** $-12 \times 4 = -48$ and $12 \times -4 = -48$.

2. **C** $\dfrac{-16}{8} = -2$ and $\dfrac{16}{-2 \times 4} = \dfrac{16}{-8} = -2$.

3. **A, B, D, E, G** Eliminate choice F immediately, because squaring, or multiplying a number by itself, will always give a positive result, because you multiply numbers with the same sign. Scan the answer choices for others that can be eliminated. Choice C, $-4 + 14$, and choice H, $-20 + 38$, both give positive results and can be eliminated. Check the remaining choices to verify that they yield -18: $-8 - 10 = -18$, $-3 \times 6 = -18$, $2 \times -9 = -18$, $36 \div -2 = -18$, and $-90 \div 5 = -18$

4. **A, E, I** First establish the result of $4 + -3 - (-5 - 8) = 4 + -3 - (-13) = 4 + -3 + 13 = 14$. You're looking for expressions that yield 14. Eliminate choices C and D immediately because the product of 3 and 4 is 12, not 14, so these are not possible answers regardless of sign. Choose A and eliminate choice B, because $2 \times -7 = -14$, not 14. For the remaining answer choices, simplify only as far as necessary to rule out incorrect answers. Choice E, $6 \times 4 - 10 = 24 - 10 = 14$ is a second correct option. Choice F, $6 \times (4 - 10) = 6 \times -6$, can be eliminated. Choice G, $-8 \times 3 - 5 \times 2 = -24 - 10$, can be eliminated, as can choice H, $-8 \times 3 + 5 \times 2 = -24 + 10$, which will be -14. Choice I, $8 \times 3 + 5 \times -2 = 24 + -10 = 24 - 10$, is the third correct choice. It is not necessary to check choice J, because you have the three requested answers, but if you want, verify that $-8 \times 3 + 6 \times -8 = -24 + -48$ does not equal 14.

5. **E** $-4 - 5 - -5 - 8 + 12 - -4 = -4 + -5 + 5 + -8 + 12 + 4 = (-4 + 4) + (-5 + 5) + (-8 + 12) = 0 + 0 + 4 = 4$.

6. **D** $62° + 4° - 7° + 0° + 10° = 66° - 7° + 0° + 10° = 59° + 0° + 10° = 69°.$

7. **E** The average monthly change in Carl's weight is $+9 - 3 + 6 = +12$ pounds, divided by 3 months, which equals +4 pounds per month.

8. **D** The sum of -7 and -4 times the quotient of -8 and $+2$ is equal to $(-7 + -4) \times (-8 \div +2) = (-11) \times (-4) = +44.$

9. **2** $\dfrac{(5 \times -7) - (2 \times -10) + 1}{(-3 \times 5) + (-2 \times -4)} = \dfrac{-35 - -20 + 1}{-15 + +8} = \dfrac{-35 + 20 + 1}{-15 + 8} = \dfrac{-15 + 1}{-7} = \dfrac{-14}{-7} = +2.$

10. $\dfrac{1}{2}$ Because $-4 + 3 = -1$, you follow the second rule and divide the sum by -2, so $-1 \div -2 = \dfrac{-1}{-2} = \dfrac{1}{2}.$

C. Number Theory

1. Odds and evens

Integers can be classified as odd or even. An even number is a number that is a multiple of 2. It can be expressed as $2n$, for some integer n. Numbers that are not even are called odd numbers. Odd numbers fall just before and just after even numbers, so they can be expressed as $2n + 1$ or $2n - 1$.

Here are the rules to keep in mind when you're adding odd and even numbers:

- Even + even = even (for example, $12 + 14 = 36$).
- Odd + odd = even (for example, $13 + 19 = 32$).
- Even + odd = odd (for example, $14 + 15 = 29$).

Here are the rules to keep in mind when you're multiplying odd and even numbers:

- Even $\times$ even = even (for example $8 \times 6 = 48$).
- Odd $\times$ odd = odd (for example, $7 \times 9 = 63$).
- Even $\times$ odd = even (for example, $6 \times 11 = 66$).

EXAMPLE:

If r is even and t is odd, which of the following is odd?

A. rt
B. $5r^2t$
C. $6r^2t$
D. $5r + 6t$
E. $6r + 5t$

The correct answer is **E**. In choice A, because r is even and t is odd, rt is even. In choice B, r^2 is even $\times$ even, which is even, and r^2t is even $\times$ odd, which is even; so, $5r^2t$ is odd $\times$ even, which is even. In choice C, you already know that r^2t is even, so $6r^2t$ is even $\times$ even, which is even. In choice D, $5r$ is odd $\times$ even, which is even, and $6t$ is even $\times$ odd, which is even, so you're adding even + even, which is even. In choice E, $6r$ is even $\times$ even, which is even, and $5t$ is odd $\times$ odd, which is odd, so you're adding even + odd, which is odd; this makes choice E the correct answer.

2. Factors

When you multiply two numbers, each number is called a *factor,* and the answer you produce is called the *product. Factorization* is the process of expressing a number as a multiplication problem or rewriting it as a product of factors.

Sometimes you want to consider different factor pairs for a number. The number 24, for example, can be expressed as 1×24, or 2×12, or 3×8, or 4×6. Each of these is a pair of factors that equal 24. Other times, you'll want to find the prime factorization of a number, expressing it as a product of prime numbers.

3. Primes

Whole numbers, except for the number 1, can be classified as prime or composite. Prime numbers are numbers whose only factors are themselves and one. The number 41, for example, is a prime number, because the only factor pair that will produce 41 is 1×41. Composite numbers have other factor pairs. For example, 51 could be written as 1×51 or 3×17, so 51 is composite.

Small prime numbers (like 2, 3, 5, and 7) are usually easy to recognize and remember, but you may come across a test question that asks about larger primes. To locate primes quickly, list all the numbers in the range described in the question and then cross out multiples of small primes. This should leave just a few numbers that require further testing. For example, if you're looking for all the primes between 40 and 60, make a list of the integers from 40 to 60:

40 41 42 43 44 45 46 47 48 49 50 51 52 53 54 55 56 57 58 59 60

Now cross out all the multiples of 2:

~~40~~ 41 ~~42~~ 43 44 45 ~~46~~ 47 ~~48~~ 49 ~~50~~ 51 ~~52~~ 53 ~~54~~ 55 ~~56~~ 57 ~~58~~ 59 ~~60~~

Next cross out the multiples of 3. (Check to see if a number is a multiple of 3 by adding the digits. If they add to a number that's divisible by 3, the number is a multiple of 3.)

~~40~~ 41 ~~42~~ 43 ~~44~~ ~~45~~ ~~46~~ 47 ~~48~~ 49 ~~50~~ ~~51~~ ~~52~~ 53 ~~54~~ 55 ~~56~~ ~~57~~ ~~58~~ 59 ~~60~~

Cross out the multiples of 5, which end in 0 or 5, and you'll have narrowed the list down quite a bit:

~~40~~ 41 ~~42~~ 43 ~~44~~ ~~45~~ ~~46~~ 47 ~~48~~ 49 ~~50~~ ~~51~~ ~~52~~ 53 ~~54~~ ~~55~~ ~~56~~ ~~57~~ ~~58~~ 59 ~~60~~

The only numbers left are 41, 43, 47, 49, 53, and 59. You probably realize 49 is a multiple of 7. The rest of the numbers are prime.

Remember that 2 is the only even prime. All other primes are odd. Note, too, that 1 is neither prime nor composite.

4. Divisors

Questions about number relationships often will require that you determine whether one number is divisible by another, or whether one is a factor of another. You may be asked that question directly, or you may need to determine that in the process of finding a common denominator or factoring a polynomial. Several quick tests can help you:

- **Divisible by 2:** Any number divisible by 2 ends in 0, 2, 4, 6, or 8. These are the even numbers.
- **Divisible by 3:** To determine if a number is divisible by 3, add the digits. If the sum of the digits is divisible by 3, so is the original number. (Not sure whether the sum is divisible by 3? Add its digits until you get to a small enough number that you can tell whether it's divisible by 3.)
- **Divisible by 4:** Just test the last two digits. If the final two digits form a number that is divisible by 4, then the entire number is divisible by 4 as well.
- **Divisible by 5:** All numbers divisible by 5 end in either 5 or 0.
- **Divisible by 6:** A number will be divisible by 6 only if it is divisible by both 2 and 3.
- **Divisible by 9:** You can test for divisibility by 9 the same way you test for divisibility by 3. Add the digits of the number. If the sum is divisible by 9, so is the original number.
- **Divisible by 10:** All numbers divisible by 10 end in 0. (And all numbers divisible by powers of 10 end in zeros. The number of zeros is the power.)

Practice

Directions (1–2): You are given two quantities, one in Column A and one in Column B. You are to compare the two quantities and choose one of the following:

- A. The quantity in Column A is greater.
- B. The quantity in Column B is greater.
- C. The two quantities are equal.
- D. The relationship cannot be determined from the information given.

	Column A	Column B
1.	The smallest prime greater than 20	The largest prime less than 30

	Column A	Column B
2.	The number of primes between 10 and 15	The number of primes between 15 and 20

Directions (3–10): Unless otherwise directed, select a single answer choice. For numeric-entry questions, enter a number in the box(es) below the question. Equivalent forms of the correct answer, such as 2.5 and 2.50, are all correct. Fractions do not need to be reduced to lowest terms. Enter the exact answer unless the question asks you to round your answer.

3. Select all the numbers that are divisors of 270.

   A. 2
   B. 3
   C. 5
   D. 7
   E. 9
   F. 11
   G. 13
   H. 15
   I. 17
   J. 18

4. The symbol $a \bigcirc b$ is defined to mean the largest prime factor of a minus the largest prime factor of b. Select all the true statements.

   A. $121 \bigcirc 49 = 4$
   B. $35 \bigcirc 12 = 3$
   C. $100 \bigcirc 15 = 0$
   D. $45 \bigcirc 27 = 2$
   E. $81 \bigcirc 16 = 1$

5. All the following are prime *except:*

   A. 31
   B. 41
   C. 51
   D. 61
   E. 71

6. Marilyn baked brownies to give as gifts at holiday time. If she packaged the brownies five to a package, she had three brownies left over. If she put seven in a package, she had three left over. If she put six in a package, there were only two left over. How many brownies did Marilyn bake?

   A. 35
   B. 36
   C. 37
   D. 38
   E. 39

7. Which of the following is divisible by 6?

   A. 826
   B. 723
   C. 624
   D. 555
   E. 428

8. What is the sum of the primes greater than 30 and less than 40?

   A. 31
   B. 37
   C. 68
   D. 64
   E. 1,011

9. Find the largest prime number that divides both 35 and 98.

                                              [   ]

10. Find the smallest number divisible by both 11 and 17.

                                              [   ]

Answers

1. B The smallest prime greater than 20 is an odd number (because 2 is the only even prime), but it's not 21, because 21 is divisible by 3 and 7. Therefore, the smallest prime greater than 20 is 23. The largest prime less than 30 is also an odd number in the 20s. Working back from 30, the first odd number is 29, which is prime. Therefore, choice B is the correct answer, because 29 is larger than 23.

2. C The prime numbers between 10 and 15 are 11 and 13, so there are two primes between 10 and 15. The prime numbers between 15 and 20 are 17 and 19, so there are also two primes between 15 and 20 as well. This makes choice C the correct answer.

3. A, B, C, E, H, J Instead of dividing 270 by each of the answer choices, factor 270 to primes: $270 = 2 \times 135 = 2 \times 5 \times 27 = 2 \times 5 \times 9 \times 3 = 2 \times 5 \times 3 \times 3 \times 3$. This prime factorization makes it clear that 2, 3, 5, and 9 are factors or divisors of 270. Notice that 7, 11, 13, and 17, which are primes, are not factors of 270. Because both 3 and 5 are factors, so is 15. That leaves only 18, which is $2 \times 3 \times 3$, and 270 has all those factors, so 18 is also a factor.

4. A, C, D, E Take the time to think about the prime factorization of each of the numbers involved and translate each expression to a subtraction. The prime factorization of 121 is 11×11, so the largest (and only) prime factor of 121 is 11. The prime factorization of 49 is 7×7, so the largest prime factor of 49 is 7. Subtracting $11 - 7 = 4$, so choice A is true. Choice B, $35 \bigcirc 12 = 7 - 3 = 4$, not 3, so choice B is not true. Remember that although 4 is a factor of 12, it is not a *prime* factor. The remaining statements are true. Choice C is $100 \bigcirc 15 = 5 - 5 = 0$, choice D is $45 \bigcirc 27 = 5 - 3 = 2$, and choice E is $81 \bigcirc 16 = 3 - 2 = 1$.

5. **C** To figure out which number isn't prime, divisibility tests are the best method. None of the choices is even, and none ends in 0 or 5, so try adding the digits: $3 + 1 = 4, 4 + 1 = 5, 5 + 1 = 6, 6 + 1 = 7$, and $7 + 1 = 8$. Because 6 is divisible by 3, 51 is divisible by 3, which means it isn't prime.

6. **D** The question tells you that if Marilyn packaged the brownies five to a package, she had three brownies left over, so the number of brownies is 3 more than a multiple of 5. If Marilyn put seven brownies in a package, she had three left over, so the number of brownies is 3 more than a multiple of 7. And, if she put six brownies in a package, there were only two left over, so the number of brownies was 2 more than a multiple of 6. If you look at the answer choices, 35 is a multiple of 5 and a multiple of 7, not 3 more than those multiples, and 36 and 37 are only 1 more and 2 more, respectively. The best choice looks like 38, which is 3 more than 35, and is also 2 more than 36, a multiple of 6.

7. **C** A number is divisible by 6 if it is divisible by 2 and by 3. So, you can eliminate choices B and D right off the bat, because they're odd and, therefore, not divisible by 2. Then check the remaining choices for divisibility by 3 by adding the digits: $8 + 2 + 6 = 16, 6 + 2 + 4 = 12$, and $4 + 2 + 8 = 14$. Because 12 is divisible by 3, but 14 and 16 are not, only 624 is divisible by 2 and by 3. So, only 624 is divisible by 6.

8. **C** To find the primes greater than 30 and less than 40, start by eliminating the even numbers. That leaves 31, 33, 35, 37, and 39. You can eliminate 35, which is a multiple of 5 (so not prime), and you can eliminate 33 and 39, both of which are multiples of 3 (so not prime). That leaves you with 31 and 37, and $31 + 37 = 68$.

9. **7** To find a prime number that divides both 35 and 98, start by listing the prime factors of 35, which are 5 and 7. You know that 98 is not divisible by 5. But $98 \div 7 = 14$, so the prime that divides both 35 and 98 is 7.

10. **187** Because 11 and 17 are both prime, the smallest common multiple is their product: $11 \times 17 = 187$.

D. Fractions

1. Equivalent fractions

Equivalent fractions have the same value, but their appearance is altered by multiplying by a fraction equal to 1. Changing the appearance of a fraction without changing its value requires that the numerator and denominator of the fraction be multiplied by the same number. The fraction $\frac{3}{4}$ is equivalent to $\frac{3}{4} \cdot \frac{5}{5} = \frac{15}{20}$. The fraction $\frac{8}{14} = \frac{2}{2} \cdot \frac{4}{7}$, so $\frac{8}{14}$ is equivalent to $\frac{4}{7}$.

2. Comparing fractions

If you're asked to compare fractions, first be sure the fractions have a common denominator. When you're working with fractions in longer calculations, it's wise to choose the lowest common denominator, but if all you're asked to do is compare, any common denominator will do. Often, the common denominator that is quickest to find is the product of the two denominators.

EXAMPLE:

> Which of the following statements is true?
>
> A. $\frac{5}{8} < \frac{19}{32}$
>
> B. $\frac{7}{16} < \frac{3}{8}$
>
> C. $\frac{5}{8} < \frac{7}{16}$
>
> D. $\frac{3}{8} < \frac{19}{32}$
>
> E. $\frac{19}{32} < \frac{7}{16}$

The correct answer is **D.** Changing all the fractions to a denominator of 32 simplifies the comparison. Your choices then become:

> A. $\frac{20}{32} < \frac{19}{32}$
>
> B. $\frac{14}{32} < \frac{12}{32}$
>
> C. $\frac{20}{32} < \frac{14}{32}$
>
> D. $\frac{12}{32} < \frac{19}{32}$
>
> E. $\frac{19}{32} < \frac{14}{32}$

If you compare the numerators, you can see that only choice D is true.

3. Addition and subtraction

Adding and subtracting fractions requires that the fractions have the same denominator. When they do, you simply add or subtract the numerators and keep the denominator. Your real work comes if they do not have a common denominator to start.

A common denominator is a number that is a multiple of each of the denominators you were given. Ideally, you should choose the lowest number that all your denominators divide evenly, but larger multiples will work—you'll just have to reduce to lowest terms at the end.

EXAMPLES:

> 1. Add $\frac{1}{3} + \frac{2}{7}$.

The lowest common multiple of 3 and 7 is 21. Multiply $\frac{1}{3} \cdot \frac{7}{7} = \frac{7}{21}$ and $\frac{2}{7} \cdot \frac{3}{3} = \frac{6}{21}$. Then $\frac{1}{3} + \frac{2}{7} = \frac{7}{21} + \frac{6}{21} = \frac{13}{21}$.

2. Add $\dfrac{7}{30} + \dfrac{5}{42}$.

To find the lowest common denominator, take a moment first to factor each denominator:

$$
\begin{array}{c}
30 = \boxed{2} \cdot 5 \cdot \boxed{3} \\
42 = \boxed{2} \cdot 7 \cdot \boxed{3}
\end{array}
$$

The factors in the boxes are already common to both denominators, so they should be factors of the common denominator, but each of them needs to appear only once. In addition, the 5 and 7 that are *not* in boxes should be factors of the common denominator. So, the lowest common denominator is $2 \times 3 \times 5 \times 7 = 210$. Multiply $\dfrac{7}{2 \cdot 3 \cdot 5} \cdot \dfrac{7}{7} = \dfrac{49}{210}$ and $\dfrac{5}{2 \cdot 3 \cdot 7} \cdot \dfrac{5}{5} = \dfrac{25}{210}$ and the problem becomes $\dfrac{49}{210} + \dfrac{25}{210} = \dfrac{74}{210} = \dfrac{2 \cdot 37}{2 \cdot 105} = \dfrac{37}{105}$.

You don't always need to find the lowest common denominator. Sometimes you simply want to add or subtract the fractions as quickly as possible. In these cases, you can fall back on a strategy commonly referred to as the bow tie and symbolized by this set of three arrows:

Each arrow represents a multiplication that needs to be done, and the place to put that answer.

3. Add $\dfrac{5}{8} + \dfrac{5}{6}$.

The double-pointed arrow at the bottom tells you to multiply the two denominators for a common denominator:

$$\frac{5}{8} + \frac{5}{6} = \frac{}{48}$$
$$\longleftrightarrow$$

The arrow slanting from the lower right to the upper left tells you to multiply the second denominator by the first numerator and put the result in the first numerator's position:

$$\frac{5}{8} \nwarrow \frac{5}{6} = \frac{30 + ?}{48}$$

The arrow slanting from the lower left to the upper right tells you to multiply the first numerator times the second denominator and put the result in the second numerator's position:

$$\frac{5}{8} \nearrow \frac{5}{6} = \frac{30 + 40}{48} = \frac{70}{48}$$

4. Multiplication

The basic rule for multiplication of fractions calls for multiplying numerator × numerator and denominator × denominator and reducing if possible.

EXAMPLE:

> Multiply $\frac{1}{9} \times \frac{3}{7}$.

Multiply 1×3 and 9×7. This gives you $\frac{3}{63}$, which reduces to $\frac{1}{21}$.

Much of the work of multiplying and dividing fractions can be made easier by canceling before multiplying. *Canceling* is dividing a numerator and a denominator by the same number. You can think of it as reducing before you multiply instead of after.

EXAMPLE:

> Multiply $\frac{3}{8} \cdot \frac{4}{9}$.

The basic rules says to multiply 3 times 4 and 8 times 9, giving the fraction $\frac{12}{72}$, which reduces to $\frac{1}{6}$.

However, you can cancel before multiplying. Divide 3 into both 3 and 9, and divide 4 into both 4 and 8:

$$\frac{3}{8} \cdot \frac{4}{9} = \frac{{}^{1}\cancel{3}}{8} \cdot \frac{4}{\cancel{9}_{3}} = \frac{{}^{1}\cancel{3}}{{}_{2}\cancel{8}} \cdot \frac{\cancel{4}^{1}}{\cancel{9}_{3}} = \frac{1 \cdot 1}{2 \cdot 3} = \frac{1}{6}$$

5. Division

To divide fractions, multiply by the reciprocal. In other words, invert the divisor and multiply. The divisor is the second fraction. Invert only the divisor.

EXAMPLES:

> 1. Divide $\frac{1}{8} \div \frac{3}{4}$.

The fraction $\frac{3}{4}$ is the divisor. Invert $\frac{3}{4}$ to get $\frac{4}{3}$, and then multiply $\frac{1}{8} \cdot \frac{4}{3} = \frac{4}{24} = \frac{1}{6}$.

> 2. Divide $\frac{15}{14} \div \frac{3}{7}$.

Invert the divisor, $\frac{3}{7}$, and multiply, so the problem becomes $\frac{15}{14} \cdot \frac{7}{3}$. Divide 3 into both 15 and 3, and divide 7 into both 7 and 14: $\frac{15}{14} \cdot \frac{7}{3} = \frac{{}^{5}\cancel{15}}{14} \cdot \frac{7}{\cancel{3}_{1}} = \frac{{}^{5}\cancel{15}}{{}_{2}\cancel{14}} \cdot \frac{\cancel{7}^{1}}{\cancel{3}_{1}} = \frac{5 \cdot 1}{2 \cdot 1} = \frac{5}{2} = 2\frac{1}{2}$.

6. Mixed numbers and improper fractions

A number like $2\frac{1}{2}$, which involves both a whole number and a fraction, is called a *mixed number.* A fraction in which the numerator is larger than the denominator is called an *improper fraction.* The mixed number represents a whole number plus a fraction: $2\frac{1}{2}=2+\frac{1}{2}=\frac{2}{1}+\frac{1}{2}=\frac{4}{2}+\frac{1}{2}=\frac{5}{2}$. The common shortcut for changing a mixed number to an improper fraction is to multiply the denominator of the fraction times the whole number, add the numerator of the fraction part, and place that result as a numerator over the denominator of the fraction part.

EXAMPLE:

> Change $3\frac{2}{7}$ to an improper fraction.

Multiply the denominator, 7, by the whole number, 3: $7 \times 3 = 21$. To the product, 21, add the 2 that is the numerator of the fraction: $21 + 2 = 23$. The result, 23, goes over the denominator, 7: $3\frac{2}{7}=\frac{7\times3+2}{7}=\frac{23}{7}$.

To change an improper fraction to a mixed number, divide the numerator by the denominator. The quotient becomes the whole number, and the remainder goes over the divisor to form the fraction part.

EXAMPLE:

> Change $\frac{43}{5}$ to a mixed number.

Divide 43 by 5. The quotient of 8 is the whole number. The remainder of 3 goes over the 5 to make the fraction: $\frac{43}{5}=8\frac{3}{5}$.

Adding mixed numbers is as simple as adding the whole-number parts and adding the fraction parts: $3\frac{2}{7}+2\frac{6}{7}=3+2+\frac{2}{7}+\frac{6}{7}=5\frac{8}{7}$. If this results in an improper fraction, as in this example, change the improper fraction to a mixed number: $\frac{8}{7}=1\frac{1}{7}$. Add this to the 5 that was the whole-number part: $5\frac{8}{7}=5+1\frac{1}{7}=6\frac{1}{7}$.

Subtracting mixed numbers can often be done by subtracting whole number from whole number and fraction from fraction as in $4\frac{7}{10}-2\frac{3}{10}$. Subtracting $4 - 2 = 2$ and subtracting $\frac{7}{10}-\frac{3}{10}=\frac{4}{10}=\frac{2}{5}$, so $4\frac{7}{10}-2\frac{3}{10}=2\frac{4}{10}=2\frac{2}{5}$. But in some cases, this strategy runs into a problem.

EXAMPLE:

> Subtract $8\frac{3}{10}-4\frac{7}{10}$.

In this case, the previous strategy leads to trying to subtract $\frac{7}{10}$ from $\frac{3}{10}$. One way to work around this problem is to do some regrouping: $8\frac{3}{10}=7+1+\frac{3}{10}=7+\frac{10}{10}+\frac{3}{10}=7\frac{13}{10}$. When the first number is re-expressed this way, you can subtract $7\frac{13}{10}-4\frac{7}{10}$ by subtracting $7 - 4 = 3$ and $\frac{13}{10}-\frac{7}{10}=\frac{6}{10}$. The difference is $3\frac{6}{10}$ or $3\frac{3}{5}$.

The need for regrouping can be avoided, however, by simply changing both mixed numbers to improper fractions, subtracting, and changing back to a mixed number:

$$8\frac{3}{10} - 4\frac{7}{10} = \frac{83}{10} - \frac{47}{10} = \frac{36}{10} = 3\frac{6}{10} = 3\frac{3}{5}$$

Don't try to multiply or divide mixed numbers. Change mixed numbers to improper fractions before multiplying or dividing.

Practice

Directions (1–4): You are given two quantities, one in Column A and one in Column B. You are to compare the two quantities and choose one of the following:

    A. The quantity in Column A is greater.
    B. The quantity in Column B is greater.
    C. The two quantities are equal.
    D. The relationship cannot be determined from the information given.

	Column A	Column B
1.	$\dfrac{5}{12}$	$\dfrac{3}{7}$
	Column A	**Column B**
2.	$\dfrac{7}{20}$	$\dfrac{1}{3}$
	Column A	**Column B**
3.	$\dfrac{5}{7} + \dfrac{1}{2}$	$\dfrac{2}{3} + \dfrac{5}{8}$
	Column A	**Column B**
4.	$\dfrac{4}{9} \cdot \dfrac{3}{5}$	$\dfrac{3}{5} \div \dfrac{4}{9}$

Directions (5–10): Unless otherwise directed, select a single answer choice. For numeric-entry questions, enter a number in the box(es) below the question. Equivalent forms of the correct answer, such as 2.5 and 2.50, are all correct. Fractions do not need to be reduced to lowest terms. Enter the exact answer unless the question asks you to round your answer.

5. Choose all the expressions that are equal to $\frac{5}{6}$.

   A. $\frac{4}{5} - \frac{1}{6} + \frac{2}{3}$

   B. $\frac{3}{5} - \frac{1}{2} + \frac{2}{3}$

   C. $\frac{4}{5} - \frac{1}{3} + \frac{11}{30}$

   D. $\frac{3}{5} - \frac{1}{15} + \frac{3}{10}$

   E. $\frac{4}{5} - \frac{2}{3} + \frac{7}{10}$

6. If N is less than $\frac{1}{10} \div \frac{3}{5} \times \frac{12}{13}$, which of the following are possible values of N?

   A. $\frac{1}{13}$

   B. $\frac{2}{13}$

   C. $\frac{1}{6}$

   D. $\frac{1}{12}$

   E. $\frac{1}{2}$

   F. $\frac{2}{15}$

7. $\left(\frac{3}{4} - \frac{2}{3}\right) \div \left(\frac{1}{2} + \frac{1}{5}\right) =$

   A. $\frac{5}{6}$

   B. $\frac{5}{7}$

   C. $\frac{6}{7}$

   D. $\frac{5}{42}$

   E. $\frac{7}{120}$

8. Hector's uncle gave him a baseball card collection from the 1950s. Half of the cards were from the Brooklyn Dodgers, and one-fourth of the cards were from the New York Giants. The rest were evenly divided among the Philadelphia Athletics, the St. Louis Browns, and the Washington Senators. If there were 15 cards from the Browns, how many Dodgers cards did Hector's uncle give him?

   A. 15
   B. 45
   C. 60
   D. 90
   E. 180

9. During contract negotiations, $\frac{7}{8}$ of the union members voted on a new contract proposal. Of those voting, $\frac{2}{3}$ voted to approve the contract. If there are 3,600 members in the union, how many voted to approve?

10. Half a number minus $3\frac{3}{4}$ is equal to $\frac{5}{4}$. Find the number.

Answers

1. **B** To determine which is larger, change the fractions to a common denominator, and compare the numerators: $\frac{5}{12}?\frac{3}{7} \Rightarrow \frac{5\times7}{12\times7}?\frac{3\times12}{7\times12} \Rightarrow \frac{35}{84} < \frac{36}{84}$.

2. **A** To determine which is larger, change the fractions to a common denominator, and compare the numerators: $\frac{7}{20}?\frac{1}{3} \Rightarrow \frac{7\times3}{20\times3}?\frac{1\times20}{3\times20} \Rightarrow \frac{21}{60} > \frac{20}{60}$.

3. **B** To determine which is larger, first you have to add the pairs of fractions. To add the first pair of fractions, change to a common denominator of 14: $\frac{5}{7}+\frac{1}{2} = \frac{5\times2}{7\times2} + \frac{1\times7}{2\times7} = \frac{10}{14} + \frac{7}{14} = \frac{17}{14}$. To add the second pair of fractions, change to a common denominator of 24: $\frac{2\times8}{3\times8} + \frac{5\times3}{8\times3} = \frac{16}{24} + \frac{15}{24} = \frac{31}{24}$.

   Comparing the answers requires changing $\frac{17}{14}$ and $\frac{31}{24}$ to a common denominator, but it doesn't have to be the *lowest* common denominator—it may be faster to multiply each fraction by the denominator of the other: $\frac{17}{14}\times\frac{24}{24}$ and $\frac{31}{24}\times\frac{17}{17}$. You don't need to know the simplified value of the denominator, just that the denominators of both fractions are the same. Once they have a common denominator, comparing the numerators will tell you the relationship of the fractions: $\frac{408}{14\times24} < \frac{527}{24\times17}$.

4. **B** To determine which is larger, first you have to multiply the first pair of fractions and divide the other. Multiplying allows for cancellation: $\frac{4}{9}\cdot\frac{3}{5} = \frac{4}{\underset{3}{9}}\cdot\frac{\cancel{3}}{5} = \frac{4}{15}$. Dividing requires inverting and multiplying, and the inversion eliminates the opportunity to cancel: $\frac{3}{5}\div\frac{4}{9} = \frac{3}{5}\times\frac{9}{4} = \frac{27}{20}$. You don't have to find a common denominator to see that the first equation is less than 1 and the second equation is greater than 1, which gives you the answer you need.

Beware of the assumption that multiplying makes bigger answers and dividing makes smaller ones. That pattern may be true for numbers greater than 1, but not for numbers less than 1.

5. **C, D, E** You can save time by finding a denominator that is compatible with all the fractions you'll work with. A common denominator of 30 should work. Change all your fractions to a denominator of 30 and look for results that equal $\frac{25}{30}$ or $\frac{5}{6}$. Choice A is too large: $\frac{4}{5} - \frac{1}{6} + \frac{2}{3} = \frac{24}{30} - \frac{5}{30} + \frac{20}{30} = \frac{39}{30}$. Choice B is just a bit too small: $\frac{3}{5} - \frac{1}{2} + \frac{2}{3} = \frac{18}{30} - \frac{15}{30} + \frac{20}{30} = \frac{23}{30}$. The remaining options are all equal to $\frac{5}{6}$: choice C is $\frac{4}{5} - \frac{1}{3} + \frac{11}{30} = \frac{24}{30} - \frac{10}{30} + \frac{11}{30} = \frac{25}{30}$, choice D is $\frac{3}{5} - \frac{1}{15} + \frac{3}{10} = \frac{18}{30} - \frac{2}{30} + \frac{9}{30} = \frac{25}{30}$, and choice E is $\frac{4}{5} - \frac{2}{3} + \frac{7}{10} = \frac{24}{30} - \frac{20}{30} + \frac{21}{30} = \frac{25}{30}$.

6. **A, D, F** Begin by evaluating $\frac{1}{10} \div \frac{3}{5} \times \frac{12}{13} = \frac{1}{{}_2 10} \times \frac{\cancel{5}}{\cancel{3}} \times \frac{\cancel{12}^4}{13} = \frac{\cancel{4}^2}{\cancel{2} \times 13} = \frac{2}{13}$ so that you know what you're comparing. Don't try to change all the fractions to common denominators. That will take too long. Use approximation to eliminate incorrect answers. $\frac{1}{13}$ is clearly less than $\frac{2}{13}$, and $\frac{1}{2}$ is clearly larger. Beware of choice B: $\frac{2}{13}$ is not less than $\frac{2}{13}$. Remember that if two fractions have the same numerator, the one with the smaller denominator is the larger fraction. So $\frac{1}{6} = \frac{2}{12} > \frac{2}{13}$, but $\frac{2}{15} < \frac{2}{13}$, so choice C is incorrect, but choice F is correct. That leaves just choice D, and since twelfths are only a tiny bit larger than thirteenths, $\frac{1}{12} < \frac{2}{13}$. If you don't trust your estimation, find a common denominator for those two.

7. **D** To subtract the fractions in the first set of parentheses, use a common denominator of 12: $\frac{3}{4} - \frac{2}{3} = \frac{9}{12} - \frac{8}{12} = \frac{1}{12}$. To add the fractions in the second set of parentheses, use a common denominator of 10: $\frac{1}{2} + \frac{1}{5} = \frac{5}{10} + \frac{2}{10} = \frac{7}{10}$. To divide, multiply $\frac{1}{12}$ by the reciprocal of $\frac{7}{10}$: $\frac{1}{12} \div \frac{7}{10} = \frac{1}{{}_6 \cancel{12}} \cdot \frac{\cancel{10}^5}{7} = \frac{5}{42}$.

8. **D** If there were 15 cards from the Browns, then there were also 15 from the Athletics and 15 from the Senators. Half the cards were Dodgers, one-fourth were Giants, and $\frac{1}{2} + \frac{1}{4} = \frac{2}{4} + \frac{1}{4} = \frac{3}{4}$, so the other 45 cards are the remaining one-fourth. If 45 cards are $\frac{1}{4}$ of the collection, then $2 \times 45 = 90$ cards would be $\frac{2}{4}$ or $\frac{1}{2}$ of the collection. The Dodgers cards were half of the collection, so there were 90 Dodgers cards.

9. **2,100** The question tells you that $\frac{7}{8}$ of the membership voted, and $\frac{2}{3}$ of those present voted to approve: $\frac{2}{3} \times \frac{7}{8} = \frac{\cancel{2}^1}{3} \times \frac{7}{\cancel{8}_4} = \frac{7}{12}$, so $\frac{7}{12}$ of the 3,600 members voted to approve. Multiplying, $\frac{7}{{}_1 \cancel{12}} \times \frac{\cancel{3,600}^{300}}{1} = 2,100$ members who voted to approve.

10. **10** Half a number minus $3\frac{3}{4}$ is equal to $\frac{5}{4}$, so half the number is equal to $\frac{5}{4} + 3\frac{3}{4}$. Don't worry about the fact that $\frac{5}{4}$ is an improper fraction; take advantage of the common denominator to add and then simplify: $\frac{5}{4} + 3\frac{3}{4} = 3\frac{8}{4} = 3 + 2 = 5$. Half the number is 5, so the whole number is 10.

E. Ratio and Proportion

1. Ratio

A *ratio* is a comparison of two numbers by division. If one number is three times the size of another, we say the ratio of the larger to the smaller is "3 to 1." This can be written as 3:1 or as the fraction $\frac{3}{1}$.

When you're told that the ratio of one number to another is 5:2, you aren't being told that the numbers are 5 and 2, but that when you divide the first by the second, you get a number equal to $\frac{5}{2}$. This means that the first number was 5 times some number and the second was 2 times that number. You can represent the numbers as $5x$ and $2x$.

EXAMPLE:

> Two numbers are in ratio 7:3 and their sum is 50. Find the numbers.

First, represent the numbers as $7x$ and $3x$. Then, $7x + 3x = 50$, so $10x = 50$ and $x = 5$. Don't forget to find the numbers! $7x = 7 \times 5 = 35$ and $3x = 3 \times 5 = 15$, so the numbers are 35 and 15.

2. Extended ratios

An *extended ratio* compares more than two numbers. Extended ratios are usually written with colons.

EXAMPLE:

> A punch contains grapefruit juice, orange juice, and ginger ale, in a ratio of 2:5:3. If 20 gallons of punch are needed for a party, how much orange juice is required?

Represent the amounts as $2x$ (grapefruit juice), $5x$ (orange juice), and $3x$ (ginger ale). So, $2x + 5x + 3x = 20$, which means that $10x = 20$ and $x = 2$. Be sure you answer the right question. Orange juice is $5x = 5 \times 2 = 10$ gallons.

3. Cross-multiplication

A *proportion* is a statement that two ratios are equal. The equation $\frac{1}{3} = \frac{2}{6}$ or 1:3 = 2:6 is an example of a proportion.

In any proportion, the product of the *means* (the two middle terms) is equal to the product of the *extremes* (the first and last terms). For example, in the proportion 5:8 = 15:24, $8 \times 15 = 5 \times 24$. This means that whenever you have two equal ratios, you can cross-multiply, and solve the resulting equation to find the unknown term.

EXAMPLE:

> If $\frac{7}{4} = \frac{x}{14}$, find x.

Cross-multiplying produces $4x = 7 \times 14$. Solving this equation gives $x = \frac{7 \cdot 14}{4} = \frac{98}{4} = 24.5$.

Practice

Directions (1–2): You are given two quantities, one in Column A and one in Column B. You are to compare the two quantities and choose one of the following:

- **A.** The quantity in Column A is greater.
- **B.** The quantity in Column B is greater.
- **C.** The two quantities are equal.
- **D.** The relationship cannot be determined from the information given.

Fruit is packed in crates so that the ratio of lemons to limes is 2:1

Column A	Column B
1. The number of limes in a crate containing 54 pieces of fruit	The number of lemons in a crate containing 27 pieces of fruit.

$$\frac{x}{7} = \frac{y}{12}$$
$$x > 0, \ y > 0$$

Column A	Column B
2. $24x$	$15y$

Directions (3–10): Unless otherwise directed, select a single answer choice. For numeric-entry questions, enter a number in the box(es) below the question. Equivalent forms of the correct answer, such as 2.5 and 2.50, are all correct. Fractions do not need to be reduced to lowest terms. Enter the exact answer unless the question asks you to round your answer.

3. In a certain town, all registered voters are either Democrats or Republicans. If there are 18,000 registered voters in the town, and there are more Democrats than Republicans, which of the following could be the ratio of Republicans to Democrats?

   A. 1:2
   B. 3:4
   C. 4:5
   D. 5:4
   E. 7:11
   F. 9:3

4. Miriam's CD collection consists of operas and Broadway shows in a ratio of 7:6. Which numbers could be the total number of CDs in her collection?

   A. 65
   B. 76
   C. 78
   D. 100
   E. 117
   F. 130
   G. 221

5. Each gallon of Callie's lemonade is two parts lemon juice, two parts simple syrup, and three parts water. What fraction of the lemonade mixture is simple syrup?

   A. $\frac{2}{7}$

   B. $\frac{2}{5}$

   C. $\frac{1}{2}$

   D. $\frac{2}{3}$

   E. $\frac{3}{2}$

6. If $\frac{8}{15} = \frac{x}{3}$, find x.

   A. 0.8
   B. 1
   C. 1.2
   D. 1.4
   E. 1.6

7. Rick's favorite salad dressing calls for vinegar and oil in a ratio of 3:2. If he wants to make 2 quarts of salad dressing for a picnic, how much oil will he need?

A. $\frac{1}{2}$ quart

B. $\frac{2}{5}$ quart

C. $\frac{1}{3}$ quart

D. $\frac{3}{5}$ quart

E. $\frac{4}{5}$ quart

8. Charles determined that the time he spent on homework was divided between math and physics in a ratio of 4:5. If Charles spent one and a half hours on homework last night, how many minutes did he spend on math?

A. 18
B. 22.5
C. 40
D. 50
E. 90

9. The ratio of girls to boys on the math team is 8:3. If there are 24 girls on the team, how many people are on the team?

☐

10. The ratio of blue marbles to red marbles in a certain jar is 7:5. If there are 60 marbles in the jar, how many are blue?

☐

Answers

1. **C** The number of lemons is $2x$ and the number of limes is x. If the total is 54, $2x + x = 54$, so $3x = 54$ and $x = 18$. There are 18 limes and 36 lemons. If the total is 27, $2x + x = 3x = 27$, so $x = 9$. There are 9 limes and 18 lemons. The number of limes in a crate containing 54 pieces of fruit is equal to the number of lemons in a crate containing 27 pieces of fruit.

2. **B** Cross-multiplying, $\frac{x}{7} = \frac{y}{12} \Rightarrow 12x = 7y$. Multiplying both sides of that equation by 2 give you $2(12x) = 2(7y) \Rightarrow 24x = 14y$. Because $24x$ is equal to $14y$, $24x$ is less than $15y$.

3. **A, C, E** First, eliminate choices D and F, because the ratio of Republicans to Democrats should be a smaller number to a larger one. If there are 18,000 registered voters, and the ratio of Republicans to Democrats is of the form $a:b$, you can set up an equation of the form $ax + bx = 18,000$ to find x and

then the number of Republicans and the number of Democrats. The value of x will be $18,000 \div (a + b)$. If $a + b$ is not a divisor of 18,000, you'll have a fractional number of people in each party, so check each of the remaining choices. Choice A gives you $1x + 2x = 18,000$, and $1 + 2 = 3$ is a factor of 18,000, but in choice B, $3x + 4x$ will leave you dividing 18,000 by 7, so eliminate that choice. Choices C and E are possible, however, because $4 + 5 = 9$ and $7 + 11 = 18$, both of which divide 18,000.

4. **A, C, E, F, G** The ratio of operas to Broadway shows is 7:6 so the total number will be $7x + 6x$, or a multiple of 13. Choice A, 65, is 5×13, and choice F, 130, is 10×13. The fastest tactic may be just to list multiples of 13. Starting with 65, you have 78 (choice C), 91, 104, 117 (choice E). If you don't want to keep listing all the way to the 200s, divide 221 by 13 or think of 221 as $130 + 91$, both multiples of 13, so 221 is a multiple of 13 as well.

5. **A** Each gallon is two parts lemon juice, two parts sugar, and three parts water, for a total of seven parts. Sugar is two of the seven parts, or $\frac{2}{7}$ of the mixture.

6. **E** Cross-multiplying, $\frac{8}{15} = \frac{x}{3}$ becomes $15x = 3 \cdot 8$ or $x = \frac{24}{15} = \frac{8}{5} = 1.6$.

7. **E** The dressing is three parts vinegar and two parts oil, so oil is two of a total of five parts, or $\frac{2}{5}$ of the mixture. Don't forget to convert it to quarts: $\frac{2}{5}$ of 2 quarts is $\frac{4}{5}$ of a quart.

8. **C** Let $4x$ represent the number of minutes spent on math and $5x$ represent the number of minutes spent on physics. One and a half hours is equivalent to $60 + 30 = 90$ minutes, so $4x + 5x = 90$, $9x = 90$, and $x = 10$. The number of minutes spent on math is $4x = 4(10) = 40$ minutes.

9. **33** If the ratio of girls to boys on the math team is 8:3, then $8x$ represents the number of girls and $3x$ represents the number of boys. If there are 24 girls, $8x = 24$ and $x = 3$. There are 24 girls and $3x = 3(3) = 9$ boys, for a total of $24 + 9 = 33$ team members.

10. **35** If the ratio of blue marbles to red marbles in a certain jar is 7:5, then the number of blue marbles can be represented by $7x$ and the number of red marbles can be represented by $5x$. The total $7x + 5x = 60$, so $12x = 60$ and $x = 5$. Blue marbles account for $7x = 7(5) = 35$.

F. Decimals

1. Place value

Decimals are, in truth, *decimal fractions,* fractions that use powers of ten as their denominators. Because they're based on powers of ten, they can conveniently be written in an extension of the place value system we use for whole numbers, so their denominators seem to disappear. Those denominators are still there, of course, and you hear them if you give the decimal its proper name. Many people will pronounce 0.375 as "point 375," but its technical name is "375 thousandths." The 375 names the numerator and the thousandths names the denominator.

In our decimal system of numbers, each place to the left of the decimal point represents a larger power of ten. A digit one place to the left is worth ten times as much. The 2 in 4,020 is worth 20, while the 2 in 4,002 is only worth 2. In a similar fashion, each place to the right of the decimal point represents a smaller power of ten. The 7 in 1.0007 is worth $\frac{7}{10,000}$, one-tenth of the value of the 7 in 1.007, which is $\frac{7}{1,000}$.

In the number 6,923.8471, here's what each number is

6	9	2	3	.	8	4	7	1
Thousands	Hundreds	Tens	Ones		Tenths	Hundredths	Thousandths	Ten-thousandths

2. Comparing decimals

When asked to compare decimals, arrange the numbers with the decimal points aligned one under another. Add zeros to the right end of numbers until all the numbers have the same number of digits after the decimal point. Then forget the decimal points are there; the largest number (without the decimal points) is the largest number (with the decimal points.)

EXAMPLE:

Which of the following is largest?

A.   0.043
B.   0.43
C.   0.403
D.   0.4003
E.   0.0043

To find the answer, write the numbers with the decimal points aligned (as they are in the answer choices above). Then add one zero to the end of choice A, two zeros to the end of choice B, and one zero to the end of choice C—this makes all five answer choices have the same number of digits (four after the decimal point). Finally, ignore the decimal points, and just look at the numbers you have left: 0430, 4300, 4030, 4003, and 0043. You can see that 4,300 is the largest number, so 0.4300, or 0.43, is the largest decimal.

3. Addition and subtraction

To add or subtract decimals, arrange the numbers with the decimal points aligned one under another. This assures that you're adding the digits with the same place value. You may want to add zeros to the right of the number to give them the same number of digits, especially if you're subtracting. Add or subtract as you would if the decimal points were not there, doing any carrying or borrowing just as you would for whole numbers. Add a decimal point to your answer directly under the decimal points in the problem.

EXAMPLE:

Add 34.82 + 9.7.

To find the answer, align the decimal points. (Add zeros if you like.) Add normally and bring the decimal point straight down.

$$\begin{array}{r} 34.82 \\ +9.70 \\ \hline 44.52 \end{array}$$

4. Multiplication

Multiplying decimals requires a slightly more complicated algorithm. You perform the actual multiplication as though the decimal points were not present. If you were multiplying 3.1×2, you would first think of it as 31×2, and if you were multiplying 3.1×0.002, you would also think of that as 31×2 to begin. The difference comes in placing the decimal point.

To place the decimal point in the product, first count the number of digits to the right of the decimal point in each of the factors. Add these up to find the number of decimal places in the product. Start from the far right end of the answer and count that many places to the left to place your decimal point. If you run out of digits, add zeros to the left end of the number until you have enough places.

EXAMPLES:

> **1.** Multiply 3.1×2.

To find the answer, first think of the problem as $31 \times 2 = 62$. Then count the decimal places. There is one digit after the decimal point in 3.1. There are no digits after the decimal point in 2, so the answer must have one digit after the decimal point. Place the decimal between the 6 and the 2 for an answer of 6.2.

> **2.** Multiply 3.1×0.002.

To find the answer, first think of the problem as $31 \times 2 = 62$. Then count the decimal places. There is one digit after the decimal point in 3.1. There are three digits after the decimal point in 0.002, so the answer must have a total of four digits after the decimal point. Start from the right side and count to the left. The 2 in 62 is one digit, the 6 is a second digit, but there must be four digits to the right of the decimal point, so place zeros for the third and fourth, giving an answer of 0.0062.

Estimation skills are useful in placing decimal points. For example, 3.1×2 should be approximately $3 \times 2 = 6$, but 3.1×0.002 should give a much smaller result.

5. Division

To divide a decimal fraction by a whole number, divide normally and bring the decimal point straight up into your quotient.

To divide a decimal by another decimal you probably learned a process that involved moving decimal points. You never actually divide by a decimal. You change the appearance of the problem so that its divisor is a whole number. This is the same process as changing the appearance of a fraction. The task of dividing 502.5 by 0.25 can be thought of as simplifying a fraction with 502.5 in the numerator and 0.25 in the denominator. Multiplying both the numerator and the denominator by 100 makes the fraction 50,250 divided by 25. That is still a bit of work, but at least the divisor is now a whole number.

To divide decimals, move the decimal point in the divisor to the right until the divisor is a whole number. Move the decimal point in the dividend the same number of places to the right. Divide normally and bring the decimal point straight up into the quotient.

EXAMPLE:

> Divide 17.835 by 2.05.

Move the decimal point in the divisor two places right so that 2.05 becomes 205. Move the decimal point in 17.835 two places to the right as well, making it 1,783.5:

$$
\begin{array}{r}
8.7 \\
205\overline{)1783.5} \\
\underline{1640} \\
1435 \\
\underline{1435} \\
0
\end{array}
$$

Divide normally, and let the decimal point in the dividend (between 3 and 5) move straight up into the quotient, for a result of 8.7.

6. Scientific notation

Scientific notation is a method of representing very large or very small numbers as the product of a number greater than or equal to one and less than ten, times a power of 10. A large number would be represented as a number between one and ten times a positive power of 10, whereas a small number (a fraction or decimal) would be some number times a negative power of 10. You can think of the sign of the exponent as an indicator of which way to move the decimal point: Positive exponents tell you to move the decimal to the right; negative exponents tell you to move to the left. The number 5,400,000 can be represented as 5.4×10^6. The number 0.00071 is 7.1×10^{-4}.

To change a number from standard form to scientific notation, place a decimal point after the first nonzero digit. Drop leading or trailing zeros. This will give you the number between one and ten. To find the appropriate power of 10, count the number of places from where you placed the decimal to where it actually should appear. If you must count to the right, the exponent will be positive. If you count to the left, the exponent will be negative.

$$
\underbrace{58,400,000}_{\text{7 places right}} = 5.84 \times 10^7
$$

$$
\underbrace{0.000000000693}_{\text{10 places left}} = 6.93 \times 10^{-10}
$$

To multiply numbers in scientific notation, multiply the front numbers normally, and multiply the powers of ten by adding the exponents: $(5 \times 10^3)(7 \times 10^9) = 35 \times 10^{12}$. Because the front number is now greater than ten, rewrite $35 \times 10^{12} = 3.5 \times 10 \times 10^{12} = 3.5 \times 10^{13}$.

To divide numbers in scientific notation, divide the front numbers normally, and divide the powers of 10 by subtracting the exponents. Remember to adjust so that the answer is in correct scientific notation:

$$
\frac{4.8 \times 10^{12}}{1.2 \times 10^8} = 4 \times 10^{12-8} = 4 \times 10^4
$$

$$
\frac{1.2 \times 10^8}{4.8 \times 10^{12}} = 0.25 \times 10^{8-12} = 0.25 \times 10^{-4} = 2.5 \times 10^{-1} \times 10^{-4} = 2.5 \times 10^{-5}
$$

Practice

Directions (1–4): You are given two quantities, one in Column A and one in Column B. You are to compare the two quantities and choose one of the following:

    A. The quantity in Column A is greater.
    B. The quantity in Column B is greater.
    C. The two quantities are equal.
    D. The relationship cannot be determined from the information given.

	Column A	**Column B**
1.	0.05003	0.0503

	Column A	**Column B**
2.	$\frac{13}{17}$	0.76

	Column A	**Column B**
3.	0.000037	3.7×10^{-6}

	Column A	**Column B**
4.	0.001 + 0.1	0.01 + 0.101

Directions (5–10): Unless otherwise directed, select a single answer choice. For numeric-entry questions, enter a number in the box(es) below the question. Equivalent forms of the correct answer, such as 2.5 and 2.50, are all correct. Fractions do not need to be reduced to lowest terms. Enter the exact answer unless the question asks you to round your answer.

5. The sum of $46.A5$, $9.B07$, and 107.6, rounded to the nearest tenth, is 164.0. Choose the three pairs of possible values for A and B.

    A. $A = 4, B = 9$
    B. $A = 1, B = 2$
    C. $A = 2, B = 1$
    D. $A = 8, B = 5$
    E. $A = 7, B = 6$

6. The decimal portion of the result of two-tenths plus two-thousandths minus two-hundredths contains which of the following digits?

   A. 0
   B. 1
   C. 2
   D. 3
   E. 4
   F. 5
   G. 6
   H. 7
   I. 8
   J. 9

7. Calculate $4.65 \div 9.3 \times 4.8$.

   A. 0.8
   B. 1.8
   C. 2.4
   D. 2.5
   E. 3.2

8. If the speed of sound is slightly more than 900 feet/second, how fast would you be traveling if you reached Mach 4, or four times the speed of sound?

   A. 3.6×10^2
   B. 3.6×10^3
   C. 3.6×10^4
   D. 9×10^4
   E. 9×10^8

9. $0.0009 \times 500 \times 0.04 \times 20 =$

   [ ]

10. The product $(4.8 \times 10^{-3}) \div (1.2 \times 10^{-5})$ is

   [ ]

Answers

1. **B** To compare 0.05003 and 0.0503, align the decimal points and add a zero to 0.0503 to make both numbers the same length. Then ignore decimal points and leading zeros. Because the number 5,030 is larger than 5,003, 0.0503 is larger than 0.05003.

2. **A** Change $\frac{13}{17}$ to a decimal by dividing 13 by 17. The decimal equivalent of $\frac{13}{17}$ is greater than 0.76.

3. **A** You can convert either Column A or Column B to the format of the other column, but the fastest approach may be to convert 0.000037 to scientific notation, counting from the current position of the decimal point to the position after 3, the first nonzero digit. This is a move of five places right, so $0.000037 = 3.7 \times 10^{-5}$. Because 3.7×10^{-5} is larger than 3.7×10^{-6}, Column A is larger.

4. **B** Add the decimals by aligning decimal points:

$$
\begin{array}{r} 0.001 \\ + \ 0.100 \\ \hline 0.101 \end{array}
\qquad
\begin{array}{r} 0.010 \\ + \ 0.101 \\ \hline 0.111 \end{array}
$$

5. **A, D, E** Although actually adding $46.A5$, $9.B07$, and 107.6 is not possible, think about the process and what the result must be to round to 164.0.

$$
\begin{array}{r} 46.A5 \\ 9.B07 \\ 107.6 \\ \hline 162.?57 \end{array}
$$

The hundredths digit is a 5, so you'll round up, and because you'll round up to 164.0, the tenths digit must be 5 or greater. $A + B + 6$ could equal 6, 7, 8, 9, 15, 16, 17, 18 or 19. If $A + B + 6 = 6, 7, 8,$ or 9, the sum will be 162 plus a decimal, and would round to 163.0. If $A + B + 6$ is greater than or equal to 15, the carry makes the sum round to 164.0. You're looking for values of A and B that add to 9, 10, 11, 12, or 13, so the correct choices are A, D, and E.

6. **B, C, I** Two-tenths plus two-thousandths minus two-hundredths is $0.2 + 0.002 - 0.02 = 0.202 - 0.020 = 0.182$.

7. **C** Dividing 4.65 by 9.3, and then multiplying by 4.8, is an appropriate job for a calculator, but you can use some simple math to make the task easier. Imagine the calculation in fraction form, and divide 9.3 and 4.8 by 3 to make the numbers smaller and easier to manage:

$$
\frac{4.65}{\underset{3.1}{9.3}} \times \frac{\overset{1.6}{4.8}}{1} = \frac{4.65 \times 1.6}{3.1}
$$

Because 1.6 is just slightly more than half of 3.1, you can estimate the result as approximately half of 4.65, but notice that $4.65 \div 3.1 = 1.5$, and the problem becomes 1.5×1.6 or one and one-half of 1.6. That's $1.6 + 0.8$ or 2.4.

8. **B** If you reached Mach 4, you would be traveling at over $4 \times 900 = 3,600$ feet/second. Because the choices are in scientific notation, convert 3,600 to a number between one and ten, 3.6, times a power of ten, 10^3.

9. **0.36** Multiply the nonzero digits, $9 \times 5 \times 4 \times 2 = 9 \times 4 \times 5 \times 2 = 36 \times 10 = 360$. Add the two zeros from the 500 and the one zero from the 20, and you have 360000. Then count the digits to the right of the decimal point in each of the factors. There are four digits to the right of the decimal point in 0.0009 and two in 0.04, so the product should have $4 + 2 = 6$ decimal places: $0.\underset{\text{6 places}}{360000}$ The trailing zeros can be dropped.

10. **400 or 4×10^2** Divide 4.8 by 1.2 and use rules for exponents to divide 10^{-3} by 10^{-5}. Keep the base of 10 and subtract the exponents: $-3 - -5 = -3 + 5 = 2$.

$$\left(4.8 \times 10^{-3}\right) \div \left(1.2 \times 10^{-5}\right) = \left(4.8 \div 1.2\right) \times \left(10^{-3} \div 10^{-5}\right)$$
$$= 4 \times 10^{-3-(-5)} = 4 \times 10^2 = 4 \times 100 = 400$$

G. Percent

1. Meaning of percent

Ratios can be hard to compare if they are "out of" different numbers. Which is larger: 4 out of 9 or 5 out of 12? If you compare them as fractions, $\frac{4}{9}$ and $\frac{5}{12}$, it might help to change to a common denominator.

Changing ratios to percents is like changing to a common denominator. Percent makes it easier to compare, because everything is out of 100. Percent means "out of 100."

2. Using proportions to change a ratio to a percent

The basic rule to remember is $\frac{\text{part}}{\text{whole}} = \frac{\%}{100}$. This proportion can be used to solve most percent problems.

EXAMPLE:

> The by-laws of the town council require that a candidate receive at least 51% of the vote to be elected council president. If the council membership is 1,288, what is the minimum number of votes a candidate must receive to be elected president?

Start with $\frac{\text{part}}{\text{whole}} = \frac{\%}{100}$ or $\frac{p}{1,288} = \frac{51}{100}$. Cross-multiplying, $100p = 1,288 \times 51$. Then $100p = 65,688$, and $p = 656.88$. Because no one can cast a fraction of a vote, round this to 657 votes.

When you use the $\frac{\text{part}}{\text{whole}} = \frac{\%}{100}$ rule, the only trick is determining which number is the part and which is the whole. Certain words in the problem can signal this for you. The word *of* usually precedes the whole amount, and the word *is* can generally be found near the part.

EXAMPLES:

> 1. What percent of 58 is 22?

Look for *of*, and you find that 58 is the whole. Look for *is*, and you find that 22 is the part.

$$\frac{\text{part}}{\text{whole}} = \frac{\%}{100}$$
$$\frac{22}{58} = \frac{x}{100}$$
$$58x = 2,200$$
$$x \approx 37.9$$

2. 46 is 27% of what number?

Look for *of,* and you find that the whole is "what number," which means it is unknown. Look for *is,* and you find that 46 is the part. Both 46 and 27 are near the *is,* but 27 has the % sign, so you know it's the percent.

$$\frac{\text{part}}{\text{whole}} = \frac{\%}{100}$$

$$\frac{46}{x} = \frac{27}{100}$$

$$27x = 4,600$$

$$x \approx 170.4$$

3. What is 83% of 112?

Look for *of,* and you find that 112 is the whole. Look for *is,* and you find that the part is "what," which means the part is unknown.

$$\frac{\text{part}}{\text{whole}} = \frac{\%}{100}$$

$$\frac{x}{112} = \frac{83}{100}$$

$$100x = 112 \cdot 83$$

$$100x = 9,296$$

$$x = 92.96$$

3. Percent increase or decrease

Some problems ask you to compute the percent increase or percent decrease. Percent increase and percent decrease—or, in general, percent change—problems compare the change in a quantity, whether increase or decrease, to the original amount. The original amount is the whole, and the change is the part.

Identify the original amount. Calculate increase or decrease, and then use $\frac{\text{change}}{\text{original}} = \frac{\%}{100}$ to calculate the percent.

EXAMPLES:

1. Allison invests $857 in a stock she researched. After a year, her investment is worth $911. What is the percent increase in the value of her investment?

The original investment is $857 and it increases $911 – $857 = $54.

$$\frac{\text{change}}{\text{original}} = \frac{\%}{100}$$

$$\frac{54}{857} = \frac{x}{100}$$

$$857x = 5400$$

$$x \approx 6.3$$

The percent increase was approximately 6.3%.

> **2.** Melissa buys $320 worth of collectibles at a flea market and tucks them away, hoping they'll increase in value. Unfortunately, when she tries to sell them, she finds that they're only worth $275. What is the percent decrease in the value of her investment?

The original cost was $320, but decreased $320 − $275 = $45.

$$\frac{change}{original} = \frac{\%}{100}$$

$$\frac{45}{320} = \frac{x}{100}$$

$$320x = 4{,}500$$

$$x \approx 14$$

Her investment decreased approximately 14%.

4. Changing to a decimal

Percent problems can also be solved by using decimal equivalents. To change a percent to a decimal, drop the percent sign and move the decimal point two places to the left: 14.5% = 0.145 and 8% = 0.08. To change a decimal to a percent, move the decimal point two places to the right and add a percent sign. Leading zeros can be dropped: 0.497 = 49.7% and 5.983 = 598.3%.

When solving percent problems using decimal equivalents, remember that *of* generally signals multiplication. So, 15% of 300 becomes 0.15×300. In the terminology used earlier, percent × whole = part.

Practice

Directions (1–2): You are given two quantities, one in Column A and one in Column B. You are to compare the two quantities and choose one of the following:

- **A.** The quantity in Column A is greater.
- **B.** The quantity in Column B is greater.
- **C.** The two quantities are equal.
- **D.** The relationship cannot be determined from the information given.

	Column A	Column B
1.	20% of 40	40% of 20

20% of x is 25

	Column A	Column B
2.	105% of x	105

Directions (3–10): Unless otherwise directed, select a single answer choice. For numeric-entry questions, enter a number in the box(es) below the question. Equivalent forms of the correct answer, such as 2.5 and 2.50, are all correct. Fractions do not need to be reduced to lowest terms. Enter the exact answer unless the question asks you to round your answer.

3. Jason paid for his new Blu-Ray player over a year in monthly installments of between $34 and $35. The list price of the Blu-Ray player was $389.50 and tax was added before the installment amounts were calculated. Choose all the possible tax rates.

    A. 4.5%
    B. 5.1%
    C. 6.3%
    D. 7.4%
    E. 8.1%.

4. $A\%$ of $B\%$ of C is 60. If $C = 500$, choose all the possible pairs of values for A and B.

    A. $A = 15, B = 80$
    B. $A = 16, B = 75$
    C. $A = 18, B = 70$
    D. $A = 20, B = 60$
    E. $A = 24, B = 50$
    F. $A = 25, B = 48$
    G. $A = 27, B = 45$
    H. $A = 30, B = 40$
    I. $A = 35, B = 50$

5. Magdalena bought several shares of stock in a small company for $350. She held the stock for a year and then sold it for $910. What was the percent increase in Magdalena's investment?

    A. 2.6
    B. 26
    C. 38
    D. 160
    E. 260

6. When Laura bought a new DVD player, the player was marked at 45% off the list price. Because she had a coupon for a special sale, she then received an additional 15% off the already reduced price. If the original list price of the DVD player was $148, what did Laura actually pay?

    A. $88
    B. $69.19
    C. $56.61
    D. $12.21
    E. $9.99

7. The constitution of a town requires that 60% of the residents vote in favor of a proposal before it can become law in the town. Maya's initiative to ban smoking in all town restaurants did not pass in the last election. If there are 9,670 residents in the town, what is the minimum number of residents who voted against Maya's proposal?

   A. 5,802
   B. 4,835
   C. 3,869
   D. 3,868
   E. 3,481

8. In a recent survey, voters in a town were asked what political party they voted for most often, and 368 people indicated they voted Republican. If this represents about 46% of the town's voters, how many voters are there in the town?

   A. 169
   B. 537
   C. 800
   D. 1,168
   E. 16,928

9. A pair of boots originally priced at $100 went on sale at 20% off. Later in the season, there was an additional markdown of 15% off the current (already reduced) price. If you buy the boots at the end of the season, what percent of the original price have you saved?

   ☐

10. Glen finds a $40 sweater on sale for 15% off, but he must pay 5% sales tax. If he hands the cashier $40, how much change will he receive?

    ☐

Answers

1. **C** To find the answer, figure 20% of 40 = 0.2 × 40 = 8 and 40% of 20 = 0.4 × 20 = 8.

2. **A** If 20% of x is 25, then $x = 5 \times 25 = 125$. You know that 105% of x is more than 125, which means it's greater than 105. (You don't have to figure out 105% of x to know the answer.)

3. **B, C, D** The total amount paid was between 12 × $34 and 12 × $35, or between $408 and $420. Subtract the list price of the DVR, and the tax is between $408 – $389.50 = $18.50 and $420 –$389.50 = $30.50. Divide $18.50 by $389.50 to find the minimum tax rate is 4.7% and divide $30.50 by $389.50 to find the maximum tax rate of 7.8%.

4. **A, B, D, E, F, H** If $A\%$ of $B\%$ of 500 is 60, then $A\% \times B\% = \dfrac{60}{500} = 12\%$. You're looking for pairs of numbers that multiply to 1,200, so that $\dfrac{A}{100} \times \dfrac{B}{100} = \dfrac{1,200}{10,000} = \dfrac{12}{100}$. Choice C, 18 × 70 = 1,260, is not correct, nor is choice G, 27 × 45 = 1,215, or choice I, 35 × 50 = 1,750.

5. **D** Magdalena's original investment of $350 increased by $910 – $350 = $560.

$$\frac{\text{change}}{\text{original}} = \frac{\%}{100}$$

$$\frac{560}{350} = \frac{x}{100}$$

$$350x = 560 \cdot 100$$

$$x = \frac{\overset{8}{560} \cdot 100}{\underset{5}{350}} = \frac{800}{5} = 160$$

Her investment increased 160%.

6. **B** List price was $148, and 45% of $148 is 0.45 × 148 = $66.60, so the marked price was $148 – $66.60 = $81.40. The additional 15% off the reduced price would be 0.15 × $81.40 = $12.21, making her cost $81.40 – $12.21 = $69.19.

7. **C** To pass, Maya's proposal would have needed 60% of the 9,670 votes, or 5,802 votes. That would leave 9,670 – 5,802 = 3,868 votes against the proposal. Because the proposal did not pass, there must have been at least one more vote against, so a minimum of 3,869 residents voted against Maya's proposal.

8. **C** If the 368 people who said they voted Republican are 46% of the town's voters, and x represents the number of voters, then 368 is the part, x is the whole, and 46 is the percent.

$$\frac{\text{part}}{\text{whole}} = \frac{\%}{100}$$

$$\frac{368}{x} = \frac{46}{100}$$

$$46x = 368 \cdot 100$$

$$x = \frac{\overset{184}{368} \cdot 100}{\underset{23}{46}} = \frac{\overset{8}{184} \cdot 100}{\underset{1}{23}} = 800$$

9. **32%** Because 20% of $100 is $20, the first markdown of 20% off reduces the price from $100 to $80. The additional discount is 15% of $80.

$$\frac{\text{part}}{\text{whole}} = \frac{\%}{100}$$

$$\frac{x}{80} = \frac{15}{100}$$

$$100x = 80 \cdot 15$$

$$x = \frac{\overset{4}{80} \cdot 15}{\underset{5}{100}} = \frac{4 \cdot \overset{3}{15}}{\underset{1}{5}} = 12$$

This means that you pay $80 – $12 = $68. You've saved $100 – $68 = $32 off the original price, or $\frac{32}{100} = 32\%$.

10. $4.30 10% of $40 is $4, so 15% will be $4 + $2 = $6. Glen will pay $40 – $6 = $34 plus 5% sales tax.

$$\frac{\text{part}}{\text{whole}} = \frac{\%}{100}$$

$$\frac{x}{34} = \frac{5}{100}$$

$$100x = 5 \cdot 34 = 170$$

$$x = \frac{170}{100} = 1.70$$

His total cost is $34 + $1.70 = $35.70. If he hands over $40, he'll receive $40 – $35.70 = $4.30.

H. Exponents

Exponents are symbols for repeated multiplication. When you write b^n you say that you want to use b as a factor n times. The number b is the base, n is the exponent, and b^n is the power. The expression 5^3, for example, means $5 \times 5 \times 5$.

You should remember some special exponents:

- For any number a, $a^1 = a$.
- For $a \neq 0$:

$$a^0 = 1$$

$$a^{-1} = \frac{1}{a}$$

$$a^{-n} = \frac{1}{a^n}$$

Notice that the negative exponents a^{-1} and a^{-n} don't affect the sign of the number. $a^{-1} \neq -a$ and $a^{-n} \neq -a^n$. The negative on the exponent signals a reciprocal, not a change in sign.

People are sometimes confused about exactly what the base is when they look at expressions like $(3x)^2$ or $3x^2$. Looking at what is immediately left of the exponent will help sort that out. The expression $(3x)^2 = (3x)(3x)$ because the parenthesis is immediately left of the exponent, and so the whole quantity in the parentheses is squared, but $3x^2 = 3 \cdot x \cdot x$ because only the x is immediately left of the exponent.

Avoid the common error that occurs when working with powers of signed numbers. Remember that to multiply –5 by –5, you must write $(-5)^2$ with parentheses. If you write -5^2 without parentheses, the exponent only touches the 5 and you get $-(5 \times 5)$.

1. Multiplication

When you multiply powers of the same base, keep the base and add the exponents.

EXAMPLES:

---

1. Simplify $x^7 \cdot y^3 \cdot x^5$.

You can use the rules for exponents on powers of the same base. Rearrange $x^7 \cdot y^3 \cdot x^5 = x^7 \cdot x^5 \cdot y^3$ and multiply the powers of x by keeping the base and adding the exponents: $x^7 \cdot x^5 \cdot y^3 = x^{12} \cdot y^3$. You cannot apply the rule to different bases, so it isn't possible to simplify any further.

---

2. Which of the following is equivalent to $2^3 \times 3^2 \times 2^2 \times 3^1$?

    A. 2^8

    B. 3^8

    C. 6^8

    D. $2^5 \times 3^3$

    E. $4^5 \times 9^3$

The correct answer is **D.** Rearrange to group powers with the same base: $2^3 \times 3^2 \times 2^2 \times 3^1 = 2^3 \times 2^2 \times 3^2 \times 3^1$. Multiply the powers of 2 by keeping the base of 2 and adding the exponents: $2^3 \times 2^2 \times 3^2 \times 3^1 = 2^5 \times 3^2 \times 3^1$. Multiply the powers of 3 by keeping the base of 3 and adding the exponents: $2^5 \times 3^2 \times 3^1 = 2^5 \times 3^3$.

The most common errors with exponents are made by students who learn only half the rule. The active part of the rule, add the exponents, is what most people remember, but the other part, keep the base, is just as important. Asked to multiply $2^3 \times 2^4$, many people will try to add the exponents *and* multiply the 2s, giving an answer of 4^7 instead of 2^7. Keep the base and add the exponents.

2. Division

When you divide powers of the same base, keep the base and subtract the exponents.

EXAMPLE:

Which of the following is another way to write $\dfrac{7^{10} \cdot 5^{12}}{7^6 \cdot 5^4}$?

    A. $7^{\frac{5}{3}} \cdot 5^3$

    B. $\dfrac{35^{22}}{35^{10}}$

    C. $7^4 \times 5^8$

    D. $1^4 \times 1^8$

    E. 35^{12}

The rules for exponents only work for powers of the same base, so there is nothing that can conveniently be done to $7^{10} \times 5^{12}$ or $7^6 \times 5^4$. Instead, divide 7^{10} by 7^6, keeping the base of 7 and subtracting the exponent of the denominator from the exponent in the numerator: $7^{10} \div 7^6 = 7^{(10-6)} = 7^4$. Then divide 5^{12} by 5^4, keeping the base of 5 and subtracting the exponents: $5^{12} \div 5^4 = 5^{(12-4)} = 5^8$. The best answer is $7^4 \times 5^8$.

3. Powers

When you raise a power to a power, keep the base and multiply the exponents.

EXAMPLE:

Which of the following is *not* equivalent to 5^{24}?

   A. $(125)^8$
   B. $(5^{12})^2$
   C. $(5^6)^4$
   D. $(5^{20})^4$
   E. $(25)^{12}$

Consider the answer choices that are conveniently written as powers of powers first. Raising a power to a power means keeping the base and multiplying the exponents, so $(5^{12})^2 = 5^{12 \times 2} = 5^{24}$ and $(5^6)^4 = 5^{6 \times 4} = 5^{24}$, but $(5^{20})^4 = 5^{20 \times 4} = 5^{80}$. Choice D is not equal to 5^{24}. If it had become necessary to test the other options, 125 could be rewritten as 5^3 and 25 rewritten as 5^2.

4. Power of a product

When a product is raised to a power, each factor is raised to that power.

EXAMPLE:

Simplify $(5a^3b^2c^4)^3$.

$(5a^3b^2c^4)^3 = 5^3 (a^3)^3 \times (b^2)^3 \times (c^4)^3$. Then apply the power of a power rule, and you have $5^3 (a^3)^3 \times (b^2)^3 \times (c^4)^3 = 125a^9b^6c^{12}$.

5. Power of a quotient

When a quotient is raised to a power, both the numerator and the denominator are raised to that power.

EXAMPLE:

Simplify $\left(\dfrac{7x^2y^{-3}z^4}{2x^{-1}y^2z^5} \right)^2$.

First, apply the power of a quotient rule:

$$\left(\frac{7x^2y^{-3}z^4}{2x^{-1}y^2z^5} \right)^2 = \frac{\left(7x^2y^{-3}z^4\right)^2}{\left(2x^{-1}y^2z^5\right)^2}$$

Then apply the power of a product rule, first to the numerator and then to the denominator:

$$\frac{\left(7x^2 y^{-3} z^4\right)^2}{\left(2x^{-1} y^2 z^5\right)^2} = \frac{7^2 \cdot \left(x^2\right)^2 \cdot \left(y^{-3}\right)^2 \cdot \left(z^4\right)^2}{2^2 \cdot \left(x^{-1}\right)^2 \cdot \left(y^2\right)^2 \cdot \left(z^5\right)^2}$$

Simplify both the numerator and the denominator:

$$\frac{7^2 \cdot \left(x^2\right)^2 \cdot \left(y^{-3}\right)^2 \cdot \left(z^4\right)^2}{2^2 \cdot \left(x^{-1}\right)^2 \cdot \left(y^2\right)^2 \cdot \left(z^5\right)^2} = \frac{49 x^4 y^{-6} z^8}{4 x^{-2} y^4 z^{10}}$$

Finally, divide powers of the same base by keeping the base and subtracting the exponents:

$$\frac{49 x^4 y^{-6} z^8}{4 x^{-2} y^4 z^{10}} = \frac{49}{4} x^{(4-(-2))} y^{(-6-4)} z^{(8-10)} = \frac{49}{4} x^6 y^{-10} z^{-2}$$

Remember that this answer could also be expressed without negative exponents:

$$\frac{49}{4} x^6 y^{-10} z^{-2} = \frac{49}{4} x^6 \cdot \frac{1}{y^{10}} \cdot \frac{1}{z^2} = \frac{49 x^6}{4 y^{10} z^2}$$

Practice

Directions (1–4): You are given two quantities, one in Column A and one in Column B. You are to compare the two quantities and choose one of the following:

    A. The quantity in Column A is greater.
    B. The quantity in Column B is greater.
    C. The two quantities are equal.
    D. The relationship cannot be determined from the information given.

	Column A	Column B
1.	5^2	2^5

	Column A	Column B
2.	$(-3)^2$	-3^2

	Column A	Column B
3.	$(2^2 - 5)^x$	$(5 - 2^2)^x$

	Column A	Column B
4.	$3^7 \times 5^7$	15^7

Directions (5–10): Unless otherwise directed, select a single answer choice. For numeric-entry questions, enter a number in the box(es) below the question. Equivalent forms of the correct answer, such as 2.5 and 2.50, are all correct. Fractions do not need to be reduced to lowest terms. Enter the exact answer unless the question asks you to round your answer.

5. Choose all the expressions with products equal to $24x^4y^7$.

    A. $(-8x^3y^5)(-3xy^2)$
    B. $(-8x^4y^5)(-3y^2)$
    C. $(6x^3y^4)(4xy^3)$
    D. $(12x^2y^2)(-2x^2y^5)$
    E. $(-12xy^3)(-2x^3y^3)$
    F. $(-6x^2y^4)(4x^3y^3)$
    G. $(8x^4)(3y^7)$
    H. $24(xy)^4y^3$

6. Choose the three expressions whose product is equal to $(-8\,a^7b^5)^2$.

    A. $2a^2b^2$
    B. $2a^3b^2$
    C. $4a^{11}b^8$
    D. $4a^{12}b^8$
    E. $8a^5b^4$
    F. $16a^9b^6$

7. $\dfrac{18xy^2z^5}{6x^3y^2z^2} =$

    A. $3x^2z^3$
    B. $12x^2z^3$
    C. $\dfrac{3z^3}{x^2}$
    D. $\dfrac{12z^3}{x^2}$
    E. $\dfrac{3y^4z^3}{x^2}$

8. $-\left(\dfrac{r^4 t}{5rt^3}\right)^2 =$

    A. $\dfrac{-r^4}{5t^2}$

    B. $\dfrac{r^6}{5t^4}$

    C. $\dfrac{-r^6}{5t^4}$

    D. $\dfrac{r^6}{25t^4}$

    E. $\dfrac{-r^6}{25t^4}$

9. $\left(\dfrac{7^0 \cdot (-4)^2}{2^3}\right)^5 =$

    [   ]

10. The quotient of 27 squared and 15 squared is the square of what number?

Answers

1. **B** $5^2 = 5 \times 5 = 25$, but $2^5 = 2 \times 2 \times 2 \times 2 \times 2 = 32$.

2. **A** Because $(-3)^2 = (-3)(-3)$, the quantity in Column A is $+9$. But $-3^2 = -(3 \times 3)$, so Column B is -9.

3. **D** The two expressions being raised to the x power differ in sign: $2^2 - 5 = -1$ and $5 - 2^2 = 1$. If x is an even number, the quantity in Column A will equal that in Column B; if x is odd, however, they will have opposite signs. Because you can't know whether x is odd or even, you can't determine which expression is larger.

4. **C** Don't spend time evaluating seventh powers. Just note that $15^7 = (3 \times 5)^7 = 3^7 \times 5^7$.

5. **A, B, C, G, H** Eliminate choices D and F, because their results will have coefficients of -24. Then check the exponents. All remaining options will have x^4, but eliminate choice E, because it will have y^6, rather than y^7.

6. **A, B, F** First, simplify $(-8a^7b^5)^2 = 64a^{14}b^{10}$; then look for expressions whose product will be $64a^{14}b^{10}$. Looking at coefficients first, you can obtain a product of 64 by $2 \times 2 \times 16$, $2 \times 2 \times 4 \times 4$, or $2 \times 4 \times 8$. Then check the powers that result from each of those combinations. If you begin with $2a^2b^2 \times 2a^3b^2 = 4a^5b^4$, you'll need $16a^9b^6$ to complete the product. The expressions with coefficients of 4 will be too large. So A, B, and F will give you the desired product.

7. C $\dfrac{18xy^2z^5}{6x^3y^2z^2} = \dfrac{18}{6}\cdot\dfrac{x}{x^3}\cdot\dfrac{y^2}{y^2}\cdot\dfrac{z^5}{z^2} = 3\cdot\dfrac{1}{x^2}\cdot 1\cdot\dfrac{z^3}{1} = \dfrac{3z^3}{x^2}.$

8. E $-\left(\dfrac{r^4t}{5rt^3}\right)^2 = -\left(\dfrac{r^3}{5t^2}\right)^2 = -\left(\dfrac{r^6}{5^2t^4}\right) = -\dfrac{r^6}{25t^4}.$

9. 32 $\left(\dfrac{7^0\cdot(-4)^2}{2^3}\right)^5 = \left(\dfrac{1\cdot16}{8}\right)^5 = 2^5 = 32.$

10. $\dfrac{9}{5}$ The quotient of 27 squared and 15 squared can be written as $\dfrac{27^2}{15^2} = \dfrac{(3\cdot9)^2}{(3\cdot5)^2} = \dfrac{3^{\cancel{2}}\cdot9^2}{3^{\cancel{2}}\cdot5^2} = \dfrac{9^2}{5^2} = \left(\dfrac{9}{5}\right)^2.$

I. Roots

Exponents talk about repeated multiplication; roots take you in the other direction. A number, r, is called the nth root of a number, x, if $r^n = x$. The number 5 is the third root, or cube root, of 125 because $5^3 = 125$. The square root of 49 is 7 because $7^2 = 49$.

The symbol for the nth root of x is $\sqrt[n]{x}$. The sign is called a *radical.* The small number in the crook of the sign is called the *index,* and the index tells what power of the root produces x. If no index is shown, it's a square root.

Positive real numbers have two square roots: a positive root and a negative root. Both 7^2 and $(-7)^2$ will produce 49, so both 7 and –7 are square roots of 49. When you see the symbol $\sqrt{49}$, however, you may assume it means the principal, or positive, square root, so $\sqrt{49} = 7$. Remember that $\left(\sqrt{x}\right)^2 = \sqrt{x}\cdot\sqrt{x} = x$ and that roots can be written as fractional exponents: $\sqrt{x} = x^{\frac{1}{2}}$. Only nonnegative numbers have square roots in the real-number system, so $\sqrt{x}$ and $x^{\frac{1}{2}}$ make sense only if $x \geq 0$.

1. Simplifying radicals

Most positive real numbers have square roots that are *irrational numbers,* numbers that cannot be expressed as fractions. Such numbers are non-terminating, non-repeating decimals, and can be written only in approximate form. So, it's often simpler and more useful to leave the numbers in simplest radical form. *Simplest radical form* means no radicals in the denominator and the smallest possible number under the radical sign.

To simplify a radical:

1. **Express the number under the radical as the product of a perfect square and some other factor.**
2. **Give each factor its own radical.**
3. **Take the known square root.**

EXAMPLE:

Which of the following is the simplest radical form of $\sqrt{128}$?

A. $2\sqrt{32}$
B. $4\sqrt{8}$
C. $32\sqrt{2}$
D. $8\sqrt{4}$
E. $8\sqrt{2}$

The number 128 could be factored as 4×32, 16×8, or 64×2, but because you want the smallest number left under the radical, you should choose the largest perfect square factor: $\sqrt{128} = \sqrt{64 \cdot 2} = \sqrt{64} \cdot \sqrt{2} = 8\sqrt{2}$.

2. Rationalizing denominators

Eliminating a radical from the denominator is essentially the same process as finding an equivalent fraction with a different denominator. You change the appearance of the fraction without changing its value by multiplying by a disguised form of 1. If the denominator is a single term, multiply the numerator and denominator by the radical in the denominator.

EXAMPLE:

Which of the following is equivalent to $\dfrac{5}{3\sqrt{7}}$?

A. $\dfrac{5\sqrt{7}}{21}$

B. $\dfrac{35}{21}$

C. $\dfrac{5}{21}$

D. $\dfrac{5\sqrt{7}}{147}$

E. $\dfrac{5 - \sqrt{7}}{3}$

The correct answer is **A.** Multiply both the numerator and the denominator by $\sqrt{7}$: $\dfrac{5}{3\sqrt{7}} \cdot \dfrac{\sqrt{7}}{\sqrt{7}} = \dfrac{5\sqrt{7}}{3 \cdot 7} = \dfrac{5\sqrt{7}}{21}$.

If the denominator has two terms, and one or both of them are radicals, multiply the numerator and denominator by the conjugate of the denominator. The *conjugate* is the same two terms connected by the opposite sign. The conjugate of $3 + \sqrt{5}$ is $3 - \sqrt{5}$. The conjugate of $\sqrt{2} - \sqrt{3}$ is $\sqrt{2} + \sqrt{3}$. The conjugate of $-7 + \sqrt{23}$ is $-7 - \sqrt{23}$.

EXAMPLE:

Which of these is equivalent to $\dfrac{5}{3+\sqrt{2}}$?

A. $\sqrt{2}$

B. $\dfrac{15-5\sqrt{2}}{7}$

C. $\dfrac{15+5\sqrt{2}}{13}$

D. $\dfrac{15+5\sqrt{2}}{11}$

E. $\dfrac{15-5\sqrt{2}}{11}$

The correct answer is **B**. Multiply the numerator and denominator by the conjugate of $3+\sqrt{2}$:

$$\frac{5}{3+\sqrt{2}}\cdot\frac{3-\sqrt{2}}{3-\sqrt{2}}=\frac{5\left(3-\sqrt{2}\right)}{\left(3+\sqrt{2}\right)\left(3-\sqrt{2}\right)}$$

Multiplying out the numerator and denominator produces the following:

$$\frac{5\left(3-\sqrt{2}\right)}{\left(3+\sqrt{2}\right)\left(3-\sqrt{2}\right)}=\frac{5\cdot3-5\sqrt{2}}{3\cdot3-3\sqrt{2}+3\sqrt{2}-\sqrt{2}\cdot\sqrt{2}}=\frac{15-5\sqrt{2}}{9-2}=\frac{15-5\sqrt{2}}{7}$$

3. Adding and subtracting

When adding (or subtracting) variable terms, you add only like terms; to do that you add the numerical coefficient and keep the same variable. When adding (or subtracting) radicals, add only like radicals, and do so by adding the coefficient and keeping the radical.

$$4x + 5y + 3x = 7x + 5y$$
$$4\sqrt{3}+5\sqrt{2}+3\sqrt{3}=7\sqrt{3}+5\sqrt{2}$$

When multiplying or dividing radicals, remember that radicals can be re-expressed as powers, and the rules for exponents apply.

$$5x \cdot 3y = 15xy \qquad 5\sqrt{2}\cdot3\sqrt{3}=15\sqrt{6}$$
$$4x \cdot 5x = 20x^2 \qquad 4\sqrt{3}\cdot5\sqrt{3}=20\left(\sqrt{3}\right)^{2}=20\cdot3=60$$

Practice

Directions (1–2): You are given two quantities, one in Column A and one in Column B. You are to compare the two quantities and choose one of the following:

  A. The quantity in Column A is greater.
  B. The quantity in Column B is greater.
  C. The two quantities are equal.
  D. The relationship cannot be determined from the information given.

	Column A	Column B
1.	$\sqrt{72}$	$12\sqrt{6}$

	Column A	Column B
2.	$20\sqrt{5}$	$2\sqrt{50}$

Directions (3–10): Unless otherwise directed, select a single answer choice. For numeric-entry questions, enter a number in the box(es) below the question. Equivalent forms of the correct answer, such as 2.5 and 2.50, are all correct. Fractions do not need to be reduced to lowest terms. Enter the exact answer unless the question asks you to round your answer.

3. Choose all the true statements about $\sqrt{125} - \sqrt{5}$.

   A. $\sqrt{125} - \sqrt{5}$ is equivalent to $\sqrt{120}$.
   B. $\sqrt{125} - \sqrt{5}$ is equal to 5.
   C. The simplest form of $\sqrt{125} - \sqrt{5}$ is $4\sqrt{30}$.
   D. $\sqrt{125} - \sqrt{5}$ can be simplified to $4\sqrt{5}$.
   E. $\sqrt{125} - \sqrt{5}$ cannot be simplified.

4. Select all the expressions equivalent to $\dfrac{\sqrt{162}}{\sqrt{72}}$.

   A. $\dfrac{9\sqrt{2}}{6\sqrt{2}}$

   B. $\dfrac{3}{2}\sqrt{2}$

   C. $\dfrac{3}{2}$

   D. $\dfrac{9}{6}$

   E. $\dfrac{\sqrt{81}\sqrt{2}}{\sqrt{8}\sqrt{9}}$

5. Simplify: $\sqrt{8} - \sqrt{9} + \sqrt{16} - \sqrt{18}$.

    A. $2\sqrt{3}$
    B. $2\sqrt{6} - 3\sqrt{3}$
    C. $1 - \sqrt{2}$
    D. $\sqrt{2} - 1$
    E. Cannot be simplified

6. Express in simplest form: $\dfrac{-2}{\sqrt{12}}$.

    A. $\dfrac{-1}{6}$

    B. -2

    C. $\dfrac{-\sqrt{3}}{3}$

    D. $\sqrt{3}$

    E. $\dfrac{-1}{\sqrt{6}}$

7. Express in simplest form: $\dfrac{5}{\sqrt{3} + 2}$.

    A. $5\sqrt{3} - 10$
    B. $10 - 5\sqrt{3}$
    C. $2 - \sqrt{3}$
    D. $-2 + \sqrt{3}$
    E. Cannot be simplified

8. Express in simplest form: $\dfrac{5 - \sqrt{6}}{5 + \sqrt{6}}$.

    A. $\dfrac{-1}{11}$

    B. -1

    C. 1

    D. $\dfrac{31 - 10\sqrt{6}}{19}$

    E. $\dfrac{10\sqrt{6} - 31}{11}$

9. Simplify: $\left(\dfrac{-2\sqrt{2}}{\sqrt{5}} \right)^{2}$.

$$\dfrac{\square}{\square}$$

10. Express in simplest form: $\dfrac{3\sqrt{2}}{\sqrt{27}} - \dfrac{2\sqrt{2}}{\sqrt{12}}$.

$$\boxed{}$$

Answers

1. **B** $\sqrt{72} = \sqrt{36 \cdot 2} = \sqrt{36}\sqrt{2} = 6\sqrt{2}$, which is less than $12\sqrt{6}$.

2. **A** Reverse the process of simplifying to make these easier to compare:
   $20\sqrt{5} = \sqrt{20^2}\sqrt{5} = \sqrt{400}\sqrt{5} = \sqrt{400 \cdot 5} = \sqrt{2000}$, but $2\sqrt{50} = \sqrt{2^2}\sqrt{50} = \sqrt{4}\sqrt{50} = \sqrt{4 \cdot 50} = \sqrt{200}$.

   Alternately, use estimation: $\sqrt{5}$ is between 2 and 3, so $20\sqrt{5}$ is between 40 and 60. $\sqrt{50}$ is between 7 and 8, so $2\sqrt{50}$ is between 14 and 16.

3. **D** Unlike radicals cannot be combined, so start by simplifying $\sqrt{125}$: $\sqrt{125} = \sqrt{25}\sqrt{5} = 5\sqrt{5}$. Then subtract $\sqrt{125} - \sqrt{5} = 5\sqrt{5} - \sqrt{5} = 4\sqrt{5}$. Only choice D is true.

4. **A, C, D, E** Don't try to rationalize the denominator until you've simplified the radicals:
   $\dfrac{\sqrt{162}}{\sqrt{72}} = \dfrac{\sqrt{81}\sqrt{2}}{\sqrt{36}\sqrt{2}} = \dfrac{9\sqrt{2}}{6\sqrt{2}} = \dfrac{9}{6} = \dfrac{3}{2}$. As you do that, you'll see that choice A is true, but choice B is

   not true; choices C and D are also true. The simplest way to check is to multiply the radicals in

   the numerator and denominator: $\dfrac{\sqrt{81}\sqrt{2}}{\sqrt{8}\sqrt{9}} = \dfrac{\sqrt{162}}{\sqrt{72}}$. So, choice E also works.

5. **C** Simplify radicals, and then combine like terms:
   $\sqrt{8} - \sqrt{9} + \sqrt{16} - \sqrt{18} = \sqrt{4}\sqrt{2} - 3 + 4 - \sqrt{9}\sqrt{2} = 2\sqrt{2} + 1 - 3\sqrt{2} = 1 - \sqrt{2}$.

6. **C** Expressing $\dfrac{-2}{\sqrt{12}}$ in simplest form calls for rationalizing the denominator, as well as simplifying

   radicals: $\dfrac{-2}{\sqrt{12}} \cdot \dfrac{\sqrt{12}}{\sqrt{12}} = \dfrac{-2\sqrt{12}}{12} = \dfrac{-\sqrt{12}}{6} = \dfrac{-\sqrt{4}\sqrt{3}}{6} = \dfrac{-2\sqrt{3}}{6} = \dfrac{-\sqrt{3}}{3}$.

7. **B** Rationalize the denominator of $\dfrac{5}{\sqrt{3}+2}$ by multiplying both the numerator and the
   denominator by the conjugate of the denominator, $\sqrt{3} - 2$:

   $\dfrac{5}{\sqrt{3}+2} \cdot \dfrac{\sqrt{3}-2}{\sqrt{3}-2} = \dfrac{5(\sqrt{3}-2)}{3+2\sqrt{3}-2\sqrt{3}-4} = \dfrac{5(\sqrt{3}-2)}{-1} = -5(\sqrt{3}-2) = -5\sqrt{3}+10 = 10-5\sqrt{3}$.

8. **D** Multiply the numerator and the denominator by the conjugate of the denominator:
   $\dfrac{(5-\sqrt{6})}{(5+\sqrt{6})} \cdot \dfrac{(5-\sqrt{6})}{(5-\sqrt{6})} = \dfrac{25-5\sqrt{6}-5\sqrt{6}+6}{25-5\sqrt{6}+5\sqrt{6}-6} = \dfrac{31-10\sqrt{6}}{19}$. Don't be distracted by the similarity
   of the numerator and denominator.

9. $\dfrac{8}{5}\left(\dfrac{-2\sqrt{2}}{\sqrt{5}}\right)^2 = \dfrac{(-2)^2(\sqrt{2})^2}{(\sqrt{5})^2} = \dfrac{4 \times 2}{5} = \dfrac{8}{5}$.

10. **0** Simplify the radicals in the denominators, and reduce each fraction to lowest terms:
    $\dfrac{3\sqrt{2}}{\sqrt{27}} - \dfrac{2\sqrt{2}}{\sqrt{12}} = \dfrac{3\sqrt{2}}{\sqrt{9}\sqrt{3}} - \dfrac{2\sqrt{2}}{\sqrt{4}\sqrt{3}} = \dfrac{\cancel{3}\sqrt{2}}{\cancel{3}\sqrt{3}} - \dfrac{\cancel{2}\sqrt{2}}{\cancel{2}\sqrt{3}} = \dfrac{\sqrt{2}}{\sqrt{3}} - \dfrac{\sqrt{2}}{\sqrt{3}} = 0$.

XI. Algebra

The Quantitative Reasoning questions on the GRE assess your ability to think through a problem involving numerical information. Manipulating that information quickly and efficiently often involves basic algebra. Solving equations and inequalities, simplifying expressions, and understanding graphs are key skills.

A. Linear Equations and Inequalities

Linear equations and inequalities are mathematical sentences that contain variables and constants. Variables are letters or other symbols that take the place of numbers, because the value of the number is unknown, or because a pattern is being represented in which different values are possible. Constants are numbers; their value is fixed.

The verb in an equation is the equal sign; in an inequality, it is the less than (<) or greater than (>), or less than or equal to (≤) or greater than or equal to (≥) symbol. Linear equations and inequalities take their name from the fact that their graphs are lines.

1. Distributing

Before you begin the actual work of solving an equation, you'll want to make the equation as simple as possible. Focus on one side of the equation at a time, and if parentheses or other grouping symbols are present, remove them. You may do this by simplifying the expression inside the parentheses, by using the distributive property, or, occasionally, by deciding that the parentheses are not necessary and just removing them. For example, the parentheses in the following equation help to organize your thinking but serve no other mathematical purpose: $x + (x + 1) + (x + 2) = 18$. You can remove the parentheses: $x + x + 1 + x + 2 = 18$.

EXAMPLE:

Use the distributive property to simplify: $5(x + 3) = 4 - (5 - x)$.

To distribute, focus on the left side of the equation and multiply $5(x + 3)$:

$$5x + 15 = 4 - (5 - x)$$

Now focus on the right side of the equation and change the signs of the terms in parentheses:

$$5x + 15 = 4 - 5 + x$$

2. Combining like terms

After parentheses have been cleared, take the time to combine like terms (and *only* like terms) before you begin solving. Each side of the equation should have no more than one variable term and one constant term when you begin to solve.

EXAMPLES:

---

1. Combine like terms: $5x + 15 = 4 - 5 + x$.

To combine like terms, on the right side, combine $4 - 5$:

$$5x + 15 = -1 + x$$

---

2. Combine like terms: $x + x + 1 + x + 2 = 18$.

To combine like terms, combine the x terms and add $1 + 2$:

$$x + x + x + 1 + 2 = 18$$
$$3x + 3 = 18$$

3. Solving equations

In solving an equation, your job is to undo the arithmetic that has been performed and get the variable alone, or isolated, on one side of the equation. Because you're undoing, you do the opposite of what has been done. To keep the equation balanced, you perform the same operation on both sides of the equation.

If there are variable terms on both sides of the equation, add or subtract to eliminate one of them. Next, add or subtract to eliminate the constant term that is on the same side as the variable term. You want to have one variable term equal to one constant term. Finally, divide both sides by the coefficient of the variable term.

EXAMPLE:

Solve: $5x + 15 = -1 + x$.

In this equation, variables appear on both sides. Subtract x from both sides:

$$4x + 15 = -1$$

Constants appear on both sides. Subtract 15 from both sides:

$$4x = -16$$

A single variable term equals a single constant term. Divide both sides by 4:

$$\frac{4x}{4} = \frac{-16}{4}$$
$$x = -4$$

4. Identities and other oddities

Sometimes when you try to isolate the variable, all the variable terms disappear. There are two reasons why this may happen. If all the variables disappear and what is left is *true,* you have an identity, an equation that is true for all real numbers. It has infinitely many solutions.

EXAMPLE:

> Solve: $5x + 3 - x = 1 + 4x + 2$.

To solve this equation, combine like terms:

$$4x + 3 = 4x + 3$$

Subtract $4x$ from both sides:

$$3 = 3$$

What is left is true, so the solution set is all real numbers.

If all the variables disappear and what is left is *false,* the equation has no solution.

EXAMPLE:

> Solve: $5x + 3 - x = 1 + 4x$.

To solve this equation, combine like terms:

$$4x + 3 = 4x + 1$$

Subtract $4x$ from both sides:

$$3 = 1$$

What is left is false, so there is no solution.

5. Absolute value

Equations that involve the absolute value of a variable expression generally have two solutions. Use simplifying and solving techniques to isolate the absolute value, and then consider that the expression between the absolute-value signs might be a positive number or a negative number. Each possibility will produce a different solution.

EXAMPLE:

> Solve: $-3|4 - 5x| + 12 = 6$.

To solve this equation, first isolate the absolute value by subtracting 12 from both sides and dividing both sides by -3:

$$-3|4 - 5x| = -6$$
$$|4 - 5x| = 2$$

If $4 - 5x$ is equal to 2, its absolute value will be 2, but the absolute value will also be 2 if $4 - 5x$ is equal to -2, so consider both possibilities:

$$4 - 5x = 2 \qquad\qquad\qquad 4 - 5x = -2$$
$$-5x = -2 \qquad\qquad\qquad -5x = -6$$
$$x = \frac{2}{5} \qquad\qquad\qquad x = \frac{6}{5}$$

6. Simple inequalities

The rules for solving inequalities are the same as those for solving equations, except at the last step. When you multiply or divide both sides of an inequality by the coefficient of the variable term, you have to make a decision about the inequality sign.

If you multiply or divide both sides of an inequality by a positive number, leave the inequality sign as is. If you multipy or divide both sides of an inequality by a negative number, reverse the inequality sign.

EXAMPLES:

1. Solve: $5x - 7 > 2x + 5$.

To solve this inequality, subtract $2x$ from both sides:

$$3x - 7 > 5$$

Add 7 to both sides:

$$3x > 12$$

Divide both sides by positive 3:

$$\frac{3x}{3} ? \frac{12}{3}$$

The inequality sign stays as is:

$$x > 4$$

2. Solve: $5t - 9 \leq 8t + 15$.

To solve this inequality, subtract $8t$ from both sides:

$$-3t - 9 \leq 15$$

Add 9 to both sides:

$$-3t \leq 24$$

Divide both sides by –3:

$$\frac{-3t}{-3} ? \frac{24}{-3}$$

Dividing by a negative reverses the direction of the inequality sign:

$$t \geq -8$$

7. Compound inequalities

Statements that condense two inequalities into a single statement are referred to as *compound inequalities.* Generally, these compound inequalities set upper and lower boundaries on the value of an expression. If it is known that the expression $5x + 4$ is between –1 and 19, inclusive, that information can be expressed by the inequality $-1 \leq 5x + 4 \leq 19$. This compound inequality condenses two statements: $5x + 4 \geq -1$ (or $-1 \leq 5x + 4$) and $5x + 4 \leq 19$.

Solving a compound inequality requires solving each of the inequalities it contains.

EXAMPLE:

> Solve $-1 \leq 5x + 4 \leq 19$.

See the compound inequality as two simple inequalities: $-1 \leq 5x + 4$ and $5x + 4 \leq 19$. Solve each inequality.

$$
\begin{array}{ll}
-1 \leq 5x + 4 & 5x + 4 \leq 19 \\
-5 \leq 5x & 5x \leq 15 \\
-1 \leq x & x \leq 3
\end{array}
$$

If desired, the two solutions can be condensed into a compound inequality: $-1 \leq x \leq 3$.

8. Absolute-value inequalities

When an equation contains an absolute-value expression, two cases must be considered. The same is true of inequalities containing absolute-value expressions, and since each case becomes an inequality, the direction of the inequality must be considered carefully.

It's important to isolate the absolute value first, as with equations, and then translate the absolute-value inequality into a compound inequality. If the absolute value of the expression is less than a constant, the value of the expression is bounded by that constant and its opposite. For example, if $|3x - 7| < 4$, then $-4 < 3x - 7 < 4$. If the absolute value of an expression is greater than a constant, as in $|8 - 2x| > 9$, then the expression itself is either greater than that constant or less than its opposite. $|8 - 2x| > 9$ translates to $8 - 2x > 9$ or $8 - 2x < -9$.

EXAMPLES:

> 1. Solve: $4 + 9|3 - 5x| \leq 22$.

Isolate the absolute value by subtracting 4 and dividing by 9. The resulting inequality, $|3-5x| \leq 2$, translates into the compound inequality $-2 \leq 3 - 5x \leq 2$. Solve each of the inequalities contained in the compound inequality:

$$-2 \leq 3 - 5x \quad \text{and} \quad 3 - 5x \leq 2$$
$$-5 \leq -5x \qquad\qquad -5x \leq -1$$
$$1 \geq x \qquad\qquad x \geq \frac{1}{5}$$

$$1 \geq x \geq \frac{1}{5}$$

Traditionally, compound inequalities like this are arranged from low to high, so it would be rewritten as $\frac{1}{5} \leq x \leq 1$, so look at answer choices carefully.

---

2. Solve $|8x+9| \geq 1$.

Since the absolute value is greater than 1, the expression $8x + 9$ is either greater than 1 or less than its opposite, so $8x + 9 \geq 1$ or $8x + 9 \leq -1$;

$$8x + 9 \geq 1 \quad \text{or} \quad 8x + 9 \leq -1$$
$$8x \geq -8 \qquad\qquad 8x \leq -10$$
$$x \geq -1 \qquad\qquad x \leq \frac{-5}{4}$$

Practice

Directions (1–2): You are given two quantities, one in Column A and one in Column B. You are to compare the two quantities and choose one of the following:

- **A.** The quantity in Column A is greater.
- **B.** The quantity in Column B is greater.
- **C.** The two quantities are equal.
- **D.** The relationship cannot be determined from the information given.

Solve: $-2(5t - 7) + 3(4 + 2t) = 38$

	Column A	Column B
1.	t	0

Solve: $(9 + 5a) - (3 - 6a) = 28$

	Column A	Column B
2.	a	0

Directions (3–10): Unless otherwise directed, select a single answer choice. For numeric-entry questions, enter a number in the box(es) below the question. Equivalent forms of the correct answer, such as 2.5 and 2.50, are all correct. Fractions do not need to be reduced to lowest terms. Enter the exact answer unless the question asks you to round your answer.

3. Choose all the equations equivalent to $2x - 5 + 3x = 7 - 4x + 78$.

    A. $0 = 7 - 4x + 78$
    B. $2x - 5 + 3x = 3x + 78$
    C. $9x - 5 = 85$
    D. $2x - 8x = 7 - 4x + 78$
    E. $5x - 5 = 7 - 4x + 78$
    F. $9x = 90$
    G. $5x - 5 = -4x + 85$
    H. $x = 10$

4. Select all the numbers that solve the inequality $2(-7z - 5) < -3(4z + 6)$.

    A. $z = -4$
    B. $z = -7$
    C. $z = -14$
    D. $z = 4$
    E. $z = 7$
    F. $z = 14$
    G. $z = 28$

5. Solve : $1 - (2y - 1) = -4(y - 3)$.

    A. $y = 6$
    B. $y = 5$
    C. $y = 2$
    D. $y = -5$
    E. $y = -6$

6. Solve $ad - bc = x$ for d.

    A. $d = \dfrac{x + bc}{a}$
    B. $d = x + bc - a$
    C. $d = \dfrac{x - a}{bc}$
    D. $d = \dfrac{x}{a} + bc$
    E. $d = \dfrac{x}{a} - bc$

7. Solve: $-5p + 12 \geq -p + 8$.

   A. $p \leq 1$
   B. $p \geq 1$
   C. $p \leq -1$
   D. $p \geq -1$
   E. $p \geq \frac{2}{3}$

8. Solve: $15 - 8y \leq 3y + 4$.

   A. $y \leq 1$
   B. $y \geq 1$
   C. $y \leq \frac{11}{5}$
   D. $y \leq -1$
   E. $y \geq -1$

9. Solve: $4|9 - 2x| - 7 = 1$.

10. Solve: $2|3x - 7| + 5 = 37$.

Answers

1. **B** Remove parentheses by applying the distributive property, and combine like terms on the left side: $-2(5t - 7) + 3(4 + 2t) = -10t + 14 + 12 + 6t = -4t + 26$. Subtract 26 from both sides and divide by -4:

$$-4t + 26 = 38$$
$$-4t = 12$$
$$t = \frac{12}{-4} = -3$$

   Because $0 > -3$, Column B is larger.

2. **A** The first set of parentheses has no real purpose, but the second set indicates that the minus sign applies to the entire quantity, so remove the parentheses by "distributing the minus"—multiplying the quantity by -1.

$$(9 + 5a) - (3 - 6a) = 28$$
$$9 + 5a - 3 + 6a = 28$$

Combine like terms on the left side. Subtract 6 from both sides and divide by 11.

$$6 + 11a = 28$$
$$11a = 22$$
$$a = 2$$

Because $2 > 0$, Column A is larger.

3. **C, E, F, G, H** The most common way to produce an equivalent equation is to perform one or more of the steps required to solve the equation, so work through your solution, and look for your steps among the choices. Combine like terms on each side of the equation to simplify before beginning to solve.

$$2x - 5 + 3x = 7 - 4x + 78$$
$$5x - 5 = 7 - 4x + 78$$
$$5x - 5 = -4x + 85$$

Simplifying the left side produces choice E, and combining like terms on the right side gives you choice G.

Eliminate one of the variable terms; by adding $4x$ to both sides, you have choice C. Add 5 to both sides, and you have choice F. Finally, divide both sides by 9, and you have choice H.

$$5x - 5 = -4x + 85$$
$$9x - 5 = 85$$
$$9x = 90$$
$$x = 10$$

4. **E, F, G** Remove the parentheses by distributing.

$$2(-7z - 5) = -3(4z + 6)$$
$$-14z - 10 = -3(4z + 6)$$
$$-14z - 10 = -12z - 18$$

Add $12z$ to both sides to eliminate a variable term, and then add 10 to both sides to eliminate a constant term. Finally, divide both sides by –2, and remember to reverse the inequality when you divide by a negative.

$$-2z - 10 > -18$$
$$-2z < -8$$
$$z > 4$$

The solution set for this inequality includes all numbers greater than 4, so choices E, F, and G all solve the inequality.

5. **B** On the left side, "distribute the negative"—that is, multiply by –1—and combine like terms. On the right side, distribute the –4.

$$1 - (2y - 1) = -4(y - 3)$$
$$1 - 2y + 1 = -4(y - 3)$$
$$2 - 2y = -4(y - 3)$$
$$2 - 2y = -4y + 12$$

Add $4y$ to both sides, then subtract 2 from both sides, and finally divide both sides by 2.

$$2 - 2y + 4y = 12$$
$$2 + 2y = 12$$
$$2y = 10$$
$$y = 5$$

6. **A** Don't be distracted by the use of letters rather than numbers. Your task is to solve for d, so treat that as the variable, and treat everything else as numbers. If it helps you, make up numbers for the other parameters and think about what steps you would take to solve. Follow those steps here as well. To get the d term by itself, add bc to both sides.

$$ad - bc = x$$
$$ad = x + bc$$

Then divide both sides by a.

$$d = \frac{x + bc}{a}$$

7. **A** Solve inequalities just as you solve equations, but if you divide both sides by a negative number, reverse the inequality. Add p to both sides, and then subtract 12 from both sides.

$$-5p + 12 \geq -p + 8$$
$$-5p + 12 + p \geq 8$$
$$-4p + 12 \geq 8$$
$$-4p \geq -4$$

Divide both sides by –4, and reverse the direction of the inequality sign.

$$\frac{-4p}{-4} \leq \frac{-4}{-4}$$
$$p \leq 1$$

8. **B** Add $8y$ to both sides, and then subtract 4 from both sides. Divide both sides by 11. Since you're dividing by a positive number, there is no change in the inequality sign.

$$15 - 8y \leq 3y + 4$$
$$15 \leq 3y + 4 + 8y$$
$$15 \leq 11y + 4$$
$$11 \leq 11y$$
$$1 \leq y$$

9. $\frac{11}{2}$ **or** $\frac{7}{2}$ Begin by isolating the absolute value. Add 7 to both sides, and divide both sides by 4.

$$4|9 - 2x| - 7 = 1$$
$$4|9 - 2x| = 8$$
$$|9 - 2x| = 2$$

Since the absolute value is equal to 2, the expression between the absolute value signs is either 2 or –2.

$$-2 = 9 - 2x \text{ or } 9 - 2x = 2$$

Solve each equation by subtracting 9 from both sides and dividing by –2.

$$-2 = 9 - 2x \quad \text{or} \quad 9 - 2x = 2$$
$$-11 = -2x \qquad\qquad -2x = -7$$
$$\frac{11}{2} = x \qquad\qquad x = \frac{7}{2}$$

10. –3 or $\frac{23}{3}$ Isolate the absolute value by subtracting 5 from both sides and dividing both sides by 2.

$$2|3x - 7| + 5 = 37$$
$$2|3x - 7| = 32$$
$$|3x - 7| = 16$$

Since the absolute value is equal to 16, the expression in the absolute value signs must be either 16 or –16. Solve both equations by adding 7 to both sides and dividing by 3.

$$-16 = 3x - 7 \quad \text{or} \quad 3x - 7 = 16$$
$$-9 = 3x \qquad\qquad 3x = 23$$
$$-3 = x \qquad\qquad x = \frac{23}{3}$$

B. Simultaneous Equations

When you're presented with several equations involving several variables and asked to find the values of the variables that will make all the equations true at the same time, the equations are referred to as simultaneous equations or a system of equations. In order to arrive at a unique solution, you have to have as many equations as variables. Fortunately, most of the systems you'll see on the GRE are sets of two equations with two variables. The solution of such a system of equations is a pair of values that makes both equations true. A system of equations may have one solution, no solution, or infinitely many solutions.

It is not possible to solve for the values of two variables in the same equation. So, solving a system of equations requires that you eliminate one variable and solve for the variable remaining. Once you've found the value of one variable, you can substitute to find the other.

1. Substitution

To solve a system by substitution, choose one equation and isolate a variable. Then go to the other equation and replace that variable with the equivalent expression. You should have an equation with only one variable, which you can solve. When you know the value of one variable, choose an equation, replace the known variable by its value, and solve for the variable remaining:

EXAMPLE:

Solve: $\begin{cases} 3x - y = -15 \\ 5x + 2y = -14 \end{cases}$

To solve this system, choose one equation and isolate a variable. Isolate y in the first equation:

$$3x - y = -15$$
$$3x = -15 + y$$
$$3x + 15 = y$$

Use this expression for y to replace y in the second equation. Substitute $3x + 15$ for y in the second equation. Clear parentheses and combine like terms. Solve for x:

$$5x + 2y = -14$$
$$5x + 2(3x + 15) = -14$$
$$5x + 6x + 30 = -14$$
$$11x + 30 = -14$$
$$11x = -44$$
$$x = -4$$

Substitute the value found into one of the original equations. Substitute -4 for x in the first equation. Solve for y:

$$3x - y = -15$$
$$3(-4) - y = -15$$
$$-12 - y = -15$$
$$-y = -3$$
$$y = 3$$

2. Elimination

The elimination method uses addition or subtraction to eliminate one of the variables. If the coefficient of one variable is the same in both equations, subtracting one equation from the other will eliminate that variable. If the coefficients are opposites, adding will eliminate the variable. When you've eliminated one variable, solve and then use substitution to find the value of the other variable.

EXAMPLE:

Solve: $\begin{cases} 8a - 2b = 18 \\ 3a + 2b = -7 \end{cases}$

Adding the equations eliminates b.

$$8a - 2b = 18$$
$$\underline{3a + 2b = -7}$$
$$11a = 11$$

Solve for a.

$$\frac{11a}{11} = \frac{11}{11}$$
$$a = 1$$

Substitute 1 for a in the second equation.

$$3a + 2b = -7$$
$$3(1) + 2b = -7$$
$$3 + 2b = -7$$

Solve for b.

$$2b = -10$$
$$b = -5$$

EXAMPLE:

Solve: $\begin{cases} -5p + 4t = -21 \\ 3p + 4t = 19 \end{cases}$

Subtracting the equations eliminates t.

$$-5p + 4t = -21$$
$$\underline{3p + 4t = 19}$$
$$-8p = -40$$

Solve for p.

$$p = \frac{-40}{-8}$$
$$p = 5$$

Substitute 5 for p in the second equation.

$$3p + 4t = 19$$
$$3(5) + 4t = 19$$
$$15 + 4t = 19$$

Solve for t.

$$4t = 4$$
$$t = 1$$

3. Elimination with multiplication

If neither adding nor subtracting will eliminate a variable (because the coefficients don't match), it's still possible to use the elimination method. First, you must multiply each equation by a constant to produce more agreeable coefficients. The fastest way to do this is generally to choose the variable you want to eliminate, and then multiply each equation by the coefficient of that variable from the other equation:

Solve: $\begin{cases} 3x + 4y = -34 \\ 2x - 5y = 31 \end{cases}$

In order to eliminate y, multiply the first equation by 5 and the second equation by 4.

$$5(3x + 4y = -34)$$
$$4(2x - 5y = 31)$$

Adding the equations eliminates y.

$$15x + 20y = -170$$
$$\underline{8x - 20y = 124}$$
$$23x = -46$$

Solve for x.

$$x = -2$$

Substitute -2 for x in the first equation.

$$3x + 4y = -34$$
$$3(-2) + 4y = -34$$
$$-6 + 4y = -34$$

Solve for y.

$$4y = -28$$
$$y = -7$$

Practice

Directions (1–4): You are given two quantities, one in Column A and one in Column B. You are to compare the two quantities and choose one of the following:

    A.   The quantity in Column A is greater.
    B.   The quantity in Column B is greater.
    C.   The two quantities are equal.
    D.   The relationship cannot be determined from the information given.

$$-x + 2y = -5$$
$$7x - 3y = 2$$

Column A	Column B
1. x	y

$$\frac{1}{2}x - \frac{1}{3}y = 14$$
$$\frac{1}{5}x + \frac{3}{4}y = -5$$

Column A	Column B
2. $-3x$	$-5y$

$$1.5x - 3.75y = 15$$
$$-2.5x + 7.5y = 35$$

Column A	Column B
3. $x - y$	$y - x$

$$3x - 5y = -4$$
$$7x + 2y = 18$$

Column A	Column B
4. x	y

Directions (5–10): Unless otherwise directed, select a single answer choice. For numeric-entry questions, enter a number in the box(es) below the question. Equivalent forms of the correct answer, such as 2.5 and 2.50, are all correct. Fractions do not need to be reduced to lowest terms. Enter the exact answer unless the question asks you to round your answer.

5. A box containing one drill and two hammers weighs 10 pounds. A box containing three drills and one hammer weighs 25 pounds. Choose all the correct statements below.

   A. Two drills and two hammers weigh 18 pounds.
   B. A drill and a hammer weigh 10 pounds.
   C. A drill weighs 9 pounds.
   D. A drill and 5 hammers weigh 13 pounds.
   E. A hammer weighs 1 pound.
   F. Three drills and five hammers weigh 29 pounds.
   G. Five drills and two hammers weigh 37 pounds.

6. Cereal is sold in large and small boxes. The large box holds 6 ounces less than twice the small box, and costs $1.39 more than the small box. Three large boxes and five small boxes contain a total of 290 ounces. You need at least 500 ounces of cereal and you cannot spend more than $60. If the small box sells for $3.79, choose all the combinations that meet your needs and budget.

A. 4 large boxes and 10 small boxes
B. 5 large boxes and 9 small boxes
C. 6 large boxes and 7 small boxes
D. 7 large boxes and 5 small boxes
E. 8 large boxes and 4 small boxes

7. Solve: $\begin{cases} x + y = -8 \\ x - y = 8 \end{cases}$

A. $(0, 8)$
B. $(0, -8)$
C. $(-8, 0)$
D. $(8, 0)$
E. $(-8, 8)$

8. Solve: $\begin{cases} 5x + 2y = -14 \\ 8x - 9y = -59 \end{cases}$

A. $(-3, 4)$
B. $(3, -4)$
C. $(-4, 3)$
D. $(4, -3)$
E. $(-4, -3)$

9. Find the value of x and the value of y: $\begin{cases} y = 2x - 17 \\ x - y = 4 \end{cases}$

$x = \boxed{}$

$y = \boxed{}$

10. Find the value of x and the value of y: $\begin{cases} x + 5y = 27 \\ 9y - 2x = 3 \end{cases}$

$x = \boxed{}$

$y = \boxed{}$

Answers

1. **A** Multiply the first equation by 7 and add to eliminate the x terms.

$$\begin{aligned}-x+2y&=-5\\7x-3y&=2\end{aligned} \Rightarrow \begin{aligned}7(-x+2y=-5)\\7x-3y=2\end{aligned} \Rightarrow \begin{aligned}-7x+14y=-35\\\underline{7x-3y=2}\\11y=-33\end{aligned}$$

Divide both sides by 11 to solve for y.

$$11y=-33$$
$$y=-3$$

Choose one of the original equations and replace y with -3, and solve for x.

$$-x+2y=-5$$
$$-x+2(-3)=-5$$
$$-x-6=-5$$
$$-x=1$$
$$x=-1$$

2. **B** It may be helpful to clear the fractions before attempting to solve. For each equation, find the common denominator of the fractions, and multiply through by that number.

$$\begin{aligned}\frac{1}{2}x-\frac{1}{3}y&=14\\\frac{1}{5}x+\frac{3}{4}y&=-5\end{aligned} \Rightarrow \begin{aligned}6\left(\frac{1}{2}x-\frac{1}{3}y=14\right)\\20\left(\frac{1}{5}x+\frac{3}{4}y=-5\right)\end{aligned} \Rightarrow \begin{aligned}3x-2y=84\\4x+15y=-100\end{aligned}$$

Multiply the top equation by 15 and the bottom equation by 2; then add to eliminate the y terms. Divide by 53 to solve for x.

$$\begin{aligned}15(3x-2y=84)\\2(4x+15y=-100)\end{aligned} \Rightarrow \begin{aligned}45x-30y=1260\\\underline{8x+30y=-200}\\53x\qquad=1060\\x\qquad=20\end{aligned}$$

Choose one of the original equations, replace x with 20, and solve for y.

$$\frac{1}{2}x-\frac{1}{3}y=14$$
$$\frac{1}{2}(20)-\frac{1}{3}y=14$$
$$10-\frac{1}{3}y=14$$
$$-\frac{1}{3}y=4$$
$$y=4\div-\frac{1}{3}=\frac{4}{1}\cdot\frac{-3}{1}=-12$$

Since $x=20$ and $y=-12$, $-3x=-60$ and $-5y=60$, so $-5y>-3x$.

3. **A** If the decimals make the problem seem difficult, multiply both equations by 100 to move the decimal points two places right and eliminate the decimals.

$$
\begin{array}{c}
1.5x - 3.75y = 15 \\
-2.5x + 7.5y = 35
\end{array}
\Rightarrow
\begin{array}{c}
150x - 375y = 1{,}500 \\
-250x + 750y = 3{,}500
\end{array}
$$

Multiply the top equation by 2, then add to eliminate the y terms, and solve for x by dividing by 50.

$$
\begin{array}{c}
150x - 375y = 1{,}500 \\
-250x + 750y = 3{,}500
\end{array}
\Rightarrow
\begin{array}{c}
2(150x - 375y = 1{,}500) \\
-250x + 750y = 3{,}500
\end{array}
\Rightarrow
\begin{array}{c}
300x - 750y = 3{,}000 \\
-250x + 750y = 3{,}500 \\
\hline
50x = 6{,}500 \\
x = \dfrac{6{,}500}{50} = 130
\end{array}
$$

Replace x with 130 in one of the original equations, and solve for y.

$$
\begin{aligned}
1.5x - 3.75y &= 15 \\
1.5(130) - 3.75y &= 15 \\
195 - 3.75y &= 15 \\
-3.75y &= 15 - 195 \\
-3.75y &= -180 \\
y = \frac{-180}{-3.75} = \frac{18{,}000}{375} &= \frac{25 \cdot 3 \cdot 5 \cdot 48}{25 \cdot 3 \cdot 5} = 48
\end{aligned}
$$

Then realize that $x - y = -1(y - x)$, so evaluate $x - y = 130 - 48 > 0$. Since $x - y$ is positive, $y - x$ will be negative, and $x - y$ is larger.

4. **C** To eliminate the y terms, multiply the top equation by 2 and the bottom equation by 5, and then add. Divide both sides by 41 to solve for x.

$$
\begin{array}{c}
3x - 5y = -4 \\
7x + 2y = 18
\end{array}
\Rightarrow
\begin{array}{c}
2(3x - 5y = -4) \\
5(7x + 2y = 18)
\end{array}
\Rightarrow
\begin{array}{c}
6x - 10y = -8 \\
35x + 10y = 90 \\
\hline
41x = 82 \\
x = 2
\end{array}
$$

To find the value of y, choose one of the original equations, replace x with 2, and solve for y.

$$
\begin{aligned}
3x - 5y &= -4 \\
3(2) - 5y &= -4 \\
6 - 5y &= -4 \\
-5y &= -10 \\
y &= 2
\end{aligned}
$$

5. A, D, E, F Let d be the weight of a drill and h be the weight of a hammer. Then $1d + 2h = 10$ and $3d + 1h = 25$. Solve the first equation for d: $d = 10 - 2h$. Substitute into the second equation.

$$3d + 1h = 25$$
$$3(10 - 2h) + 1h = 25$$
$$30 - 6h + 1h = 25$$
$$30 - 5h = 25$$
$$-5h = -5$$
$$h = 1$$

A hammer weighs 1 pound, so choice E is true. Replace h with 1 in one of the original equations.

$$1d + 2h = 10$$
$$1d + 2(1) = 10$$
$$d = 8$$

A drill weighs 8 pounds, so choice C is not true. Calculate the weight of each combination.

- **Choice A:** Two drills and two hammers: $2 \times 8 + 2 \times 1 = 16 + 2 = 18$ pounds
- **Choice B:** A drill and a hammer: $8 + 1 = 9$ pounds
- **Choice D:** A drill and 5 hammers: $8 + 5 \times 1 = 8 + 5 = 13$ pounds
- **Choice F:** Three drills and five hammers: $3 \times 8 + 5 \times 1 = 24 + 5 = 29$ pounds
- **Choice G:** Five drills and two hammers: $5 \times 8 + 2 \times 1 = 40 + 2 = 42$ pounds

Choices A, D, and F are also true.

6. E Let x be the number of ounces in each large box and y be the number of ounces in each small box. Then $x = 2y - 6$ and $3x + 5y = 290$. Substitute for x in the second equation.

$$3x + 5y = 290$$
$$3(2y - 6) + 5y = 290$$
$$6y - 18 + 5y = 290$$
$$11y - 18 = 290$$
$$11y = 308$$
$$y = 28$$

The small box contains 28 ounces, so the large box contains $2(28) - 6 = 56 - 6 = 50$ ounces.

Check each choice to see if it gives you the required 500 ounces.

- **Choice A:** 4 large and 10 small = $4 \times 50 + 10 \times 28 = 200 + 280 = 480$
- **Choice B:** 5 large and 9 small = $5 \times 50 + 9 \times 28 = 250 + 252 = 502$
- **Choice C:** 6 large and 7 small = $6 \times 50 + 7 \times 28 = 300 + 196 = 496$
- **Choice D:** 7 large and 5 small = $7 \times 50 + 5 \times 28 = 350 + 140 = 490$
- **Choice E:** 8 large and 4 small = $8 \times 50 + 4 \times 28 = 400 + 112 = 512$

Only B and E meet the requirement for 500 ounces. Check the cost on those two. The small box is $3.79 and the large box is $3.79 + $1.39 = $5.18. Choice B will cost 9($3.79) + 9($5.18) = $60.01. Choice D will cost 4($3.79) + 8($5.18) = $56.60. Only E fits in the $60 budget.

7. **B** Add the two equations to eliminate y. The value of x can be found by dividing.

$$
\begin{aligned}
x + y &= -8 \\
\underline{x - y = 8} \\
2x \quad &= 0 \\
x \quad &= 0
\end{aligned}
$$

Substitute 0 for x in one of the original equations, and the value of y becomes clear: $y = -8$.

8. **C** Multiply the first equation by 9, multiply the second equation by 2, and then add to eliminate the y terms. Divide by 61 to solve for x.

$$
\begin{array}{ccc}
\begin{aligned}
5x + 2y &= -14 \\
8x - 9y &= -59
\end{aligned}
&\Rightarrow&
\begin{aligned}
9(5x + 2y = -14) \\
2(8x - 9y = -59)
\end{aligned}
&\Rightarrow&
\begin{aligned}
45x + 18y &= -126 \\
\underline{16x - 18y = -118} \\
61x \quad &= -244 \\
x &= -4
\end{aligned}
\end{array}
$$

Replace x with -4 in one of the original equations, and solve for y.

$$
\begin{aligned}
5x + 2y &= -14 \\
5(-4) + 2y &= -14 \\
-20 + 2y &= -14 \\
2y &= 6 \\
y &= 3
\end{aligned}
$$

9. **$x = 13$, $y = 9$** The first equation gives an expression for y that can be substituted into the other equation. Solve for y.

$$
\begin{aligned}
y &= 2x - 17 \\
x - y &= 4 \\
x - (2x - 17) &= 4 \\
x - 2x + 17 &= 4 \\
-x + 17 &= 4 \\
-x &= -13 \\
x &= 13
\end{aligned}
$$

Substitute 13 for x in the first equation to find that y is 9.

$$
\begin{aligned}
y &= 2x - 17 \\
y &= 2(13) - 17 \\
y &= 26 - 17 = 9
\end{aligned}
$$

10. $x = 12, y = 3$ Solve the first equation for x, and substitute the resulting expression into the second equation. Solve for y.

$$x + 5y = 27$$
$$x = 27 - 5y$$
$$9y - 2x = 3$$
$$9y - 2(27 - 5y) = 3$$
$$9y - 54 + 10y = 3$$
$$19y - 54 = 3$$
$$19y = 57$$
$$y = \frac{57}{19} = 3$$

Return to the original equation and replace y with 3. Solve for x.

$$x + 5y = 27$$
$$x + 5(3) = 27$$
$$x + 15 = 27$$
$$x = 12$$

C. Multiplying and Factoring

Just as two numbers can be multiplied and a single number can be expressed as a product of factors, polynomials can be multiplied and factored as well.

1. The distributive property

To multiply a single term times a sum or difference, distribute the multiplication to each term of the sum or difference.

EXAMPLE:

Simplify $-7x^2(5x^3 - 4x^2 + 8x - 1)$.

The term $-7x^2$ must be multiplied by each of the four terms in the parentheses:

$$-7x^2(5x^3 - 4x^2 + 8x - 1) = (-7x^2 \cdot 5x^3) - (-7x^2 \cdot 4x^2) + (-7x^2 \cdot 8x) - (-7x^2 \cdot 1)$$

Simplify each term, paying careful attention to signs:

$$(-7x^2 \cdot 5x^3) - (-7x^2 \cdot 4x^2) + (-7x^2 \cdot 8x) - (-7x^2 \cdot 1) = -35x^5 + 28x^4 - 56x^3 + 7x^2$$

157

2. Greatest common factor

Expressing a polynomial as the product of a single term and a simpler polynomial requires using the distributive property in reverse. You know the answer to the multiplication problem and you're trying to re-create the question.

To factor out a greatest common factor:

1. **Determine the largest number that will divide the numerical coefficient of every term.**
2. **Determine the highest power of each variable that is common to all terms.**
3. **Place the common factor outside the parentheses.**
4. **Inside the parentheses, create a new polynomial by dividing each term of the original by the common factor.**

EXAMPLE:

Factor $6x^5y^2 - 9x^4y^4 + 27x^3y^7$.

The largest number that divides 6, 9, and 27 is 3; the largest power of x common to all terms is x^3; and the largest power of y common to all terms is y^2. So the greatest common factor is $3x^3y^2$.

$$\frac{6x^5y^2}{3x^3y^2} = 2x^2 \qquad \frac{-9x^4y^4}{3x^3y^2} = -3xy^2 \qquad \frac{27x^3y^7}{3x^3y^2} = 9y^5$$

Place the common factor outside the parentheses, and the simpler polynomial inside:

$$6x^5y^2 - 9x^4y^4 + 27x^3y^7 = 3x^3y^2(2x^2 - 3xy^2 + 9y^5)$$

3. FOIL

The FOIL rule is a memory device to help you multiply two binomials. The letters in FOIL stand for:

First $\quad (x+5)(x-3) \Rightarrow x \cdot x$

Outer $\quad (x+5)(x-3) \Rightarrow x \cdot -3$

Inner $\quad (x+5)(x-3) \Rightarrow 5 \cdot x$

Last $\quad (x+5)(x-3) \Rightarrow 5 \cdot -3$

To multiply binomials, multiply the first terms of the binomials, multiply the outer terms, multiply the inner terms, and multiply the last terms of the binomials. Combine like terms (usually the inner and the outer).

EXAMPLE:

Multiply $(2x - 7)(3x + 4)$.

First: $2x \cdot 3x$. Outer: $2x \cdot 4$. Inner: $-7 \cdot 3x$. Last: $-7 \cdot 4$.

$$(2x - 7)(3x + 4) = (2x \cdot 3x) + (4 \cdot 2x) + (-7 \cdot 3x) + (-7 \cdot 4)$$
$$= 6x^2 + 8x - 21x - 28$$
$$= 6x^2 - 13x - 28$$

4. Factoring

The FOIL rule helps you multiply two binomials to get a trinomial. To go backward and turn a trinomial into the product of two binomials, begin by putting the trinomial in standard form ($ax^2 + bx + c$). List the factors of the squared term and the factors of the constant term. Set up parentheses with spaces for the two binomials. Put factors of the squared term in the FIRST positions and factors of the constant term in the LAST positions. Try different arrangements of these factors, checking to see if the INNER and OUTER products can combine to produce the desired middle term. When you've found the correct combination, place signs. If the constant term is positive, both signs will be the same as the sign of the middle term. If the constant term is negative, one factor should have a plus and the other a minus. Place the signs so that the larger of the INNER and the OUTER has the sign of the middle term.

EXAMPLE:

Factor $6x^2 + 5x - 56$.

Possible factors for $6x^2$ are $3x \cdot 2x$ or $6x \cdot x$. The possible factors of 56 are $1 \cdot 56$, $2 \cdot 28$, $4 \cdot 14$, or $7 \cdot 8$. There are many possible arrangements, but the fact that the middle term is small is a hint that you want factors that are close together, so start with $3x \cdot 2x$ and $7 \cdot 8$.

$(3x \underline{} 7)(2x \underline{} 8)$ produces an OUTER of $24x$ and an INNER of $14x$. While $24x$ and $14x$ could add to $38x$ or subtract to $10x$, they cannot produce a middle term of $5x$, so switch the 7 and the 8.

$(3x \underline{} 8)(2x \underline{} 7)$ produces an OUTER of $21x$ and an INNER of $16x$, which will subtract to $5x$.

The constant term is negative, -56, so place one $-$ and one $+$. The middle term, $5x$, is positive, so the larger of the INNER and the OUTER must be positive. $21x$ is larger than $16x$, so you want $+21x$ and $-16x$, which means the factors are $(3x - 8)(2x + 7)$.

5. Special factoring patterns

You should memorize certain patterns of multiplication, either because they give surprising results or because they appear frequently. The most important is the **difference of squares:**

$$(a + b)(a - b) = a^2 - b^2$$

This form is surprising because the product of two binomials usually produces a trinomial, but here the INNER and the OUTER add to zero, leaving only two terms. It is also a common form, used, for example, when rationalizing denominators.

EXAMPLES:

1. Multiply: $(5x + 4)(5x - 4)$.

Since the two factors are the sum and difference of the same two terms, the difference of squares rule applies: $(5x + 4)(5x - 4) = (5x)^2 - 4^2 = 25x^2 - 16$.

2. Factor: $(3x - 7)^2 - 36$.

Don't let the extra quantity intimidate you—this is a difference of squares: The quantity $(3x - 7)^2$ minus 6^2. So, $a = 3x - 7$ and $b = 6$. Then the factors are $(a + b)(a - b)$ or $[(3x - 7) + 6] \times [(3x - 7) - 6]$. Simplifying each factor gives you $(3x - 1)(3x - 13)$.

Another form commonly encountered is the **perfect square trinomial.** Of course, you can always square a binomial by using the FOIL rule, and you can factor a perfect square trinomial by trial and error, but recognizing the form will help you get through problems faster.

$$(a + b)^2 = a^2 + 2ab + b^2$$
$$(a - b)^2 = a^2 - 2ab + b^2$$

Notice that the first and last terms are squares and the middle term is twice the product of the terms of the binomial. The sign of the middle term matches the sign connecting the terms of the binomial.

EXAMPLE:

$(8x - 9)^2 =$

A. $8x^2 - 81$
B. $8x^2 + 81$
C. $64x^2 - 81$
D. $64x^2 + 144x - 81$
E. $64x^2 - 144x + 81$

The correct answer is **E.** The first term must be $(8x)^2$ or $64x^2$ so you can eliminate choices A and B immediately. Squaring a binomial produces a trinomial, not a binomial, so eliminate choice C. In choosing between D and E, check the signs. The last term of a square trinomial should always be positive, and the middle term should match the connecting sign of the binomial. Therefore, $(8x - 9)^2 = 64x^2 - 144x + 81$.

You also may want to know the forms of the **sum and difference of cubes.**

$$a^3 + b^3 = (a + b)(a^2 - ab + b^2)$$
$$a^3 - b^3 = (a - b)(a^2 + ab + b^2)$$

The rules are similar, which means less to memorize but trouble keeping them straight. Remember that the binomial factor gets the same sign as the original expression. Each rule is entitled to one minus sign, so the sum of cubes must use its minus sign in the trinomial.

EXAMPLE:

$(3t + 5p)(9t^2 - 15tp + 25p^2) =$

A. $3t^3 + 5p^3$
B. $3t^3 - 5p^3$
C. $27t^3 + 125p^3$
D. $27t^3 - 125p^3$
E. $27t^3 + 5p^3$

The correct answer is **C**. If you multiply $(3t + 5p)(9t^2 - 15tp + 25p^2)$, you'll invest far too much time and risk making mistakes. Instead, recognize the form. The trinomial has squares as its first and last term, and the middle term is the product of their square roots. This will be either a sum or a difference of cubes, and the answer choices confirm that analysis. The binomial terms are connected by a plus, so it is a sum of cubes, eliminating choices B and D. The first term must be $(3t)^3$, or $27t^3$, and a quick look at the problem, which would require you to begin by multiplying $3t$ by $9t^2$, will remind you of this. Eliminate choice A, and carefully compare choices C and E. The numerical coefficient of p^3 is wrong in choice E, so the correct answer is C.

Many complicated-looking expressions can be factored by applying the special forms. The expression $(3x - 1)^2 - \dfrac{4x^2}{9y^2}$ might look impossible at first glance, but the first term is a square, and so is the second— it can be rewritten as $\left(\dfrac{2x}{3y}\right)^2$. The whole expression is a difference of squares with $a = 3x - 1$ and $b = \dfrac{2x}{3y}$. The factors are $\left((3x - 1) + \dfrac{2x}{3y}\right)$ and $\left((3x - 1) - \dfrac{2x}{3y}\right)$.

Tip: Learning to look for patterns will help you solve many problems.

Practice

Directions (1–2): You are given two quantities, one in Column A and one in Column B. You are to compare the two quantities and choose one of the following:

    A.   The quantity in Column A is greater.
    B.   The quantity in Column B is greater.
    C.   The two quantities are equal.
    D.   The relationship cannot be determined from the information given.

$$24x^5 - 32x^8 = ax^5(b - cx^3)$$

Column A	Column B
$c - b$	$c - a$

1.

$$(-2x - 3)(2x + 5) = ax^2 + bx + c$$

Column A	Column B
b	c

2.

Directions (3–10): Unless otherwise directed, select a single answer choice. For numeric-entry questions, enter a number in the box(es) below the question. Equivalent forms of the correct answer, such as 2.5 and 2.50, are all correct. Fractions do not need to be reduced to lowest terms. Enter the exact answer unless the question asks you to round your answer.

3. Which of the following are possible factorizations of $8x^2 - 200y^2$?

   A. $(x + 5y)(8x - 40y)$
   B. $(4x + 20y)(2x - 10y)$
   C. $(4x + 100y)(4x - 100y)$
   D. $2(2x + 5y)(2x - 15y)$
   E. $2(2x + 10y)(2x - 10y)$
   F. $8(x + 25y)(x - y)$
   G. $8(x + 5y)(x - 5y)$

4. Which of the following are possible factorizations of $9x^2 - 30x + 25$?

   A. $(3x + 5)^2$
   B. $(3x - 5)^2$
   C. $(3x + 5)(3x - 5)$

5. The product $\left(\frac{1}{2}t + 12\right)\left(\frac{1}{2}t - 12\right)$ is equal to which of the following?

   A. $\frac{1}{2}t^2 + 144$

   B. $\frac{1}{2}t^2 - 144$

   C. $t^2 - 144$

   D. $\frac{1}{4}t^2 + 144$

   E. $\frac{1}{4}t^2 - 144$

6. $-3t^3(2t - 1) =$

   A. $-6t^4 - 1$
   B. $-6t^4 - 3t^3$
   C. $-6t^4 + 3t^3$
   D. $-t^4 + 3t^3$
   E. $-5t^4 - 3t^3$

7. Which of the following is the correct factorization for $32x^2 - 72$?

   A. $(16x - 36)^2$
   B. $(16x + 36)^2$
   C. $(16x + 36)(16x - 36)$
   D. $8(2x - 3)(2x + 3)$
   E. $(8x + 3)(4x - 3)$

8. $(5x + 3)(2x - 1) =$

    A. $10x^2 + x - 3$
    B. $10x^2 - 3$
    C. $10x^2 + 11x - 3$
    D. $10x^2 - 11x - 3$
    E. $7x^2 - 3$

9. $2x^2 - 11x - 21 = (x + a)(2x + b)$. Find a and b.

$$a = \boxed{}$$

$$b = \boxed{}$$

10. Find the coefficient of x when the product $(4x - 7)(2x + 5)$ is expressed in $ax^2 + bx + c$ form.

$$\boxed{}$$

Answers

1. **A** $24x^5 - 32x^8 = 8x^5(3 - 4x^3)$, so $a = 8$, $b = 3$, and $c = 4$. Then $c - b = 4 - 3 = 1$ and $c - a = 4 - 8 = -4$.

2. **B** $(-2x - 3)(2x + 5) = -4x^2 - 10x - 6x - 15 = -4x^2 - 16x - 15$, so $b = -16$ and $c = -15$.

3. **A, B, E, G** Note that the question asks for possible factorizations, not the best factorization or a complete factorization. Checking the choices by multiplying is probably faster than trying to think of all the different way you could factor $8x^2 - 200y^2$. First check choices A, B, and C, to see if the FIRSTs multiply to $8x^2$.

  ■ **Choice A:** $(x + 5y)(8x - 40y)$
  ■ **Choice B:** $(4x + 20y)(2x - 10y)$
  ■ **Choice C:** $(4x + 100y)(4x - 100y)$

The FIRSTs multiply to $8x^2$ for choices A and B but not choice C, so eliminate C. Continue checking choices A and B. The LASTs multiply to $-200y^2$, and the INNER and OUTER are $40xy$ and $-40xy$, so they add to zero. Choices A and B will work.

Choices D through F have a common factor as well as a pair of binomials, so the check is a little more complicated. Do the FOIL first.

  ■ **Choice D:** $2(2x + 5y)(2x - 15y) = 2(4x^2 - 30xy + 10xy - 75y^2)$. You can see that the INNER and OUTER won't add to zero, so eliminate choice D.
  ■ **Choice E:** $2(2x + 10y)(2x - 10y) = 2(4x^2 - 20xy + 20xy - 100y^2)$.
  ■ **Choice F:** $8(x + 25y)(x - y) = 8(x^2 - xy + 25xy - 25y^2)$. The middle terms won't add to zero, so eliminate choice F.
  ■ **Choice G:** $8(x + 5y)(x - 5y) = 8(x^2 - 5xy + 5xy - 25y^2)$.

Finish multiplying E and G to verify that both are factorizations of $8x^2 - 200y^2$.

4. **B** $9x^2 - 30x + 25$ is a perfect square trinomial, and so equal to $(3x - 5)^2$. Choice A will produce $9x^2 + 30x + 25$, and choice C will produce $9x^2 - 25$.

5. **E** Recognize this as the sum and difference of the same two terms and, therefore, equal to the difference of squares:

$$\left(\frac{1}{2}t + 12\right)\left(\frac{1}{2}t - 12\right) = \left(\frac{1}{2}t\right)^2 - (12)^2 = \frac{1}{4}t^2 - 144$$

6. **C** $-3t^3(2t - 1) = (-3t^3)(2t) - (-3t^3)(1) = -6t^4 + 3t^3$.

7. **D** Look at the answer choices and apply what you know about factoring patterns. The square of a binomial will always have an x term, and $32x^2 - 72$ does not, so you can eliminate choices A and B. Choice C would be equal to $(16x)^2 - (36)^2$, and $(36)^2$ is far larger than 72. Since $32x^2 - 72 = 8(4x^2 - 9) = 8(2x + 3)(2x - 3)$, you can choose D, but you can also verify that choice E will have an x term.

8. **A** $(5x + 3)(2x - 1) = (5x)(2x) + (5x)(-1) + 3(2x) + 3(-1) = 10x^2 - 5x + 6x - 3 = 10x^2 + x - 3$.

9. $a = -7, b = 3$ $2x^2 - 11x - 21 = (x - 7)(2x + 3) = (x + a)(2x + b)$ so $a = -7$ and $b = 3$.

10. **6** $(4x - 7)(2x + 5) = 8x^2 + 20x - 14x - 35 = 8x^2 + 6x - 35$.

D. Applications of Factoring

1. Quadratic equations

Equations of the form $ax^2 + bx + c = 0$ are called *quadratic equations*. You may encounter quadratic equations that are not perfectly aligned to this definition, so it's good to develop the habit of immediately transforming the equation to this form when you see an x^2 term.

a. Taking the root of both sides

Quadratic equations that consist only of a variable expression squared and a constant term can be solved by taking square roots. If you can transform the equation so that you have a square on one side equal to a constant on the other, you can take the square root of both sides. This may give you an irrational result; if so, you can leave it in simplest radical form, or use your calculator for an approximation.

EXAMPLE:

> Solve $3(x + 1)^2 - 48 = 0$.

While you could FOIL out $(x + 1)^2$, simplify, and solve the simplified version of the equation, taking the root of both sides may be easier. Add 48 to both sides, and divide both sides by 3.

$$3(x + 1)^2 - 48 = 0$$
$$3(x + 1)^2 = 48$$
$$(x + 1)^2 = 16$$

Take the square root of both sides: $x + 1 = \pm 4$. This produces two solutions: $x + 1 = 4$ gives $x = 3$ and $x + 1 = -4$ gives $x = -5$.

b. Solving by factoring

The zero product property says something you know almost instinctively. If the product of two factors is zero, then one or both factors will be zero. Transform a quadratic equation so that one side of the equation is zero, and see if you can factor the other side. If you can, use the zero product property to create two simple equations, each of which produces one of the solutions of your quadratic equation.

EXAMPLE:

Solve $3x^2 + 2x - 6 = 50 - 3x - 3x^2$.

First, bring all the terms to one side, equal to zero.

$$3x^2 + 2x - 6 = 50 - 3x - 3x^2$$
$$6x^2 + 2x - 6 = 50 - 3x$$
$$6x^2 + 5x - 6 = 50$$
$$6x^2 + 5x - 56 = 0$$

Factor the polynomial to $(3x - 8)(2x + 7) = 0$ and set each factor equal to zero.

$$(3x - 8) = 0 \quad (2x + 7) = 0$$
$$3x = 8 \quad\quad 2x = -7$$
$$x = \frac{8}{3} \quad\quad x = \frac{-7}{2}$$

EXAMPLE:

If the product of two positive integers is 54 and their sum is 15, find the larger number.

If you write a system of equations, using x for the larger number and y for the smaller one, you get $xy = 54$ and $x + y = 15$. The second equation is linear, but the first is not. Don't let that stop you. Solve the second equation for y, and use the fact that $y = 15 - x$ to substitute into the first equation. The first equation becomes $x(15 - x) = 54$, which can be simplified to $x^2 - 15x + 54 = 0$ and solved by factoring to give you $(x - 6)(x - 9) = 0$ and $x = 6$ or $x = 9$. Therefore, the larger number is 9.

2. Rational expressions

Factoring is an important tool in working with rational expressions, sometimes called *algebraic fractions*.

a. Simplifying rational expressions

To reduce an algebraic fraction to lowest terms, factor the numerator and the denominator and cancel any factors that appear in both.

EXAMPLE:

Which of the following is *not* equal to $\frac{x+1}{x+2}$?

A. $\frac{3x+3}{3x+6}$

B. $\frac{x^2+x}{x^2+2x}$

C. $\frac{x^2-1}{x^2+x-2}$

D. $\frac{x^2-x-2}{x^2-4}$

E. $\frac{x^2+x+1}{x^2+x+2}$

Factor the numerator and denominator of each fraction, if possible.

- **Choice A:** $\frac{3x+3}{3x+6} = \frac{3(x+1)}{3(x+2)}$

- **Choice B:** $\frac{x^2+x}{x^2+2x} = \frac{x(x+1)}{x(x+2)}$

- **Choice C:** $\frac{x^2-1}{x^2+x-2} = \frac{(x+1)(x-1)}{(x+2)(x-1)}$

- **Choice D:** $\frac{x^2-x-2}{x^2-4} = \frac{(x+1)(x-2)}{(x+2)(x-2)}$

All these fractions can be reduced to $\frac{x+1}{x+2}$, but choice E is a fraction in which neither the numerator nor the denominator can be factored, so it cannot be reduced to $\frac{x+1}{x+2}$.

b. Multiplying and dividing rational expressions

To multiply rational expressions, factor all numerators and denominators, cancel any factor that appears in both a numerator and a denominator, and multiply numerator times numerator and denominator times denominator. To divide rational expressions, invert the divisor and multiply.

EXAMPLE:

Express in simplest form: $\frac{x^2-25}{x^2+8x+15} \div \frac{3x+15}{x^2+6x+9}$.

Invert the divisor and multiply.

$$\frac{x^2-25}{x^2+8x+15} \cdot \frac{x^2+6x+9}{3x+15}$$

Factor all numerators and denominators.

$$\frac{(x+5)(x-5)}{(x+3)(x+5)}\cdot\frac{(x+3)(x+3)}{3(x+5)}$$

Cancel and multiply.

$$\frac{(x+5)(x-5)}{(x+3)(x+5)}\cdot\frac{(x+3)(x+3)}{3(x+5)}=\frac{(x-5)(x+3)}{3(x+5)}$$

c. Adding and subtracting rational expressions

Adding and subtracting algebraic fractions calls upon the same skills as adding and subtracting numeric fractions. If the fractions have different denominators, they must be transformed to have a common denominator. Once the denominators are the same, add or subtract the numerators, and reduce if possible. Because the numerators and denominators are polynomials, factoring is essential to the process.

If the fractions have different denominators:

1. **Factor the denominators.**
2. **Identify any factors common to both denominators.**
   The lowest common denominator is the product of each factor that is common, and any remaining factors of either denominator.
3. **Transform each fraction by multiplying the numerator and denominator by the same quantity.**

When the fractions have common denominators, add or subtract the numerators. For subtraction, use parentheses around the second numerator to avoid sign errors. Finally, factor the numerator and denominator and reduce if possible.

EXAMPLE:

Express in simplest form: $\frac{5x}{3x-3}-\frac{2}{3x}$.

Factor each denominator: $3x-3=3(x-1)$ and $3x=3\cdot x$. The denominators have the factor 3 in common.

The lowest common denominator is $3(x-1)\cdot x$ or $3x(x-1)$. Transform each fraction:

$$\frac{5x}{3(x-1)}\cdot\frac{x}{x}=\frac{5x^2}{3x(x-1)}\text{ and }\frac{2}{3x}\cdot\frac{(x-1)}{(x-1)}=\frac{2x-2}{3x(x-1)}$$

The problem now becomes:

$$\frac{5x}{3x-3}-\frac{2}{3x}=\frac{5x^2}{3x(x-1)}-\frac{2x-2}{3x(x-1)}$$

Put parentheses around the second numerator, as a reminder to change all the signs:

$$\frac{5x^2-(2x-2)}{3x(x-1)}=\frac{5x^2-2x+2}{3x(x-1)}$$

167

Practice

Directions (1–2): You are given two quantities, one in Column A and one in Column B. You are to compare the two quantities and choose one of the following:

    A.   The quantity in Column A is greater.
    B.   The quantity in Column B is greater.
    C.   The two quantities are equal.
    D.   The relationship cannot be determined from the information given.

$$5x^2 + 20x + 20 = 0$$

	Column A	**Column B**
1.	The sum of the solutions	The product of the solutions

$$x^2 + 18x + 81 = 0$$

	Column A	**Column B**
2.	x	9

Directions (3–10): Unless otherwise directed, select a single answer choice. For numeric-entry questions, enter a number in the box(es) below the question. Equivalent forms of the correct answer, such as 2.5 and 2.50, are all correct. Fractions do not need to be reduced to lowest terms. Enter the exact answer unless the question asks you to round your answer.

3. The solutions of the equation $3x^2 - 5x + 4 = 6$ are

    A. -2
    B.   2
    C. $-\dfrac{4}{3}$
    D. $\dfrac{4}{3}$
    E. -4
    F.   4
    G. -6
    H.   6
    I. -3
    J.   3
    K. $-\dfrac{1}{3}$
    L. $\dfrac{1}{3}$

4. If an object is thrown upward from ground level with an initial velocity of v_0 feet per second, its height after t seconds is given by the formula $h = -16t^2 + v_0t$. Which of the following pairs of values represent an initial velocity and the correct resulting time to hit the ground?

   A. $v_0 = 40, t = 2.5$
   B. $v_0 = 48, t = 3$
   C. $v_0 = 50, t = 3.25$
   D. $v_0 = 60, t = 3.75$
   E. $v_0 = 64, t = 4$

5. $\dfrac{x^2 - 1}{x^2 + 11x + 28} \div \dfrac{x^2 + 6x - 7}{x^2 + 5x + 4} =$

   A. $\left(\dfrac{x-1}{x+4}\right)^2$

   B. $\left(\dfrac{x+1}{x+7}\right)^2$

   C. $\dfrac{x^2+1}{x^2+49}$

   D. $\dfrac{-1(5x+4)}{(11x+28)(6x-7)}$

   E. $\dfrac{-1(6x-7)}{(11x+28)(5x+4)}$

6. $\dfrac{x}{3a} - \dfrac{y}{5a} =$

   A. $\dfrac{x-y}{8a}$

   B. $\dfrac{x-y}{15a}$

   C. $\dfrac{5x-3y}{15a}$

   D. $\dfrac{5x-3y}{8a}$

   E. $\dfrac{x-y}{-2a}$

7. $\dfrac{x^2-1}{x^2-8x+16} \div \dfrac{x^2+3x-4}{x^2-16}$

   A. $\dfrac{(x+1)(x-1)^2}{(x-4)^3}$

   B. $\dfrac{(x-1)(x+1)^2}{(x+4)(x-4)^2}$

   C. $\dfrac{x-4}{x+1}$

   D. $\dfrac{x+1}{x-4}$

   E. $\dfrac{(x-1)(x+4)}{(x-4)^2}$

8. The product of two consecutive positive odd numbers is one less than nine times their sum. Find the smaller of the two numbers.

   A. 15
   B. 16
   C. 17
   D. 18
   E. 19

9. Find the largest of three consecutive positive odd numbers for which the product of the smallest and the largest is 117.

   ☐

10. Three less than the square of a positive number is five more than twice the number. Find the number.

   ☐

Answers

1. **B** Solve the equation by factoring.

$$5x^2 + 20x + 20 = 0$$
$$5(x^2 + 4x + 4) = 0$$
$$5(x + 2)^2 = 0$$
$$x + 2 = 0$$
$$x = -2$$

Since the two solutions are identical, the sum of the solutions is $-2 + -2 = -4$, and the product of the solutions is $(-2)(-2) = 4$.

2. B The polynomial $x^2 + 18x + 81$ is a perfect square trinomial, so its two factors will be identical, $(x + 9)^2 = 0$, and produce only one solution, $x = -9$. Therefore $x < 9$.

3. B, K The list may seem intimidating, but a quadratic equation will have no more than two solutions. Solve the equation by factoring.

$$3x^2 - 5x + 4 = 6$$
$$3x^2 - 5x - 2 = 0$$
$$(3x + 1)(x - 2) = 0$$

$$3x + 1 = 0 \qquad x - 2 = 0$$
$$3x = -1 \qquad x = 2$$
$$x = \frac{-1}{3}$$

4. A, B, D, E When the object hits the ground, its height is zero, so you can find the time it takes to hit the ground by solving $0 = -16t^2 + v_0 t$. At first glance, it seems you need to solve five different equations, but the similarities will make your task easier: $0 = -16t^2 + v_0 t = t(-16t + v_0)$. Setting each factor to zero gives you $t = 0$—when the object leaves the ground—and $-16t + v_0 = 0$, which solves to $t = \frac{v_0}{16}$. Divide each value of v_0 by 16 to find the time to hit the ground: $\frac{40}{16} = 2.5$, $\frac{48}{16} = 3$, $\frac{50}{16} = 3.125 \neq 3.25$, $\frac{60}{16} = 3.75$, and $\frac{64}{16} = 4$.

5. B To divide, multiply by the reciprocal, and factor all the numerators and denominators to locate opportunities for cancellation.

$$\frac{x^2 - 1}{x^2 + 11x + 28} \div \frac{x^2 + 6x - 7}{x^2 + 5x + 4} = \frac{x^2 - 1}{x^2 + 11x + 28} \cdot \frac{x^2 + 5x + 4}{x^2 + 6x - 7}$$

$$= \frac{(x+1)\cancel{(x-1)}}{\cancel{(x+4)}(x+7)} \cdot \frac{\cancel{(x+4)}(x+1)}{(x+7)\cancel{(x-1)}}$$

$$= \frac{(x+1)^2}{(x+7)^2} = \left(\frac{x+1}{x+7}\right)^2$$

6. C In order to subtract, you'll need a common denominator. Multiply the first fraction by $\frac{5}{5}$ and the second by $\frac{3}{3}$: $\frac{x}{3a} - \frac{y}{5a} = \frac{5x}{5(3a)} - \frac{3y}{3(5a)} = \frac{5x - 3y}{15a}$.

7. D To divide, invert the divisor and multiply. Factor all the numerators and denominators and look for factors to cancel.

$$\frac{x^2 - 1}{x^2 - 8x + 16} \div \frac{x^2 + 3x - 4}{x^2 - 16}$$

$$\frac{x^2 - 1}{x^2 - 8x + 16} \cdot \frac{x^2 - 16}{x^2 + 3x - 4}$$

$$\frac{(x+1)\cancel{(x-1)}}{(x-4)\cancel{(x-4)}} \cdot \frac{(x+4)\cancel{(x-4)}}{(x+4)\cancel{(x-1)}}$$

$$\frac{x+1}{x-4}$$

8. C Let the two numbers be x and $x + 2$. Then *the product is one less than nine times their sum* becomes:

$$x(x+2)=9(x+x+2)-1$$
$$x^2+2x=9(2x+2)-1$$
$$x^2+2x=18x+18-1$$
$$x^2+2x=18x+17$$
$$x^2-16x-17=0$$
$$(x-17)(x+1)=0$$
$$x-17=0 \qquad x+1=0$$
$$x=17 \qquad x=-1$$

The numbers are 17 and 19.

9. 13 Call the three consecutive odd numbers x, $x + 2$, and $x + 4$. The product of the smallest and the largest is 117 becomes:

$$x(x + 4) = 117$$
$$x^2 + 4x = 117$$
$$x^2 + 4x - 117 = 0$$

This will factor as $(x + 13)(x - 9) = 0$, giving solutions of $x = -13$ or $x = 9$. Since the consecutive odd numbers are positive, the numbers are 9, 11, and 13.

10. 4 *Three less than the square of a positive number is five more than twice the number* can be written as

$$x^2-3=5+2x$$
$$x^2-2x-3-5=0$$
$$x^2-2x-8=0$$
$$(x-4)(x+2)=0$$
$$x-4=0 \qquad x+2=0$$
$$x=4 \qquad x=-2$$

XII. Geometry

The need to build a strong foundation of logical argument has always been one of the key arguments for teaching geometry, so it's not surprising to find geometry on a test meant to assess your reasoning skills. Don't expect to be asked to prove any theorems, though. The geometry on the GRE will focus on figures, their measurements, and their relationships.

A. Lines, Rays, Segments, and Angles

One of the fundamental concepts in geometry is a line. A *line* has infinite length but no width or thickness. The term *straight line* is redundant, because all lines are straight. A *ray,* sometimes called a *half-line,* has one endpoint but continues; it resembles an arrow. A *line segment* is a portion of a line between two endpoints. Most work in geometry deals with line segments.

1. Length

It isn't possible to assign lengths to lines or rays because they go on forever, but it is possible to talk about the length of a line segment. That length is the distance between its endpoints. What we call a ruler is simply a way of assigning numbers to points on a line segment, so that the distance between two points can be found by subtracting the numbers assigned to those points. Distance and length are always positive numbers. Two segments that have the same length are *congruent segments.*

2. Angle measurement and classification

An *angle* is made up of two rays that share an endpoint called the *vertex.* When you measure an angle, you're measuring the rotation from one ray, or side, of the angle to the other. In geometry, angles are measured in degrees; in trigonometry, they're often measured in radians, but the GRE uses degree measurement.

A full rotation is 360°. Half of this, or 180°, is the measure of a *straight angle.* The straight angle takes its name from the fact that it looks like a straight line.

An angle of 90°, or a quarter rotation, is called a *right angle.*

Angles between 0° and 90° are called *acute angles.* (One definition of *acute* is "sharp." Acute angles have a sharp point.)

Angles with measurements greater than 90° but less that 180° are *obtuse angles.* ("Thick" is a synonym for *obtuse.* Obtuse angles are thick.)

3. Midpoints and segment bisectors

The *midpoint* of a segment is the point on the segment that is equidistant from the endpoints. It sits exactly at the middle of the segment and divides the segment into two congruent segments. Each of the two congruent segments is half as long as the original segment.

A *segment bisector* is a line, ray, or segment that passes through the midpoint. A bisector divides the segment into two congruent segments, each half as long as the original. If a bisector intersects the segment to form 90-degree angles, it is called a *perpendicular bisector.* Note that not all bisectors are perpendicular.

4. Angle bisectors

An *angle bisector* is a line, ray, or segment that passes through the vertex and divides an angle into two congruent angles. Each of those congruent angles is half the size of the original angle.

EXAMPLE:

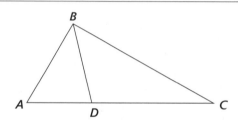

$\overline{BD}$ bisects $\angle ABC$ and $m\angle ABD = 44°$. Find the measure of $\angle ABC$.

Because $\overline{BD}$ bisects $\angle ABC$, $\angle ABD \cong \angle CBD$, so each is 44°. That measurement is half of the measure of $\angle ABC$, so $\angle ABC$ measures 88°.

Be careful not to assign other jobs to an angle bisector. It bisects the angle, but it does not necessarily bisect the opposite side of the triangle.

5. Angle pair relationships

When two lines intersect, four angles are formed. Each pair of angles across the intersection from one another is a pair of *vertical angles.* Vertical angles are congruent.

Two angles whose measurements total 90° are called *complementary angles.* If two angles are complementary, each is the *complement* of the other.

Two angles whose measurements total 180° are called *supplementary angles.* If two angles are supplementary, each is the *supplement* of the other.

EXAMPLES:

1. Find the complement of an angle of 25°.

To find the complement, subtract the known angle from 90°: 90° – 25° = 65°.

> **2.** Find the supplement of an angle of 132°.

To find the supplement, subtract the known angle from 180°: 180° – 132° = 48°.

6. Parallel lines

Lines that are always the same distance apart and, therefore, never intersect are called *parallel lines.* When a pair of parallel lines is cut by another line, called a *transversal,* eight angles are formed. Different pairs from this group of eight are classified in different ways.

As the transversal crosses the top line, it creates a cluster of four angles, here labeled $\angle 1$, $\angle 2$, $\angle 3$, and $\angle 4$. As it crosses the lower line, it creates another cluster of four angles, labeled $\angle 5$, $\angle 6$, $\angle 7$, and $\angle 8$. In each cluster, there is an angle in the upper-left position ($\angle 1$ from the top cluster or $\angle 5$ from the bottom cluster). There are also angles in the upper-right, lower-left, and lower-right positions. The angle from the upper cluster and the angle from the lower cluster that are in the same position are called *corresponding angles.*

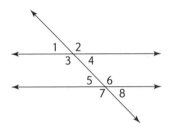

When parallel lines are cut by a transversal, corresponding angles are congruent. They have the same measurements. $\angle 1 \cong \angle 5$, $\angle 2 \cong \angle 6$, $\angle 3 \cong \angle 7$, and $\angle 4 \cong \angle 8$.

Consider only the angles that are between the parallel lines: $\angle 3$, $\angle 4$, $\angle 5$, and $\angle 6$. These are called *interior angles.* Choose one from the top cluster (say, $\angle 3$) and one from the bottom cluster on the other side of the transversal (in this case, $\angle 6$), and you have a pair of alternate interior angles.

When parallel lines are cut by a transversal, alternate interior angles are congruent. They have the same measurements: $\angle 3 \cong \angle 6$ and $\angle 4 \cong \angle 5$. Alternate interior angles are easy to spot because they form a Z (or a backward Z).

When parallel lines are cut by a transversal, alternate exterior angles are congruent: $\angle 1 \cong \angle 8$ and $\angle 2 \cong \angle 7$.

Using these facts, and the fact that vertical angles are congruent, you can quickly deduce that $\angle 1 \cong \angle 4 \cong \angle 5 \cong \angle 8$ and $\angle 2 \cong \angle 3 \cong \angle 6 \cong \angle 7$. Add the fact that $\angle 1$ and $\angle 2$ are supplementary, and it becomes possible to assign each of the angles one of two measurements: $m\angle 1 = m\angle 4 = m\angle 5 = m\angle 8 = n°$ and $m\angle 2 = m\angle 3 = m\angle 6 = m\angle 7 = (180 - n)°$.

EXAMPLE:

> Transversal $\overrightarrow{PQ}$ intersects $\overrightarrow{AB}$ at point M and intersects $\overrightarrow{CD}$ at point N. If $\overrightarrow{AB} \parallel \overrightarrow{CD}$, and $m\angle PMB = 35°$, find the measure of $\angle MNC$.

Draw a diagram to show the situation, and mark the congruent angles: $\angle PMB$ and $\angle MNC$ are not congruent, so they must be supplementary. Therefore, $m\angle MNC = 180° - m\angle PMB = 180° - 35° = 145°$.

7. Perpendicular lines

Perpendicular lines are lines that intersect at right angles. The symbol for "is perpendicular to" is $\perp$. Remember that all right angles are congruent, because all right angles measure 90°. When a line segment is drawn from a vertex of a triangle perpendicular to the opposite side, that segment is called an *altitude* of the triangle.

If a line is perpendicular to one of two parallel lines, it is perpendicular to the other.

If a line is parallel to one of two perpendicular lines, it is perpendicular to the other.

EXAMPLE:

> $\overrightarrow{AB} \perp \overrightarrow{CD}$ at point N. Line $\overrightarrow{PQ}$ intersects $\overrightarrow{AB}$ at P and $\overrightarrow{CD}$ at Q. What is $m\angle NPQ + m\angle NQP$?
>
> **A.**   45°
> **B.**   60°
> **C.**   90°
> **D.**   180°
> **E.**   Cannot be determined

Draw the diagram to help you see the situation. The perpendicular lines form right angles at N, so $\triangle PNQ$ is a right triangle. Since $\angle N$ is 90°, the other two angles in the triangle make up the rest of the 180°, so $m\angle NPQ + m\angle NQP = 90°$.

Practice

Directions (1–2): You are given two quantities, one in Column A and one in Column B. You are to compare the two quantities and choose one of the following:

A.   The quantity in Column A is greater.
B.   The quantity in Column B is greater.
C.   The two quantities are equal.
D.   The relationship cannot be determined from the information given.

Questions 1–3 refer to the following diagram. Line m is parallel to line n. The figure is not drawn to scale.

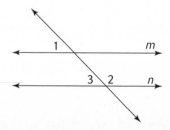

	Column A	Column B
1.	$m\angle 1$	$m\angle 3$

	Column A	Column B
2.	$m\angle 1$	$m\angle 2$

Directions (3–10): Unless otherwise directed, select a single answer choice. For numeric-entry questions, enter a number in the box(es) below the question. Equivalent forms of the correct answer, such as 2.5 and 2.50, are all correct. Fractions do not need to be reduced to lowest terms. Enter the exact answer unless the question asks you to round your answer.

3. If line m is parallel to line n, which of the following are true? Select all the true statements.

    A. $\angle 1 \cong \angle 2$.
    B. $\angle 1 \cong \angle 3$.
    C. $\angle 2 \cong \angle 3$.
    D. $\angle 1$ and $\angle 2$ are supplementary.
    E. $\angle 2$ and $\angle 3$ are supplementary.
    F. $\angle 1$ and $\angle 3$ are supplementary.

Question 4 refers to the following figure.

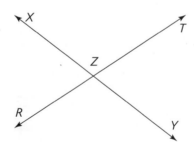

4. If $\overleftrightarrow{XY} \perp \overleftrightarrow{RT}$, which of the following statements are true? Select all the true statements.

    A. $\angle YZT$ is supplementary to $\angle XZR$.
    B. $\angle XZR$ is complementary to $\angle RZY$.
    C. $\angle XZT \cong \angle RZY$.
    D. $\angle XZR$ is a right angle.
    E. $\angle XZY$ is a straight angle.
    F. $\angle XZT \cong \angle RZX$.
    G. $\angle YZT$ is supplementary to $\angle XZT$.

Question 5 refers to the following figure.

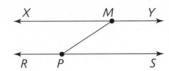

5. If $\overleftrightarrow{XY}$ is parallel to $\overleftrightarrow{RS}$ and $\angle XMP$ measures 24°, find the measure of $\angle RPM$.

   A. 24°
   B. 48°
   C. 66°
   D. 156°
   E. 336°

6. $m\angle A = 89°$. Which of the following is the measure of the supplement of $\angle A$?

   A. 189°
   B. 91°
   C. 89°
   D. 44.5°
   E. 1°

7. Find the complement of an angle of 9°.

   A. 9°
   B. 18°
   C. 81°
   D. 171°
   E. 351°

8. $\angle V$ and $\angle W$ are complementary. Which of the following best describes $\angle W$?

   A. Acute
   B. Right
   C. Obtuse
   D. Reflex
   E. Straight

9. $\triangle XYZ$ is drawn with $\angle X \cong \angle Z$. If the measure of $\angle X$ is 40°, find the measure of $\angle Y$.

   ☐

10. $\triangle ABC$ has a right angle at B and $\angle C$ measures 15°. Find the measure of $\angle A$.

    ☐

Answers

1. **C** When parallel lines are cut by a transversal, corresponding angles are congruent. $\angle 1$ and $\angle 3$ are corresponding angles, so $m\angle 1 = m\angle 3$.

2. **D** Because $\angle 2$ and $\angle 3$ are a linear pair, they're supplementary, and because $\angle 1$ and $\angle 3$ are congruent, you can show by substitution that $\angle 1$ and $\angle 2$ are supplementary. But without knowing the measure of any of the angles, you can't determine which is larger.

3. **B, D, E** When parallel lines are cut by a transversal, corresponding angles are congruent, so $\angle 1 \cong \angle 3$. $\angle 2$ and $\angle 3$, a linear pair, are supplementary, but they would only be congruent if the transversal were perpendicular to the parallel lines. Because $\angle 2$ and $\angle 3$ are supplementary and $\angle 1 \cong \angle 3$, $\angle 2$ and $\angle 1$ are supplementary as well.

4. **A, C, D, E, F, G** If $\overline{XY} \perp \overline{RT}$, all four angles are right angles, and all right angles are congruent, so choices C, D, and F are true. Any two right angles are supplementary, so choices A and G are true. Adjacent right angles form a straight angle, making choice E true. Complementary angles total $90°$, so it's impossible for two right angles to be complementary; therefore, choice B is not true.

5. **D** $\angle XMP$ and $\angle RPM$ are supplementary, so $m\angle RPM = 180° - 24° = 156°$.

6. **B** The measure of the supplement of $\angle A$ is $180° - 89° = 91°$.

7. **C** The complement of an angle of $9°$ is $90° - 9° = 81°$.

8. **A** If $\angle V$ and $\angle W$ are complementary, their measurements total $90°$, so each must be less than $90°$.

9. **100°** If $\angle X \cong \angle Z$ and the measure of $\angle X$ is $40°$, then the measure of $\angle Z$ is also $40°$. That leaves $180° - (40° + 40°) = 180° - 80° = 100°$ for the measure of $\angle Y$.

10. **75°** The three angles of the triangle total $180°$. $m\angle B + m\angle C = 90° + 15° = 105°$, leaving $180° - 105° = 75°$ for $\angle A$.

B. Triangles

1. Classifying triangles

Right triangles are triangles that contain one right angle. *Obtuse triangles* contain one obtuse angle, and *acute triangles* contain three acute angles.

Isosceles triangles are triangles with two congruent sides. The angles opposite the congruent sides, often called the *base angles,* are congruent to each other. In an isosceles triangle, the altitude drawn from the vertex to the base bisects the base and the vertex angle.

An *equilateral triangle* is one in which all three sides are the same lengths. Each of its angles measures $60°$. Any altitude bisects the side to which it is drawn and the angle from which it is drawn.

EXAMPLE:

In $\triangle$ABC, $\overline{AB} \cong \overline{BC}$ and $\overline{BD}$ is an altitude.

Column A	Column B
$m\angle ABD$	$m\angle CBD$

Draw the triangle. The angles being compared make up the vertex angle. Because we know that an altitude from the vertex of an isosceles triangle bisects the vertex angle, the two angles are equal.

2. Angles in triangles

a. Sum of the angles of a triangle

In any triangle, the sum of the measures of the three angles is 180°. In a right triangle, the two acute angles are complementary.

b. Exterior angles

An *exterior angle* of a triangle is formed by extending one side of the triangle. The exterior angle is supplementary to the interior angle adjacent to it. Because the three interior angles of the triangle add up to 180°, it's easy to show that the measure of an exterior angle of a triangle is equal to the sum of the two remote interior angles.

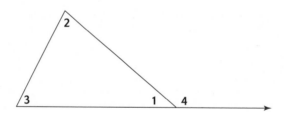

$m\angle 1 + m\angle 2 + m\angle 3 = 180°$

$m\angle 1 + m\angle 4 = 180°$

$m\angle 1 + m\angle 2 + m\angle 3 = m\angle 1 + m\angle 4$

$m\angle 2 + m\angle 3 = m\angle 4$

EXAMPLE:

In $\triangle ABC$, $m\angle A = 43°$ and $m\angle B = 28°$. What is the measure of the exterior angle of the triangle at C?

Sketch the triangle. The exterior angle is equal to the sum of the two remote interior angles, so $m\angle BCD = 43° + 28° = 71°$.

Alternatively, you could calculate the measure of $\angle BCA$ ($180° - 43° - 28° = 109°$) and, because $\angle BCD$ is supplementary to $\angle BCA$, it will be $180° - 109° = 71°$.

3. Triangle inequality

In any triangle, the sum of the lengths of any two sides will be greater than the length of the third. Put another way, the length of any side of a triangle is less than the sum of the other two sides but more than the difference between them.

EXAMPLE:

> Gretchen lives 5 miles from the library and 2 miles from school. Which of the following cannot be the distance from the library to school?
>
> **A.**   4 miles
> **B.**   5 miles
> **C.**   6 miles
> **D.**   7 miles
> **E.**   8 miles

The correct answer is **E**. If Gretchen's house, the library, and the school are the vertices of a triangle, then the distance from the library to school must be greater than 5 – 2 and less than 5 + 2. So the distance is between 3 and 7 miles. Choice E, 8 miles, would not be possible. It's wise to consider the possibility that Gretchen's house, the library, and the school lie in a straight line, but even if that were the case, the maximum distance from the library to the school would be 7 miles.

4. Pythagorean theorem

The Pythagorean theorem is a statement about the relationship among the sides of a right triangle. A *right triangle* is one that contains one right angle; the side opposite the right angle is called the *hypotenuse*. The other two sides, which form the right angle, are called *legs*. The Pythagorean theorem states that in any right triangle, the square of the hypotenuse is equal to the sum of the squares of the other two sides. Most people remember it in symbolic form, though.

If the legs of the right triangle are a and b and the hypotenuse is c, then $a^2 + b^2 = c^2$.

EXAMPLE:

> Dorothy walks to school every morning and, on sunny days, she cuts through a rectangular vacant lot. On snowy days, she must go around the block. One side of the rectangular lot measures 5 meters and the other measures 12 meters. How much shorter is Dorothy's walk on sunny days?

The path through the lot is the hypotenuse of a right triangle, so its length can be found using the Pythagorean theorem: $5^2 + 12^2 = c^2$, so $c^2 = 25 + 144 = 169$, and $c = 13$ meters. On sunny days, she takes the path through the lot, which is 13 meters, but on snowy days, she must walk around the legs of the triangle, a total of 17 meters. On sunny days, her walk is 4 meters shorter.

5. Special right triangles

When an altitude is drawn in an equilateral triangle, it divides the triangle into two congruent right triangles. Each of these smaller triangles has an angle of 60° and an angle of 30° in addition to the right angle.

The hypotenuse of the 30°-60°-90° triangle is the side of the original equilateral triangle. The side opposite the 30° angle is half as large as the hypotenuse. Using the Pythagorean theorem, you can determine that the side opposite the 60° angle must be half the hypotenuse times the square root of 3. If s is the side of the equilateral triangle, and the side opposite the 30° angle is the a leg of the right triangle, then:

$$a^2 + b^2 = c^2$$

$$\left(\frac{1}{2}s\right)^2 + b = s^2$$

$$\frac{1}{4}s^2 + b^2 = s^2$$

$$b^2 = \frac{3}{4}s^2$$

$$b = \sqrt{\frac{3}{4}s^2}$$

$$b = \frac{\sqrt{3}}{2}s = \frac{1}{2}s\sqrt{3}$$

In an isosceles right triangle, the two legs are of equal length. Apply the Pythagorean theorem and you can see that the hypotenuse must be equal to the leg times the square root of 2. If s is the leg of the isosceles right triangle,

$$a^2 + b^2 = c^2$$

$$s^2 + s^2 = c^2$$

$$2s^2 = c^2$$

$$\sqrt{2s^2} = c$$

$$s\sqrt{2} = c$$

EXAMPLES:

1. Find the area of a square whose diagonal is $15\sqrt{2}$.

The diagonal of a square divides it into two isosceles right triangles, and the diagonal is the hypotenuse of each. If the hypotenuse is $15\sqrt{2}$, the sides must be 15, so the area is 225 square units.

2. The altitude of an equilateral triangle is 7 cm. Find the perimeter of the triangle.

The altitude divides the equilateral triangle into two 30°-60°-90° triangles. The altitude is the side opposite the 60° angle, so its length is $\frac{1}{2}h\sqrt{3}$, where h is the length of a side of the triangle.

$$\frac{1}{2}h\sqrt{3} = 7$$

$$h\sqrt{3} = 14$$

$$h = \frac{14}{\sqrt{3}} = \frac{14\sqrt{3}}{3}$$

Be sure to answer the question asked. The perimeter of the triangle is $3 \cdot \frac{14\sqrt{3}}{3} = 14\sqrt{3}$.

6. Congruence and similarity

a. Congruence

Triangles are *congruent* if they are the same shape and the same size. Because the size of the angles controls the shape of the triangle, in a pair of congruent triangles, corresponding angles are congruent. Because the length of sides controls size, corresponding sides are of equal length.

To conclude that triangles are congruent, you must have evidence that certain combinations of sides and angles of one triangle are congruent to the corresponding parts of the other triangle. Here are the minimums required to prove that triangles are congruent:

- **Three sides: SSS**
- **Two sides and the included angle: SAS**
- **Two angles and the included side: ASA**
- **Two angles and the non-included side: AAS**

b. Similarity

Triangles are similar if they are the same shape, but not necessarily the same size. Corresponding angles are congruent and corresponding sides are in proportion.

To conclude that triangles are similar you must know that two angles of one triangle are congruent to the corresponding angles of the other (AA).

EXAMPLE:

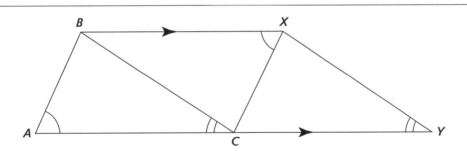

Given that $\angle A \cong \angle BXC$, $\angle BCA \cong \angle XYC$, and $\overline{BX} \parallel \overline{AY}$, which of the following is true?

A. $\triangle CXY$ is isosceles.
B. $\triangle XCB$ is isosceles.
C. $\triangle ABC$ is equilateral.
D. $\triangle ABC$ is isosceles.
E. $\triangle ABC \sim \triangle CXY$.

Mark the diagram to show the given information. Because $\overline{BX} \parallel \overline{AY}$, it is possible to conclude that $\angle BCA \cong \angle CBX$ and $\angle BXC \cong \angle XCY$. Therefore, choice E is true by AA.

7. Area

The area of a triangle is equal to half the product of the length of the base and the height. Any side may be considered the base, but the height must be drawn from the opposite vertex, perpendicular to the base. This can sometimes cause the altitude to fall outside the triangle.

EXAMPLE:

$\triangle PQR$ has an area of 24 square units. If the lengths of its sides are 3 cm, 6 cm, and 8 cm, find the length of the longest altitude.

The area of the triangle will be the same no matter which side is called the base, provided that the altitude is drawn correctly. If we say the base is the side of length 3, then $A = \frac{1}{2}bh$ becomes $24 = \frac{1}{2} \cdot 3 \cdot h$ and $h = 16$.

Logically, the longest altitude will be drawn to the shortest side, but repeating the calculation with other sides as bases will show that the altitude drawn to the 6 cm side is 8 cm long, and the altitude to the longest side is 6 cm long. The longest altitude is 16 cm.

Practice

Directions (1–2): You are given two quantities, one in Column A and one in Column B. You are to compare the two quantities and choose one of the following:

    A.   The quantity in Column A is greater.
    B.   The quantity in Column B is greater.
    C.   The two quantities are equal.
    D.   The relationship cannot be determined from the information given.

Questions 1–2 refer to the following diagram. $\overline{RS} \parallel \overline{TU}$. The figure is not drawn to scale.

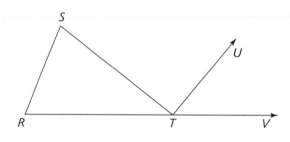

	Column A	**Column B**
1.	$m\angle SRT$	$m\angle UTV$

	Column A	**Column B**
2.	$m\angle STV$	$m\angle S$

184

Directions (3–10): Unless otherwise directed, select a single answer choice. For numeric-entry questions, enter a number in the box(es) below the question. Equivalent forms of the correct answer, such as 2.5 and 2.50, are all correct. Fractions do not need to be reduced to lowest terms. Enter the exact answer unless the question asks you to round your answer.

3. $\triangle CDE$ is an isosceles triangle in which $CD = DE$ and side $\overline{CE}$ is extended through E to F, forming exterior $\angle DEF$. Which of the following must be true? Select all the true statements.

   A. $m\angle DEF > m\angle CDE$.
   B. $\angle DEF$ and $\angle DEC$ are supplementary.
   C. $\angle DEC$ and $\angle DCE$ are congruent.
   D. $m\angle DEF > m\angle DEC$.
   E. $m\angle CDE < m\angle DEC$.
   F. $m\angle DEF = m\angle CDE + m\angle DCE$.

4. If $\triangle PQR \cong \triangle MNO$ and both are isosceles triangles, which of the following must be true? Select all the true statements.

   A. $PQ = MN$
   B. $PQ = NO$
   C. $NO = QR$
   D. $QR = MO$
   E. $\angle Q \cong \angle O$
   F. $\angle M \cong \angle P$
   G. $\angle Q \cong \angle N$
   H. $\angle O \cong \angle R$

5. $\triangle RST \sim \triangle MNP$. $RS = 12$ and $ST = 18$. Find the length of $\overline{MN}$ if $NP = 6$.

   A. 4
   B. 9
   C. 12
   D. 24
   E. 48

6. The town of Treadway is 40 miles north of Centerville and 30 miles east of Dodge. Which of the following is the best estimate of the distance from Centerville to Dodge?

   A. 10 miles
   B. 30 miles
   C. 40 miles
   D. 50 miles
   E. 70 miles

7. $\triangle RST$ is a scalene triangle. If $RS = 7$ and $RT = 4$, which of the following is *not* true?

    A. $TS > 3$
    B. $TS < 11$
    C. $TS \neq 7$
    D. $TS \neq 4$
    E. $TS = \sqrt{65}$

8. The area of a square is 100 square meters. Find the length of its diagonal.

    A. 10m
    B. 15m
    C. $10\sqrt{2}$ m
    D. $5\sqrt{3}$ m
    E. 20m

9. $\triangle RST \cong \triangle MNP$. If $RS = 12$ and $ST = 18$, find the length of $\overline{MN}$.

    [ ]

10. $\triangle PRT$ is a right triangle with $\overline{PR} \perp \overline{RT}$. Side $\overline{RT}$ is extended through R to S. Find the measure of $\angle PRS$.

    [ ]

Answers

1. **C** $\angle SRT$ and $\angle UTV$ are corresponding angles. When parallel lines are cut by a transversal, corresponding angles are congruent.

2. **A** $m\angle STV = m\angle STU + m\angle UTV$ and $m\angle S = m\angle STU$ because they are alternate interior angles. Since the whole is greater than the part, $m\angle STV > m\angle S$.

3. **A, B, C, F** $m\angle DEF > m\angle CDE$ because the measure of an exterior angle of a triangle is greater than the measure of either remote interior angle and $m\angle DEF = m\angle CDE + m\angle DCE$ because the measure of the exterior angle is the sum of the two remote interior angles. $\angle DEF$ and $\angle DEC$ are supplementary because they're a linear pair. $\angle DEC$ and $\angle DCE$ are congruent because base angles of an isosceles triangle are congruent. The relative size of $\angle DEF$ and $\angle DEC$ cannot be determined, nor can the relative size of $\angle CDE$ and $\angle DEC$.

4. **A, C, F, G, H** If $\triangle PQR \cong \triangle MNO$, the correspondence described by that statement tells us that choices A, C, F, G, and H must be true. Because the triangles are isosceles, there are congruent sides and congruent angles, and other choices may be true, but without knowing which two sides of each triangle are congruent, you can't be certain.

5. **A** Because $\triangle RST \sim \triangle MNP$, the triangle's corresponding sides are in proportion.

$$\frac{RS}{ST} = \frac{MN}{NP}$$
$$\frac{12}{18} = \frac{x}{6}$$
$$18x = 72$$
$$x = 4$$

$MN = 4$.

6. **D** The distance from Centerville to Dodge is the third side of a triangle, so its length is more than $40 - 30 = 10$ miles and less than $40 + 30 = 70$ miles. The description suggests that the triangle is a right triangle, so by the Pythagorean theorem, $c^2 = 30^2 + 40^2 = 900 + 1{,}600 = 2{,}500$ and $c = \sqrt{2{,}500} = 50$ miles.

7. **E** If $RS = 7$ and $RT = 4$, the length of the third side is greater than the difference of the two known sides but less than their sum, so choices A and B are true. Because the triangle is scalene, side ST cannot be the same length as RS or RT, so choices C and D are true. Choice E would be true only if TS were the hypotenuse of a right triangle, which we know is not true.

8. **C** The area of a square is the square of the length of its side, so if the area is 100 square meters, the side is 10 meters long. Use the Pythagorean theorem to find the length of its diagonal:

$$a^2 + b^2 = c^2$$
$$10^2 + 10^2 = c^2$$
$$200 = c^2$$
$$\sqrt{200} = 10\sqrt{2} = c$$

9. **12** Since $\triangle RST \cong \triangle MNP$, $\overline{MN} \cong \overline{RS}$ so $MN = RS = 12$.

10. **90°** $\angle PRS$ is an exterior angle of $\angle PRT$ and is adjacent to the right angle at R. The measure of $\angle PRS$ is 90°.

C. Quadrilaterals

The term *quadrilateral* denotes any four-sided polygon, but most of the attention falls on the members of the parallelogram family.

1. Parallelograms

A *parallelogram* is a quadrilateral with two pairs of opposite sides parallel and congruent. In any parallelogram, consecutive angles are supplementary and opposite angles are congruent. Drawing one diagonal in a parallelogram divides it into two congruent triangles. When both diagonals are drawn in the parallelogram, the diagonals bisect each other.

EXAMPLE:

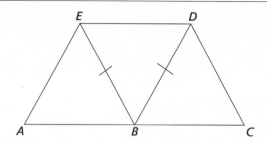

ABDE and *BCDE* are parallelograms with *BD* = *BE*. Which of the following are true?

A. $\angle A \cong \angle C$

B. $AE = CD$

C. $\triangle AEB \cong \triangle CDB$

Since $BD = BE$, $\triangle EBD$ is isosceles, and $\angle DEB \cong \angle EDB$. Because opposite angles of a parallelogram are congruent, $\angle A \cong \angle EDB \cong \angle DEB \cong \angle C$, so choice A is true. Because opposite sides of a parallelogram are congruent, $AE = BE = BD = CD$, so choice B is true. Because $\triangle AEB$, $\triangle EBD$, and $\triangle BDC$ are all isosceles triangles, $\angle A \cong \angle EBA \cong \angle DBC \cong \angle C$, and $\triangle AEB \cong \triangle CDB$ by AAS. Therefore, choice C is also true.

The area of a parallelogram is found by multiplying the base times the height: $A = bh$. Remember that the height must be measured as the perpendicular distance between the bases. Don't confuse the side with the height.

EXAMPLE:

Find the area of parallelogram *ABCD* if *AB* = 13, *BC* = 10, and altitude *BX* = 12.

BX is the height and *BC* is the base, so the area is $12 \times 10 = 120$ square units.

2. Rhombuses

A *rhombus* is a parallelogram with four sides of the same length. Because the rhombus is a parallelogram, it has all the properties of a parallelogram. The diagonals of a rhombus are perpendicular to one another.

Because the diagonals of a rhombus are perpendicular bisectors of one another, they divide the rhombus into four congruent right triangles. The area of each right triangle can be easily found. The legs of the right triangle are $\frac{1}{2}d_1$ and $\frac{1}{2}d_2$, so the area of each right triangle is $\frac{1}{2} \cdot \frac{1}{2}d_1 \cdot \frac{1}{2}d_2 = \frac{1}{8}d_1 d_2$. Because there are four triangles making up the rhombus, the area of the rhombus is $4 \cdot \frac{1}{8}d_1 \cdot d_2 = \frac{1}{2}d_1 \cdot d_2$. The area of a rhombus is one-half the product of the diagonals.

EXAMPLE:

> Find the area of a rhombus whose diagonals are 12 cm and 20 cm.

The area of the rhombus is $\frac{1}{2} \cdot 12 \cdot 20 = 120 \text{cm}^2$.

3. Rectangles and squares

A *rectangle* is a parallelogram with four right angles. Because the rectangle is a parallelogram, it has all the properties of a parallelogram. The perimeter of any figure is the sum of the lengths of its sides. Because opposite sides of a rectangle are congruent, this can be expressed as $P = 2l + 2w$.

A *square* is a parallelogram that is both a rhombus and a rectangle. Squares have four right angles and four equal sides.

EXAMPLES:

> 1. Marianna wants to build a fence around her vegetable garden. If the garden is a rectangle 30 feet long and 15 feet wide, and fencing costs $1.25 per foot, how much will it cost to fence the garden?

The perimeter of a rectangle is $2l + 2w$, so she'll need $(2 \times 30) + (2 \times 15) = 60 + 30 = 90$ feet of fencing. You're asked the cost of the fencing, however, not how much fencing is needed. So, 90 feet of fencing at $1.25 per foot will cost $90 \times \$1.25 = \$112.50$.

The diagonals of a rectangle are congruent, and because the rectangle is a parallelogram, the diagonals bisect each other.

> 2. In rectangle $ABCD$, the diagonals intersect at E. If $BE = 8$, find AE.

Because the diagonals are congruent and bisect each other, $AE = EC = BE = ED$. So $AE = 8$.

Since the rectangle is a parallelogram, its area is base times height. But because the adjacent sides of the rectangle are perpendicular, the length and width are the base and the height, so $A = lw$.

EXAMPLE:

> What is the area in square yards of Marianna's garden if the garden plot is 30 feet long and 15 feet wide?

The dimensions of the garden are given in feet, but the answer must be in square yards. You can convert to square yards at the end, but it may be simpler to convert the length and width to yards before finding the area. Because there are 3 feet in a yard, 30 feet = 10 yards and 15 feet = 5 yards. The area is $10 \times 5 = 50$ square yards.

Alternatively, you can find the area as $30 \times 15 = 450$ square feet. There are 9 square feet in one square yard, so $450 \div 9 = 50$ square yards.

4. Trapezoids

A *trapezoid* is a quadrilateral with one pair of parallel sides and one pair of nonparallel sides. If the nonparallel sides are congruent, the trapezoid is an *isosceles trapezoid*. Base angles of an isosceles trapezoid are congruent, and in any trapezoid, the angle at one end of the top base is supplementary to the angle at the same end of the bottom base. In an isosceles trapezoid, diagonals are congruent. Diagonals of other trapezoids are not congruent. Diagonals of a trapezoid do not necessarily bisect one another.

The line segment joining the midpoints of the nonparallel sides is called the *median* of the trapezoid. The median is parallel to the bases. Its length is the average of the bases.

If you cut the top off a trapezoid by cutting along the median, and rotate the top piece over and set it next to the bottom piece, you create a parallelogram. The height of the parallelogram is half the height of the trapezoid. The base of the parallelogram is the sum of the length of the long base and the short base of the trapezoid. So, the area of a trapezoid is equal to half the height times the sum of the bases. Some people remember this formula as the average of the bases times the height, or the length of the median times the height.

EXAMPLE:

> The area of a trapezoid is 40 square centimeters. If the bases are 3 cm and 5 cm, how high is the trapezoid?

$A = \frac{1}{2}h(b_1 + b_2)$ and you know the bases are 3 and 5, so:

$$40 = \frac{1}{2}h(3+5)$$
$$40 = \frac{1}{2}h \cdot 8$$
$$40 = 4h$$
$$h = 10$$

Practice

Directions (1–2): You are given two quantities, one in Column A and one in Column B. You are to compare the two quantities and choose one of the following:

- A. The quantity in Column A is greater.
- B. The quantity in Column B is greater.
- C. The two quantities are equal.
- D. The relationship cannot be determined from the information given.

RSTU is a rhombus, with *UV* = 4 cm and *RV* = 6 cm.

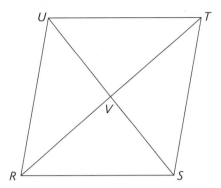

Column A	Column B
1. The number of square centimeters in the area of the rhombus	The number of centimeters in the perimeter of the rhombus

In rectangle *ABCD*, *BC* = 30 inches and *AC* = 50 inches.

Column A	Column B
2. The number of inches in the perimeter of rectangle *ABCD*	The number of square inches in the area of rectangle *ABCD*

Directions (3–10): Unless otherwise directed, select a single answer choice. For numeric-entry questions, enter a number in the box(es) below the question. Equivalent forms of the correct answer, such as 2.5 and 2.50, are all correct. Fractions do not need to be reduced to lowest terms. Enter the exact answer unless the question asks you to round your answer.

3. In rectangle *ABCD*, diagonals $\overline{AC}$ and $\overline{BD}$ intersect at *E*. Select all the true statements.

   A. *AD* = *BC*.
   B. ∠*ABC* is a right angle.
   C. $\overline{CD} \perp \overline{DA}$.
   D. *AB* = *AE*.
   E. ∠*EAB* ≅ ∠*EBA*.

4. *ABCD* is a trapezoid with $\overline{BC} \parallel \overline{AD}$. *BC* = 8 cm and *AD* = 22 cm. The area of the trapezoid is 150 square centimeters. Select all the true statements.

   A. *ABCD* is an isosceles trapezoid.
   B. The median of trapezoid *ABCD* is 15 cm.
   C. The height of trapezoid *ABCD* is 10 cm.
   D. *m*∠*A* = *m*∠*D*
   E. ∠*A* and ∠*B* are supplementary.

5. Find the perimeter of isosceles trapezoid *ABCD* if the median is 18 units long and each of the nonparallel sides is 6 units long.

   A. 24
   B. 30
   C. 42
   D. 48
   E. 108

Question 6 refers to the following figure.

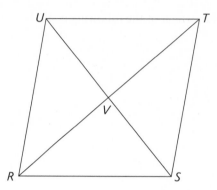

6. *RSTU* is a rhombus. *UV* = 5 m and *RT* = 24 m. Find the area of the rhombus.

   A. 120 m²
   B. 240 m²
   C. 360 m²
   D. 480 m²
   E. 600 m²

Question 7 refers to the following figure.

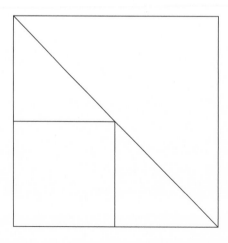

7. The diagonal of a square is $9\sqrt{2}$ cm. If another square is drawn with one vertex at a vertex of the large square and the opposite vertex on the diagonal as shown, find the perimeter of the smaller square.

   A. 18 cm
   B. $18\sqrt{2}$ cm
   C. 36 cm
   D. $36\sqrt{2}$ cm
   E. 72 cm

8. A parallelogram has a base equal in length to its shorter diagonal. If the angle formed by that base and the shorter diagonal is 40°, which of the following could be the measure of an angle of the parallelogram?

   A. 40°
   B. 70°
   C. 80°
   D. 100°
   E. 140°

Question 9 refers to the following figure.

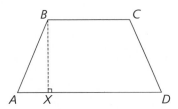

9. Find the area of trapezoid $ABCD$ if the median = 18 and height $BX = 6$.

   [   ]

10. A rhombus has diagonals of 8 cm and 6 cm. Find the side of the rhombus, in centimeters.

   [   ]

Answers

1. **A** The area of a rhombus is equal to half the product of the lengths of the diagonals. Because the rhombus is a parallelogram, the diagonals bisect each other, so you can conclude from the given information that the lengths of the diagonals are 8 and 12. Then the area is $\frac{1}{2}(8)(12) = 48$. The diagonals of the rhombus are perpendicular, so use the Pythagorean theorem to find the length of a side: $4^2 + 6^2 = c^2$ so $c = \sqrt{16 + 36} = \sqrt{52} \approx 7.211$. If one side is slightly longer than 7, the perimeter is between 28 and 29, so the value of the area is larger.

2. **B** Use the Pythagorean theorem to find AB:

$$(AB)^2 + (BC)^2 = (AC)^2$$
$$(AB)^2 + 30^2 = 50^2$$
$$(AB)^2 + 900 = 2,500$$
$$(AB)^2 = 1,600$$
$$AB = 40$$

Then the perimeter is 2(30) + 2(40) = 60 + 80 = 140 inches and the area is $30 \times 40 = 1,200$ square inches.

3. **A, B, C, E** Choice A is true because AD and BC are opposite sides of the rectangle, so $AD = BC$. Because any pair of adjacent sides of a rectangle meet at right angles, both choices B and C are true. $\angle EAB \cong \angle EBA$ because the diagonals of a rectangle are congruent and bisect each other, so $\triangle AEB$ is isosceles with $AE = BE$, and the angles opposite those sides are congruent. However, AB will be equal to AE only if $\triangle AEB$ is equilateral, and there is not sufficient information to know if that is true.

4. **B, C, E** There is not enough information to determine if the nonparallel sides are congruent, so the truth of choices A and D cannot be determined. The length of the median is the average of the bases, $\frac{8 + 22}{2} = 15$ cm. The area of the trapezoid is $\frac{1}{2}(b_1 + b_2)h$. The bases are 8 cm and 22 cm long, and the area is 150 cm².

$$A = \frac{1}{2}(b_1 + b_2)h$$
$$150 = \frac{1}{2}(8 + 22)h$$
$$150 = \frac{1}{2}(30)h$$
$$150 = 15h$$
$$10 = h$$

The height is 10 cm. $\angle A$ and $\angle B$ are consecutive angles between the parallels, so they are supplementary.

5. **D** The length of the median is half the sum of the two bases, so if the median is 18, the sum of the two bases is 36. Add to that the two nonparallel sides, each 6, to find the perimeter: 36 + 2(6) = 48.

6. **A** The area of the rhombus is equal to half the product of the diagonals. The diagonals are $2 \times 5 = 10$ and 24, so $\frac{1}{2} \times 10 \times 24 = 120$ m².

7. **A** The diagonal of the square is $9\sqrt{2}$ cm, so the side of the larger square is 9. The smaller square has a side half as long as the larger square, so its perimeter is $4(4.5) = 18$ cm.

8. **B** The shorter diagonal divides the parallelogram into two triangles and because the shorter diagonal is congruent to the base, the triangle is isosceles. The angle formed by the two congruent line segments is the vertex angle of the isosceles triangle, so the two congruent base angles of the isosceles triangle total 140°. This means that each of those angles is 70°, and one of them is an angle of the parallelogram. The angles of the parallelogram are 70° and 110°.

9. **108** The length of the median is equal to half the sum of the bases, so the area of the trapezoid is equal to $18 \times 6 = 108$ square units.

10. **5** The diagonals of a rhombus are perpendicular and bisect each other; therefore, they create four congruent right triangles, each with legs of 3 cm and 4 cm. Using the Pythagorean theorem, or Pythagorean triples, those triangles would be 3-4-5 right triangles, so each side of the rhombus will be 5 cm long.

D. Other Polygons

1. Names

Polygons are named according to the number of sides. *Triangles* have three sides, and *quadrilaterals* have four sides. A polygon with five sides is a *pentagon,* and a polygon with six sides is a *hexagon. Octagons* have eight sides, and *decagons* have ten sides.

2. Diagonals

The number of diagonals that can be drawn in a polygon with n sides is $n(n-3) \div 2$. That formula comes from the realization that there are n vertices, and from each of them there are $n-3$ vertices to which you can draw. It is not possible to draw a diagonal to the vertex you start from, nor to either of the adjacent vertices, since those would be sides, not diagonals. The reason for dividing by 2 is to eliminate repetition, such as counting both the diagonal from A to E and the diagonal from E to A.

3. Angles

The sum of the interior angles of any convex polygon can be found with the formula $s = 180°(n-2)$, where n is the number of sides. If the convex polygon is divided into triangles by drawing all the possible diagonals from a single vertex, there are $n-2$ triangles, each with angles totaling 180°.

If the polygon is regular—that is, all sides are congruent and all angles are congruent—then the measure of any interior angle can be found by dividing the total number of degrees by the number of angles. The sum of the exterior angles of any polygon is 360°.

EXAMPLE:

> Find the measure of the interior angle of a regular pentagon.

The total of the measures of the five angles of a pentagon is $180(5-2) = 180(3) = 540°$. The pentagon is regular so all the angles are the same size. Divide $540°$ by 5 to find that each angle is $108°$.

4. Area

You'll sometimes be asked to find the area of polygons for which you have not learned a specific formula. Use a diagram to try to divide the figure into sections whose areas you *do* know how to calculate.

EXAMPLE:

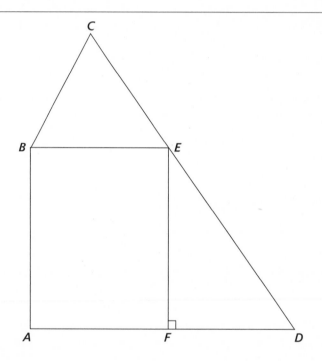

> Find the area of quadrilateral $ABCD$ if $AB = AD = 6$ cm, $\overline{EF}$ is the perpendicular bisector of $\overline{AD}$, and $\triangle BEC$ is equilateral.

Break the polygon into two triangles and a rectangle. The area of the rectangle is $6 \cdot 3 = 18$. $\triangle DFE$ is a right triangle with legs of 6 and 3, so its area is $\frac{1}{2} \cdot 6 \cdot 3 = 9$. $\triangle BEC$ is equilateral with a base of 3 and a height of $\frac{3}{2}\sqrt{3}$, so its area is $\frac{1}{2} \cdot 3 \cdot \frac{3}{2}\sqrt{3} = \frac{9}{4}\sqrt{3}$. The total area is $18 + 9 + \frac{9}{4}\sqrt{3} = 27 + \frac{9}{4}\sqrt{3} \approx 30.9$.

In regular polygons, you can easily divide the figure into congruent triangles. Find the area of one triangle and multiply by the number of triangles present. If the regular polygon is divided as shown, the height of each little triangle is called the *apothem* of the polygon. The area of each little triangle is half the apothem times a side of the polygon. The area of a regular polygon is half the product of the apothem and the perimeter.

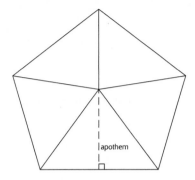

Practice

Directions (1–2): You are given two quantities, one in Column A and one in Column B. You are to compare the two quantities and choose one of the following:

    A.   The quantity in Column A is greater.
    B.   The quantity in Column B is greater.
    C.   The two quantities are equal.
    D.   The relationship cannot be determined from the information given.

Column A	Column B
1. The sum of the interior angles of a triangle	The sum of the exterior angles of a triangle

Column A	Column B
2. The sum of the interior angles of a pentagon	The sum of the exterior angles of a pentagon

Directions (3–10): Unless otherwise directed, select a single answer choice. For numeric-entry questions, enter a number in the box(es) below the question. Equivalent forms of the correct answer, such as 2.5 and 2.50, are all correct. Fractions do not need to be reduced to lowest terms. Enter the exact answer unless the question asks you to round your answer.

3. The symbol $t\underline{|s|}$ is defined to mean "t is the total of the interior angles of a polygon with s sides." Select all the true statements.

   A. $180°\underline{|3|}$

   B. $360°\underline{|4|}$

   C. $450°\underline{|5|}$

   D. $720°\underline{|6|}$

   E. $1,080°\underline{|8|}$

   F. $1,760°\underline{|10|}$

   G. $1,800°\underline{|12|}$

4. Select all the statements that correctly match the number of sides of a regular polygon with the measure of one of its interior angles.

   A. A regular polygon with five sides has interior angles that each measure 108°.
   B. A regular polygon with six sides has interior angles that each measure 120°.
   C. A regular polygon with eight sides has interior angles that each measure 132°.
   D. A regular polygon with ten sides has interior angles that each measure 140°.

5. The number of sides in a decagon minus the number of sides in a hexagon equals:

   A. The number of sides in an octagon
   B. The number of sides in a pentagon
   C. The number of sides in a quadrilateral
   D. The number of diagonals in a rectangle
   E. The number of diagonals in a hexagon

6. Find the number of diagonals in a polygon of 20 sides.

   A. 400
   B. 360
   C. 340
   D. 180
   E. 170

Question 7 refers to the following figure.

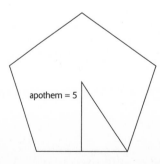

apothem = 5

7. Find the perimeter of a regular pentagon if its area is 50 square meters and the length of the *apothem* (distance from center to edge) is 5 meters.

   A.   4 meters
   B.   5 meters
   C.   10 meters
   D.   20 meters
   E.   50 meters

8. Find the area of a regular hexagon 4 inches on each side.

   A.   16 in.^{2}
   B.   24 in.^{2}
   C.   36 in.^{2}
   D. $16\sqrt{3}$ in.^{2}
   E. $24\sqrt{3}$ in.^{2}

9. The length of each outer wall of the Pentagon in Washington, D.C., is 921 feet, and the structure, including its inner courtyard, covers an area of 1,481,000 square feet. Find the length of the apothem to the nearest foot.

   ┌──────────┐
   └──────────┘

10. Find the measure of an interior angle of a dodecagon, a regular polygon with 12 sides.

   ┌──────────┐
   └──────────┘

Answers

1. **B** The sum of the interior angles of a triangle is 180°. The sum of the exterior angles of a triangle is 360°.

2. **A** The sum of the interior angles of a pentagon is $(5 - 2) \times 180° = 540°$. The sum of the exterior angles of a pentagon—the sum of the exterior angles of any polygon—is 360°.

3. **A, B, D, E, G** The sum of the measures of the interior angles of a polygon with s sides is $(s - 2) \times 180°$, so $180°\boxed{3}$ is true, because the three angles of a triangle total 180°, and $360°\boxed{4}$ is true, because $(4 - 2) \times 180° = 360°$. Check the remaining choices. $(5 - 2) \times 180° = 540°$, not 450°. $(6 - 2) \times 180° = 720°$ and, $(8 - 2) \times 180° = 1,080°$, but $(10 - 2) \times 180° = 1,440°$, not 1,760°. However, $(12 - 2) \times 180° = 1,800°$.

4. **A, B** If the polygon is regular, the measure of one interior angle can be found by finding the total of all the interior angles and dividing by the number of angles. A regular polygon with five sides has interior angles of $540° \div 5 = 108°$, and one with six sides has $720° \div 6 = 120°$: A regular polygon with eight sides has $1,080° \div 8 = 135°$, and one with ten sides has $1,440° \div 10 = 144°$.

5. **C** The number of sides in a decagon is ten and the number of sides in a hexagon is six, so the difference is 4.

6. **E** From each of the vertices of a polygon, you can draw a number of diagonals that is three fewer than the number of vertices. So, from each of the 20 vertices you can draw 17 diagonals. At first

glance, the answer would seem to be $20 \times 17 = 340$. But that counts each diagonal twice—once from one end and again from the other end. To eliminate the duplication, divide $340 \div 2 = 170$.

7. **D** The area of the hexagon is half the product of the apothem and the perimeter, so if the area is 50, the apothem times the perimeter equals 100. Since the apothem is 5, the perimeter is 20.

8. **E** A regular hexagon can be divided into six identical equilateral triangles by drawing diagonals. Each of these triangles has a base of 4 inches and, by using 30-60-90 right-triangle relationships, a height of $2\sqrt{3}$. The area of each equilateral triangle is $\frac{1}{2} \cdot 4 \cdot 2\sqrt{3} = 4\sqrt{3}$ and there are six of them so the area of the hexagon is $6 \cdot 4\sqrt{3} = 24\sqrt{3}$.

9. **643 feet** The area is made up of five triangles, so each triangle has an area of $1{,}481{,}000 \div 5 = 296{,}200$ square feet. Each of the triangles has a base of 921 feet and a height that is the apothem of the pentagon.

$$A = \frac{1}{2}bh$$
$$296{,}200 = \frac{1}{2} \cdot 921h$$
$$2(296{,}200) = 921h$$
$$h = \frac{2(296{,}200)}{921} \approx 643.2$$

10. **150°** The measure of an interior angle of a regular dodecagon is $\frac{(12-2) \cdot 180°}{12} = \frac{1800°}{12} = 150°$.

E. Areas of Shaded Regions

Problems that ask you to find the area of a shaded region are a favorite of most test writers. Sometimes these areas can be found by calculating the area of the shaded region directly, and other times it's easier to calculate the area of the overall figure and then subtract the area of the unshaded region.

EXAMPLES:

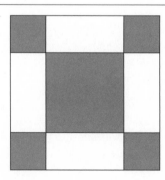

1. The whole figure is a square with side of length 4 centimeters. The shaded center square has a side of 2 centimeters, and all the shaded regions are squares. Find the total shaded area.

If the center square has a side of 2 centimeters, then each of the small shaded squares in the corners has a side of 1 centimeter. The shaded area is the area of the center square plus the areas of the four corner squares: $2^2 + (4 \times 1^2) = 4 + 4 = 8$ cm^2.

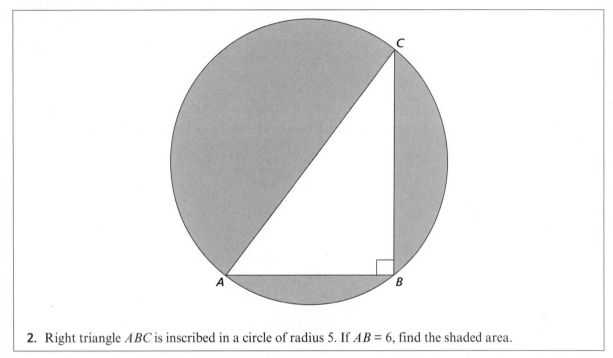

2. Right triangle ABC is inscribed in a circle of radius 5. If $AB = 6$, find the shaded area.

The area of the circle is πr^2 or 25π square units. When a right triangle is inscribed in a circle, the inscribed right angle intercepts a semicircle, so the hypotenuse of the triangle is a diameter. The diameter is 10 and leg AB is 6, so the remaining leg of the triangle is 8. The area of the triangle is $\frac{1}{2}bh = \frac{1}{2} \cdot 6 \cdot 8 = 24$ square units.

The shaded area is the area of the circle minus the area of the triangle or $25\pi - 24$.

Practice

Directions (1–2): You are given two quantities, one in Column A and one in Column B. You are to compare the two quantities and choose one of the following:

A. The quantity in Column A is greater.
B. The quantity in Column B is greater.
C. The two quantities are equal.
D. The relationship cannot be determined from the information given.

Question 1 refers to the following figure. The circles in the figure are congruent to one another, and tangent to one another and to the rectangle. The diameter of each circle is 4 inches.

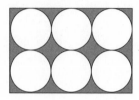

	Column A	**Column B**
1.	The shaded area	The unshaded area

Question 2 refers to the following figure. In the figure, the large circle has a radius of 10 cm. The two smaller circles are tangent to the large circle and to each other.

	Column A	**Column B**
2.	The shaded area	The unshaded area

Directions (3–10): Unless otherwise directed, select a single answer choice. For numeric-entry questions, enter a number in the box(es) below the question. Equivalent forms of the correct answer, such as 2.5 and 2.50, are all correct. Fractions do not need to be reduced to lowest terms. Enter the exact answer unless the question asks you to round your answer.

Question 3 refers to the following figure. The unshaded areas are quarter-circles.

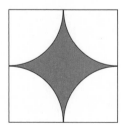

3. If the side of the square is 4 cm, select all the true statements.

    A.   The shaded area is one-fifth of the square.

    B.   The perimeter of the square is 16 cm.

    C.   The unshaded area is equivalent to the area of a circle of radius 2 cm.

    D.   The unshaded area is 4π cm^2.

    E.   The shaded area is $16 - 4\pi$ cm^2.

Question 4 refers to the following figure.

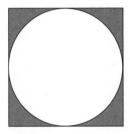

4. If the circle is tangent to the sides of the square, select all the statements that would provide enough information to find the area of the shaded region.

    A.   The perimeter of the square is 48 inches.

    B.   The circumference of the circle is 12π inches.

    C.   The side of the square is 12 inches.

    D.   The radius of the circle is 6 inches.

Question 5 refers to the following figure.

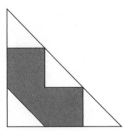

5. Each triangle in the figure is an isosceles right triangle. The large triangle has legs 30 cm long, and the small unshaded triangles have legs 10 cm long. Find the area of shaded polygon.

    A.   100 cm^2

    B.   150 cm^2

    C.   200 cm^2

    D.   250 cm^2

    E.   300 cm^2

Question 6 refers to the following figure.

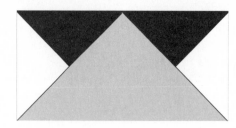

6. In the rectangle shown, the black triangles are congruent isosceles triangles, each with an area of 12 in.^{2}. What is the area of the gray-shaded region?

   A. 12 in.^{2}
   B. 18 in.^{2}
   C. 24 in.^{2}
   D. 36 in.^{2}
   E. 48 in.^{2}

Question 7 refers to the following figure.

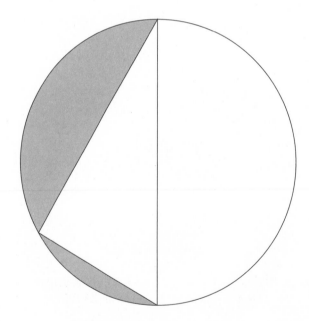

7. A right triangle with sides of 6 inches, 8 inches, and 10 inches is inscribed in a circle. Find the shaded area ($\pi \approx 3.14$).

   A. 15.3 in.^{2}
   B. 24 in.^{2}
   C. 48 in.^{2}
   D. 54.5 in.^{2}
   E. 266.2 in.^{2}

Question 8 refers to the following figure.

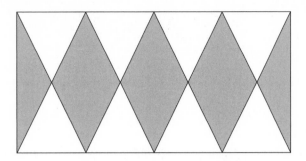

8. If the rectangle measures 4 feet by 2 feet, and all the white triangles are congruent, find the shaded area.

   A. 1 ft.^{2}
   B. 2 ft.^{2}
   C. 4 ft.^{2}
   D. 6 ft.^{2}
   E. 7 ft.^{2}

Questions 9–10 refer to the following figure. In the figure, a target formed from concentric circles has a diameter of 4 feet. The innermost circle has a diameter of 1 foot, and each ring has the same width.

9. Find the white area in the figure ($\pi \approx 3.14$).

$\boxed{}$

10. Find the black area in the figure ($\pi \approx 3.14$).

$\boxed{}$

Answers

1. **B** The diameter of each circle is 4 inches, so the radius of each circle is 2 inches, and the area of each circle is $\pi r^2 = 4\pi$ square inches. The total unshaded area is $6 \times 4\pi$, or about 75.4 square inches. The diameters of the circles also allow you to determine that the rectangle measures 12 inches by 8 inches, so it has an area of 96 in.². The shaded region has an area equal to the area of the rectangle minus the area of the six circles. This is $96 - 6(4\pi) = 96 - 75.4 = 20.6$ in.².

2. **C** If the large circle has a radius of 10 cm, then each of the small circles has a diameter of 10 cm and a radius of 5 cm. The area of the large circle is 100π cm², and the total area of the two smaller circles is $2(25\pi) = 50\pi$ cm². Subtracting the combined area of the small circles from the area of the large circle leaves a shaded area of 50π cm², or half the large circle.

3. **B, C, D, E** The shaded region is the area of the square minus the four quarter-circles, which make one full circle; choice C is true. The radius of that circle is half the side of the square, or 2. The area of the square is 16 square units, so choice E is true. The area of the circle is 4π, so choice D is true. The shaded area is $16 - 4\pi \approx 3.4$. One-fifth of the square would be 3.2, so choice A is not true. The perimeter of the square is 4×4, so choice B is true.

4. **A, B, C, D** To find the shaded area, you need to subtract the area of the circle from the area of the square. If you know the perimeter, you can divide by 4 to find the side of the square. The side of the square is equal to the diameter of the circle, and the radius of the circle is half the diameter, so any one of the choices will provide sufficient information to find the necessary areas.

5. **D** The area of the largest triangle is $\frac{1}{2}(30)^2 = \frac{1}{2} \cdot 900 = 450$ cm². The area of each of the small triangles is $\frac{1}{2}(10)^2 = \frac{1}{2} \cdot 100 = 50$. The shaded region is the area of the large triangle minus the combined area of the four small triangles, so the shaded area is $450 - 4(50) = 250$ cm².

6. **E** The gray shaded triangle has a base equal to the total of the bases of the two black triangles, and a height twice the height of the black triangles. The area of a black triangle is $\frac{1}{2}bh = 12$. The gray triangle has an area equal to $\frac{1}{2}(2b)(2h) = 4 \cdot \frac{1}{2}bh = 4 \cdot 12 = 48$.

7. **A** The triangle is a right triangle, because its sides are a Pythagorean triple. Its hypotenuse is a diameter of the circle. The shaded area is half the area of the circle minus the area of the triangle: $\frac{1}{2}\pi \cdot 5^2 - \frac{1}{2} \cdot 6 \cdot 8 = \frac{25\pi}{2} - 24 \approx 15.3$ in.².

8. **C** The total area of the rectangle is $4 \times 2 = 8$ square feet, and each white triangle has a base of 1 foot and a height of 1 foot, so each white triangle has an area of 0.5 ft.². There are eight white triangles for a total area of 4 ft.², so the shaded area is the remaining 4 ft.².

9. **4.71** The smallest white circle has a radius of $\frac{1}{2}$, so its area is $\frac{\pi}{4}$ square feet. The area of the white ring is the area of a circle of radius $\frac{3}{2}$, minus the area of a circle of radius 1. $\pi\left(\frac{3}{2}\right)^2 - \pi \cdot 1^2 = \frac{9\pi}{4} - \pi = \frac{9\pi}{4} - \frac{4\pi}{4} = \frac{5\pi}{4}$ square feet. The total white area is $\frac{\pi}{4} + \frac{5\pi}{4} = \frac{6\pi}{4} = \frac{3\pi}{2} \approx 4.71$ square feet.

10. **7.85 ft.²** The black area is the area of the entire target, $\pi \times 2^2 = 4\pi$, minus the white area found in question 9. You also can find it by adding the areas of the two black rings. The larger black ring has an area of $\pi \cdot 2^2 - \pi\left(\frac{3}{2}\right)^2 = \frac{16\pi}{4} - \frac{9\pi}{4} = \frac{7\pi}{4}$, and the area of the smaller black ring is $\pi \cdot 1^2 - \pi\left(\frac{1}{2}\right)^2 = \frac{4\pi}{4} - \frac{\pi}{4} = \frac{3\pi}{4}$. Add the two rings to get $\frac{7\pi}{4} + \frac{3\pi}{4} = \frac{10\pi}{4} = \frac{5\pi}{2} \approx 7.85$ ft.².

F. Circles

A circle is the set of all points in a plane at a fixed distance from a given point, called the *center.*

1. Lines and segments in a circle

The fixed distance that determines the size of the circle is called the *radius;* all radii of a circle are the same length. A *chord* is a line segment whose endpoints lie on the circle; the longer the chord, the closer it is to the center of the circle. The *diameter* is the longest chord of a circle. It passes through the center of the circle; the diameter is twice as long as the radius. Congruent chords cut off congruent arcs. If two chords intersect in a circle, each chord is divided into two sections by the other chord, and the product of the lengths of the sections of one chord is equal to the product of the lengths of the sections of the other. A *secant* is a line that contains a chord; it's a line that intersects the circle in two distinct points. A *tangent* is a line that touches the circle in exactly one point. The radius drawn to the point of tangency is perpendicular to the tangent line. Two tangent segments drawn to a circle from the same point are congruent.

EXAMPLE:

> In circle O, chords $\overline{AB}$ and $\overline{CD}$ intersect at E. If $AE = 4$, $BE = 10$, and $CE = 8$, find the length of DE.

The segments of chord $\overline{AB}$ are 4 units and 10 units long. Multiplying 4×10 gives a product of 40. The known segment of $\overline{CD}$ is 8 units. If the other is x, then $8x = 40$, so $x = 5$.

2. Angles

A **central angle** is an angle formed by two radii. Its vertex is at the center of the circle. A measure of a central angle is equal to the measure of its intercepted arc. An *inscribed angle* is an angle whose sides are chords, and whose vertex lies on the circle. The measure of an inscribed angle is equal to one-half the measure of its intercepted arc.

EXAMPLE:

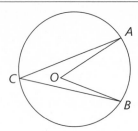

In circle O, $\overline{OA}$ and $\overline{OB}$ are radii, and $\overline{AC}$ and $\overline{BC}$ are chords. If $\overset{\frown}{AB} = 50°$, find $m\angle AOB$ and $m\angle ACB$.

$\overset{\frown}{AB}$ is the intercepted arc for both angles. $\angle AOB$ is a central angle, so its measure is the same as the measure of the arc. $m\angle AOB = 50°$. $\angle ACB$ is an inscribed angle, so its measure is half the measure of the arc: $m\angle ACB = 25°$.

When two chords intersect within a circle, they form four angles. Vertical angles are congruent, and adjacent angles are supplementary. The measure of an angle formed by two chords (and of its vertical angle partner) is one-half the sum of the two intercepted arcs. To find the measure of an angle formed by two chords, average the arcs intercepted by the two vertical angles.

EXAMPLE:

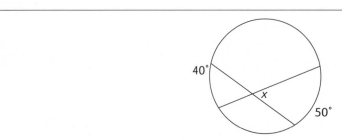

Two chords intersect in the circle as shown. Find the value of x.

The two vertical angles whose measure is x intercept arcs of 40° and 50°. $x = \frac{1}{2}(40 + 50) = 45°$.

Angles formed by two secants, a tangent and a secant, or two tangents intercept two arcs. The arc nearer to the vertex of the angle is smaller. The measure of the angle is one-half the difference of the two arcs it intercepts.

EXAMPLE:

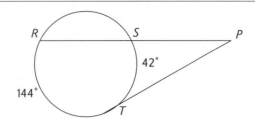

A secant and a tangent both drawn from point P intersect the circle as shown. Find the measure of $\angle P$.

The measure of $\angle P$ is half the difference of $\overset{\frown}{RT}$ and $\overset{\frown}{ST}$. $\angle P = \frac{1}{2}\left(\overset{\frown}{RT} - \overset{\frown}{ST}\right) = \frac{1}{2}(144 - 42) = \frac{1}{2}(102) = 51°$.

3. Circumference

The circumference of a circle is the distance around the circle. The circumference of the circle is similar to the perimeter of a polygon. The formula for the circumference of a circle is $C = 2\pi r = \pi d$, where r is the radius of the circle, d is the diameter of the circle, and π is a constant approximately equal to 3.14159. For most questions, you can use 3.14 or $\frac{22}{7}$ as approximate values of π.

EXAMPLE:

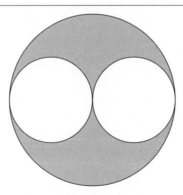

If the radius of the large circle is equal to the diameter of the smaller circles, then the circumference of the large circle is equal to:

A. The circumference of a small circle
B. Half the circumference of a small circle
C. Twice the circumference of a small circle
D. Four times the circumference of a small circle
E. None of the above

The correct answer is **C.** For convenience, make up a radius for the large circle, say 10 cm. The circumference of the large circle is $2\pi \times 10 = 20\pi$. The circumference of the small circle is $\pi \times 10 = 10\pi$, so the circumference of the large circle is twice the circumference of the small circle.

4. Area

The area of a circle is the product of π and the square of the radius: $A = \pi r^2$.

EXAMPLE:

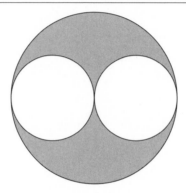

If the radius of the large circle is equal to the diameter of the smaller circles, then the area of the large circle is equal to:

A. The area of a smaller circle
B. Half the area of a smaller circle
C. Twice the area of a smaller circle
D. Four times the area of a smaller circle
E. None of the above

Make up a value for the radius of the large circle—say, 10. The area of the large circle is $\pi \times 10^2 = 100\pi$. The diameter of the small circle is 10, so its radius is 5. The area of the small circle is $\pi \times 5^2 = 25\pi$. The area of the large circle is four times as large as the area of the small circle.

Practice

Directions (1–2): You are given two quantities, one in Column A and one in Column B. You are to compare the two quantities and choose one of the following:

    A.   The quantity in Column A is greater.
    B.   The quantity in Column B is greater.
    C.   The two quantities are equal.
    D.   The relationship cannot be determined from the information given.

Column A	Column B
1. The number of centimeters in the circumference of a circle of radius 5 cm	The number of square centimeters in the area of a circle of diameter 10 cm

Column A	Column B
2. The area of a circle whose radius is 7	The area of a rhombus whose side is 7

Directions (3–10): Unless otherwise directed, select a single answer choice. For numeric-entry questions, enter a number in the box(es) below the question. Equivalent forms of the correct answer, such as 2.5 and 2.50, are all correct. Fractions do not need to be reduced to lowest terms. Enter the exact answer unless the question asks you to round your answer.

Question 3 refers to the following figure.

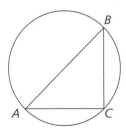

3. $\triangle ABC$ with $\overline{AC} \perp \overline{BC}$ is inscribed in the circle. Select all the true statements.

    A. $\overline{AB}$ is a diameter.
    B. $\triangle ACB$ is isosceles.
    C. $\angle B$ is acute.
    D. $m\angle B = \frac{1}{2}\widehat{AC}$.
    E. $AC = BC$.

Question 4 refers to the following figure.

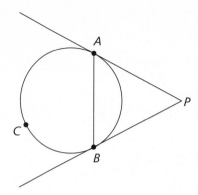

4. Two tangents are drawn to the circle from point P. $m\angle P = 60°$, and $m\overarc{ACB} = 240°$. Select all the true statements.

    A. $\triangle APB$ is a scalene triangle.

    B. $\triangle APB$ is a right triangle.

    C. $\triangle APB$ is an equilateral triangle.

    D. $\overline{AB}$ is a diameter.

Questions 5–6 refer to the following figure.

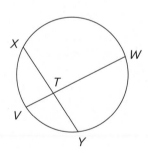

5. $\overarc{XW} = 120°$ and $\overarc{VY} = 40°$. Find $m\angle YTW - m\angle XTW$.

    A.   20°

    B.   45°

    C.   85°

    D.   100°

    E.   120°

6. In the circle, $XY = 12$, $TW = 16$, and $VT = 2$. find TX.

   A. 5
   B. 6
   C. 7
   D. 8
   E. 9

Questions 7–8 refer to the following figure.

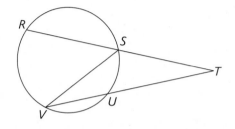

7. $\triangle STV$ is isosceles, with $ST = SV$. $\overset{\frown}{RV} = 110°$. Find the measure of $\overset{\frown}{SU}$.

   A. 35°
   B. 45°
   C. 55°
   D. 65°
   E. 105°

8. In the circle, secant $RT = 10$ and $VT = 8$. If $ST = 6$, Find TU.

   A. 5
   B. 7.5
   C. 10
   D. 12.5
   E. 15

9. The radius of a circle is $\frac{2}{\pi}$. Find its area to the nearest hundredth ($\pi \approx 3.14$).

10. A central angle and an inscribed angle both intercept an arc of 86°. Find the difference in their measures.

Answers

1. **B** The number of centimeters in the circumference of a circle of radius 5 cm is $2\pi r = 10\pi$. The number of square centimeters in the area of a circle of diameter 10 cm is $\pi r^2 = 25\pi$.

2. **A** Estimation is enough to allow you to decide. The area of a circle whose radius is 7 is 49π, and the area of a rhombus whose side is 7 is 7 times the height. The height of the rhombus will be less than or equal to the side, since the perpendicular distance between the parallel sides is the shortest distance. That means the height will be less than 7 and the area will be less than 49.

3. **A, C, D** An angle inscribed in a circle will intercept an arc equal to twice its measure, so a right angle will intercept a semicircle and $\overline{AB}$ will be a diameter, so choice A is true. The same relationship tells you that choice D is true. The other two angles of the right triangle must be acute, so choice C is true, but it is not possible to determine whether they're equal or whether the triangle is isosceles.

4. **C** When two tangents are drawn to a circle from the same point, the tangent segments are congruent, so $\triangle APB$ is not scalene. In order for $\triangle APB$ to be a right triangle, the vertex angle, $\angle P$, would have to be the right angle, but you know that $m\angle P = 60°$. Since $m\angle P = 60°$ and the remaining angles of the triangle are congruent, because they are opposite congruent sides, all three angles are 60° and the triangle is equilateral. $\overline{AB}$ cannot be a diameter, because $m\overparen{ACB} = 240°$.

5. **A** $m\angle XTW = \frac{1}{2}\left(\overparen{XW} + \overparen{VY}\right) = \frac{1}{2}(120 + 40) = \frac{1}{2}(160) = 80$. $\angle YTW$ and $\angle XTW$ are supplementary, so $m\angle YTW = 180° - 80° = 100°$. Then $m\angle YTW - m\angle XTW = 100° - 80° = 20°$.

6. **D** When two chords intersect within a circle, the product of the lengths of the two pieces of one chord is equal to the product of the lengths of the two pieces of the other. So, $TW \times VT = TX \times TY$, and if you let x represent the length of TX, that means $16 \times 2 = x(12 - x)$. Solve the quadratic equation, to find that $x = 8$ or $x = 4$.

7. **C** Let x represent the measure of $\overparen{SU}$. The measure of $\angle V$ is half of $\overparen{SU}$ and the measure of $\angle T$ is half the difference of $\overparen{RV}$ and $\overparen{SU}$. Since $m\angle V = m\angle T$, $\frac{1}{2}x = \frac{1}{2}\left(110 - x\right)$ and that means $x = 110 - x$, so $2x = 110$ and $x = 55°$.

8. **B** When two secants are drawn to a circle from the same point, the product of the lengths of the secant and its external segment are constant, so $RT \times ST = VT \times TU$. Substituting known values, $10 \times 6 = 8 \times TU$, or $TU = 60 \div 8 = 7.5$.

9. **1.27** The area of the circle is $\pi r^2 = \pi \cdot \left(\frac{2}{\pi}\right)^2 = \pi \cdot \frac{4}{\pi^2} = \frac{4}{\pi} \approx 1.27$.

10. **43°** The central angle has a measure equal to its intercepted arc, 86°, and the inscribed angle has a measure equal to half the intercepted arc, or 43°, so the difference between them is 43°.

G. Solids

1. Volume

Instead of memorizing numerous volume formulas, remember that the volume of a prism or a cylinder is $V =$ area of the base $\times$ height. The volume of a pyramid or cone is $V = \frac{1}{3} \times$ area of the base $\times$ height.

EXAMPLE:

> Find the volume of a triangular prism 4 inches high, whose base is an equilateral triangle with sides 6 inches long.

First, you need to find the area of the base. Because it is an equilateral triangle, you can use the 30°-60°-90° triangle relationship to find the height. The altitude of the equilateral triangle is half the side times the square root of 3, or $3\sqrt{3}$. The area of the triangle is $\frac{1}{2} bh = \frac{1}{2} \cdot 6 \cdot 3\sqrt{3} = 9\sqrt{3}$. Finally, the volume of the prism is the area of the base times the height, or $9\sqrt{3} \cdot 4 = 36\sqrt{3}$.

2. Surface area

Questions about surface area can be answered by finding the area of each surface of the solid and adding. The surface area of a rectangular solid, for example, is $SA = 2lw + 2lh + 2wh$.

The surface area of a cylinder is the total of the areas of the two circles at the ends, plus the area of the rectangle that forms the cylindrical wall. (Think about a label on a can.) The area of each circle is πr^2. The rectangle has a height equal to the height of the cylinder and a base equal to the circumference of the circle, so its area is $2\pi rh$. The total surface area is $SA = 2\pi r^2 + 2\pi rh$.

EXAMPLE:

	Column A	Column B
1.	The surface area of a cylinder of diameter 4 cm and height 4 cm	The surface area of a cube of side 4 cm

The diameter is 4 cm, so the radius is 2, and the surface area of the cylinder is

$$SA = 2\pi r^2 + 2\pi rh$$
$$= 2 \cdot \pi \cdot 2^2 + 2 \cdot \pi \cdot 2 \cdot 4$$
$$= 8\pi + 16\pi = 24\pi \approx 75.4$$

The surface area of the cube is the total of the areas of six identical squares, each with an area of 16 cm². The total surface area is $6 \times 16 = 96$ cm², so the cube has the larger surface area.

Practice

Directions (1–2): You are given two quantities, one in Column A and one in Column B. You are to compare the two quantities and choose one of the following:

A. The quantity in Column A is greater.
B. The quantity in Column B is greater.
C. The two quantities are equal.
D. The relationship cannot be determined from the information given.

	Column A	Column B
1.	The surface area of a cube with an edge of 2 cm	The surface area of a cylinder with a radius of 2 cm and a height of 2 cm

	Column A	Column B
2.	The edge of a cube whose volume is 64 cm^3	The edge of a cube whose surface area is 64 cm^2

Directions (3–10): Unless otherwise directed, select a single answer choice. For numeric-entry questions, enter a number in the box(es) below the question. Equivalent forms of the correct answer, such as 2.5 and 2.50, are all correct. Fractions do not need to be reduced to lowest terms. Enter the exact answer unless the question asks you to round your answer.

Question 3 refers to the following figure.

3. A hexagonal paving stone is made by pouring concrete into a mold. The area of the hexagonal face is 54 square inches and the block is 2 inches thick. One cubic foot is 1,728 cubic inches. Which of the following statements correctly state the volume of concrete required? Select all the true statements.

   A. 420 pavers require 25 ft.^{3} of concrete.
   B. 650 pavers require 40 ft.^{3} of concrete.
   C. 1,200 pavers require 75 ft.^{3} of concrete.
   D. 2,800 pavers require 175 ft.^{3} of concrete.
   E. 5,000 pavers require 312 ft.^{3} of concrete.

Question 4 refers to the following figure.

4. A beam is formed from metal in the shape of a cross. Each "arm" of the cross is a square, as is the center section. Each of these squares has a side of 6 inches, and the beam is 6 feet long. The metal from which it is formed weighs 1.5 ounces per cubic inch. Select all the true statements.

    A. The height of the beam is 1 foot.
    B. The width of the beam is 18 inches.
    C. The surface area of the cross-shaped face of the beam is 180 in.^{2}.
    D. The volume of the beam is 1,080 in.^{3}.
    E. The weight of the beam is 19,440 ounces.

Question 5 refers to the following figure.

5. Find the volume of the washer shown if the outer diameter is 10 inches, the inner diameter (the diameter of the hole) is 6 inches, and the washer is $\frac{1}{4}$ inch thick.

    A. 6.28 in.^{3}
    B. 9.42 in.^{3}
    C. 12.57 in.^{3}
    D. 15.71 in.^{3}
    E. 18.85 in.^{3}

6. Find the volume of a cylinder with a diameter of 18 feet and a height of 25 feet ($\pi \approx = 3.14$).

    A. 25,446.90 ft.^{3}
    B. 6,361.73 ft.^{3}
    C. 8,100 ft.^{3}
    D. 2,025 ft.^{3}
    E. 1,413.72 ft.^{3}

7. How many boxes, each a cube with a volume of 8 in.³, can be packed into a crate 2 feet wide, 3 feet long, and 1 foot high?

    A.   60
    B.   600
    C.   1,296
    D.   5,184
    E.   10,368

8. A cylindrical container must have a volume of 200 cm³, but shelf space requires that the height of the container cannot exceed 12 cm. What should be the radius of the container?

    A.   16.67 cm
    B.   5.31 cm
    C.   4.08 cm
    D.   2.30 cm
    E.   1.18 cm

Questions 9–10 refer to the following figure. The prism shown has a base that is a right triangle.

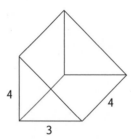

9. Find the surface area of the prism.

    [ ]

10. Find the volume of the prism.

    [ ]

Answers

1. **B** The surface area of a cube with an edge of 2 cm is $6(2^2) = 24$ cm². The surface area of a cylinder with a radius of 2 cm and a height of 2 cm $= 2\pi r^2 + 2\pi rh = 2\pi \times 2^2 + 2\pi \times 2 \times 2 = 8\pi + 8\pi = 16\pi$ cm², which is greater than 48.

2. **A** The edge of a cube whose volume is 64 cm³ is 4 cm, since $4^3 = 64$. If a cube has surface area of 64 cm², that represents the total area of the six faces, all identical squares. Each square would have an area of $\frac{64}{6} = 10\frac{2}{3}$ cm², and so the edge would be between 3 and 4.

3. **C, D** The volume of one paving stone is the area of the base, 54 in.^{2}, times the height, 2 in., or 108 in.^{3}. To find the number of cubic feet of concrete required for a number of pavers, multiply the number of pavers times 108 and divide by 1,728: $420 \times 108 \div 1,728 = 26.25$, so choice A is incorrect. $650 \times 108 \div 1,728 = 40.625$, so choice B is incorrect. $1,200 \times 108 \div 1,728 = 75$ and $2,800 \times 108 \div 1,728 = 175$, so choices C and D are correct. $5,000 \times 108 \div 1,728 = 312.5$, so choice E is incorrect.

4. **B, C, E** The height and width of the beam are both three of the squares that make up the cross, and each square is 6 inches, so the height and width are 18 inches, not 1 foot. The face of the beam has a surface area of $5(6)^2$ in.^{2} or 180 in.^{2}. Multiply this by the length of the beam, 6 feet or 72 inches, to find the volume of the beam: $180 \times 72 = 12,960$ in.^{3} is the volume of the beam. (So, choice D is incorrect.) To find the weight of the beam, multiply the volume by 1.5 ounces per cubic inch. The weight is 12,960 in.$^3 \times 1.5$ ounces per cubic inch = 19,440 ounces, so choice E is correct.

5. **C** First, calculate the volume of the outer cylinder, and then subtract the volume of the hole in the washer. The outer cylinder has a volume of $\pi r^2 h \approx \frac{22}{7} \cdot 5^2 \cdot \frac{1}{4} = \frac{550}{28} = \frac{275}{14}$, and the hole has a volume of $\pi r^2 h \approx \frac{22}{7} \cdot 3^2 \cdot \frac{1}{4} = \frac{99}{14}$. Subtracting, $\frac{275}{14} - \frac{99}{14} = \frac{176}{14} = \frac{88}{7} = 12\frac{4}{7}$.

6. **B** The volume of a cylinder is $V = \pi r^2 h$. The diameter is 18 feet, so the radius is 9 feet, and the height is 25 feet. $V = \pi \times 9^2 \times 25 = \pi \times 81 \times 25 \approx 6,361.5$ ft.^{3}.

7. **C** The crate has a volume of 2 ft. $\times$ 3 ft. $\times$ 1 ft. = 24 in. $\times$ 36 in. $\times$ 12 in. = 10,368 in.^{3}. Divide by 8 to find the crate will hold 1,296 boxes.

8. **D** The volume of a cylinder is $V = \pi r^2 h$. Set volume to 200 and height to 12, and solve for the radius.

$$V = \pi r^2 h$$
$$200 = \pi r^2 \cdot 12$$
$$\frac{200}{12\pi} \approx 5.31 = r^2$$
$$r \approx \sqrt{5.31} \approx 2.31$$

9. **60 square units** The surface area can be broken down into the area of the two 3-4-5 right triangles plus the areas of the three rectangular faces. The area of each right triangle is $\frac{1}{2} \cdot 3 \cdot 4 = 6$, so the two right triangles have a total area of 12. The rectangular faces are 3×4, 4×4, and 5×4 and, therefore, total $12 + 16 + 20 = 48$. The total surface area is $12 + 48 = 60$ square units.

10. **24 cubic units** The volume is the area of the right triangle times the height of 4. Volume is $V = \left(\frac{1}{2} \cdot 3 \cdot 4\right) \cdot 4 = 24$.

H. Coordinate Geometry

In coordinate geometry, the plane is divided into four quadrants by two perpendicular number lines called the x-axis and the y-axis. The x-axis is horizontal; the y-axis is vertical. These axes intersect at their zero points. The point $(0, 0)$ is called the *origin*. Every point in the plane can be represented by a set of numbers or coordinates (x, y). This ordered pair allows you to locate the point by counting from the origin. The x-coordinate indicates the left/right movement. The y-coordinate indicates the up/down movement.

1. Midpoints

To find the midpoint of the segment connecting two points in the plane, average the x-coordinates of the two points, and average the y-coordinates. The resulting ordered pair gives the coordinates of the midpoint.

The midpoint, M, of the segment joining (x_1, y_1) with (x_2, y_2) is the point $\left(\dfrac{x_1 + x_2}{2}, \dfrac{y_1 + y_2}{2} \right)$.

EXAMPLE:

> Find the midpoint of the segment that joins the points $(-7, 5)$ and $(4, -6)$.

The midpoint is the point whose x-coordinate is midway between -7 and 4, and whose y-coordinate is the average of 5 and -6. So, $M = \left(\dfrac{-7+4}{2}, \dfrac{5+-6}{2} \right) = \left(\dfrac{-3}{2}, \dfrac{-1}{2} \right)$.

2. Distances

The formula for the distance between two points in the coordinate plane is a disguised version of the Pythagorean theorem. To find the distance between the points (x_1, y_1) and (x_2, y_2), imagine a right triangle with vertices (x_1, y_1), (x_2, y_2), and (x_1, y_2). The length of the vertical leg is $y_1 - y_2$ and the length of the horizontal leg is $x_2 - x_1$. Using the Pythagorean theorem, the distance, d, between (x_1, y_1) and (x_2, y_2) is $a^2 + b^2 = c^2$ or $(x_2 - x_1)^2 + (y_2 - y_1)^2 = d^2$.

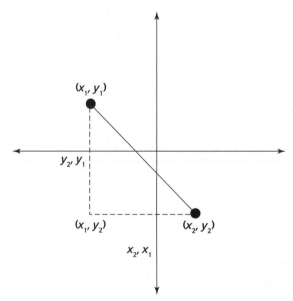

To find d, take the square root of both sides and you have the distance formula: $d = \sqrt{(x_2 - x_1)^2 + (y_2 - y_1)^2}$.

EXAMPLE:

> Find the distance from the point $(-7, 5)$ to the point $(4, -6)$.

Call $(-7, 5)$ the first point, so $x_1 = -7$ and $y_1 = 5$. The second point is $(4, -6)$ so $x_2 = 4$ and $y_2 = -6$. Use the distance formula $d = \sqrt{(x_2 - x_1)^2 + (y_2 - y_1)^2}$ and substitute $x_1 = -7$, $y_1 = 5$, $x_2 = 4$, and $y_2 = -6$:

$$
\begin{aligned}
d &= \sqrt{(-7-4)^2 + (5--6)^2} \\
&= \sqrt{(-11)^2 + (11)^2} \\
&= \sqrt{121 + 121} \\
&= \sqrt{121 \times 2} \\
&= \sqrt{121}\sqrt{2} \\
&= 11\sqrt{2} \approx 15.56
\end{aligned}
$$

3. Slope

The slope of a line is a means of talking about whether the line is rising or falling, and how quickly it's doing so. In the coordinate plane, slope can be expressed as the ratio of rise to run—that is, the amount of vertical change to the amount of horizontal change. If two points on the line are known to be (x_1, y_1) and (x_2, y_2), then the slope, m, of the line is given by the following formula:

$$
m = \frac{\text{rise}}{\text{run}} = \frac{\Delta y}{\Delta x} = \frac{y_2 - y_1}{x_2 - x_1}
$$

EXAMPLE:

> Find the slope of the line through the points $(-4, -4)$ and $(7, 3)$.

From a sketch, you can count the rise and the run. The rise is 7 and the run is 11. Or, using the formula, let $x_1 = 7$, $y_1 = 3$, $x_2 = -4$, $y_2 = -4$:

$$
m = \frac{\text{rise}}{\text{run}} = \frac{\Delta y}{\Delta x} = \frac{y_2 - y_1}{x_2 - x_1}
$$

$$
m = \frac{3 - (-4)}{7 - (-4)} = \frac{3 + 4}{7 + 4} = \frac{7}{11}
$$

A horizontal line has a rise of 0; therefore, its slope is 0. A vertical line has a run of 0; because of the zero in the denominator, the slope of a vertical line is undefined. We say a vertical line has no slope.

4. Finding the equation of a line

The slope-intercept form of a linear equation is $y = mx + b$, where m is the slope and b is the y-intercept. If the slope and y-intercept of a line are known, you can write the equation by simply putting these numbers into the correct positions. In other situations, it's more helpful to use the point-slope form, $y - y_1 = m(x - x_1)$. In this form, m is the slope and (x_1, y_1) is a point on the line.

EXAMPLE:

Find the equation of the line through the points (2, 5) and (–7, 23).

First, find the slope:

$$m = \frac{y_2 - y_1}{x_2 - x_1} = \frac{23 - 5}{-7 - 2} = \frac{18}{-9} = -2$$

Use the point-slope form with $m = -2$ and either point:

$$y - y_1 = m(x - x_1)$$
$$y - 5 = -2(x - 2)$$
$$y - 5 = -2x + 4$$
$$y = -2x + 9$$

5. Parallel and perpendicular lines

Parallel lines have the same slope. You can decide whether two lines are parallel by finding the slope of each line. If the slopes are the same, the lines are parallel. You can use this fact to help find the equation of a line parallel to a given line. In order to be parallel, the lines must have the same slope.

EXAMPLE:

Find the equation of a line through the point (–1, 3) parallel to $3x + 2y = 7$.

First, find the slope of the line $3x + 2y = 7$. Rearranging into $y = mx + b$ form, you get $y = \frac{-3}{2}x + \frac{7}{2}$, so the slope is $\frac{-3}{2}$. Use point-slope form with $m = \frac{-3}{2}$ and the point $(x_1, y_1) = (-1, 3)$.

$$y - y_1 = m(x - x_1)$$
$$y - 3 = \frac{-3}{2}\left(x - (-1)\right)$$
$$y - 3 = \frac{-3}{2}x - \frac{3}{2}$$
$$y = \frac{-3}{2}x + \frac{3}{2}$$

If two lines are perpendicular, their slopes will be negative reciprocals. You can determine if two lines are perpendicular by looking at their slopes, or you can use the relationship between the slopes of the lines to help you find the equation of a line perpendicular to a given line.

EXAMPLE:

Find the equation of a line through the point (–1, 3) perpendicular to $3x + 2y = 7$.

First, find the slope of the line $3x + 2y = 7$. Rearranging into $y = mx + b$ form, you get $y = \dfrac{-3}{2}x + \dfrac{7}{2}$, so the slope is $\dfrac{-3}{2}$. The slope of the line perpendicular to this will be $\dfrac{2}{3}$. Use point-slope form with $m = \dfrac{2}{3}$ and the point $(x_1, y_1) = (-1, 3)$.

$$y - y_1 = m(x - x_1)$$
$$y - 3 = \frac{2}{3}\left(x - (-1)\right)$$
$$y - 3 = \frac{2}{3}x + \frac{2}{3}$$
$$y = \frac{2}{3}x + \frac{11}{3}$$

6. Transformations

In transformational geometry, objects are moved about the plane by different methods.

a. Reflection

Anyone who has used a mirror has some experience with reflection. Reflection preserves distances, so objects stay the same size, and angle measure remains the same. Orientation changes, however, as you know if you've ever tried to do something that requires a sense of left and right while watching yourself in a mirror. The reflection of an object is congruent to the original.

On the coordinate plane, the most common reflections are reflection across the x-axis, reflection across the y-axis, and reflection across the line $y = x$. Reflection across the x-axis inverts the image. Under such a reflection, the image of the point (x, y) is the point $(x, -y)$. Reflection across the y-axis flips the image left to right. The image of the point (x, y) under a reflection across the y-axis is $(-x, y)$. Reflection across the line $y = x$ swaps the x- and y-coordinates. If the point (x, y) is reflected across the line $y = x$, its image is (y, x).

b. Translation

Translation is moving an object by sliding it across the plane. Translating a point left or right causes a change in the x-coordinate, while translating it up or down changes the y-coordinate. What appears to be a diagonal slide can be resolved into a horizontal and a vertical component. If the point (x, y) is translated h units horizontally and k units vertically, the image is $(x + h, y + k)$. Translation preserves distances, so objects stay the same size, and angle measure remains the same.

c. Rotation

Rotation is the transformation that moves an object in a circular fashion about the origin. Because rotation is really a series of reflections across intersecting lines, you can predict coordinates as you did with reflections.

Rotation Counterclockwise	Image of (x, y)
90°	(–y, x)
180°	(–x, –y)
270°	(y, –x)

Practice

Directions (1–4): You are given two quantities, one in Column A and one in Column B. You are to compare the two quantities and choose one of the following:

- **A.** The quantity in Column A is greater.
- **B.** The quantity in Column B is greater.
- **C.** The two quantities are equal.
- **D.** The relationship cannot be determined from the information given.

A is the point (7, –3) and B is the point (–1, 5).

	Column A	**Column B**
1.	The x-coordinate of the midpoint of $\overline{AB}$	The y-coordinate of the midpoint of $\overline{AB}$

A is the point (–3, 2) and B is the point (4, 7).

	Column A	**Column B**
2.	The distance from A to B	The distance from the origin to B

Line m has the equation $x + y = 5$.

	Column A	**Column B**
3.	The slope of a line parallel to m	The slope of a line perpendicular to m

P is the point (–5, 0).

	Column A	**Column B**
4.	The x-coordinate of the image of P under a rotation of 90° about the origin	The x-coordinate of the image of P under a rotation of 270° about the origin

Directions (5–10): Unless otherwise directed, select a single answer choice. For numeric-entry questions, enter a number in the box(es) below the question. Equivalent forms of the correct answer, such as 2.5 and 2.50, are all correct. Fractions do not need to be reduced to lowest terms. Enter the exact answer unless the question asks you to round your answer.

5. A line passing through the point $(0, -5)$ has a slope of 4. Which of the following are points on that line? Select all the correct answers.

    A. $(1, -1)$
    B. $(12, 43)$
    C. $(-1, -9)$
    D. $(-5, -5)$
    E. $(3, 7)$

6. The line segment connecting points $(4, 1)$ and $(x, -3)$ has its midpoint at $(8, -1)$. Which of the following points lie on the line containing that segment? Select all the correct answers.

    A. $(-3, 0)$
    B. $(-1, 4)$
    C. $(2, 2)$
    D. $(3, 1)$
    E. $(6, -2)$

7. Find the equation of a line through the point $(0, -4)$ perpendicular to $3x - 2y = 7$.

    A. $y = 3x - 4$
    B. $y = -3x - 4$
    C. $y = \dfrac{-3}{2}x - 4$
    D. $y = \dfrac{2}{3}x - 4$
    E. $3y = -2x - 12$

8. The midpoint of the segment that connects the origin with point P is $(7, -5)$. Find point P.

    A. $(14, -5)$
    B. $(7, -10)$
    C. $(14, -10)$
    D. $(3.5, -2.5)$
    E. $(7, -5)$

9. $\overrightarrow{AB}$ is parallel to the line $5x - 4y = 20$. What is the slope of $\overrightarrow{AB}$?

10. The image of the point $(6, -3)$ under translation 4 units left and 5 units up is what point?

Answers

1. **A** If A is the point $(7, -3)$ and B is the point $(-1, 5)$, the midpoint is $\left(\frac{7+-1}{2}, \frac{-3+5}{2}\right) = \left(\frac{6}{2}, \frac{2}{2}\right) = (3,1)$.

2. **A** The distance from A to B is $\sqrt{(-3-4)^2 + (2-7)^2} = \sqrt{49+25} = \sqrt{74}$. The distance from the origin to B is $\sqrt{(0-4)^2 + (0-7)^2} = \sqrt{16+49} = \sqrt{65}$.

3. **B** Line m has the equation $x + y = 5$ or $y = -x + 5$ and, therefore, a slope of -1. The slope of a line parallel to m is -1 and the slope of a line perpendicular to m is 1.

4. **C** The image of P under a rotation of $90°$ about the origin is $(0, -5)$ so its x-coordinate is 0, and the image of P under a rotation of $270°$ about the origin is $(0, 5)$ so its x-coordinate is 0.

5. **A, B, C, E** The y-intercept of the line is -5 and the slope is 4, so the equation of the line is $y = 4x - 5$. Points on the line fit the equation. When $x = 1$, $y = 4(1) - 5 = -1$, and when $x = 12$, $y = 4(12) - 5 = 43$. When $x = -1$, $y = 4(-1) - 5 = -9$, but when $x = -5$, $y = 4(-5) - 5 = -25$. When $x = 3$, $y = 4(3) - 5 = 7$.

6. **C** If the line segment connecting points $(4, 1)$ and $(x, -3)$ has its midpoint at $(8, -1)$, the slope of the line is $m = \frac{-1-1}{8-4} = \frac{-2}{4} = -\frac{1}{2}$. Using the point $(4, 1)$ and the slope, the equation of the line is $y - 1 = -\frac{1}{2}(x - 4)$ or $y = -\frac{1}{2}x + 3$. When x is an odd number, the value of y will not be an integer, so only choices C and E can possibly be on the line. When $x = 2$, $y = -\frac{1}{2}(2) + 3 = 2$ so choice C is correct. When $x = 6$, $y = -\frac{1}{2}(6) + 3 = 0$, so choice E is not correct.

7. **E** Find the slope of $3x - 2y = 7$ by putting the equation in slope-intercept form:

$$3x - 2y = 7$$
$$-2y = -3x + 7$$
$$y = \frac{3}{2}x - \frac{7}{2}$$

A line perpendicular to this will have a slope equal to the negative reciprocal of $\frac{3}{2}$, so the slope will be $-\frac{2}{3}$, since $(0, -4)$ is the y-intercept, the equation of the line is $y = -\frac{2}{3}x - 4$. Because that does not appear as a choice, multiply through by 3 to get $3y = -2x - 12$.

8. **C** The origin is the point $(0, 0)$. Call point P the point (x, y). Then $\left(\dfrac{0+x}{2}, \dfrac{0+y}{2}\right) = (7, -5)$ and $\dfrac{x}{2} = 7$ and $\dfrac{y}{2} = -5$, so P is the point $(14, -10)$:

$$5x - 4y = 20$$
$$-4y = -5x + 20$$
$$y = \frac{-5x + 20}{-4}$$
$$y = \frac{5}{4}x - 5$$

9. $\dfrac{5}{4} = 1.25$ Since $\overleftrightarrow{AB}$ is parallel to the line $5x - 4y = 20$, the slope of $\overleftrightarrow{AB}$ is equal to the slope of $5x - 4y = 20$. Put $5x - 4y = 20$ into slope-intercept form:

$$5x - 4y = 20$$
$$-4y = -5x + 20$$
$$y = \frac{-5x + 20}{-4}$$
$$y = \frac{5}{4}x - 5$$

The slope is $\dfrac{5}{4} = 1.25$.

10. **(2, 2)** The image of the point $(6, -3)$ under translation 4 units left and 5 units up is the point $(6 - 4, -3 + 5) = (2, 2)$.

XIII. Applications

All the math skills you've acquired, whether from arithmetic, algebra, or geometry, have a common purpose: to allow you to solve problems. You'll be asked to use your skills to investigate patterns and trends, draw conclusions, and piece together missing information. The GRE will ask you to demonstrate your mathematical proficiency by drawing conclusions from data in charts and graphs, by making predictions based on probabilities, and by solving a variety of problems, some familiar, some inventive.

A. Data Interpretation

The changes to the GRE in 2011 include increased emphasis on interpretation of data. In every field of study and every career path, you face tremendous amounts of categorical and quantitative information. Visual representations of data are often easier to understand than tables full of numbers.

Read the graphs carefully to be sure you understand what they're telling you. Read the labels, check the scales, notice units of measurement. Recognize that not all graphs are well constructed, and poorly drawn graphs can misrepresent information, intentionally or unintentionally.

1. Bar graphs

Bar graphs are used to compare different quantities. Each bar represents a quantity or a category, and the height of the bar corresponds to the size of the quantity or the frequency of items in the category. You may need to estimate the quantities when you read the height of the bars, if exact values are not given. Be sure to read scales carefully, and watch for units of measurement. Scales should start at zero, but if the frequencies, or heights, are large numbers, the graph may use a broken scale. A symbol on the vertical axis indicates a break in the scale or a jump between values. The use of a broken scale may make it difficult to compare bars visually, so pay close attention to labels.

EXAMPLE:

The bar graph below summarizes the sales of various lunches offered in a school cafeteria. Based upon this information, chicken outsells pasta by approximately what percent?

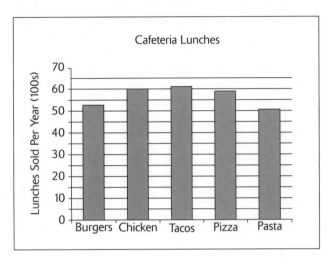

A. 10
B. 16
C. 20
D. 50
E. 60

The correct answer is **C.** The bar representing sales of chicken appears to reach 60, making sales of chicken approximately 6,000 lunches, since the scale tells you that each unit on the graph is 100. Pasta is just above 50, so pasta sales are slightly more than 5,000 lunches. The difference is 1,000 lunches. Compare this to the sales of pasta, for an answer of $\frac{1,000}{5,000} = 20\%$.

2. Line graphs

Line graphs are generally used to show the change in a quantity over time. The horizontal axis is labeled in time units, such as days, months, or years. The vertical axis measures the value of the quantity represented by the graph. A point is placed on the graph for each time unit, and the points are connected by line segments. This allows you to see the rise and fall of the quantity over time.

EXAMPLE:

The graph below shows the sales of hot dogs at Jenny's Beach Bungalow over the course of the last year. Over which period did sales have the greatest change?

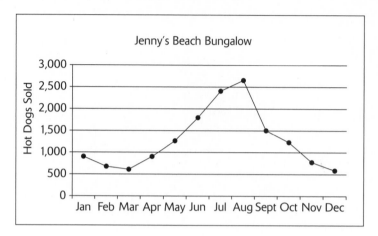

A.   May to June
B.   June to July
C.   July to August
D.   August to September
E.   September to October

The correct answer is **D.** Estimate the sales for May, June, July, August, September, and October from the graph. May is approximately 1,250. June is approximately 1,800. The change from May to June is 1,800 – 1,250 = 550. July is approximately 2,500. The change from June to July is 2,500 – 1,800 = 700. August is approximately 2,700. The change from July to August is 2,700 – 2,500 = 200. September is approximately 1,500. The change from August to September is 1,500 – 2,700 = –1,200. October is approximately 1,200. The change from September to October is 1,200 – 1,500 = –300. The question doesn't specify whether the change must be positive or negative, so the greatest change is from August to September, a decline of 1,200.

Alternatively, examine the graph. The greatest change will be represented by the line segment with the longest and steepest slope. A positive slope represents an increase in sales, while a negative slope is a decrease in sales.

3. Circle graphs

Circle graphs, sometimes called pie charts, are used to represent quantities as fractions of a whole. The size of each wedge or sector is a number of degrees, a portion of the circle, that corresponds to the percent of the whole that quantity represents.

EXAMPLES:

The example questions refer to the following graph showing the enrollment in various arts electives last year.

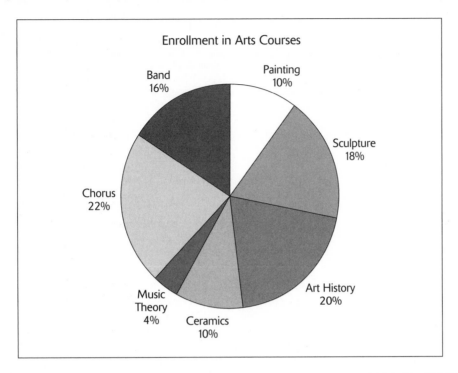

Enrollment in Arts Courses

1. What percent of the enrollment was in music courses?

Add the percents for Band, Chorus, and Music Theory: 16% + 22% + 4% = 42%.

2. If a total of 461 students signed up for arts electives, how many students took Art History?

Twenty percent of the students took Art History, and 20% of 461 is approximately 92 students.

4. Means and medians

Statistics are numbers that represent collections of data or information. They help you to draw conclusions about the data. One of the ways you can represent a set of data is by giving an average of the data.

There are three different averages in common use:

- **Mean:** The mean is the number most people think of when you say "average." The mean is found by adding all the data items and dividing by the number of items.
- **Mode:** The mode is the most common value, the one that occurs most frequently.
- **Median:** The median is the middle value when a set of data has been ordered from smallest to largest or largest to smallest. If there is an even number of data points, and two numbers seem to be in the middle, the mean of those two is the median.

231

EXAMPLE:

> Find the mean and median of the number of acres in rural parks and wildlife areas in 2002 for the states shown in the table below.

Land in Rural Parks and Wildlife Areas in 2002	
State	Acres (in thousands of acres)
Michigan	1,436
Wisconsin	1,000
Minnesota	2,959
Ohio	372
Indiana	264
Illinois	432
Iowa	327
Missouri	649

To find the mean, add the entries for all states, and divide by 8, the number of states shown in the table: 1,436 + 1,000 + 2,959 + 372 + 264 + 432 + 327 + 649 = 7,439 and 7,439 ÷ 8 = 929.875. The states shown have a mean of 929,875 acres of land in rural parks and wildlife areas. (**Remember:** The acres listed in the table are in thousands.) To find the median, place the entries in order: 2,959; 1,436; 1,000; 649; 432; 372; 327, 264. Because there are an even number of entries, average the two middle entries: (649 + 432) ÷ 2 = 1,081 ÷ 2 = 540.5, so 540,500 acres is the median.

Practice

Directions (1–2): You are given two quantities, one in Column A and one in Column B. You are to compare the two quantities and choose one of the following:

    A.   The quantity in Column A is greater.
    B.   The quantity in Column B is greater.
    C.   The two quantities are equal.
    D.   The relationship cannot be determined from the information given.

$$A = \{2, 2, 2, 3, 3, 4, 4, 4, 4\}$$

	Column A	Column B
1.	The mode of set A	The median of set A

	Column A	Column B
2.	The mean of the prime numbers less than 10	The median of the prime numbers less than 10

Directions (3–10): Unless otherwise directed, select a single answer choice. For numeric-entry questions, enter a number in the box(es) below the question. Equivalent forms of the correct answer, such as 2.5 and 2.50, are all correct. Fractions do not need to be reduced to lowest terms. Enter the exact answer unless the question asks you to round your answer.

Questions 3–4 refer to the following chart, which shows the number of books sold each day from Monday through Friday.

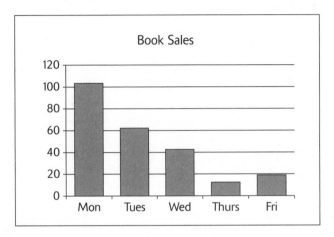

3. Over which of the following periods did book sales drop 25% or more? Choose all correct answers.

   A. Monday to Tuesday
   B. Tuesday to Wednesday
   C. Wednesday to Thursday
   D. Thursday to Friday
   E. None of the above

4. Choose all the values that represent the average sales over two consecutive days.

   A. 17.5
   B. 25.6
   C. 28.5
   D. 34.5
   E. 39.6

Questions 5–6 refer to the following graph, which shows the number of students who were reported absent due to illness each month of the second term.

Absences Due to Illness

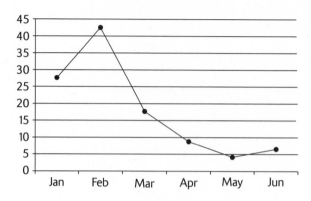

5. The lowest incidence of absences occurred in which month?

    A. January
    B. March
    C. April
    D. May
    E. June

6. The largest single drop in absences occurred between which two months?

    A. January and February
    B. February and March
    C. March and April
    D. April and May
    E. May and June

Questions 7–8 refer to the following circle graph, which shows the membership of the high school honor roll, broken down by class.

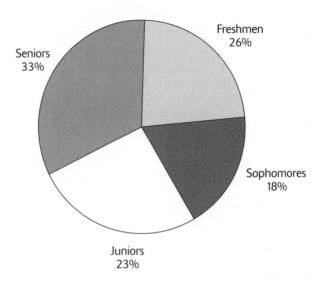

Honor Roll Membership

7. The class with the most honor roll members exceeds the class with the fewest honor roll members by what percent?

   A. 15
   B. 18
   C. 23
   D. 26
   E. 33

8. If there are 300 students on the honor roll, how many juniors are honor roll members?

   A. 23
   B. 54
   C. 69
   D. 78
   E. 99

9. Find the mean of the set of numbers {34, 54, 78, 92, 101}.

10. Find the median of the set of numbers {3,4, 5, 4, 7, 8, 9, 2, 10, 1}.

Answers

1. **A** The mode of set A is 4 because there are four 4s, three 2s, and two 3s. The median of set A is 3, because 3 is the fifth of the nine numbers.

2. **A** The prime numbers less than ten are 2, 3, 5, and 7. The mean is $(2 + 3 + 5 + 7) \div 4 = 17 \div 4 = 4.25$. The median is the average of 3 and 5, which is $(3 + 5) \div 2 = 8 \div 2 = 4$.

3. **A, B, C** You can eliminate choice D immediately, because there is an increase from Thursday to Friday. The decrease from Monday to Tuesday is a bit more than 40, from about 105 to about 62. This is a change of close to 40%. From Tuesday to Wednesday, there is a change of less than 20, from about 62 to about 42, a change of about 33%. Wednesday to Thursday is a little less than 30, from 42 to about 15, representing a decrease of more than 70%.

4. **A, C** Estimate the sales each day from the chart and average the values for consecutive days. Monday to Tuesday is $\frac{105+62}{2} = 83.5$. Tuesday to Wednesday is $\frac{62+42}{2} = 52$. Wednesday to Thursday is $\frac{42+15}{2} = 28.5$. Thursday to Friday is $\frac{15+20}{2} = 17.5$.

5. **D** The lowest point on the graph occurs in May.

6. **B** Look for the line segment with the steepest negative slope. This occurs from February to March.

7. **A** The class with the most honor roll members is the senior class, with 33%. The class with the fewest honor roll members is the sophomore class, with 18%. The difference is $33\% - 18\% = 15\%$.

8. **C** Juniors represent 23% of the 300 members, and $0.23 \times 300 = 69$.

9. **71.8** $(34 + 54 + 78 + 92 + 101) \div 5 = 71.8$.

10. **4.5** Arrange the numbers in order: $\{1, 2, 3, 4, 4, 5, 7, 8, 9, 10\}$. Then average the two middle numbers, 4 and 5. The average of 4 and 5 is $(4 + 5) \div 2 = 9 \div 2 = 4.5$.

B. Functions and Invented Functions

You've probably already seen questions about functions that assume you're familiar with the $f(x)$ notation. On many tests, similar questions are slipped in without the function notation. Instead, new and sometimes odd-looking symbols are invented that do the same job. Don't be intimidated by the strange symbols. Take the time to understand how the function—whether normal or invented—is defined, and you'll be able to answer the questions.

1. Evaluation

To find the value of the function for a given input, simply replace the variable with the given value and simplify.

EXAMPLES:

1. If $f(x) = x^2 - 5$, find $f(3)$.

In the rule $x^2 - 5$, replace x with 3: $3^2 - 5 = 9 - 5 = 4$.

2. $\lceil a$ is defined to mean $a^2 - 3a$. Find $\lceil 5$.

In the rule $a^2 - 3a$, replace a with 5: $5^2 - 3 \times 5 = 25 - 15 = 10$.

2. Solution

In some problems the value of the function is known and you're asked to find the value of the input. Set the expression equal to the given value and solve the equation.

EXAMPLES:

1. If $f(x) = \dfrac{3}{x}$, find the value of x for which $f(x) = 6$.

Set $\dfrac{3}{x} = 6$, cross-multiply, and solve: $6x = 3$, and $x = \dfrac{1}{2}$.

2. $[n] = 2n - 1$. If $[t] = 15$, find t.

Set $2t - 1 = 15$ and solve: $2t = 16$ and $t = 8$.

3. Composition

If you think of a function as a machine that takes in a number, works on it according to some rule, and gives out a new number, then composition of functions can be thought of as two machines on an assembly line. The first takes in a number, works on it, and gives an output, which it passes to the second function. The second function accepts that value, works on it according to its own rule, and puts out a new value.

EXAMPLES:

1. If $f(x) = 3x - 7$ and $g(x) = x^2 + 1$, find $g(f(2))$.

Work from the inside out. Put 2 in place of x in the rule for f: $f(2) = 3 \times 2 - 7 = -1$. The function f passes this value to g: $g(-1) = (-1)^2 + 1 = 2$.

2. $\boxed{x} = 2x - 9$ and $\nabla y = 4y + 5$. Find the value of $\boxed{\nabla 2}$.

Work from the inside out: $\nabla 2 = 4 \times 2 + 5 = 13$ and then $\boxed{13} = 2(13) - 9 = 17$.

Practice

Directions (1–2): You are given two quantities, one in Column A and one in Column B. You are to compare the two quantities and choose one of the following:

A. The quantity in Column A is greater.
B. The quantity in Column B is greater.
C. The two quantities are equal.
D. The relationship cannot be determined from the information given.

$$f(x) = 5 - x$$

Column A	Column B
1. $f(3)$	$f(-3)$

$$\frac{\Theta}{a} = a^2 - 4a$$

Column A	Column B
2. $\dfrac{\Theta}{4}$	$\dfrac{\Theta}{0}$

Directions (3–10): Unless otherwise directed, select a single answer choice. For numeric-entry questions, enter a number in the box(es) below the question. Equivalent forms of the correct answer, such as 2.5 and 2.50, are all correct. Fractions do not need to be reduced to lowest terms. Enter the exact answer unless the question asks you to round your answer.

3. If $g(x) = 9 - 5x$, select all the true statements.

   A. $g(1) = 4$
   B. $g(2) = -1$
   C. $g(3) = 24$
   D. $g(-1) = 14$
   E. $g(-2) = 19$
   F. $g(0) = 9$

4. If $\left|\dfrac{a}{b}\right|$ is defined to be $\sqrt{a^2+b^2}$, select all the true statements.

A. $\left|\dfrac{2}{3}\right| \approx 3.6$

B. $\left|\dfrac{5}{2}\right| \approx 5.4$

C. $\left|\dfrac{3}{5}\right| = 4$

D. $\left|\dfrac{1}{1}\right| = 1$

E. $\left|\dfrac{4}{3}\right| = 5$

5. The function f is defined as $f(x) = 17 - 3x$. At a certain value, h, $f(h) = -1$. Find h.

   A.   3
   B.   6
   C.   12
   D.   17
   E.   20

6. Define $\dfrac{a\;|\;b}{c\;|\;d}$ to be $\dfrac{a}{b} - \dfrac{c}{d}$. Find x if $\dfrac{3\;|\;2}{x\;|\;4}$ is equal to 1.

   A.   2
   B.   3
   C.   4
   D.   5
   E.   6

7. If $f(x) = 7 - 2x^2$ and $g(x) = 5x - 3$, then what is $f\left(g(1)\right)$?

   A. -5
   B. -3
   C. -1
   D.   1
   E.   3

8. If $℧a$ is defined to mean $\sqrt{a+9}$ and $℧p = 7$, which of the following could be the value of p?

   A.   20
   B.   30
   C.   40
   D.   50
   E.   60

9. When an object is thrown upward from the roof of a 90-foot building with an initial velocity of 10 feet per second, its height is a function of time. If $h(t) = 90 + 10t - 16t^2$, what is the height of the object after 1 second?

10. Define $\bigcap_{\,b}^{\,a}$ as $a^2 - b^2$ and $\boxed{x}$ as $x - 1$. Find $\boxed{\bigcap_{\,2}^{\,3}}$.

Answers

1. **B** $f(3) = 5 - 3 = 2$, but $f(-3) = 5 - (-3) = 8$.

2. **C** $\underset{4}{\Theta} = 4^2 - 4 \cdot 4 = 0$ and $\underset{0}{\Theta} = 0^2 - 4 \cdot 0 = 0$.

3. **A, B, D, E, F** If $g(x) = 9 - 5x$, $g(1) = 9 - 5(1) = 4$, $g(2) = 9 - 5(2) = -1$, $g(3) = 9 - 5(3) = -6$, $g(-1) = 9 - 5(-1) = 14$, $g(-2) = 9 - 5(-2) = 19$, and $g(0) = 9 - 5(0) = 9$.

4. **A, B, E** If $\lfloor_b^a$ is defined to be $\sqrt{a^2 + b^2}$, $\lfloor_3^2 = \sqrt{2^2 + 3^2} = \sqrt{13} \approx 3.6$, and $\lfloor_2^5 = \sqrt{5^2 + 2^2} = \sqrt{29} \approx 5.4$. But $\lfloor_5^3 = \sqrt{3^2 + 5^2} = \sqrt{34} \neq 4$ and $\lfloor_1^1 = \sqrt{1^2 + 1^2} = \sqrt{2} \neq 1$. However, $\lfloor_3^4 = \sqrt{4^2 + 3^2} = \sqrt{25} = 5$.

5. **B** $f(h) = 17 - 3h = -1$ so $-3h = -18$ and $h = 6$.

6. **A** $\dfrac{3 \mid 2}{x \mid 4} = \dfrac{3}{2} - \dfrac{x}{4} = 1$, so $-\dfrac{x}{4} = -\dfrac{1}{2}$ and $x = 2$.

7. **C** To find $f(g(1))$ evaluate $g(1)$ and then evaluate f at the resulting value: $g(1) = 5 \times 1 - 3 = 2$ and $f(2) = 7 - 2 \times 2^2 = 7 - 8 = -1$.

8. **C** $\mho p = \sqrt{p + 9} = 7$, so $p + 9 = 49$ and $p = 40$.

9. **84 feet** $h(1) = 90 + 10 \times 1 - 16 \times 1^2 = 90 + 10 - 16 = 84$ feet.

10. **4** $\boxed{\bigcap_{\,2}^{\,3}} = \boxed{3^2 - 2^2} = \boxed{9 - 4} = \boxed{5} = 5 - 1 = 4$.

C. Combinatorics and Probability

The probability of an event is a number between 0 and 1 that indicates how likely the event is to happen. An impossible event has a probability of 0. An event with a probability of 1 is certain to happen.

1. Basic counting principle

In order to determine probability, you often need to count quickly the number of different ways something can happen. If, for example, you were asked about the probability of pulling a certain two-card combination from a standard deck of 52 cards, you would need to calculate the number of different ways to pull two cards. In some situations, you can quickly list all the possible outcomes, but when that isn't possible, the counting principle provides a convenient alternative.

1. **Create a slot for each choice that needs to be made.**
2. **Fill each slot with the number of options for that choice.**
3. **Multiply the numbers you've entered to find the total number of ways your choices can be made.**

EXAMPLE:

> Susan has 4 skirts, 7 blouses, and 3 jackets. If all these pieces coordinate, how many different outfits—each consisting of skirt, blouse, and jacket—can Susan create?

Create a slot for each choice that needs to be made. Susan must choose three items of clothing, so three slots are needed: (___)(___)(___). Fill each slot with the number of options for that choice. There are 4 options for the skirt, 7 options for the blouse, and 3 options for the jacket: (4)(7)(3). Multiply the numbers you've entered to find the total number of ways the choices can be made: $4 \times 7 \times 3 = 84$ different outfits.

2. Permutations and combinations

A *permutation* is an arrangement of items in which order matters. If you were asked, for example, how many different ways John, Martin, and Andrew could finish a race, the order of finish would matter, so you would want all the permutations of these three items.

The formula for the number of permutations of n things taken t at a time is $_nP_t = \dfrac{n!}{(n-t)!}$.

A *combination* is a group of objects in which the order does *not* matter. If you were asked to select a team of five students to represent your class of 40 students, and the order in which you chose them did not matter, the number of different such teams would be the combinations of 40 students taken 5 at a time.

The number of combinations of n things taken t at a time is $_nC_t = \dfrac{n!}{(n-t)!\,t!}$.

In each of these formulas, the symbol $n!$ means the product of the whole numbers from n down to 1. The symbol $n!$ is read "n factorial." Although the formulas for permutations and combinations may look complicated, the properties of factorials work to cut the calculations down to size.

EXAMPLES:

---

1. Find the number of permutations of eight things taken three at a time.

$$_8P_3 = \frac{8!}{(8-3)!} = \frac{8!}{5!} = \frac{8 \cdot 7 \cdot 6 \cdot \cancel{5} \cdot \cancel{4} \cdot \cancel{3} \cdot \cancel{2} \cdot \cancel{1}}{\cancel{5} \cdot \cancel{4} \cdot \cancel{3} \cdot \cancel{2} \cdot \cancel{1}} = 336$$

---

2. Find the number of combinations of seven things taken two at a time.

$$_7C_2 = \frac{7!}{(7-2)!2!} = \frac{7!}{5!2!} = \frac{7 \cdot 6 \cdot \cancel{5} \cdot \cancel{4} \cdot \cancel{3} \cdot \cancel{2} \cdot \cancel{1}}{\cancel{5} \cdot \cancel{4} \cdot \cancel{3} \cdot \cancel{2} \cdot \cancel{1} \cdot 2 \cdot 1} = \frac{7 \cdot \cancel{6}^3}{\cancel{2} \cdot 1} = 21$$

Most of the questions you'll encounter, however, are simple enough not to require a formula. You can adapt the basic counting principle.

EXAMPLES:

---

1. In how many different ways can John, Martin, and Andrew finish a race?

You could tackle this just by listing: JMA, JAM, AMJ, AJM, MJA, MAJ. There are six different orders. Alternatively, you could say there are three choices for the first place finisher, leaving two choices for second place, and one for third, so (3)(2)(1) = 6.

---

2. A class of 20 students is asked to select a team of five to represent the class. How many different teams are possible?

Using the counting principle, set up five slots: (___)(___)(___)(___)(___). There are 20 choices for the first slot, 19 for the second, and so on: (20)(19)(18)(17)(16). Before you start to multiply out this extremely large number, remember that order does not matter here. To eliminate the extra arrangements of the same five people, divide by $5 \times 4 \times 3 \times 2 \times 1$ or $5!$. $\dfrac{(20)(19)(18)(17)(16)}{5 \cdot 4 \cdot 3 \cdot 2 \cdot 1}$ is still a large number, but canceling can help to make it more manageable:

$$\frac{\cancel{(20)}(19)\cancel{(18)}(17)(16)}{\cancel{5} \cdot \cancel{4} \cdot \cancel{3} \cdot \cancel{2} \cdot 1} = 19 \cdot 3 \cdot 17 \cdot 16 = 15,504$$

3. Simple probability

The probability of an event is defined as the number of successes divided by the number of possible outcomes.

The probability of choosing the ace of spades from a standard deck of 52 cards is $\frac{1}{52}$, while the probability of choosing any ace is $\frac{4}{52} = \frac{1}{13}$.

4. Probability of compound events

The probability of two events occurring is the product of the probability of the first and the probability of the second. The word *and* signals that you should multiply.

EXAMPLE:

> A card is drawn from a standard deck of 52 cards, recorded, and replaced in the deck. The deck is shuffled and a second card is drawn. What is the probability that both cards are hearts?

The probability of drawing a heart is $\frac{13}{52} = \frac{1}{4}$. Since the first card drawn is replaced before the second draw, the probability of drawing a heart on the second try is the same, so the probability of drawing two hearts is $P(\text{heart}) \cdot P(\text{heart}) = \frac{1}{4} \cdot \frac{1}{4} = \frac{1}{16}$.

Independent and dependent events

Be sure to think about whether the first event affects the probability of the second. In the previous example, the deck was restored to its original condition before the second card was drawn, so the two draws were independent, or unaffected by one another. If cards are drawn without replacement, however, the events are dependent. The result of the first may change the probability of the second.

EXAMPLE:

> Two cards are drawn at random from a standard deck of 52 cards. The first card is not returned to the deck before the second card is drawn. What is the probability that both cards will be hearts?

The probability of the first card being a heart is $\frac{13}{52} = \frac{1}{4}$, but the probability of drawing a heart on the second try is not the same, because the removal of the first card changes the deck. The probability that the second card will be a heart is $\frac{12}{51} = \frac{4}{17}$, because there are 12 hearts left among the 51 remaining cards. The probability of drawing two hearts without replacement is $\frac{1}{4} \cdot \frac{4}{17} = \frac{1}{17}$, slightly less than with replacement.

The probability that one event or another will occur is the probability that the first will occur plus the probability that the second will occur, minus the probability that both will occur.

EXAMPLE:

> A card is drawn at random from a standard deck, recorded, and returned to the deck. What is the probability that the card is either an ace or a heart?

The probability that the card is an ace is $\frac{4}{52} = \frac{1}{13}$. The probability that the card is a heart is $\frac{13}{52} = \frac{1}{4}$. One card, however, fits into both categories—the ace of hearts—so it gets counted twice. To eliminate that duplication, you need to subtract $\frac{1}{52}$. The probability that the card is an ace or a heart is $\frac{4}{52} + \frac{13}{52} - \frac{1}{52} = \frac{16}{52} = \frac{4}{13}$.

Mutually exclusive events

Two events are mutually exclusive if it's impossible for them to happen at the same time. If a card is chosen at random from a standard deck of 52 cards, it's possible for it to be a 5 or a 6, but it isn't possible for it to be a 5 *and* a 6. The events "draw a 5" and "draw a 6" are mutually exclusive. By contrast, the events "draw a 5" and "draw a heart" are not mutually exclusive. It is possible to draw one card that is a 5 of hearts.

When events A and B are mutually exclusive, the probability of A and B is zero, so the probability of A or B is simply the probability of A plus the probability of B.

Practice

Directions (1–2): You are given two quantities, one in Column A and one in Column B. You are to compare the two quantities and choose one of the following:

A. The quantity in Column A is greater.
B. The quantity in Column B is greater.
C. The two quantities are equal.
D. The relationship cannot be determined from the information given.

Column A	Column B
1. The permutations of five things taken two at a time	The combinations of seven things taken three at a time

A bag contains four blue marbles and three white marbles

Column A	Column B
2. The probability of choosing a blue marble	The probability of choosing a white marble

Directions (3–10): Unless otherwise directed, select a single answer choice. For numeric-entry questions, enter a number in the box(es) below the question. Equivalent forms of the correct answer, such as 2.5 and 2.50, are all correct. Fractions do not need to be reduced to lowest terms. Enter the exact answer unless the question asks you to round your answer.

3. A jar contains 20 marbles, of which 2 are white, 10 are yellow, 5 are blue, and 3 are red. If one marble is selected at random, which of the following statements are true? Choose all that apply.

   A. The probability of drawing a white marble is $\frac{1}{10}$.

   B. The probability of drawing a red marble is $\frac{3}{20}$.

   C. The probability of drawing a blue marble is $\frac{1}{4}$.

   D. The probability of drawing a yellow marble is $\frac{1}{2}$.

   E. The probability of drawing a marble that is not green is 1.

4. If 3 cards are selected at random from a standard deck of 52 cards, without replacement, which of the following can be used to calculate the probability that all 3 cards are aces? Choose all that apply.

   A. $\frac{4}{52} \times \frac{3}{52} \times \frac{2}{52}$

   B. $\frac{4}{52} \times \frac{4}{52} \times \frac{4}{52} \times \frac{4}{52}$

   C. $\frac{4}{52} \times \frac{3}{51} \times \frac{2}{50}$

   D. $\frac{1}{13} \times \frac{2}{13} \times \frac{3}{13}$

   E. $\frac{1}{13} \times \frac{1}{17} \times \frac{1}{25}$

5. Kijana has been observing the weather for several months and recording whether it was sunny, cloudy, or rainy. He has determined that there is a 38% chance that it will be cloudy, a 21% chance that it will rain, and a 41% chance that it will be sunny. What is the probability that it will not rain tomorrow?

   A. 21%
   B. 38%
   C. 41%
   D. 50%
   E. 79%

6. A bag contains 12 marbles, of which 4 are red, 3 are white, and 5 are blue. What is the probability that a marble selected at random will be red or blue?

   A. $\frac{1}{4}$

   B. $\frac{1}{3}$

   C. $\frac{5}{12}$

   D. $\frac{3}{4}$

   E. $\frac{5}{36}$

7. Two members of the science club must be selected to represent the school in a competition. Four members are seniors, three are juniors, two are sophomores, and five are freshmen. If the two representatives are chosen at random, what is the probability that the pair will be composed of one freshman and one senior?

    A. $\frac{1}{2}$

    B. $\frac{9}{14}$

    C. $\frac{10}{91}$

    D. $\frac{14}{91}$

    E. $\frac{20}{91}$

8. Jennifer owns a pair of "trick" dice. Each die has six faces, numbered 1 through 6, but one die is fair—that is, there is an equal probability of it landing on each number—and one die is not fair. The unfair die always lands on 6. What is the probability that a roll of these dice will produce a total of ten or more?

    A. $\frac{5}{6}$

    B. $\frac{1}{4}$

    C. $\frac{1}{3}$

    D. $\frac{1}{2}$

    E. $\frac{1}{6}$

9. Find the probability that a single card drawn from a standard deck of 52 cards will be a face card (jack, queen, or king.)

$$\frac{\square}{\square}$$

10. A fair die, numbered 1 through 6, is rolled. Find the probability that the die shows a prime number.

$$\frac{\square}{\square}$$

Answers

1. **B** The permutations of five things taken two at a time is $5 \times 4 = 20$, and the combinations of seven things taken three at a time is $(7 \times 6 \times 5) \div (3 \times 2 \times 1) = 35$.

2. **A** The probability of choosing a blue marble is $\frac{4}{7}$, and the probability of choosing a white marble is $\frac{3}{7}$.

3. **A, B, C, D, E** The probability of drawing a white marble is $\frac{2 \text{ white marbles}}{20 \text{ marbles}} = \frac{1}{10}$, the probability of drawing a red marble is $\frac{3 \text{ red marbles}}{20 \text{ marbles}} = \frac{3}{20}$, the probability of drawing a blue marble is $\frac{5 \text{ blue marbles}}{20 \text{ marbles}} = \frac{1}{4}$, and the probability of drawing a yellow marble is $\frac{10 \text{ yellow marbles}}{20 \text{ marbles}} = \frac{1}{2}$. Because there are no green marbles, drawing a green marble is impossible, so drawing a marble that is not green is certain, a probability of 1.

4. **C, E** If 3 cards are selected at random from a standard deck of 52 cards, without replacement, the probability that the first is an ace is $\frac{4}{52} = \frac{1}{13}$. The second draw is drawn from 51 remaining cards, and there are three aces remaining, so the probability of drawing the second ace is $\frac{3}{51} = \frac{1}{17}$, and the probability of drawing the third ace would be $\frac{2}{50} = \frac{1}{25}$. The probability is found by multiplying these. Choices A and B do not change the denominators to account for the changing number of cards in the deck. Choice c is a correct option, $\frac{4}{52} \times \frac{3}{51} \times \frac{2}{50}$, as is choice E, which is the same product in lowest terms.

5. **E** The probability that it will not rain is 1– probability of rain = 100% – 21% = 79%.

6. **D** The probability that a marble selected at random will be red or blue is $P(\text{red}) + P(\text{blue}) = \frac{4}{12} + \frac{5}{12} = \frac{9}{12} = \frac{3}{4}$.

7. **E** There are $4 + 3 + 2 + 5 = 14$ people to choose from, so the number of possible teams is the combinations of 14 people taken two at a time: $(14 \times 13) \div (2 \times 1) = 91$. The number of teams composed of a senior and a freshman is $(4 \times 5) = 20$. So the probability is $\frac{20}{91}$.

8. **D** Because one die will always land on 6, a total of ten or more will be produced by $6 + 4$, $6 + 5$, or $6 + 6$. The question, therefore, becomes what is the probability of a 4, 5, or 6 on the fair die?

$$P(4 \text{ or } 5 \text{ or } 6) = P(4) + P(5) + P(6) = \frac{3}{6} = \frac{1}{2}$$

9. $\frac{12}{52} = \frac{3}{13}$ The probability of choosing a face card (jack, queen, or king) from a standard deck of 52 cards is $\frac{12}{52}$ because there are 12 face cards, three in each suit. $\frac{12}{52} = \frac{3}{13}$.

10. $\frac{3}{6} = \frac{1}{2}$ Possible prime numbers are 2, 3, and 5, so the probability that the die shows a prime number is $\frac{3}{6} = \frac{1}{2}$.

D. Common Problem Formats

1. Mixtures

Problems about mixtures often can be simplified by organizing the information into a chart.

Amount of substance	×	Cost per unit (or percent purity)	=	Value of substance

Generally, the amounts of the component substances must total the amount of the mixture, and the values of the components must total the value of the mixture.

EXAMPLE:

A merchant wants to make 10 pounds of a mixture of raisins and peanuts. Peanuts can be purchased for $2.50 per pound and raisins for $1.75 per pound. How much of the mix should be peanuts and how much should be raisins if the mixture is to be sold for $2.25 per pound?

	Amount of substance	×	Cost per unit (or percent purity)	=	Value of substance
Peanuts	x	×	2.50	=	2.50x
Raisins	y	×	1.75	=	1.75y
Mixture	10	×	2.25	=	22.50

Adding down the first column, $x + y = 10$. Adding the last column, $2.50x + 1.75y = 22.50$. Solve the system by substitution, using $y = 10 - x$.

$$2.50x + 1.75y = 22.50$$
$$2.50x + 1.75(10 - x) = 22.50$$
$$2.50x + 17.50 - 1.75x = 22.50$$
$$0.75x = 5.00$$
$$x = \frac{5.00}{0.75} = 6\frac{2}{3}$$

The mixture should be made from $6\frac{2}{3}$ pounds of peanuts and $3\frac{1}{3}$ pounds of raisins.

2. Distance, rate, and time

Like mixture problems, problems involving distance, rate, and time often can be simplified by organizing the information into a chart.

Rate	×	Time	=	Distance

Either the times or the distances generally can be added.

EXAMPLE:

> One car leaves Chicago at noon heading east at 55 mph. One hour later, another car leaves Chicago traveling west at 50 mph. When will the cars be 400 miles apart?

Let x represent the number of hours the first car travels. Then the second car travels one hour less, or $x - 1$ hours. The distances traveled by both cars must add up to 400.

Rate	×	Time	=	Distance
55	×	x	=	$55x$
50	×	$x - 1$	=	$50(x - 1)$
				400

Adding the distance column, $55x + 50(x - 1) = 400$. Solve for x.

$$55x + 50(x - 1) = 400$$
$$55x + 50x - 50 = 400$$
$$105x = 450$$
$$x = 4\frac{30}{105} = 4\frac{2}{7}$$

The cars will be 400 miles apart in $4\frac{2}{7}$ hours.

3. Work

When problems talk about the amount of time required to complete a job, reframe the information in terms of the part of the job that can be completed in one unit of time. This will give you a fraction less than 1. Since the entire job, the whole job, is represented by 1, the part of the job completed in one unit of time multiplied by the time spent should equal 1.

EXAMPLES:

> 1. Greg can paint a room in three hours and Harry can paint the same room in four hours. How long will it take them to paint the room if they work together?

In one hour, Greg paints $\frac{1}{3}$ of the room and Harry paints $\frac{1}{4}$ of the room. Working together, they paint $\frac{1}{3} + \frac{1}{4} = \frac{4+3}{12} = \frac{7}{12}$ of the room in one hour, so it will take them x hours to paint the room, where $\frac{7}{12}x = 1$.
Solving, $x = 1 \div \frac{7}{12} = \frac{12}{7} = 1\frac{5}{7}$ hours.

> 2. When both drain pipes are opened, a tank empties in 45 minutes. When only the first drain is open, the draining process takes 60 minutes. How long will it take to drain the tank if only the second pipe is opened?

Let x equal the number of minutes it takes the second pipe to drain the tank. Then the first pipe can drain $\frac{1}{60}$ of the tank per minute and the second pipe can drain $\frac{1}{x}$ of the tank per minute. In order to drain the whole tank in 45 minutes when working together, they must be able to drain $\frac{1}{45}$ of the tank per minute, which means that $\frac{1}{60} + \frac{1}{x} = \frac{1}{45}$. Solve the equation to find x.

$$\frac{1}{60} + \frac{1}{x} = \frac{1}{45}$$
$$\frac{x+60}{60x} = \frac{1}{45}$$
$$45(x+60) = 60x$$
$$45x + 2{,}700 = 60x$$
$$2{,}700 = 15x$$
$$180 = x$$

It will take the second pipe 180 minutes, or three hours, to drain the tank.

Practice

Directions (1–5): Give your answer as a number.

1. A jet plane flying with the wind went 2,600 miles in five hours. Against the wind, the plane could fly only 2,200 miles in the same amount of time. Find the rate of the plane in calm air and the rate of the wind.

   Plane: ☐

   Wind: ☐

2. Flying with the wind, a plane flew 1,080 miles in three hours. Against the wind, the plane required four hours to fly the same distance. Find the rate of the plane in calm air and the rate of the wind.

   Plane: ☐

   Wind: ☐

3. How many liters of a 70% alcohol solution must be added to 50 liters of a 40% alcohol solution to produce a 50% alcohol solution?

   ☐

4. Find the selling price per pound of a coffee mixture made from 8 pounds of coffee that sells for $9.20 per pound and 12 pounds of coffee that costs $5.50 per pound.

   ☐

5. An executive drove from home at an average speed of 30 mph to an airport where a helicopter was waiting. The executive boarded the helicopter and flew to the corporate offices at an average speed of 60 mph. The entire distance was 150 miles; the entire trip took three hours. Find the distance from the airport to the corporate offices.

Answers

1. **480 mph, 40 mph** The speed of the plane is 480 mph, and the wind speed is 40mph.

Rate	×	Time	=	Distance
$x + y$	×	5	=	2,600
$x - y$	×	5	=	2,200

$$\begin{array}{l} 5(x+y)=2,600 \\ 5(x-y)=2,200 \end{array} \Rightarrow \begin{array}{l} 5x+5y=2,600 \\ 5x-5y=2,200 \end{array} \Rightarrow 10x=4,800 \Rightarrow 480$$

Then substitute $5(x + y) = 2,600 \rightarrow 5(480 + y) = 2,600 \rightarrow 480 + y = 520 \rightarrow y = 40$.

2. **315 mph, 45 mph** Flying with the wind, a plane flew 1,080 miles in three hours, so $x + y = 1,080 \div 3 = 360$. Since $3(x + y) = 4(x - y)$, $3x + 3y = 4x - 4y$, and $x = 7y$. Substituting, $7y + y = 360$ so $y = 45$ and $x = 315$.

3. **25 liters**

Amount of Substance	×	Percent Purity	=	Value of Substance
x	×	0.70	=	$0.70x$
50	×	0.40	=	20
$x + 50$	×	0.50	=	$0.50(x + 50)$

$0.70x + 20 = 0.50x + 25 \rightarrow 0.20x = 5 \rightarrow x = 25$.

4. **$6.98**

Amount of Substance	×	Cost per Unit (or Percent Purity)	=	Value of Substance
8	×	9.20		73.60
12	×	5.50		66.00
20	×	x		139.60

$20x = 139.60 \rightarrow x = 6.98$.

5. **120 miles** Let x represent the number of hours she drove and $3 - x$ represent the number of hours she flew: $30x + 60(3 - x) = 150 \rightarrow 30x + 180 - 60x = 150 \rightarrow -30x = -30$ so $x = 1$. She drove one hour and flew for two, so the offices were $2(60) = 120$ miles from the airport.

E. Set Theory

1. Sets and set notation

A *set* is simply a collection of objects, but in math we're generally concerned with sets of numbers. A set can be denoted by listing the elements, or members, of the set between a set of braces, or can be described verbally or by a formula. The set {2, 3, 5, 7, 11, 13, 17, 19} might also be indicated as {prime numbers less than 20}. A set is named by an uppercase letter—for example P—and the notation $t \in P$ says "t is an element of set P."

Set A is a subset of set B if every element of A is also an element of B. Set A is contained in set B and B contains A.

EXAMPLE:

Which of the following is a subset of P = {2, 3, 6, 7, 11, 13, 17, 19}?

A. {2, 3, 4}
B. {6, 7, 16, 17}
C. {11, 13, 19}
D. {2, 3, 6, 7, 8}
E. {17, 18, 19}

The correct answer is **C**. Choice A contains 4, which is not in P, and choice B includes 16, which is also not in P. Each of the elements of choice C is also an element of P, so this is a subset. Choice D contains 8 and choice E contains 19, neither of which is in P, so only choice C is a subset of P.

2. Venn diagrams

A Venn diagram can be a convenient way of understanding set relationships. The Venn diagram consists of a rectangle, representing the universe—that is, all items being considered. Inside this rectangle, circles represent different sets. They may overlap if they have elements in common or may not overlap if they don't share any elements. Sets with no elements in common are disjoint.

EXAMPLE:

A group of 100 people was surveyed and asked what pets they owned. Of the group, 28 said they did not own a pet, 38 said they owned a cat, and 9 of those said they owned both a dog and a cat. If all the members of the group gave some response, how many owned dogs?

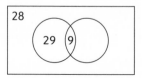

The rectangle represents the 100 people surveyed and the two circles represent cat owners and dog owners. The circles overlap because 9 people own both a dog and a cat. The 38 cat owners include 9 who own a dog and a cat and 29 others who own only a cat. This accounts for 28 + 29 + 9 = 66 people, so there are 100 – 66 = 34 people still uncounted. There is only one answer they could have given, which is that they owned a dog. Those 34 plus the 9 people who own both dogs and cats make a total of 43 dog owners.

3. Intersection

The intersection of two sets is the set of elements that belong to both sets. It represents the overlap of the two sets. If there is no overlap, the intersection is an empty set and the two sets are disjoint. The symbol for the intersection of A and B is $A \cap B$.

EXAMPLE:

> If P = {prime numbers less than 20} and Q = {odd numbers less than 20}, find $P \cap Q$.

P = {2, 3, 5, 7, 11, 13, 17, 19} and Q = {3, 5, 7, 9, 11, 13, 15, 17, 19}. The elements that appear in both sets are 3, 5, 7, 11, 13, 17, and 19 so $P \cap Q$ = {3, 5, 7, 11, 13, 17, 19}.

4. Union

The union of two sets is a new set formed by combining the elements of the two sets. If an element appears in both sets, it does not need to be duplicated in the union. The symbol for the union of A and B is $A \cup B$.

EXAMPLE:

> If R = {perfect squares less than 30} and T = {positive multiples of 5 less than 20}, find $R \cup T$.

R = {1, 4, 9, 16, 25} and T = {5, 10, 15} so $R \cup T$ = {1, 4, 5, 9, 10, 15, 16, 25}.

Practice

Directions (1–2): You are given two quantities, one in Column A and one in Column B. You are to compare the two quantities and choose one of the following:

    A.   The quantity in Column A is greater.
    B.   The quantity in Column B is greater.
    C.   The two quantities are equal.
    D.   The relationship cannot be determined from the information given.

$$A = \{2, 7, 10, 15, 22\}$$
$$B = \{2, 10, 22\}$$

Column A	Column B
1. The number of elements in A	The number of elements in $A \cup B$

$$P = \{\text{prime numbers between 20 and 30}\}$$
$$R = \{\text{odd numbers between 20 and 30}\}$$

Column A	Column B
2. The number of elements in P	The number of elements in R

Directions (3–4): Unless otherwise directed, select a single answer choice.

3. If $A = \{\text{positive multiples of 3 less than 25}\}$ and $B = \{\text{positive multiples of 4 less than 25}\}$, choose all the numbers in the intersection $A \cap B$.

A. 8
B. 9
C. 12
D. 20
E. 21
F. 24
G. 36

4. A survey of 50 people found that 28 people liked vanilla ice cream, 37 people liked chocolate ice cream, and 8 did not like either. Which of the following conclusions can be drawn? Select all that apply.

A. Five people like vanilla but not chocolate.
B. Twenty-two people prefer some other flavor.
C. Fourteen people like chocolate but not vanilla.
D. Eleven people like both vanilla and chocolate.
E. None of the above.

Answers

1. **C** $A \cup B = \{2, 7, 10, 15, 22\} = A$, since B is a subset of A. The number of elements in A is 5 and the number of elements in $A \cup B$ is 5.

2. **B** $P = \{23, 29\}$ and $R = \{21, 23, 25, 27, 29\}$. The number of elements in P is 2 and the number of elements in R is 5.

3. **C, F** $A = \{3, 6, 9, 12, 15, 18, 21, 24\}$ and $B = \{4, 8, 12, 16, 20, 24\}$, so $A \cap B = \{12, 24\}$.

4. **A, C** There were 50 people in the survey, and 8 did not like either vanilla or chocolate, so 42 liked one or the other or both. Since 37 liked chocolate, there are $42 - 37 = 5$ who like only vanilla. A total of 28 liked vanilla, so there must be $28 - 5 = 23$ who like both vanilla and chocolate. That leaves $37 - 23 = 14$ who like only chocolate.

F. Sequences

A sequence is an ordered list of numbers. Questions about sequences generally involve predicting the value of terms not shown. This requires that you determine a pattern underlying the terms shown. Commonly, sequences are *arithmetic* (which means that each new term is found by adding a set value to the previous term) or *geometric* (in which each term is multiplied by a number to produce the next term).

The sequence 3, 7, 11, 15, 19, . . . is an example of an arithmetic sequence. Each term is 4 more than the previous term. The terms in the sequence can be denoted a_1, a_2, a_3, . . . and if the common difference—in this case, 4—is d, then $a_n = a_1 + (n - 1)d$.

EXAMPLE:

> Find the 100th term of the sequence 9, 6, 3, 0, –3, . . .

The first term is 9 and the common difference is –3. To find the 100th term, you need to add –3 to each term, and do that a total of 99 times. $a_{100} = a_1 + (100 - 1)d = 9 + (99)(-3) = 9 - 297 = -288$. The 100th term is –288.

The geometric sequence 7, 35, 175, 875, . . . has a common ratio of 5. The common ratio can be found by dividing a term by the previous term. To calculate later terms, you need to multiply repeatedly by 5, which means multiplying the first term by a power of 5: $a_n = a_1 r^{(n-1)}$.

EXAMPLE:

> Find the eighth term of the sequence 40, 20, 10, 5, . . .

The common ratio is $\frac{1}{2}$, and the first term is 40, so the eighth term will be $a_8 = a_1 r^{(8-1)} = 40\left(\frac{1}{2}\right)^7 = \frac{5}{16}$.

Sequences can be formed with patterns that are variations and combinations of these. The sequence 3, 5, 12, 14, 21, 23, 30, . . . alternates between adding 2 and adding 7. The sequence 8, 16, 19, 38, 41, 82, 85, . . . combines multiplying by 2 with adding 3. A famous sequence known as the Fibonacci sequence adds two adjacent terms to create the next term, starting with two ones: 1, 1, 2, 3, 5, 8, 13, . . .

Practice

Directions (1–2): You are given two quantities, one in Column A and one in Column B. You are to compare the two quantities and choose one of the following:

   A.   The quantity in Column A is greater.
   B.   The quantity in Column B is greater.
   C.   The two quantities are equal.
   D.   The relationship cannot be determined from the information given.

	Column A	**Column B**
1.	The tenth term in the sequence 3, 7, 11, 15, 19, . . .	The eighth term in the sequence 3, 6, 12, 24, . . .

	Column A	**Column B**
2.	The twelfth term in the sequence 20, 17, 14, 11, 8, . . .	The seventh term in the sequence 18, 16, 14, 12, 10, . . .

Directions (3–10): Unless otherwise directed, select a single answer choice.

3. Find the tenth term in the sequence 1,024; 512; 256; 128; . . .

   A.   0
   B.   1
   C.   2
   D.   4
   E.   8

4. Find the 12th term in the sequence 7, 9, 3, 5, –1, 1, . . .

   A.   –3
   B.   –5
   C.   –7
   D.   –8
   E.   –11

5. Find the product of the eighth and ninth terms of the sequence 40, 20, 18, 9, 7, . . .

   A.   5.25
   B.   0.75
   C.   –1.25
   D.   –0.9375
   E.   1.125

Answers

1. **B** The sequence 3, 7, 11, 15, 19, . . . has a common difference of 4, so the tenth term will be $3 + 9 \times 4 = 39$. The sequence 3, 6, 12, 24, . . . has a common ratio of 2, so the eighth term is $3 \times 2^7 = 3 \times 128 = 384$.

2. **B** The twelfth term in the sequence 20, 17, 14, 11, 8, . . . is $20 + 11(-3) = -13$. The seventh term in the sequence 18, 16, 14, 12, 10, . . . is $18 + 6(-2) = 6$.

3. **C** The sequence 1,024; 512; 256; 128; . . . is a geometric sequence with a common ratio of $\frac{1}{2}$, so the tenth term is $1,024\left(\frac{1}{2}\right)^9 = 1,024\left(\frac{1}{512}\right) = 2$.

4. **E** Two rules are at work here: $\underbrace{7, 9}_{+2}, \underbrace{3, 5}_{+2}, \underbrace{-1, 1}_{+2}, \ldots$ and $7, \underbrace{9, 3}_{-6}, \underbrace{5, -1}_{-6}, 1, \ldots.$ Continue the sequence to the twelfth term: 7, 9, 3, 5, –1, 1, –5, –3, –9, –7, –13, –11.

5. **D** Two rules are at work: $\underbrace{40, 20}_{\times\frac{1}{2}}, \underbrace{18, 9}_{\times\frac{1}{2}}, 7,\ldots$ and $40, \underbrace{20, 18}_{-2}, \underbrace{9, 7}_{-2},\ldots.$ Continue the sequence to the ninth term: 40, 20, 18, 9, 7, 3.5, 1.5, 0.75, –1.25. Then the product of the eighth and ninth terms is $0.75 \times -1.25 = -0.9375$.

XIV. Full-Length Practice Test with Answer Explanations

Section 1: Analytical Writing

Essay 1: "Analyze an Issue"

You will have 30 minutes to organize and write a response that shows your point of view on the issue in the prompt. You will receive a zero if you write about another topic. You can support, deny, or qualify the claim made in the prompt, as long as the concepts you present are relevant to the topic. Substantiate your ideas or views with strong reasons and solid examples based on general knowledge, direct experience, and/or academic studies.

The GRE readers will grade your writing based on how well you:

- Recognize the intricacies and implications of the issue.
- Organize your thoughts in a coherent outline in your essay.
- Substantiate your response to the prompt with strong, relevant examples.
- Edit and proofread your writing.

Organize your thoughts, write out a quick outline, make sure you have strong examples, and analyze the issue from different angles. Think logically. Then compose your stand on the issue. Give yourself a few minutes to edit and proofread to avoid careless errors.

Time: 30 minutes

1 essay

> In this day and age, specialists are overrated because they cannot give broader viewpoints like generalists. Our society needs more generalists rather than experts.

Directions: Consider the extent to which you agree or disagree with the claim in the statement and write a response in which you explain your reasoning for the position. As you develop your position, evaluate the ramifications of the issue and the way these possibilities have shaped your position.

Essay 2: "Analyze an Argument"

You will have 30 minutes to prepare and compose a critique of a particular argument presented as a short passage about the size of a paragraph or less. You must write a critique on that argument or you will receive a score of zero.

Scrutinize the logic and reasoning in the argument. Think about and write down notes about the evidence needed to refute or support the argument, as well as any questionable assumptions. Consider any alternative explanations as well.

It is important to organize and write using strong examples or evidence that supports your case. The evidence should analyze the credibility of the argument. *This is not about your personal views, but an objective critique of an argument.*

The GRE readers will grade your writing based on how well you:

- Recognize or list the significant aspects of the argument that need to be analyzed.
- Organize your thoughts in a coherent outline in your critique.
- Substantiate your critique of the argument with strong examples.
- Edit and proofread your writing.

Organize your thoughts, write out a quick outline, make sure you have strong examples, and analyze the argument from different angles. Think logically. Then compose your critique of the argument. Give yourself a few minutes to edit and proofread to avoid careless errors.

Time: 30 minutes

1 essay

The following appeared as a feature article in a family health magazine:

> Approximately 80 percent of people who visit emergency rooms after a skateboarding accident did not use protective gear or light-reflecting material. The risk of injury could be avoided by wearing protective gear with light reflectors when skateboarding, so clearly this statement proves that taking these precautions will reduce the risk of being hurt in a skateboarding accident.

In a well-reasoned essay, examine the stated and/or unstated assumptions of the argument. Consider how the argument depends on these assumptions, and what the implications are for the argument if the assumptions prove unwarranted.

IF YOU FINISH BEFORE TIME IS CALLED, CHECK YOUR WORK ON THIS SECTION ONLY. DO NOT WORK ON ANY OTHER SECTION IN THE TEST.

Section 2: Quantitative Reasoning

Time: 40 minutes

25 questions

Numbers: All numbers used are real numbers.

Figures: Figures are intended to provide useful positional information, but they are not necessarily drawn to scale. Unless a note states that a figure is drawn to scale, you should not solve these problems by estimating sizes or by measurements. Use your knowledge of math to solve the problems. Angle measures can be assumed to be positive. Lines that appear straight can be assumed to be straight. Unless otherwise indicated, figures lie in a plane.

Directions (1–9): You are given two quantities, one in Column A and one in Column B. You are to compare the two quantities and choose one of the following:

    A.   The quantity in Column A is greater.

    B.   The quantity in Column B is greater.

    C.   The two quantities are equal.

    D.   The relationship cannot be determined from the information given.

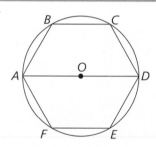

ABCDEF is a regular hexagon inscribed in circle *O*

$\overline{AD}$ is a diameter of circle *O*

	Column A	**Column B**
1.	The length of radius $\overline{OD}$	The length of arc $\overarc{FE}$

A television with a list price of $300 is advertised at 15% off

The final cost reflects that discount and a 6% sales tax on the discounted price

	Column A	**Column B**
2.	The final cost	$273

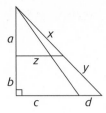

	Column A	**Column B**
3.	$(x + y)^2$	$a^2 + b^2 + c^2 + d^2$

A manufacturer produces plastic boxes that are cubes, 2 inches on each edge

	Column A	**Column B**
4.	The number of cubes that can be packed into a shipping carton that is a cube 1 foot on each edge	The number of cubes that can be packed into a shipping carton 2 feet long, 1 foot wide, and 6 inches high

	Column A	**Column B**
5.	$\frac{2}{5}(0.001)$	$\frac{1}{5}(0.002)$

Yvonne bought a refrigerator at 15% off the regular price

Alicia bought the same refrigerator at 95% of what Yvonne paid

	Column A	**Column B**
6.	The cost of the refrigerator at 20% off regular price	The price Alicia paid for the refrigerator

p, q, and r are positive integers

$$p = 3q$$
$$q = 5r$$

	Column A	**Column B**
7.	The remainder when pq is divided by r	The remainder when pr is divided by q

	Column A	**Column B**
8.	$(6 + 3) \times 5 - 6 \div 2 + 3^2$	$6 + 3 \times 5 - 6 \div 2 + 3^2$

	Column A	**Column B**
9.	x if $x^3 = 125$	y if $y^2 = 25$

Directions (10–25): Unless otherwise directed, select a single answer choice. For numeric-entry questions, enter a number in the box(es) below the question. Equivalent forms of the correct answer, such as 2.5 and 2.50, are all correct. Fractions do not need to be reduced to lowest terms. Enter the exact answer unless the question asks you to round your answer.

Questions 10–14 refer to the following graphs.

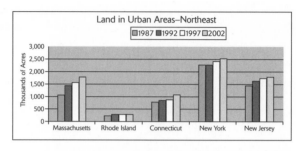

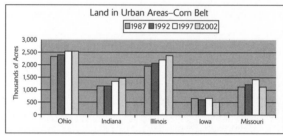

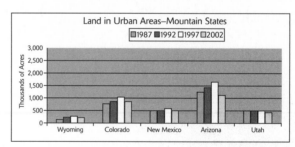

10. Which two states have an overall pattern of approximately equal amounts of land in urban areas?

    A. Arizona
    B. Colorado
    C. Indiana
    D. Massachusetts
    E. Missouri
    F. New Jersey
    G. New York
    H. Ohio

11. From 1987 to 2002, the land in urban areas in Massachusetts increased by approximately what percent?

    A. 20
    B. 39
    C. 56
    D. 64
    E. 90

12. In 2002, the land in urban areas in Ohio exceeded the land in urban areas in New Mexico by approximately how many acres?

    A. 2,000
    B. 20,000
    C. 200,000
    D. 2 million
    E. 20 million

13. The average number of acres in urban areas in Arizona over the years from 1987 to 2002 was approximately:

    A. 0.6 million
    B. 1.1 million
    C. 1.3 million
    D. 1.5 million
    E. 1.8 million

14. Based on the graphs, which of the following statements are true in 2002?

    A. Urban land in Iowa and New Mexico was approximately equal.
    B. Urban land in Rhode Island exceeded that in Wyoming.
    C. Urban land in Connecticut and Colorado was approximately equal.

Questions 15–17 refer to the following table.

Life Expectancy by Age, Race, and Gender									
	All Races			White			Black		
Age	Total	Male	Female	Total	Male	Female	Total	Male	Female
0	77.8	75.2	80.4	78.3	75.7	80.8	73.1	69.5	76.3
20	78.8	76.2	81.2	79.1	76.6	81.5	74.6	71.2	77.7
40	79.9	77.6	81.9	80.1	77.9	82.1	76.3	73.4	78.8
60	82.5	80.8	84.0	82.6	80.9	84.1	80.4	78.2	82.2
80	89.1	88.2	89.8	89.1	88.1	89.7	89.1	88.0	89.6

15. The life expectancy for 40-year-old black females exceeds that for 40-year-old white males by

    A. 0.9 years
    B. 1.3 years
    C. 3.8 years
    D. 4.5 years
    E. 5.9 years

16. Life expectancy for 60-year-old females is what percent higher than that for males of the same age?

    A. 0.12
    B. 1.20
    C. 3.96
    D. 5.12
    E. 8.97

263

17. For a single demographic subgroup, the greatest percent increase in life expectancy from age 40 to age 60 is

   A. 3.9% for white males
   B. 2.4% for white females
   C. 6.5% for black females
   D. 4.3% for black females
   E. 6.5% for black males

18. If a and b are positive integers and $a \times b$ is odd, choose all the true statements.

   A. a and b are prime numbers.
   B. ab^2 is odd.
   C. $a - b$ is odd.
   D. $a + b$ is even.

19. If $xy \neq 0$ and $y = 3x$, then $\dfrac{x^2 + 2xy + y^2}{xy} =$

   A. $1\dfrac{1}{3}$

   B. $2\dfrac{4}{9}$

   C. $3\dfrac{1}{9}$

   D. $3\dfrac{1}{3}$

   E. $5\dfrac{1}{3}$

20. Two cars started from the same point and traveled on a straight course in opposite directions for exactly three hours, at which time they were 330 miles apart. If one car traveled, on average, 10 miles per hour faster than the other car, what was the average speed of the slower car for the three-hour trip?

   ☐

21. If $|a| = b$ and $a + b = 0$, then $b - 2a =$

   A. $3a$
   B. $2a$
   C. 0
   D. $2b$
   E. $3b$

22. If $2x - 5 = y + 4$, then $x - 2 =$

   A. $\dfrac{y+5}{2}$

   B. $y + 5$

   C. $\dfrac{y+9}{2}$

   D. $y + 9$

   E. $\dfrac{y-1}{2}$

23. If the mean of 6 consecutive integers is 8.5, what is the product of the first and the last?

   ☐

24. In a sample of 2,000 computer chips, 0.2% were found to be defective. What is the ratio of defective to nondefective chips?

   A. 400:1,600
   B. 40:1,960
   C. 4:1,996
   D. 4:2,000
   E. 40:2,000

25. Choose all the statements that are true about the graph of $3x - 7y - 4 = 0$.

   A. The x-intercept is $\dfrac{4}{3}$

   B. The y-intercept is $\dfrac{4}{3}$

   C. The slope is $\dfrac{3}{7}$

IF YOU FINISH BEFORE TIME IS CALLED, CHECK YOUR WORK ON THIS SECTION ONLY. DO NOT WORK ON ANY OTHER SECTION IN THE TEST.

Section 3: Verbal Reasoning

Time: 30 minutes

20 questions

Directions (1–6): For each blank, select the word or phrase that best completes the text. (Your answer will consist of one, two, or three letters, depending on the number of blanks in each question.)

1. Faced with high temperatures and rapidly increasing humidity, the tourists were overcome by _____ and felt unable to continue their climb up the pyramid.

   A. zealousness
   B. lethargy
   C. abstinence
   D. resilience
   E. antipathy

2. Her enthusiasm for the project _____ as soon as she found out that the budget had been cut in half and the deadline had been moved up by a month.

   A. dissipated
   B. retained
   C. elevated
   D. exalted
   E. disparaged

3. Hoping to reach some accord on the many issues that divided them, the delegates made every attempt to (1) _____ the opposition leader but to no avail; he remained (2) _____ in his demands.

Blank 1	Blank 2
propitiate	complaisant
encumber	intractable
foster	craven

4. Although the new leader had erstwhile (1) _____ the democratic ideals of a free press and religious freedom, his reign quickly became (2) _____.

Blank 1	Blank 2
espoused	despotic
abrogated	enlightened
burnished	egalitarian

5. Political machinery does not act of itself. As it is first made, so it has to be worked, by men, and even by ordinary men. It needs not their simple (1) _____, but their active participation; and must be adjusted to the capacities and qualities of such men as are available. This implies three conditions: The people for whom the form of government is intended must be willing to accept it, or at least not so unwilling as to (2) _____ an insurmountable obstacle to its establishment; they must be willing and able to do what is necessary to keep it standing; and they must be willing and able to do what it requires of them to enable it to (3) _____.

Blank 1	Blank 2	Blank 3
acquiescence	refine	exact a promise
repudiation	posit	establish a foothold
demurral	induce	fulfill its purpose

6. Samuel Johnson criticizes Shakespeare's characters for being less than natural, not free from (1) _____. Johnson's (2) _____ originates from a fanciless way of thinking to which everything appears (3) _____ that is not insipid.

Blank 1	Blank 2	Blank 3
disposition	censure	tepid
affectation	veneration	unnatural
stature	equivocation	imperceptible

Directions (7–10): Questions follow each of the passages. Using only the stated or implied information in each passage, answer the questions.

Questions 7–8 are based on the following passage.

The earliest form of painting, used by Egyptian artists, was with colors ground in water. Various media, such as wax and mastic, were added as a fixative. Today, this is known as tempura painting. The Greeks acquired their knowledge of the art from the Egyptians, and later the Romans dispersed it throughout Europe; they probably introduced tempura painting for decoration of the walls of their houses. The English monks visited the Continent and learned the art of miniature painting for illuminating their manuscripts by the same process. Owing to opaque white being mixed with the colors, the term of painting in *body-color* came in use. Painting, in this manner, was employed by artists throughout Europe in making sketches for their oil paintings.

Two such drawings by Albrecht Dürer, produced with great freedom in the early part of the 16th century, are in the British Museum. The Dutch masters also employed the same means. Holbein introduced the painting of miniature portraits into this country, for although the monks inserted figures in their illuminations, little attempt was made in producing likenesses. As early as the middle of the 17th century, the term *watercolors* came into use.

7. The passage states that:
   A. The Romans introduced tempura painting minimally.
   B. The Greeks dispersed tempura painting throughout the region.
   C. Tempura painting in color was employed by artists in Europe.
   D. The English monks used portraits as a means of communication.
   E. Artists disagreed about the effects of tempura painting.

8. According to the passage, which of the following are true? Consider each of the three choices and select all that apply.
   A. There was minimal attempt to produce realistic portraits by the monks.
   B. There was critical acclaim about the production-realistic portraits by the monks.
   C. There was a strong attempt to produce realistic portraits by the monks.

Questions 9–10 are based on the following passage.

The Panama Canal conflict is due to the fact that the governments of Great Britain and the United States do not agree upon the interpretation of the Hay-Pauncefote Treaty of September 18, 1901, which stipulates as follows: "The Canal shall be free and open to the vessels of commerce and of war of all nations . . . , on terms of entire equality, so that there shall be no discrimination against any such nation, or its citizens or subjects, in respect of the conditions and charges of traffic, or otherwise. Such conditions and charges of traffic shall be just and equitable." By Section 5 of the Panama Canal Act of August 24, 1912, the president of the United States is authorized to prescribe, and from time to time to change, the tolls to be levied upon vessels using the Panama Canal, but the section orders that no tolls whatever shall be levied upon vessels engaged in the coasting trade of the United States, and also that, if the tolls to be charged should be based upon net registered tonnage for ships of commerce, the tolls shall not exceed $1.25 per net registered ton nor be less, for other vessels, than those of the United States or her citizens, than the estimated proportionate cost of the actual maintenance and operation of the canal.

As regards the enactment of Section 5 of the Panama Canal Act that the vessels of the Republic of Panama shall be entirely exempt from the payment of tolls. Now Great Britain asserts that since these enactments set forth in Section 5 of the Panama Canal Act are in favor of vessels of the United States, they comprise a violation of Article III, No. 1, of the Hay-Pauncefote Treaty, which stipulates that the vessels of all nations shall be treated on terms of entire equality. This assertion made by Great Britain is met by the memorandum which, when signing the Panama Canal Act, President Taft left to accompany the act. The president contends that, in view of the fact that the Panama Canal has been constructed by the United States wholly at her own cost, upon territory ceded to her by the Republic of Panama, the United States possesses the power to allow her own vessels to use the canal upon such terms as she sees fit. Therefore, vessels pass through the canal either without the payment of any tolls, or on payment of lower tolls than those levied upon foreign vessels.

9. Which of the following statements could logically follow the last sentence of the second paragraph?

   A. In contrast, the Republic of Panama is exempt from the payment of tolls.
   B. The president denies that the U.S. is in violation of Article III, No. 1, of the Hay-Pauncefote Treaty.
   C. In other words, the United States has the privilege to use the canal as a most-favored nation.
   D. Any factors may have been levied upon them for the use of the canal.
   E. Nevertheless, Great Britain will no longer have justification to protest.

10. Which of the following could best describe the organization of the passage:

   A. An objective investigation into the conflict between Great Britain and the United States regarding the Panama Canal
   B. A critical debate into the conflict between Panama and the United States regarding the Panama Canal
   C. A biased opinion on the conflict between Great Britain and the United States regarding the Panama Canal
   D. A historical survey of the conflict between Great Britain and the United States regarding the Panama Canal
   E. An exposé of the behind-the-scenes subterfuge responsible for the conflict between Great Britain and the United States regarding the Panama Canal

Directions (11–14): Select two of the choices from the list of six that best complete the meaning of the sentence as a whole. The two words you select should produce completed sentences that are most alike in meaning. To receive credit for the question, both answers must be correct. No partial credit will be given; your answer must consist of two letters.

11. Although some economic forecasts indicate a fiscal recovery, this upswing may not come fast enough to end an _____ unemployment crisis.

   A. intransigent
   B. incredulous
   C. inimitable
   D. inviolable
   E. intractable
   F. inestimable

12. Medical schools, in an ongoing effort to make medical care more accessible, have published guidelines suggesting a limit on the physician's use of _____ while explaining treatment options to patients.

   A. oratory
   B. succinctness
   C. jargon
   D. argot
   E. solace
   F. circumspection

13. Many students currently living in dormitories are opposed to what they see as _____ curfew rules designed to tighten security on campus.

   A. anarchic
   B. invaluable
   C. inevitable
   D. terse
   E. stringent
   F. draconian

14. Vehemently opposed to the budget cuts that the central office instituted, Ms. Alexander tried cajolery and then _____; finally, she handed in her letter of resignation.

   A. austerity
   B. approbation
   C. expostulation
   D. torpidity
   E. remonstrance
   F. affluence

Directions (15–20): Questions follow each of the passages. Using only the stated or implied information in each passage, answer the questions.

Questions 15–17 are based on the following passage.

A large part of the education of humans as well as of animals consists precisely in the modification of our original responses to situations by a trial-and-error discovery of ways of attaining satisfactory and avoiding annoying situations. Both animals and humans, when they have several times performed a certain act that brings satisfaction, tend, on the recurrence of a similar situation, to repeat that action immediately and to eliminate with successive repetitions almost all the other responses which are possible, but which are ineffective in the attainment of some specific satisfaction. The whole training imposed by civilization on the individual is based ultimately on this fundamental fact that human beings can be taught to modify their behavior, to change their original response to a situation in the light of the consequences that follow it. This means that while man's nature remains on the whole constant, its operations may be indefinitely varied by the results which follow the operation of any given instinct. The child has its original tendency to reach toward bright objects checked by the experience of putting its hand in the flame. Later his tendency to take all the food within reach may be checked by the looks of scorn which follow that manifestation of man's original greed, or the punishment and privation which are correlated with it. Through experience with punishment and reward, humans may be taught to do precisely the opposite of what would have been their original impulse in any given situation, just as the monkey reported by one experimenter may be taught to go to the top of his cage whenever a banana has been placed at the bottom.

15. Which of the following, if true, would most undermine the writer's argument?

   A. Students who get gold stars from their teacher for good behavior will consistently exhibit proper decorum.
   B. Children are able to detect a negative response in the facial expression of adults.
   C. Rats who are shocked when they make a wrong turn in a maze learn more quickly than rats who aren't shocked.
   D. Research has shown that animals and human beings have analagous methods of perception.
   E. Pedagogical studies on third-graders conclude that rote memorization of mathematical processes is the most efficient method of learning multiplication.

16. The "education" described in the passage is most analogous to which of the following? Consider each of the three choices and select all that apply.

   A. The time spent by the female rhesus monkey in grooming the male fluctuates rhythmically and reaches a minimum at midcycle, at which time the male's grooming activity reaches a maximum.
   B. A troop of monkeys daily leaves the shelter of the jungle for a human encampment where the delighted tourists feed them bananas.
   C. Monkeys rub themselves with leaves from the piper plant, which are natural insect repellents and antiseptics, warding off bacterial and fungal infections.

17. Select the sentence in the passage that indicates incongruence between human nature and behavioral responses.

Question 18 is based on the following passage.

The professor of chemistry, while administering, in the course of his lectures, the protoxide of nitrogen, or, as it is commonly called, laughing gas, in order to ascertain how great an influence the imagination had in producing the effects consequent on respiring it, secretly filled the India rubber gas-bag with common air instead of gas. It was taken without suspicion, and the effects, if anything, were more powerful than upon those who had really breathed the pure gas. One complained that it produced nausea and dizziness, another immediately manifested pugilistic propensities, and before he could be restrained, tore in pieces the coat of one of the bystanders, while the third exclaimed, "This is life. I never enjoyed it before."

18. It can be inferred from the passage that the professor of chemistry would agree with which of the following statements? Consider each of the three choices and select all that apply.

   A. Expectation can play a potent role in human responses.
   B. Any drug trial with aspirations of authenticity must account for the placebo effect.
   C. Of all the sciences, chemistry is most susceptible to fraudulent claims.

Question 19 is based on the following passage.

Soil is formed by a complex process, broadly known as weathering, from the rocks that constitute the earth's crust. Soil is, in fact, only pulverized and altered rock. The forces that produce soil from rocks are of two distinct classes—physical and chemical. The physical agencies of soil production merely cause a pulverization of the rock; the chemical agencies, on the other hand, so thoroughly change the essential nature of the soil particles that they are no longer like the rock from which they were formed. Of the physical agencies, temperature changes are first in order of time, and perhaps of first importance. As the heat of the day increases, the rock expands, and as the cold night approaches, contracts. This alternate expansion and contraction, in time, cracks the surfaces of the rocks. Into the tiny crevices thus formed water enters from the falling snow or rain. When winter comes, the water in these cracks freezes to ice and, in so doing, expands and widens each of the cracks. As these processes are repeated from day to day, from year to year, and from generation to generation, the surfaces of the rocks crumble. The smaller rocks so formed are acted upon by the same agencies, in the same manner, and thus the process of pulverization goes on.

19. It can be inferred from the passage that:

   A. Chemical alterations in the rocks are a result of the alternate expansion and contraction of their surfaces.
   B. Larger rocks undergo a process of pulverization far different from that which affects smaller rocks.
   C. Although radically changed by the process of erosion, rock samples retain their original chemical properties year after year.
   D. Seasonal shifts in climate are the primary factors leading to the physical changes that occur in soil formation.
   E. Moving bodies of water produce the most dramatic changes on soil formation as they grind the rock into sediment.

Question 20 is based on the following passage.

Connected also with some of the worst parts of our social system, we see lately a most powerful impulse given to the production of costly works of art, by the various causes that promote the sudden accumulation of wealth in the hands of private persons. We have, thus, a vast and new patronage, which, in its present agency, is injurious to our schools, but which is, nevertheless, in a great degree earnest and conscientious, and far from being influenced chiefly by motives of ostentation. Most of our rich men would be glad to promote the true interests of art in this country: and even those who buy for vanity, found their vanity on the possession of what they suppose to be best. It is, therefore, in a great measure the fault of artists themselves if they suffer from this partly unintelligent, but thoroughly well-intended, patronage. If they seek to attract it by eccentricity, to deceive it by superficial qualities, or take advantage of it by thoughtless and facile production, they necessarily degrade themselves and it together, and have no right to complain afterwards that it will not acknowledge better-grounded claims. But if every painter of real power would do only what he knew to be worthy of himself, and refuse to be involved in the contention for undeserved or accidental success, there is, indeed, whatever may have been thought or said to the contrary, true instinct enough in the public mind to follow such firm guidance.

20. In the passage, the underlined sentence functions as:

A. A conclusion that represents the primary argument of the paragraph

B. A statement that opposes the main argument of the paragraph

C. An assertion that supports the qualification in the sentence immediately preceding it

D. An aside that is tangential to the main purpose of the paragraph

E. An intermediate conclusion that is refuted by the conclusion in the last sentence of the paragraph

IF YOU FINISH BEFORE TIME IS CALLED, CHECK YOUR WORK ON THIS SECTION ONLY. DO NOT WORK ON ANY OTHER SECTION IN THE TEST.

STOP

Section 4: Quantitative Reasoning

Time: 40 minutes

25 questions

Numbers: All numbers used are real numbers.

Figures: Figures are intended to provide useful positional information, but they are not necessarily drawn to scale. Unless a note states that a figure is drawn to scale, you should not solve these problems by estimating sizes or by measurements. Use your knowledge of math to solve the problems. Angle measures can be assumed to be positive. Lines that appear straight can be assumed to be straight. Unless otherwise indicated, figures lie in a plane.

Directions (1–9): You are given two quantities, one in Column A and one in Column B. You are to compare the two quantities and choose one of the following:

    A.   The quantity in Column A is greater.
    B.   The quantity in Column B is greater.
    C.   The two quantities are equal.
    D.   The relationship cannot be determined from the information given.

	Column A	**Column B**
1.	$(3^2)^2$	$(2^3)^2$

$$5x - y = 3$$
$$3x + y = 13$$

	Column A	**Column B**
2.	x	y

$$a \Xi b = a^2 - ab$$

	Column A	**Column B**
3.	$4 \Xi 3$	$3 \Xi 4$

	Column A	**Column B**
4.	$\dfrac{121}{31}$ rounded to the nearest tenth	$\dfrac{121}{31}$ rounded to the nearest hundredth

$$7x - 6y > 4$$

Column A	**Column B**
5. $18y - 21x$	-12

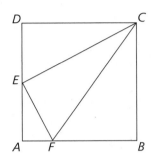

$ABCD$ is a square with side length 12

$\angle CEF$ is a right angle

$DE = 5$

$FB = 9$

Column A	**Column B**
6. Perimeter of $\triangle DEC$	Perimeter of $\triangle FEC$

p, q, and r are prime numbers less than 10, and $p < q < r$

Column A	**Column B**
7. $q - p$	$r - q$

x and y are positive integers and $\left(\dfrac{x}{y}\right)^2 > \left(\dfrac{y}{x}\right)^2$

Column A	**Column B**
8. x	y

Column A	**Column B**
9. The time needed to drive a miles at $\dfrac{b}{a}$ miles per hour	The time needed to drive $\dfrac{b}{a}$ miles at b miles per hour

Directions (10–25): Unless otherwise directed, select a single answer choice. For numeric-entry questions, enter a number in the box(es) below the question. Equivalent forms of the correct answer, such as 2.5 and 2.50, are all correct. Fractions do not need to be reduced to lowest terms. Enter the exact answer unless the question asks you to round your answer.

Question 10 refers to the following table.

Distances between Cities				
	Springfield	**Fort Wayne**	**Toledo**	**Indianapolis**
Springfield	–	254	343	186
Fort Wayne	254	–	89	101
Toledo	343	89	–	183
Indianapolis	186	101	183	–

10. If the distance in miles between cities is shown in the table above, which of the following statements are true?

   A. Springfield, Fort Wayne, and Toledo lie on a line.
   B. Indianapolis is the midpoint of the line segment connecting Toledo and Springfield.
   C. Indianapolis, Toledo, and Fort Wayne are the vertices of an equilateral triangle.

Question 11 refers to the following figure.

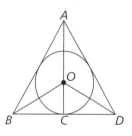

11. The sides of equilateral $\triangle ABD$ are tangent to a circle with center O. If $AB = 12\sqrt{3}$ and $OD = 12$, the circumference of the circle is

   A. 6π
   B. 12π
   C. $6\pi\sqrt{3}$
   D. $12\pi\sqrt{3}$
   E. 24π

12. Alberto saves $12 each week. Dahlia has already saved $270, and each week she spends $15 of that savings. When they both have the same amount in savings, they combine their money. What is the combined amount?

   A. $120
   B. $216
   C. $240
   D. $390
   E. $432

13. Each week, Sharon earns 2% of the first $2,500 she sells and 5% of sales beyond $2,500. How much does she earn in a week in which she sells $3,000 of goods?

A. $60
B. $75
C. $125
D. $150
E. $200

14. To choose a committee, the names of all possible members are written on identical cards, and five cards are drawn at random. If there are 14 men and 16 women among the possible members, what is the probability that all committee members are women?

A. $\dfrac{1}{2}$

B. $\dfrac{1}{32}$

C. $\dfrac{8}{15}$

D. $\left(\dfrac{8}{15}\right)^5$

E. $\dfrac{8}{261}$

15. Each member of the chorus must wear a shirt, slacks, and a sweater, but no two people should have the same outfit. If sweaters are available in five different colors, shirts in six different colors, and slacks in three different colors, how many different costumes are possible?

A. 6
B. 14
C. 30
D. 90
E. 196

16. In a hexagon, the total number of diagonals that can be drawn exceeds the total number of sides by:

A. 1
B. 2
C. 3
D. 4
E. 5

Question 17 refers to the following figure.

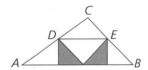

17. In right triangle $\triangle ABC$, $\angle C$ is a right angle; $\overline{DE}$ is parallel to $\overline{AB}$; and D and E are the midpoints of $\overline{CA}$ and $\overline{CB}$, respectively. Each shaded triangle is similar to $\triangle ABC$, and the shaded triangles are congruent to one another. What fraction of the area of $\triangle ABC$ is shaded?

A. $\dfrac{1}{8}$

B. $\dfrac{1}{4}$

C. $\dfrac{1}{3}$

D. $\dfrac{1}{2}$

E. $\dfrac{3}{4}$

18. A theater sells children's tickets for two-thirds of the adult ticket price. If seven adult tickets and three children's tickets cost a total of $108, what is the cost of an adult ticket?

☐

19. If S is the point $(4, 1)$, T is the point $(-2, y)$, and the slope of $\overrightarrow{ST} = \frac{2}{3}$, find y.

    A. 5
    B. 2
    C. 0
    D. −3
    E. −8

20. If $2x + 3y = 12$, find the value of $12x + 18y$.

    A. 30
    B. 60
    C. 72
    D. 144
    E. 448

21. If $a^2 + 2ab + b^2 = 9$, then $(2a + 2b)^3 =$

    A. 3
    B. 6
    C. 9
    D. 27
    E. 216

22. Two pools in the shape of rectangular prisms are being filled with water by pumps. The first pump fills its pool completely in one hour. The second pumps water twice as fast as the first pump, and fills a pool that is twice the width, twice the length, and the same depth of the first pool. How many hours does it take the second pump to fill its pool?

    A. 1
    B. 2
    C. 4
    D. 8
    E. 16

23. In the following chart, 40 people reported their age on their last birthday. Find the median age.

Age on Last Birthday	
Age	Frequency
30	5
31	7
32	3
33	12
34	9
35	4

    A. 6
    B. 6.666
    C. 32.5
    D. 32.625
    E. 33

24. A particular stock is valued at $50 per share. If the value increases 25% and then decreases 20%, what is the value of the stock per share after the decrease?

Question 25 refers to the following figure.

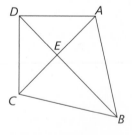

25. $\triangle ABC$ is an equilateral triangle. If $m\angle DAC = m\angle DCA = 40°$, choose all the true statements.

    A. $AD = DC$
    B. $AD < BC$
    C. $m\angle DAB = m\angle DCB$
    D. $m\angle ADC > m\angle DCB$
    E. $CE = EA$

IF YOU FINISH BEFORE TIME IS CALLED, CHECK YOUR WORK ON THIS SECTION ONLY. DO NOT WORK ON ANY OTHER SECTION IN THE TEST.

Section 5: Verbal Reasoning

Time: 30 minutes

20 questions

Directions (1–6): For each blank, select the word or phrase that best completes the text. (Your answer will consist of one, two, or three letters, depending on the number of blanks in each question.)

1. After investing in several questionable real-estate schemes, the once financially comfortable businessman found himself _____.

   A. opulent
   B. incorrigible
   C. indulgent
   D. impecunious
   E. multifarious

2. Although he had been invited to attend the conference on human social interaction as a guest, the professor's _____ was such that he assumed he was to speak from the podium.

   A. presumption
   B. compunction
   C. decorum
   D. rhetoric
   E. asceticism

3. At the conclusion of the president's speech, mostly wise and sensible but in some parts morally commonplace, even (1) _____, occurs a surprising burst of passionate (2) _____.

Blank 1	Blank 2
erudite	banality
platitudinous	eloquence
sagacity	pragmatism

4. After financial success brought her only misery, Ruta vowed to (1) _____ worldly considerations, as she embarked on a lifelong journey of (2) _____.

Blank 1	Blank 2
seek	abnegation
engender	dissolution
eschew	opportunism

5. After he was found guilty of being (1) _____, Dr. Burns admitted the results of his experimental trials were rife with (2) _____ results.

Blank 1	Blank 2
an iconoclast	irreproachable
a charlatan	conformist
a dilettante	specious

6. Sherlock Holmes, the most famous fictional detective, has delighted readers for generations with his astute (1) _____ and his brilliant deductions. An eccentric with myriad (2) _____, Holmes is nevertheless most precise in his detective work. He homes in on his suspects and (3) _____ identifies the culprit.

Blank 1	Blank 2	Blank 3
obtuseness	excoriations	unerringly
perspicacity	conundrums	injudiciously
inanity	idiosyncrasies	contritely

Directions (7–10): Questions follow each of the passages. Using only the stated or implied information in each passage, answer the questions.

Questions 7–8 are based on the following passage.

The majority of plants are adaptable to a terrestrial environment indoors, even if they are epiphytic in the wild and, thus, must be contained to propagate roots. When the nutrients in the houseplant's soil become depleted, it is necessary to artificially replace them with fertilizers that contain the essential chemical elements (macronutrients) of potassium, phosphorous, and nitrogen. Fertilizers for indoor plants are commercially available in crystalline, liquid, granular, or tablet forms and contain trace minerals as well.

Potassium (K), in the form of potash, engenders the production of fruit and flowers and aids the overall health and heartiness of the plant. Phosphorous (P), in the form of phosphate or phosphoric acid, is crucial for healthy root production. Nitrogen (N) is essential for the growth of the plant's stems and leaves and for the production of chlorophyll.

Fertilizers vary in their composition, but the majority of commercial fertilizers contains a 20-20-20 (N-P-K) formula. They are suitable for most indoor plants. Those containing more N are best for particularly leafy plants and plants nearing the peak of leaf production. If more P is prevalent, it results in a slightly slower growth rate but will aid in a well-developed root system. Fertilizers high in potash are ideal for plants that have just completed flowering and need fortifying as they prepare for the next flowering cycle.

Over-fertilization can result in an excess of soluble salts, which accumulate on the top layer of the soil, around the drainage holes in the pots or build up on the exterior of clay pots. When water evaporates from soil, the minerals remain and over time become more and more concentrated, resulting in a plant being unable to effectively absorb water. Houseplants need only be fertilized during periods of active growth.

7. A plant that is about to produce fruit should be fed a fertilizer high in:

    A.   Potassium
    B.   Phosphorous
    C.   Nitrogen
    D.   Nitrogen and phosphorous
    E.   Soluble salts

8. A fertilizer composition of 16-20-12 contains:

    A.   More potassium than nitrogen
    B.   More nitrogen than phosphate
    C.   More phosphoric acid than phosphate
    D.   Less potassium than phosphorus
    E.   Less phosphorus than nitrogen or potassium

Questions 9–10 are based on the following passage.

Scandinavian migration to the United States at the turn of the 19th century differed from other European migration patterns in that the bulk of people who made the journey were not fleeing religious or political persecution. Rather, they were abandoning an agrarian way of life threatened by an increase in the standard of living that led to huge population surges. Rural areas were greatly impacted by this increase, which was due to a decrease in infant mortality, more food production, and a lack of famine and war, which historically caused migration from other European countries to the U.S. to soar. The population growth strained social structures and exacerbated social issues as a surplus of laborers resulted in not enough work, a shrinking amount of tillable land, and an increase in landless citizens, resulting in social upheaval. Rural people attracted to land-rich America moved primarily to the upper Midwest and had a strong proclivity to re-create their traditional ways of life in their new world. The Scandinavians tended to migrate within cohesive family groups, and, thus, the balance of the sexes was even. These people clung to their religious traditions and languages and rural ways of life.

9. The primary purpose of this passage is to:

   A. Liken Scandinavian migration to other migration patterns

   B. Highlight why Scandinavians settled in the Midwest

   C. Explain the surge in Scandinavian migration to the United States at the turn of the 19th century

   D. Analyze the changing social structures in Scandinavia

   E. Clarify why most people migrating from Scandinavia to the United States came from urban rather than industrial areas

10. Which of the following statements, if true, would most undermine the argument of the passage?

   A. A decrease in infant mortality rates can have a detrimental effect on an agrarian society.

   B. Most Scandinavians migrated to the American Midwest because it was similar in topography to their native lands.

   C. Most fluctuations in emigration rates from Eastern Europe follow the patterns of famine and religious persecution.

   D. Periods of prosperity, health, and peace are always accompanied by a reduction in emigration.

   E. Scandinavian migration differed from other ethnic relocations in that entire families traveled and settled together.

Directions (11–14): Select two of the choices from the list of six that best complete the meaning of the sentence as a whole. The two words you select should produce completed sentences that are most alike in meaning. To receive credit for the question, both answers must be correct. No partial credit will be given; your answer must consist of two letters.

11. Although the twins were nearly identical in physical appearance, they could not have been more unlike in temperament; Beth was _____, while Seth was aloof and reserved.

    A. taciturn
    B. insipid
    C. contentious
    D. garrulous
    E. voluble
    F. ostentatious

12. As the country struggled with one armed conflict after another, many of the older folks would reminisce wistfully about the _____ days in their peaceful past.

    A. bellicose
    B. halcyon
    C. turbid
    D. pacific
    E. edifying
    F. monotonous

13. Storming out of the rehearsal after finding that most of his lines had been cut from the scene, the veteran actor hurled _____ at the newly hired director.

    A. opalescences
    B. acclamations
    C. obloquies
    D. invectives
    E. effulgences
    F. ubiquities

14. Once the darling of his readers for his caustic commentary on the political machinations of the incumbent, the reporter was astonished to find himself _____ for his scathing report on the governor's trip to Appalachia.

    A. vilified
    B. endangered
    C. excoriated
    D. objectified
    E. perturbed
    F. flouted

Directions (15–20): Questions follow each of the passages. Using only the stated or implied information in each passage, answer the questions.

Questions 15–17 are based on the following passage.

Hawthorne was an excellent critic of his own writings. He recognizes repeatedly the impersonal and purely objective nature of his fiction. R. H. Hutton once called him the
(5) ghost of New England; and those who love his exquisite, though shadowy, art are impelled to give corporeal substance to this disembodied spirit: to draw him nearer out of his chill aloofness, by associating him with people and
(10) places with which they, too, have associations. I heard Colonel Higginson say, in a lecture at Concord, that if a few drops of redder blood could have been added to Hawthorne's style, he would have been the foremost imaginative
(15) writer of his century. The ghosts in *The Aeneid* were unable to speak aloud until they had drunk blood. Instinctively, then, one seeks to infuse more red corpuscles into the somewhat anemic veins of these tales and romances. For
(20) Hawthorne's fiction is almost wholly ideal. He does not copy life like Thackeray, whose procedure is inductive: does not start with observed characters, but with an imagined problem or situation of the soul, inventing
(25) characters to fit. There is always a dreamy quality about the action: no violent quarrels, no passionate love scenes. Thus, it has been often pointed out that in *The Scarlet Letter* we do not get the history of Dimmesdale's and
(30) Hester's sin: not the passion itself, but only its sequels in the conscience. So in *The House of the Seven Gables* and *The Marble Faun,* a crime has preceded the opening of the story, which deals with the working out of the retri-
(35) bution.

15. According to the passage, which of the following are characteristic of Hawthorne's writings? Consider each of the three choices and select all that apply.

   A. Detached and lacking a subjective point of view
   B. Accurate in its representation of the passions of humanity
   C. Aloof and chilly in its portrayal of life

16. The allusion to "a few drops of redder blood" (line 12) suggests:

   A. The violent nature of plots of Hawthorne's fiction
   B. The dispassionate temperament of characters that inhabit Hawthorne's novels
   C. The vicious nature of the ghosts in *The Aeneid*
   D. The color of the letter *A* in *The Scarlet Letter*
   E. The love affair between Hester Prynne and Arthur Dimmesdale

17. Select the sentence in the passage that suggests that a subjective and associative response can infuse substance into objective art.

Questions 18–20 are based on the following passage.

The remains of pueblo architecture are found scattered over thousands of square miles of the arid region of the southwestern plateaus. This vast area includes the drainage
(5) of the Rio Pecos on the east and that of the Colorado on the west, and extends from central Utah on the north beyond the limits of the United States southward, in which direction its boundaries are still undefined.
(10) The descendants of those who at various times built these stone villages are few in number and inhabit about 30 pueblos distributed irregularly over parts of the region formerly occupied. Of these, the greater number are
(15) scattered along the upper course of the Rio Grande and its tributaries in New Mexico; a few of them, comprised within the ancient provinces of Cibola and Tusayan, are located within the drainage of the Little Colorado.
(20) From the time of the earliest Spanish expeditions into the country to the present day, a period covering more than three centuries, the former province has been often visited by whites, but the remoteness of Tusayan and the
(25) arid and forbidding character of its surroundings have caused its more complete isolation. The architecture of this district exhibits a close adherence to aboriginal practices, still bears the marked impress of its development under
(30) the exacting conditions of an arid environment, and is but slowly yielding to the influence of foreign ideas. The architecture of Tusayan and Cibola embraces all of the inhabited pueblos of those provinces, and includes a
(35) number of the ruins traditionally connected with them.

18. The word *marked* (line 29) most nearly means:

   A. Darkened
   B. Indicated
   C. Patent
   E. Colored
   D. Subtle

19. The passage suggests that:

   A. Pueblo architecture shows organized structures within a small region.
   B. Pueblo architecture gives clues to certain people reacting to their environment.
   C. The influence of pueblo architecture is worldwide.
   D. The descendants of the Tusayan and Cibola are the most prevalent ethnic group in Colorado.
   E. The Tusayan and Cibola were fighting nomads.

20. Select the sentence that accounts for the isolation of Tusayan.

IF YOU FINISH BEFORE TIME IS CALLED, CHECK YOUR WORK ON THIS SECTION ONLY. DO NOT WORK ON ANY OTHER SECTION IN THE TEST.

Answer Key

Section 2: Quantitative Reasoning

1. B	8. A	15. A	22. A
2. B	9. D	16. C	23. 66
3. A	10. G, H	17. E	24. C
4. C	11. D	18. B, D	25. A, C
5. C	12. D	19. E	
6. B	13. C	20. 50	
7. C	14. A, B	21. E	

Section 3: Verbal Reasoning

1. B	6. affectation, censure, unnatural	13. E, F	indefinitely varied by the results which follow the operation of any given instinct.
2. A		14. C, E	
3. propitiate, intractable	7. C	15. E	
	8. A	16. B, C	
4. espoused, despotic	9. C	17. This means that while man's nature remains on the whole constant, its operations may be	18. A, B
5. acquiescence, posit, fulfill its purpose	10. A		19. D
	11. A, E		20. C
	12. C, D		

Section 4: Quantitative Reasoning

1. A	8. A	15. D	22. B
2. B	9. D	16. C	23. E
3. A	10. A	17. B	24. $50
4. C	11. B	18. 12	25. A, B, C, E
5. B	12. C	19. D	
6. B	13. B	20. C	
7. D	14. E	21. E	

Section 5: Verbal Reasoning

1. D
2. A
3. platitudinous, eloquence
4. eschew, abnegation
5. a charlatan, specious
6. perspicacity, idiosyncrasies, unerringly
7. A
8. D
9. C
10. D
11. D, E
12. B, D
13. C, D
14. A, C
15. A, C
16. B
17. R. H. Hutton once called him the ghost of New England; and those who love his exquisite, though shadowy, art are impelled to give corporeal substance to this disembodied spirit: to draw him nearer out of his chill aloofness, by associating him with people and places with which they, too, have associations.
18. C
19. B
20. From the time of the earliest Spanish expeditions into the country to the present day, a period covering more than three centuries, the former province has been often visited by whites, but the remoteness of Tusayan and the arid and forbidding character of its surroundings have caused its more complete isolation.

Answer Explanations

Section 1: Analytical Writing

In this section, we provide sample score-6 essays. For more information on scoring the essays, see Chapter 9. For more sample essays, visit www.ets.org/gre/revised_general/prepare/analytical_writing/issue/sample_responses and www.ets.org/gre/revised_general/prepare/analytical_writing/argument/sample_responses.

Sample "Analyze an Issue" essay

Today, specialists are necessary but overrated; we need generalists as well as specialists in our society as it becomes increasingly complex with both positive and negative effects from the innovative social and technological advances.

Today there are high-speed social and technological changes with innovative ways of communication moves, which contributes to the intricacies and psychological shifts, both positive and negative effects among persons in Western cultures, demand for an equilibrium in which there are both non-experts and specialists.

Specialists are critical. Without them, society in this day and age could not properly function, nor could we digest or incorporate the heaps of new information. There is a convergence of technology, and knowledge can only be formed out of research after it's digested by specialists. In today's shrinking global world or flattening playing field, information is disseminated through mass global media at a speed hardly anyone can decipher. I paraphrase from a writer who I heard give a talk at my educational institute: "I am able to research only because so many individuals whom I know are reliable and I can turn to them for basic knowledge. Each person whom I rely on has a sharp focus in a given area so that, at each step, we can gain a full and true perspicacious understanding of the complexities of life. Each one of us adds to the tree of knowledge, leaf by leaf, and together we can reach the stars." This demonstrates the point that our society's level of knowledge and technology is in a phase now in which there simply must be experts or specialists in order for our society to use information effectively.

To state this point simply, without experts, our civilization would find itself overwhelmed in the ocean of information that piles up in excess. While it worked okay for early thinkers to learn and to comprehend the concrete laws and concepts that existed then, now, no one individual can possibly absorb and learn all the knowledge in any given field.

On the contrary, too much specialization means narrow-mindedness or too tight of a focus or lens. Then people can lose the macro ideas or larger picture. No one can wish to appreciate beauty by only viewing one's artistic masterpiece. What we study or observe from the perspective of a narrow focus may be logically coherent or sound but may be immaterial or fallacious within the broader framework. More so, if we inspect only one masterpiece—Monet's Gardens, for example—we may conclude that all Impressionist painting is similar. Another example to illustrate my point: If I read only one of my student's papers all year long, I would make a fallacious conclusion about his or her writing style and skill. So, useful conclusions and positive inventions must come by sharing among specialists perhaps. Simply throwing out various discoveries means we have a heap of useless discoveries; it is only when one can make with them a montage or medley that we can see that they may form a picture.

Overspecialization can be risky in terms of the accuracy, clarity, and cohesion of critical knowledge because it may serve to obfuscate universal or ethical issues. Only generalists can interpret a broad body of information; a narrow focus may place too much emphasis on a particle of independent knowledge while disregarding the macrocosm. The challenge is to see the holistic picture, to view progress on a global scale.

Furthermore, overspecialization in society would unfortunately rush people into making important decisions too early in life (at least by university), thus compartmentalizing their lives. It would be easier to feel isolated and on one's own. Not only does this hypothetical view create a less progressive viewpoint, but also it would generate many narrowly focused individuals who may be able to regurgitate information, but not necessarily process it well. Problem solving would suffer with people who would be generally poorly educated individuals with information but not able to use it effectively. Also, it would assure a sense of loss of community, often followed by a feeling of general dissatisfaction. Without generalists, society becomes myopic and less efficient. Thus, society needs both specialists and generalists because specialists drive us forward in the world series as in baseball, while generalists make sure we have our bases covered and apply good field strategies.

Reader response: This is a superb response because it shows strong reasoning skills and the language is sophisticated and gets its point across with both solid examples and figurative language. The issue is twofold: It presents a compelling case for specialization as well as an equally compelling, well-organized case against overspecialization. Again, this example is an exceptional written response to the topic.

Sample "Analyze an Argument" essay

In the faulty argument, there are two separate kinds of gear—preventive and protective—but it does not take into account other significant factors. Helmets are an example of protective gear, whereas light-reflecting material is considered to be preventive or to warn other people. What is the warning? A skateboarder is near a person driving a vehicle. The argument falls apart if the motorist is irresponsible or infringes upon the space of the person on the skateboard. The intention of protective gear is to decrease the margin of potential accident, whether it's caused by someone else, by the skateboarder, or by some other factor. Protective gear does little, though, to stop an accident from happening or to prevent it. However, in this argument, it is presumed to reduce the injuries. There are many statistics on injuries suffered by skateboarders showing people who were injured with protective and preventive gear. These statistics could give us a better understanding of which kinds of gear are of more assistance in a precarious situation between a motorist and skateboarder.

Thus, the idea that protective gear greatly reduces the injuries suffered in accidents is not a logical conclusion. At first glance, it sounds logical, but it is not. The argument is weakened by the patent fact that it does not take into account the vast differences between skaters who wear gear and those who do not use protective or preventive gear. Are the people who wear it more safety-conscious individuals or not? The skaters who invest in gear may be less likely to cause an accident through careless or dangerous behavior. So, it's not the gear that saves them but their attitude or cautious approach when skateboarding. It's critical to take the locale into this argument. Are people who are safety conscious by nature skating on busy streets or in the safe venues such as quiet roads or their own driveways? This is an important factor overlooked in this argument, and it needs to be taken into consideration.

This argument does not allow for one to analyze the seriousness of an injury. Not all injuries can be lumped into one category. The conclusion that safety gear prevents severe injuries implies that it is presumed that individuals who go to the hospital only suffer from severe injuries. That line of reasoning is unrealistic. It may be the fact that people are skateboarding during leisure hours when a doctor is only available in an emergency room, so their injuries are not severe, but their general-care practitioner is unavailable at the time of the injury.

Furthermore, there is insufficient evidence that proves high-quality or expensive gear works better than less-expensive models. Possibly a person did not put on their gear correctly and a wristband would not protect a break in the wrist effectively.

The case that safety gear based on emergency-room statistics could give us critical information and potentially save lives is not sound.

Reader response: This fine response shows the writer's strong reasoning and ability to analyze an argument, introducing holes or faulty assumptions. It allows the reader to see that there are missing pieces to a declarative statement because (1) individuals do not share common approaches to skateboarding, (2) the venue is significant, and (3) the statistics do not differentiate by the severity of the injuries or the different types of gear. All these points substantiated this essay very well, even though it could have been written with more eloquence.

Section 2: Quantitative Reasoning

1. **B** In the regular hexagon, if $\overline{OE}$ and $\overline{OF}$ are drawn, $\triangle OEF$ is an equilateral triangle, and so $\overline{FE} \cong \overline{OE} \cong \overline{OD}$. Because $\widehat{FE}$ is longer than $\overline{FE}$, however, $\widehat{FE}$ is longer than $\overline{OD}$. *(See Chapter XII, Section D.)*

2. **B** The final cost is $300 - (15\%$ of $\$300) + (6\%$ of the discounted price). The discount is $0.15 \times 300 = \$45$, so the discounted price is $\$255$. The tax is $0.06(255) = \$15.30$, so the final cost is $\$255 + \$15.30 = \$270.30$. *(See Chapter X, Section G.)*

3. **A** $(x + y)^2 = (a + b)^2 + (c + d)^2$, but $(a + b)^2 + (c + d)^2$ does not equal $a^2 + b^2 + c^2 + d^2$; rather, $(a + b)^2 + (c + d)^2 = a^2 + 2ab + b^2 + c^2 + 2cd + d^2$. Because a, b, c, and d are all positive, $2ab$ and $2cd$ are positive, and so $(a + b)^2 + (c + d)^2$ is larger than $a^2 + b^2 + c^2 + d^2$; therefore, $(x + y)^2$ is greater than $a^2 + b^2 + c^2 + d^2$. *(See Chapter X, Section C; Chapter 12, Section B.)*

4. **C** A shipping carton that is a cube 1 foot on each edge has a volume of 1 ft.³ or 1,728 in.³. The 2-inch cubes can be packed into the carton in six layers, each with 36 cubes, arranged 6 by 6. It holds a total of 216 cubes. A shipping carton 2 feet long, 1 foot wide, and 6 inches high can hold layers of 12 by 6 cubes, 72 cubes in each layer, but it can hold only three layers. It holds a total of 216 cubes. *(See Chapter XII, Section G.)*

5. **C** $\frac{2}{5}(0.001) = 0.4(0.001) = 0.0004$ and $\frac{1}{5}(0.002) = 0.2(0.002) = 0.0004$. *(See Chapter X, Section F.)*

6. **B** The cost of the refrigerator at 20% off the regular price is 80% of the original price. The price Yvonne paid for the refrigerator is 85% of the original price. The price Alicia paid for the refrigerator is 95% of 85% of the original price. Because $0.95 \times 0.85 = 0.8075$, or 80.75%, the price Alicia paid is greater than 20% off the regular price. *(See Chapter X, Section G.)*

7. **C** $\frac{pq}{r} = \frac{3q \cdot q}{r} = \frac{3(5r)^2}{r} = \frac{75r^2}{r} = 75r$. Because 75 and r are both positive integers, the remainder is 0. $\frac{pr}{q} = \frac{3q \cdot r}{5r} = \frac{3(5r) \cdot r}{5r} = \frac{15r^2}{5r} = 3r$. Here, too, the denominator is a factor of the numerator, so the remainder is 0. *(See Chapter 10, Sections C and H; Chapter XI, Section C.)*

8. **A** $(6 + 3) \times 5 - 6 \div 2 + 3^2 = 9 \times 5 - 6 \div 2 + 3^2 = 9 \times 5 - 6 \div 2 + 9 = 45 - 3 + 9 = 42 + 9 = 51$, but $6 + 3 \times 5 - 6 \div 2 + 3^2 = 6 + 3 \times 5 - 6 \div 2 + 9 = 6 + 15 - 3 = 9 = 21 - 3 + 9 = 18 + 9 = 27$. *(See Chapter X, Section A.)*

9. **D** If $x^3 = 125$, then $x = 5$, but if $y^2 = 25$, y may be equal to 5 or –5. *(See Chapter X, Section I; Chapter 11, Section D.)*

10. **G, H** Arizona showed increases in the first three counts but declined in 2002. No other state showed a similar pattern. Colorado and Missouri have a similar shape, but values for Missouri are higher. Indiana remained constant for 1987 and 1992 and never rose above 1,500. Massachusetts increased at each reading, with the 2002 value between 1,500 and 2,000. New Jersey also increased consistently, but not as sharply as Massachusetts. New York and Ohio are the most similar, differing only slightly in 1997. *(See Chapter XIII, Section A.)*

11. **D** From 1987 to 2002 the land in urban areas of Massachusetts increased from about 1,100,000 to about 1,800,000, an increase of about 700,000. Percent change is $\frac{700000}{1100000} = \frac{7}{11}$, which is 63.6%. The best answer is choice D, 64%. *(See Chapter X, Section G; Chapter XIII, Section A.)*

12. **D** In 2002, the land in urban areas in Ohio was slightly more than 2,500,000 acres, while the land in urban areas in New Mexico was just about 500,000 acres. The difference is $2,500,000 - 500,000 = 2,000,000$ or 2 million acres. *(See Chapter X, Section A; Chapter XIII, Section A.)*

13. **C** The land in urban areas in Arizona, in thousands of acres, was approximately 1,250 in 1987; 1,400 in 1992; 1,700 in 1996; and 1,100 in 2002. Averaging these gives $\frac{1,200 + 1,400 + 1,700 + 1,000}{4} = \frac{5,300}{4} = 1,325$ thousand acres or 1.325 million acres. *(See Chapter X, Section A; Chapter XIII, Section A.)*

14. **A, B** In 2002, urban land in Iowa and New Mexico was approximately equal, and urban land in Rhode Island did exceed that in Wyoming, but urban land in Connecticut was significantly higher than that in Colorado. *(See Chapter XIII, Section A.)*

15. **A** The life expectancy for 40-year-old black females is 78.8, while that for 40-year-old white males is 77.9. So, $78.8 - 77.9 = 0.9$ years. *(See Chapter XIII, Section A.)*

16. **C** Life expectancy for 60-year-old females is 84.0, while that for males of the same age is 80.8. The difference of $84.0 - 80.8 = 3.2$ years as a percent of the life expectancy for males is $\frac{3.2}{80.8} = \frac{32}{808} = \frac{4}{101}$, or slightly less than 4%. *(See Chapter X, Sections A and G; Chapter XIII, Section A.)*

17. **E** Percent increase is equal to 100 times the change, divided by the original value.

	White		Black	
Age	Male	Female	Male	Female
40	77.9	82.1	73.4	78.8
60	80.9	84.1	78.2	82.2
Change	3	2	4.8	3.4
Percent Change	3.85%	2.44%	6.54%	4.31%

(See Chapter X, Section G; Chapter XIII, Section A.)

18. **B, D** Because $a \times b$ is odd, both a and b must be odd. They need not be prime, simply odd, but the difference between two odd numbers will be even. Because $ab^2 = a \times b \times b$ (the product of three odd numbers), it will be odd. The sum $a + b$ of two odd numbers will be even. *(See Chapter X, Section C.)*

19. **E** If $xy \neq 0$ and $y = 3x$, then $\dfrac{x^2 + 2xy + y^2}{xy} = \dfrac{x^2 + 2x(3x) + (3x)^2}{x(3x)} = \dfrac{16x^2}{3x^2} = 5\frac{1}{3}$. *(See Chapter XI, Section D.)*

20. **50** Because the two cars were traveling in opposite directions, the distance between them is the sum of the distances traveled by each car. They were 330 miles apart after three hours, so the distance between them increased by 110 miles per hour. Because one car traveled, on average, 10 miles per hour faster than the other car, their speeds can be represented as x and $x + 10$. Then $x + x + 10 = 110$, so the slower car traveled at 50 mph and the faster car at 60 mph. *(See Chapter XI, Section A; Chapter 13, Section D.)*

21. **E** If $|a| = b$, then either $a = b$ or $a = -b$. The fact that $a + b = 0$ tells you that $a = -b$. Then $b - 2a = b - 2(-b) = b + 2b = 3b$. *(See Chapter X, Section B; Chapter XI, Section A.)*

22. **A** If $2x - 5 = y + 4$, then $2x - 4 = y + 5$, so $2(x - 2) = y + 5$ and $x - 2 = \dfrac{y + 5}{2}$. *(See Chapter XI, Section A.)*

23. **66** Represent the six consecutive integers as x, $x + 1$, $x + 2$, $x + 3$, $x + 4$, and $x + 5$. If the mean is 8.5, the sum of the six integers is $6(8.5) = 51$. Then $6x + 15 = 51$, $6x = 36$, and $x = 6$. The six integers are 6, 7, 8, 9, 10, and 11, so the product of the first and the last is 66. *(See Chapter XI, Section A; Chapter XIII, Section A.)*

24. **C** If 0.2% of 2,000 computer chips are defective, there are $0.002 \times 2,000 = 4$ defective chips, and 1,996 nondefective chips. *(See Chapter X, Section G.)*

25. **A, C** When $y = 0$, $3x = 4$ and $x = \dfrac{4}{3}$, so choice A is true. When $x = 0$, however, $-7y = 4$ and $y = -\dfrac{4}{7}$, so choice B is not true. Putting the equation in slope-intercept form gives you $y = \dfrac{3}{7}x - \dfrac{4}{7}$, showing that choice C is also true. *(See Chapter XI, Section A; Chapter XII, Section H.)*

Section 3: Verbal Reasoning

1. **B** *Lethargy* means sluggishness or lack of energy. The clue is that the tourists were overcome by heat and humidity and unable to climb. *(See Chapter V, Section B.)*

2. **A** *Dissipated* means dispersed or disintegrated. The logic of the sentence (budget cuts and deadline moved up) suggests that these factors would lower enthusiasm. *(See Chapter V, Section B.)*

3. **propitiate, intractable** *Propitiate* is to appease, which is what the delegates would do to reach an accord. The clue *no avail* suggests that the attempt at appeasement was unsuccessful, so the leader remained *intractable* (stubborn and inflexible). *(See Chapter V, Section C.)*

4. **espoused, despotic** The clue *Although* indicates a change in the leader who first *espoused* (supported) democratic ideals but then became *despotic* (tyrannical). *(See Chapter V, Section C.)*

5. **acquiescence, posit, fulfill its purpose** On the long, three-blank text completions, you have to use the entire context. The context clue to Blank 1 (which comes after the blank, not before it) is that the missing word is the opposite of active participation; *acquiescence* means submissive acceptance. Blank 2 must fit into the context of being willing to accept or not so unwilling as to *posit* (put forward) an obstacle. The entire context leads to Blank 3, *fulfill its purposes. Exact a promise* doesn't make sense in the context, and *establish a foothold* suggests something just starting out, which doesn't fit the main idea of people actively participating in their government. *(See Chapter V, Section C.)*

6. **affectation, censure, unnatural** To be less than natural is to have *affectations* (pretentiousness). The word *criticizes* is the clue to Blank 2, *censure* (disapproval). The clue to Blank 3, the opposite of *fanciless* and *insipid,* should lead you back to less than natural or *unnatural. (See Chapter V, Section C.)*

7. **C** Choice C is correct because the passage states that "Painting, in this manner, was employed by artists throughout Europe in making sketches for their oil paintings." All the other choices are contradicted by information in the passage. *(See Chapter VIII, Section B1.)*

8. **A** Both choices B and C are contradicted by the information in the passage that monks made little effort to produce realistic likenesses. *(See Chapter VIII, Section B1.)*

9. **C** Only choice C makes sense after the last sentence in the passage. All the other choices begin with a transitional word of contrast, yet no contrast exists. Choice C continues the discussion of payment of tolls, which is the main point of the paragraph. *(See Chapter VIII, Section B1.)*

10. **A** Choice A is correct because the passage is an objective presentation, without any biased opinion about the topic of the Panama Canal and the conflict between the United States and Great Britain. *(See Chapter VIII, Section B1.)*

11. **A, E** The clues in the sentence suggest that the recovery will not occur fast enough to end a crisis that is *intransigent* or *intractable* (unyielding). *(See Chapters VI and VII.)*

12. **C, D** The clue that medical schools want to make care more accessible would lead them to suggest limits on the use of *jargon* or *argot,* terminology of a particular profession. *(See Chapters VI and VII.)*

13. **E, F** The context implies that the students feel the rules are too *stringent* (strict) or *draconian* (unjustly severe). *(See Chapters VI and VII.)*

14. **C, E** The sentence implies an increasing progression of Ms. Alexander's opposition: First, she tried *cajolery* (sweet talking) and, finally, resignation. The step in the middle is *expostulation* (expression of disapproval) or *remonstrance* (protest or objection). *(See Chapters VI and VII.)*

15. **E** The writer's main argument is that most learning consists of trial-and-error. The only choice that weakens this argument is choice E, which supports rote memorization as a learning tool. *(See Chapter VIII, Section B1.)*

16. **B, C** Both choices B and C illustrate trial-and-error learning. Choice A, *instinct,* is not an example of trial-and-error learning. *(See Chapter VIII, Section B2.)*

17. **This means that while man's nature remains on the whole constant, its operations may be indefinitely varied by the results which follow the operation of any given instinct.** This sentence indicates a contrast between man's nature (constant) and his behavioral traits (varied). *(See Chapter VIII, Section B1.)*

18. **A, B** Choices A and B are correct because the passage illustrates the power of suggestion on human response. This is usually referred to as a placebo effect, a placebo being an inactive substance that can have an effect on a subject's condition. Choice C can't be supported by the information in the passage. *(See Chapter VIII, Section B2.)*

19. **D** In the sentence "Of the physical agencies, temperature changes are first in order of time, and perhaps of first importance," the writer indicates the importance of seasonal fluctuations in breaking down rocks into soil. *(See Chapter VIII, Section B1.)*

20. **C** The sentence supports the second clause of the sentence immediately preceding it. That clause is a qualification of the point that the patronage of wealthy men is harmful to society. By pointing out that most rich men would promote the "true interests of art," the author modifies his original assertion of the injurious nature of patronage. *(See Chapter VIII, Section B1.)*

Section 4: Quantitative Reasoning

1. **A** $(3^2)^2 = 9^2 = 81$ but $(2^3)^2 = 8^2 = 64$. *(See Chapter X, Section H.)*

2. **B** Adding the equations eliminates y and gives $8x = 16$ or $x = 2$. Substituting 2 for x in the first equation gives $10 - y = 3$, so $y = 7$. *(See Chapter XI, Section B.)*

3. **A** $4 \boxminus 3 = 4^2 - 4 \times 3 = 16 - 12 = 4$, but $3 \boxminus 4 = 3^2 - 3 \times 4 = 9 - 12 = -3$. *(See Chapter XIII, Section B.)*

4. **C** $\frac{121}{31} \cong 3.903225. \ldots$ Rounded to the nearest tenth, 3.903225 becomes 3.9. Rounded to the nearest hundredth, it becomes 3.90. *(See Chapter X, Section F.)*

5. **B** $18y - 21x = -3(7x - 6y)$, so you can gain information about the value of $18y - 21x$ by multiplying both sides of the given inequality by -3. That multiplication will reverse the direction of the inequality, giving you $-3(7x - 6y) < -3 \times 4$ and $18y - 21x < -12$. *(See Chapter XI, Sections A and C.)*

6. **B** Because $DE = 5$ and $DC = 12$, $\triangle DEC$ is a 5-12-13 right triangle, and with $EC = 13$, the triangle has a perimeter of 30. Because $FB = 9$ and $BC = 12$, the sides of $\triangle FBC$ are multiples of a 3-4-5 right triangle, specifically 9-12-15, with $FC = 15$. The third side of $\triangle FEC$, EF, is the hypotenuse of $\triangle FEA$ and so is longer than either of the legs; therefore, $EF > 7$. The perimeter of $\triangle FEC = EC + FC + EF > 13 + 15 + 7$; therefore, the perimeter of $\triangle FEC > 35$. *(See Chapter XII, Sections B and C.)*

7. **D** The primes less than 10 are 2, 3, 5, and 7. Four possibilities exist for the values of p, q, and r. (See the following chart.) In two cases, $q - p < r - q$; in one case, $q - p > r - q$ and in the last, $q - p = r - q$.

p	q	r	q – p	r – q
2	3	5	1	2
2	3	7	1	4
2	5	7	3	2
3	5	7	2	2

(See Chapter X, Section C.)

8. **A** If x and y were equal, both $\left(\dfrac{x}{y}\right)^2$ and $\left(\dfrac{y}{x}\right)^2$ would equal 1. Because $\left(\dfrac{x}{y}\right)^2 > \left(\dfrac{y}{x}\right)^2$, $x \neq y$. Because the numbers are not equal, one of the ratios, $\dfrac{x}{y}$ or $\dfrac{y}{x}$, will be greater than 1 and the other less than 1. The square of a number larger than 1 is larger than 1, and the square of a number less than 1 is less than 1. The given information that $\left(\dfrac{x}{y}\right)^2 > \left(\dfrac{y}{x}\right)^2$ tells you that $\dfrac{x}{y} > 1$, so $x > y$. *(See Chapter X, Section B.)*

9. **D** Using the relationship Distance = Rate × Time, the time needed to drive a miles at $\dfrac{b}{a}$ miles per hour is $a \div \dfrac{b}{a} = \dfrac{a}{1} \cdot \dfrac{a}{b} = \dfrac{a^2}{b}$. The time needed to drive $\dfrac{b}{a}$ miles at b miles per hour is $\dfrac{b}{a} \div b = \dfrac{b}{a} \cdot \dfrac{1}{b} = \dfrac{1}{a}$. It is impossible to determine which is larger without more information. *(See Chapter XIII, Section D; Chapter XI, Section A.)*

10. **A** If three points lie on a line, the distance from the first to the second plus the distance from the second to the third will equal the distance from the first to the third. Reading the distances from the table, you can see that $254 + 89 = 343$, so choice A is true. The distance from Toledo to Springfield is 343. The midpoint of the segment connecting them would be 171.5 miles from each. Indianapolis is 186 miles from Springfield and 183 miles from Toledo, so it is not the midpoint, and choice B is not true. Indianapolis, Toledo, and Fort Wayne are the vertices of a triangle, but the triangle is not equilateral. Its sides measure 89, 183, and 186, so choice C is not true. *(See Chapter XII, Section A; Chapter XIII, Section A.)*

11. **B** $\triangle ACB$ is a 30°-60°-90° right triangle with hypotenuse $AB = 12\sqrt{3}$, so $BC = 6\sqrt{3}$, and $AC = 6\sqrt{3} \cdot \sqrt{3} = 18$. $OA = OB = OD = 12$, and $OC = AC - OA = 6$, so the radius of the circle is 6, and its circumference is $C = 2\pi r = 12\pi$. *(See Chapter XII, Sections B and F.)*

12. **C** Alberto's savings can be represented by $12w$, where w is the number of weeks. Dahlia's savings can be represented by $270 - 15w$. Solve $12w = 270 - 15w$ to find that $27w = 270$ and $w = 10$. After ten weeks, they have equal savings of \$120 each, which they combine for \$240. *(See Chapter XI, Section A.)*

13. **B** In a week when she sells \$3,000 of goods, Sharon earns 2% of the first \$2,500 and 5% of the additional \$500. So, $0.02(2,500) + 0.05(500) = 50 + 25 = \$75$. *(See Chapter X, Section G.)*

14. **E** The probability that all committee members are women is the product of the probability that the first person selected is a woman, $\dfrac{16 \text{ women}}{30 \text{ people}}$, times the probability that the second person chosen is a woman, $\dfrac{15}{29}$, times the probability that the third is a woman, $\dfrac{14}{28}$, times the probability that the fourth is a woman, $\dfrac{13}{27}$, times the probability that the fifth is a woman, $\dfrac{12}{26} \cdot \dfrac{16}{30} \cdot \dfrac{15}{29} \cdot \dfrac{14}{28} \cdot \dfrac{13}{27} \cdot \dfrac{12}{26}$

$= \dfrac{16}{30} \cdot \dfrac{15}{29} \cdot \dfrac{14}{28} \cdot \dfrac{13}{27} \cdot \dfrac{12}{26} = \dfrac{16 \cdot 4}{2 \cdot 29 \cdot 2 \cdot 9 \cdot 2} = \dfrac{8}{261}$. *(See Chapter XIII, Section C.)*

15. **D** The number of different costumes is $5 \times 6 \times 3 = 90$. *(See Chapter XIII, Section C.)*

16. **C** In a hexagon, the total number of diagonals that can be drawn is $\dfrac{6 \times 3}{2} = 9$, which exceeds the total number of sides by $9 - 6 = 3$. *(See Chapter X, Section D.)*

17. **B** The shaded triangles have heights equal to half the height of $\triangle ABC$, and their combined bases are equal to $\overline{DE}$. Because it connects the midpoints of the sides, $\overline{DE}$ is half as long as $\overline{AB}$. If the area of $\triangle ABC$ is $\frac{1}{2}bh$, the area of one shaded triangle is $\frac{1}{2}\left(\frac{1}{4}b\right)\left(\frac{1}{2}h\right) = \frac{1}{16}bh$, so the shaded area of the two triangles is $\frac{1}{8}bh$. Because $\frac{1}{8}bh \div \frac{1}{2}bh = \frac{1}{4}$, one-fourth of $\triangle ABC$ is shaded. *(See Chapter X, Section E.)*

18. **12** If c is the price of a child's ticket and a is the price of an adult's ticket, $c = \frac{2}{3}a$. Seven adult tickets and three children's tickets cost \$108, so $7a + 3c = 7a + 3\left(\frac{2}{3}a\right) = 108$ or $9a = 108$ and $a = 12$. *(See Chapter XI, Section A; Chapter XIII, Section D.)*

19. **D** The slope of $\overline{ST} = \frac{1-y}{4--2} = \frac{1-y}{6} = \frac{2}{3}$. Cross-multiply to get $3(1-y) = 2 \times 6$, so $3 - 3y = 12$. Solve to find $-3y = 9$ and $y = -3$. *(See Chapter XI, Section A.)*

20. **C** $12x + 18y = 6(2x + 3y) = 6(12) = 72$. *(See Chapter XI, Sections A and C.)*

21. **E** Because $a^2 + 2ab + b^2 = (a + b)^2 = 9$, $a + b = \pm 3$. Then $2a + 2b = \pm 6$ and $(2a + 2b)^3 = (\pm 6)^3 = \pm 216$. The best answer choice is 216. *(See Chapter XI, Sections C and D.)*

22. **B** If the dimensions of the first pool are l, w, and h, the dimensions of the second pool are $2w$, $2l$, and h. The volume of the first pool is lwh, and the volume of the second is $(2l)(2w)(h)$ or $4lwh$. The second pool holds four times as much as the first. If the first pool's pump were used to fill the second, it would take four hours to fill; however, because the second pump fills twice as fast, it will take two hours. *(See Chapter XI, Section A; Chapter XIII, Section C.)*

23. **E** The median of the 40 data points will be the average of the 20th and 21st values. Because both the 20th and 21st values are 33, the median is 33. *(See Chapter XIII, Section A.)*

24. **\$50** The stock begins at \$50. A 25% increase will be an increase of \$12.50, raising the price to \$62.50. A 20% decrease—20% of \$62.50—is a decrease of \$12.50, taking the price back to \$50. *(See Chapter X, Section G.)*

25. **A, B, C, E** Start by finding the measures of all the angles. $m\angle ABC = m\angle BCA = m\angle CAB = 60°$, and $m\angle DAC = m\angle DCA = 40°$. By subtracting, $m\angle ADC = 180° - (40° + 40°) = 100°$. Because $m\angle DAC = m\angle DCA = 40°$, $AD = DC$, so choice A is true. You can order the sides of $\triangle ADC$ because the longest side will be opposite the largest angle, so AC is longer than AD or DC, and the sides of the equilateral triangle are all congruent, so $AB = BC = AC$, which means that BC is larger than AD, so choice B is true. $\angle DAB$ and $\angle DCB$ are each made up of a 40° angle and a 60° angle, so $\angle DAB = \angle DCB = 100°$, and choice C is true. You know that $m\angle ADC = 100°$, so $m\angle ADC = m\angle DCB$, and choice D is false. Finally, $\triangle DEC \cong \triangle DEA$ because two angles and the included side in one triangle are congruent to the corresponding parts in the other triangle, so $CE = ED$ and choice E is true. *(See Chapter X, Section B.)*

Section 5: Verbal Reasoning

1. **D** Choice D is correct because *impecunious* means insolvent or out of money. The questionable nature of the real-estate schemes and the words *once financially comfortable* lead you to understand that the businessman has had a change of circumstances. *(See Chapter V, Section B.)*

2. **A** Choice A is correct because *presumption* can mean overconfidence or arrogance. The professor is overly confident in assuming that he was to speak; he had been invited only as a guest. *(See Chapter V, Section B.)*

3. **platitudinous, eloquence** *Platitudinous* means dull, trite, and obvious, and *eloquence* means effective use of language. The word *even* before Blank 1 suggests that the word will be a more extreme form of morally commonplace, which makes *platitudinous* a good choice. That sets up the shift to a *surprising burst of passionate eloquence*—surprising because eloquence is the opposite of platitudinous. *(See Chapter V, Section C.)*

4. **eschew, abnegation** *Eschew* means to avoid and *abnegation* means the act of renouncing or giving up. Because financial success brought Ruta misery, she would avoid worldly considerations and live a life of abstinence. *(See Chapter V, Section C.)*

5. **a charlatan, specious** Choice B and F are correct: A *charlatan* is a fraud, and *specious* means false but having the appearance of truth. The logic of the sentence indicates that the words must have a cause-and-effect relationship. Because Dr. Burns was found guilty, he had to admit his results were false. *(See Chapter V, Section C.)*

6. **perspicacity, idiosyncrasies, unerringly** Blank 1 must be a positive word to describe Sherlock Holmes; *perspicacity* (perceptiveness or insightfulness) is the best choice to go along with brilliant deductions. The description of Holmes as eccentric suggests that Blank 2 is *idiosyncrasies* (odd quirks or personal habits). Because he is so *precise in his detective work*, he *unerringly* (flawlessly), Blank 3, identifies the culprit. *(See Chapter V, Section C.)*

7. **A** The passage indicates that "Potassium (K), in the form of potash, engenders the production of fruit and flowers." None of the other choices is supported by the information in the passage. *(See Chapter VIII, Section B1.)*

8. **D** The composition of 16-20-12 means that there are 16 units of N (nitrogen), 20 units of P (phosphate or phosphoric acid), and 12 units of K (potassium). Therefore, there is less potassium than phosphorous. None of the other choices is supported by the information in the passage. *(See Chapter VIII, Section B1.)*

9. **C** Though some of the other choices are mentioned or explained in the passage, the primary point of this brief history is to explain why so many Scandinavians emigrated to the United States at the turn of the 19th century. *(See Chapter VIII, Section B1.)*

10. **D** One of the main points in the passage is that the increase in the standard of living led to a surge in the rural population, which, in turn, led the Scandinavians to leave their native countries. None of the other choices weakens the argument in the passage. *(See Chapter VIII, Section B1.)*

11. **D, E** The context clues in the sentence suggest that the missing word is the opposite of aloof and reserved. *Garrulous* and *voluble* both mean talkative. *(See Chapters VI and VII.)*

12. **B, D** The sentence indicates that the country is now in a state of turmoil. The older folks are *reminiscing* about more peaceful (*halcyon* or *pacific*) days in their pasts. *(See Chapters VI and VII.)*

13. **C, D** The veteran actor is clearly very angry that his lines have been cut. He hurls *obloquies* (censure or abusive language) or *invectives* (insulting or violent words) at the director. *(See Chapters VI and VII.)*

14. **A, C** Because he was once the darling of his readers, the reporter is astonished to find himself *vilified* (defamed or slandered) or *excoriated* (severely denounced or berated). *(See Chapters VI and VII.)*

15. **A, C** The passage states that Hawthorne "recognizes repeatedly the impersonal and purely objective nature of his fiction" and that those who love him try to draw him out of his "chilly aloofness." Choice B is not correct because the passage states that "He does not copy life." *(See Chapter VIII, Section B2.)*

16. **B** The writer suggests that Hawthorne's style could be improved by more passion (redder blood) in the "anemic veins" of his tales. Choice A is contradicted by the information in the passage that Hawthorne's tales don't contain violence or passion. Choice C, D, and E have nothing to do with the allusion. *(See Chapter VIII, Section B1.)*

17. **R. H. Hutton once called him the ghost of New England; and those who love his exquisite, though shadowy, art are impelled to give corporeal substance to this disembodied spirit: to draw him nearer out of his chill aloofness, by associating him with people and places with which they, too, have associations.** This is the only sentence in the passage that reveals the reader's role in responding to Hawthorne's fiction "by associating" (a subjective response). *(See Chapter VIII, Section B1.)*

18. **C** *Patent* means evident or obvious, which is the closest in meaning to *marked* as it is used in this sentence. None of the other choices makes sense in the context of this sentence. *(See Chapter VIII, Section B1.)*

19. **B** Choice B is correct because the passage states that the architecture "bears the marked impress of its development under the exacting conditions of an arid environment." Choice A is contradicted the first sentence: "The remains of pueblo architecture are found scattered over thousands of square miles. . . ." Choices C, D, and E can't be supported by any evidence in the passage. *(See Chapter VIII, Section B1.)*

20. **From the time of the earliest Spanish expeditions into the country to the present day, a period covering more than three centuries, the former province has been often visited by whites, but the remoteness of Tusayan and the arid and forbidding character of its surroundings have caused its more complete isolation.** The isolation of the Tusayan is explained in this sentence. None of the other sentences in this passage explains the isolation. *(See Chapter VIII, Section B1.)*